The International Banking System

The International Banking System

Capital Adequacy, Core Businesses and Risk Management

Felix Lessambo
St John's University USA

First published 2013 by
PALGRAVE MACMILLAN

Palgrave Macmillan in the UK is an imprint of Macmillan Publishers Limited, registered in England, company number 785998, of Houndmills, Basingstoke, Hampshire RG21 6XS.

Palgrave Macmillan in the US is a division of St Martin's Press LLC, 175 Fifth Avenue, New York, NY 10010.

Palgrave Macmillan is the global academic imprint of the above companies and has companies and representatives throughout the world.

Palgrave® and Macmillan® are registered trademarks in the United States, the United Kingdom, Europe and other countries.

ISBN 978–1–137–27512–7

This book is printed on paper suitable for recycling and made from fully managed and sustained forest sources. Logging, pulping and manufacturing processes are expected to conform to the environmental regulations of the country of origin.

A catalogue record for this book is available from the British Library.

A catalog record for this book is available from the Library of Congress.

10   9   8   7   6   5   4   3   2   1
22   21   20   19   18   17   16   15   14   13

Printed and bound in Great Britain by
CPI Antony Rowe, Chippenham and Eastbourne

Contents

List of Tables

List of Figures

Acknowledgements

Writing a book is always a challenge, but writing a book on the international banking system is a particularly daring intellectual exercise, especially in the area of international finance, international economics, and risk management, where rules and regulations have been barely implemented and with secretive central banks around the globe involved in obscure practices.

I would like to thank Professors W. Jean Kwon (Chairperson of the School of Risk Management, Insurance & Actuarial Science, St. John's University, New York) and Nicos A. Scordis (The Peter J. Tobin College of Business – School of Risk Management) for their cogent advice and friendly support throughout this project. I also extend my gratitude to Ismael Rivera-Sierra (the Director of the Kathryn & Shelby Cullom-Davis Library) who provided technical support. In addition, I thank all my students at St. John's University who inspired me through their challenging questions in search of sound, precise, and comprehensive answers.

Several good friends provided me with needed guidance and materials to complete this book, while others took valuable time to review, comb through the manuscripts, and support me in their thoughts and prayers (Pastor Roland Dalo, Aline Kabongo).

Last but not least, I am grateful to various organizations, including BIS and a number of US government agencies, including the Securities and Exchange Commission, for supplying the precious data used to illustrate my analyses.

Disclaimer

While the author has made every effort to ensure that the information in this book is correct at the time of publication, he does not assume and hereby disclaims any liability to any party for any loss, damage, or disruption caused by errors or omissions, whether such errors or omissions result from negligence, accident, or any other cause.

This publication is designed to provide accurate and authoritative information in regard to the subject matter covered. It is sold on the understanding that the publisher is not engaged in rendering professional services. If professional advice or other expert assistance is required, the services of a competent professional should be sought.

Abbreviations

ADR	American Depository Receipt
ABS	asset-backed security
AIRB	advanced internal ratings-based approach
A/R	acid ratio
ARDC	American Research and Development Corporation
BHC	bank holding company
BIS	Bank for International Settlements
BoE	Bank of England
BoJ	Bank of Japan
BS	balance sheet
CAMELS	capital adequacy, asset quality, management, earnings, liquidity, and sensitivity to market risk
CBB	Central Bank of Brazil
CBR	Central Bank of Russia
CCS	Credit Card Services
CD	certificate of deposit
CDO	collateralized debt obligation
CFC	controlled foreign corporation
CPEC	convertible preferred equity certificate
CPI	Consumer Protection Index
CPM	comparable multiple method
CRR	cash reserve ratio
CVaR	conditional value-at-risk
DR	depository receipt program
EAD	exposure-at-default
ECB	European Central Bank
EL	expected loss
EMU	Economic Monetary Union
EPS	earnings per share

EU	European Union
ESCB	European System of Central Banks
Fed	Federal Reserve
FHA	Federal Housing Administration
FHC	financial holding company
FIDIC	Federal Deposit Insurance Corporation
FPHC	foreign personal holding company
FX	foreign exchange
GAAP	generally accepted accounting principle
GDP	gross domestic product
GO	general obligation (bonds)
GSE	government sponsored enterprise
HELOC	home equity line of credit
HUD	Department of Housing and Urban Development
IBF	international banking facility
IRA	individual retirement account
IRB	internal ratings-based approach
IRC	Internal Revenue Code
LAF	liquidity adjustment facility
LAVaR	liquidity-adjusted value-at-risk
LCR	liquidity coverage ratio
LGD	loss given default
LLC	limited liability company
LLP	limited liability partnership
M&A	mergers and acquisitions
MBS	mortgage-backed security
MPC	Monetary Policy Committee
MSS	Market Stabilization Scheme
NGO	non-general obligation (bonds)
NOL	net operating loss
NRSO	nationally recognized statistical rating organization
NSFR	net stable funding ratio
OBC	offshore banking center

OECD	Organization for Economic Development and Cooperation
OMO	open market operation
PBoC	People's Bank of China
PCAOB	Public Company Accounting Oversight Board
PD	probability of default
P/E	price-earnings ratio
PLS	private label securities
QSPV	qualified special purchase vehicle
RAROC	risk-adjusted return on capital
Repo	repurchase agreement
RBI	Reserve Bank of India
RFS	retail financial services
SA	Standarized approach
SAM	share appreciation mortgage
SAMA	Saudi Arabia Monetary Agency
SEC	Securities and Exchange Commission
SLR	statutory liquidity ratio
SPE	special purpose entity
SPV	special purpose vehicle
STRIPS	Separate Trading of Registered Interest and Principal Securities
TAAPS	Treasury Automated Auction Processing System
TIPS	Treasury inflation-protected securities
UFIRS	Uniform Financial Institutions Rating System
UK	United Kingdom
US	United States of America
VaR	value-at-risk

Cited Cases

1. Air Products and Chemicals, Inc., v. Airgas, Inc. (Del. Ch., C.A. N0. 5249-CC, 2/15/2011).
2. Francis v. New Jersey Bank, 432 A.2d 814 (NJ 1981)
3. Helvering v. Minnesota Tea Co., US 378 (1935)
4. Hort v. Commissioner of Internal Revenue, US S.Ct. 313 US 28 (1941)
5. Illinois Tool Works & Subs. v. Commissioner, 117 T.C., N0. 4, July 31, 2001
6. In Re Walt Disney Co. Derivative Litigation, Del. Ch.2003
7. Libson Shops, Inc. v. Koehler, S.Ct. 353 US 382 (1957)
8. Mills Acquisition Co. v. Macmillan, Inc., 559 A.2d 1261 (Del. 1989)
9. Moran v. Household International , Inc., 500 A.2d 1346 (Del. 1985)
10. New Colonial Ice Co. v. Helvering, S.Ct. 292 US 435 (1934)
11. Omnicare v. NCS Healthcare Inc., 818 A.2d 914 (Del. 2003)
12. Paramount Communications, Inc. v. QVC Network, Inc. 637 A.2d 34 (Del. 1994)
13. Phelps Dodge v. Cyprus Amax Minerals Co.,CA N0. 17398 (Del. Ch. Ct. 27 September, 1999)
14. Revlon, Inc v. MacAndrews & Forbes Holding, Inc. 506 A.2d 173 (Del. 1985)
15. Roosvelt Hotel Co., v. Commissioner, T.C. 399 (1949)
16. Smith v. Van Gorkhom, 448 A.2d 858 (Del. Supr. 1985)
17. Unocal Corp. v. Mesa Petroleum Co. 493 A.2d 946 (Del. 1985)

Preface

Financial markets have become global, and are closely interrelated. Among the big players are commercial and investment banks. They perform core banking functions and underpin the main economy. They also provide efficient payment mechanisms, facilitating transactions and extending loans to those in need of liquidity, providing value in our economies as liquidity intermediaries. The landscape of the international banking system is rapidly changing, with the world's top three banks from China, and America's largest bank down to the fifth position.[1]

The first banking activities can be traced back to around 2000 BCE, in Assyria and Babylonia. Modern banking activities date back to Medieval and early Renaissance Italy, while the development of the banking industry we recognize today started in the 19th century, when banks evolved into large commercial entities extending loans to the general public. The internationalization of business in the 20th century facilitated the emergence of universal banking activities.

The demarcation line between commercial and investment banking has become blurred in recent decades. In the United States, for example, prior to the repeal of the Glass–Steagall Act on November 12, 1999, commercial and investment banks operated in two distinct arenas. Commercial banks focused on regular individual and business activities. They collected deposits from their clients and extended loans to businesses, both new and old, to start or develop an ongoing undertaking. Investment banks, meanwhile, assisted businesses in the raising of capital. The repeal of Glass–Steagall allowed commercial banks to engage in core activities formerly restricted to investment banks and vice versa. In so doing, the Gramm–Leach–Bliley Act, also known as the Financial Services Modernization Act, created a sharp conflict of interest among commercial banks and investment banks. It altered the culture of the US banks without putting in place a clear mechanism of control to secure, or at least monitor, the overall banking system. Through mergers and acquisitions or internal restructuring, US banks were allowed to operate as both commercial and investment banks. Juggernaut banking institutions, later referred to as too big to fail, escaped almost completely from being under sound supervision. The premises upon which Gramm–Leach–Bliley relied were revealed to be illusory. The fate of the international banking system is linked to the fate of the overall financial system.

The collapse of the Bretton Woods era was followed by unfettered deregulation among various banking authorities. The phenomenon and philosophy would be accentuated in the 1990s under US Federal Reserve Chairman Alan Greenspan, who was a proponent of market fundamentalism.[2]

Non-banking institutions such as insurance companies were allowed to engage in banking operations. US banks thus become supermarket banks offering, under the same umbrella, retail and wholesale banking, investment banking and various intermediary financial institutions. Several regulatory authorities across the world followed the American path of deregulation, at the expense of their core economies. Five years after the onset of the financial crisis in 2007, the six largest American financial institutions are significantly bigger than they were before the crisis.[3] Supervising, or at least controlling, their activities has become a challenge. In the US, banks are under the supervision of at least four institutions: the Office of the Comptroller of the Currency, the Federal Reserve Board, the Federal Deposit Insurance Corporation, and the State Bank Regulators. It was the Federal Reserve that failed to detect the 2007 crash, which would lead to the rescue of the well-known "too-big-to-fail" banking institutions despite the claimed rules of the free market.

We need to ask whether the financial crisis of 2007–2009 redrew the picture of the international banking system. Many US and European Union juggernaut banks have opened their capital structures to funds from Asian sovereign funds, but they still operate under the old corporate governance structures that led to the crisis. As the world financial center of gravity has shifted eastward, major international banks are rushing to the booming Asian markets – Hong Kong, Shanghai, Singapore – to stay financially afloat. Would they commit themselves to observing laws and regulations in their new territories? The international banking system is shaped by the laws and regulations of the main financial players, including the US Federal Reserve, the European Union Central Bank, The Central Bank of Japan, the Bank of England, the People's Bank of China, the Reserve Bank of India, the Central Bank of Russia, the Central Bank of Brazil, the Saudi Arabia Monetary Authority, and the Bank for International Settlements. The regulatory efforts shaped by the Bank for International Settlement – Basel I, II, and III – if properly followed could stabilize the international banking system. Compliance with these laws and regulations is vital to all players around the world.

This book is organized into three parts. Part I analyzes the role played by the main financial players already listed. It highlights the different monetary policies pursued and their effects on the banks' business. Part II investigates capital adequacy and the main banking operations. Bank capital is a proxy, especially in the securities marketplace, for public confidence in the banking system or any specific bank. The inadequacy of capital coupled with, in some cases, managerial fraud, has created a risky situation in the international banking system, especially where domestic banking supervision is weak.[4] Part III focuses on risk management, which has become a heated topic generally, but has particular application to banking as a result of the internationalization of the system. As the trend continues, risk management becomes a core business in the banking field.

Notes

1. Joseph Stiglitz (2010) *Free Fall, America Free Markets, and the Sinking of the World Economy*, W. W. Norton & Company, p. 224.
2. Otto Hieronymi (2009) *Globalization and the Reform of the International Banking and Monetary System*, Palgrave Macmillan, p. 18.
3. Their assets are worth over 66% of the United States' GDP (US$94 trillion), 20% up from the GDP in the 1990s.
4. James C. Baker (2002) *The Bank for International Settlements*, Quorum Books, pp. 44–45.

Part I
Regulators

1
The US Federal Reserve Bank

1.1 Introduction

The Federal Reserve Bank is the central bank of the United States. It does not conduct commercial banking activities; rather, the Federal Reserve role consists of maintaining stable economic growth. The Federal Reserve originated from the Owen-Glass[1] bill introduced in both houses of Congress and became law in December 1913. From its inception, the Federal Reserve was assigned three key purposes: (a) to provide an elastic supply of currency; (b) to provide a means to discount commercial credits; and (c) to supervise and regulate the nation's banks. Later on, as a result of changes in our modern economy and needs, the Federal Reserve has been assigned to provide full employment as well. The US Federal Reserve System and its Federal Reserve Board is the most powerful central bank in the world.[2]

In order to gain a better understanding of the Federal Bank of the US, it is crucial to shed light on the historical facts that provided the framework for the Bank. The US financial industry went through several crises during the 19th and 20th centuries. Major businesses and banks faced bankruptcy during the economic turmoil. The failure of the nation's banking system to effectively provide funding to troubled depository institutions contributed significantly to the economy's vulnerability to financial panic.[3] In 1907, the economic crisis impelled Congress to establish the National Monetary Commission, which put forth proposals to create an institution that would help prevent and contain financial disruptions of this kind.[4] During this time, payments were disrupted throughout the country because many banks and clearinghouses refused to clear checks drawn on certain other banks, a practice that contributed to the failure of otherwise solvent banks.

After some consideration, Congress finally approved the Federal Reserve Act: to provide for the establishment of Federal Reserve banks; to furnish an elastic currency; to afford means of rediscounting commercial paper; to establish a more effective supervision of banking in the United States; and for other purposes.[5] President Woodrow Wilson signed the Act into law on December 23, 1913.

The Federal Reserve System is generally regarded as an independent central bank because its decisions do not have to be ratified by the President or anyone else in the executive branch of government. It is, however, subject to supervision by the US Congress. The Federal Reserve must work within the framework of the overall objectives of economic and financial policy established by the government. Almost a century after President Andrew Jackson vetoed the re-chartering of the Bank of the United States in 1832, the US government lacked a central mechanism for regulating the money supply to control inflation or deflation and to boost the economy in times of recession and depression. This resulted in conflict arising between creating a powerful private central bank and focusing on giving the job to a government agency. Finally, during the Progressive Era, President Woodrow Wilson proposed, and Congress enacted, the Federal Reserve Act of 1913, which combined private banks with government regulation.[6]

The Federal Reserve was created by Congress "to provide a safe, flexible, and stable monetary and financial system. The agency conducts the nation's monetary policies, supervises and regulates banks, guards the credit rights of consumers, and provides financial services and information to the government, financial institutions, and the general public."[7] This creates a financial system that has become the foundation of the US Federal Reserve System. The Federal Reserve Board has generally responded well to financial crises, although critics charged that the Board's tight-money policies following the stock market crash of 1929 worsened the subsequent depression. The Board's efforts to end double-digit inflation in the late 1970s triggered a severe recession. In the 1990s, the Board under Chairman Alan Greenspan was widely "credited" with keeping inflation down during the longest uninterrupted period of sustained prosperity in the nation's history.[8] Since the 2007–2009 financial crisis unfolded, many have come to express doubts concerning Mr Greenspan's monetary policy. Most economists came to vilify his actions as Chairman of the Board: the lax regulations and loose monetary policy developed under his chairmanship are seen as the direct causes of the current financial bubble.

To some economists, the Federal Reserve failed miserably to forecast the state of the US economy, and when it pretended to have a forecast, the model used was flawed. The Board of the Federal Reserve was not only discredited all around the world, but many expressed serious reservations about the intellectual capabilities of those in charge of our monetary policy. To many, the Federal Reserve is an opaque institution, not accountable to the nation for its actions. Most of the Federal Reserve's actions are and remain discretionary, and its monetary policy a mystery. As well as all these flaws, the Federal Reserve is more-or-less a club of well-connected "economists and/or lawyers" without a clear set of sound monetary policies.

1.2   The Organizational Structure of the Federal Reserve

In its two first decades, the Federal Reserve contained two loci of power: the main one was the head or the Governor of the Federal Reserve Bank of New York, and of lesser importance was the Federal Reserve Board, in Washington DC[9] It was in 1934 when Marriner Eccless, an outsider from the influential Morgan's rule in the New York Fed, posed as a pre-condition of his acceptance of his appointment as governor of the Federal Reserve Board, that the center of gravity shifted from New York to Washington DC[10] Today, the Federal Reserve is organized as follows:

- the Board of Governors;
- the Federal Open Market Committee;
- the Federal Reserve Banks; and
- the Board of Directors.

1.2.1   The Board of Governors

The Board of Governors (BoG) represents the ultimate authority of the Federal Reserve System. It was established as a Federal agency and is composed of seven Governors, mostly professional economists and jurists, appointed by the President of the United States and confirmed by the Senate for a staggered 14-year term. The Chairman (and Vice Chairman) is also appointed by the President with the advice and consent of the Senate, for four-year terms. The Board of Governors and its staff of about 1700 are located in Washington, DC.

> In selecting the members of the Board, not more than one of whom shall be selected from any one Federal Reserve District, the President shall have due regard to a fair representation of the financial, agricultural, industrial, and commercial interests, and geographical divisions of the country.[11]

However, in practice, the regional restriction placed by the Federal Reserve Act is loosely applied.[12] Ben Bernanke and Donald Kohn, for instance, represent the Atlanta and Kansas City Districts, but they neither lived nor worked in these districts at the time of their appointments. Also, despite the requirement that the members of the Federal Reserve Board reflect a range of interests, the Board is dominated by economists and bankers. The primary aim of the Board is to determine and implement monetary policy. The Board also exercises supervisory and regulatory activities over the Federal Reserve Banks, bank holding companies, and Federal Reserve System banks. The Board decides the percentage of deposits member banks must hold as reserves. It reviews and approves the interest rate, or the discount rate, and charges member banks for Federal Reserve loans.

Furthermore, there are three advisory groups that aid or assist the Board of Governors:

1. Federal Advisory Council, consisting of one member from each Federal Reserve bank. Its major concerns involve banking and economic issues.
2. Consumer Advisory Council, consisting of 30 specialists in consumer and financial matters.
3. Thrift Institutions Advisory Council, consisting of people representing thrift institutions, and is concerned with issues affecting those institutions.

At least four times per year, the 12 members of the Federal Advisory Council meet with the members of the Board of Governors to discuss and assess general economic conditions.

1.2.2   The Federal Open Market Committee

The Federal Reserve System's vital element is the Federal Open Market Committee (FOMC). The FOMC is comprised of the members of the Board of Governors, the president of the Federal Reserve Bank of New York, and presidents of four other Federal Reserve banks, who serve on a rotating basis. Its role is made up of the following responsibilities.

1. **Open market operations** consist of the purchase or sale of securities, primarily US Treasury bonds, in the open market to influence the level of balances that depository institutions hold at the Federal Reserve banks. Put differently, when the Federal Reserve buys US Treasury bonds it injects money into the economy, with an aim of keeping the interest rates at lower levels. Conversely, when the Federal Reserve sells the Treasury bonds it tends to reduce the volume of the money in circulation in order to raise the interest rates.

   In 2010, the Federal Reserve also initiated a controversial money supply approach referred to as "quantitative easing", whereby it injected money into the economy through the purchase of bonds from the market in order to balance the money supply. The effect of such a measure has been below expectations; it sent the wrong signal to the markets as to the interest rates, without boosting the key sector of economic growth in the US – construction.
2. **Reserve requirements** are requirements regarding the percentage of certain deposits that depository institutions must hold in reserve in the form of cash or in an account at a Federal Reserve bank.

3. **Contractual clearing balances** are amounts that a depository institution agrees to hold at its Federal Reserve bank in addition to any required reserve balance.
4. **Discount window lending** consists of credits extensions to depository institutions made through the primary, secondary, or seasonal lending programs. Through its "discount window", the Federal Reserve extends loans to financial institutions – solvent commercial banks – in urgent need of liquidity.

The recent 2007–2009 crisis revealed substantial corporate governance flaws within the Federal Reserve's structural organization. Power concentration and the absence of an accountability culture led those in charge of the Federal Reserve to consider themselves as "above the law" in a country which proclaims that "everybody should be bound by the rule of law".

1.2.3   The Federal Reserve Banks

The Federal Reserve banks were established by Congress as the operating arms of the United States' central banking system.

The 12 districts Federal Reserve banks are: Atlanta, Boston, Chicago, Cleveland, Dallas, Kansas City, Minneapolis, New York, Philadelphia, Richmond, San Francisco, and St. Louis (Figure 1.1). They operate under the general supervision of the Board of Governors located in Washington DC.

Federal Reserve banks generate their own income through interest earned on government securities acquired in the course of Federal Reserve monetary

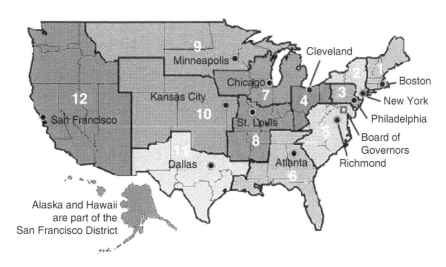

Figure 1.1   The 12 US Federal Reserve districts.

policy, and through services provided to depository institutions, as required by the Monetary Control Act of 1980. Each of the Federal Reserve banks is organized into a "corporation" whose shares are sold to the commercial banks and thrifts operating within its jurisdiction or district. However, they are neither publicly-traded corporations nor for-profit corporations. Each year, they return to the US Treasury all earnings in excess of Federal Reserve operating and other expenses.

Each Federal Reserve bank is composed of nine directors, classified into classes A, B, and C, depending on how they have been appointed. Three class A directors are selected by the member banks; three class B directors are also elected by member banks to represent the non-banking sector of the economy; and three class C directors are appointed by the Board of Governors and represent the non-bank public. Furthermore, the Federal Reserve Bank of New York is seen as the "primus inter pares" since it not only sits in the world's financial center but serves as the Federal Open Market Committee's operating arm, conducting open market operations and foreign exchange intervention. Congress chartered these banks and, consequently, has supervisory responsibilities for them.

The Board of Governors has the authority to set the interest rates that the 12 banks charge "their member banks for loans as well as determine the amount of reserves that banks must keep on hand, in order to stabilize the economy and prevent wide fluctuations. In addition, the board sets margin requirements for financial securities traded on the stock exchanges. It also establishes maximum interest rates on time deposits and savings deposits for its member banks."[13]

1.3   Role and Functions of the Federal Reserve

The original rationale behind the Federal Reserve Act of December 23, 1913 was to make certain that there will always be an available supply of money and credit in the United States with which to meet unusual banking requirements. Banks of a new class, to be known as Federal Reserve Banks, were to be established and upon these banks was to rest the heavy responsibility of supporting the structure in periods of financial strain.[14] This makes sense, since there is always a foundation that the US economy can turn to in times of financial distress.

Before the Federal Reserve Act, banks had to depend on the loan contraction and the selling of securities. Now, they resort to the Federal Reserve Banks, securing additional funds from these by rediscounting commercial loans.[15] This new system lent a helping hand in alleviating the financial pressure on the banking institutions. Other reasons, as stated in the Federal Reserve Act, were to: furnish an elastic currency; to afford means of rediscounting commercial paper; to establish a more effective supervision of banking in the United States; and for other purposes.[16]

1.4   The Federal Reserve's Policies and Processes

The Federal Reserve has several duties that it must follow:[17]

1. To conduct the nation's monetary policy by influencing the monetary and credit conditions in the economy in pursuit of maximum employment, stable prices, and moderate long-term interest rates. This is an important task that the Federal Reserve must perform to ensure that the US economy is stabilized without running into any financial crisis.
2. To regulate and supervise banking institutions to ensure the safety and soundness of the nation's banking and financial system and to protect the credit rights of consumers. This duty protects consumers so that they are not exploited by the financial institutions.
3. To maintain the stability of the financial system and contain systemic risk that might arise in financial markets. This goes hand-in-hand with the aforementioned duties that reduce the risk whilst preserving a balance.
4. To provide financial services to depository institutions, the US government, and foreign official institutions, including playing a major role in operating the nation's payments system.

All these duties emphasize the significance of the supervision and regulation of the Federal Reserve by Congress. In essence, these responsibilities state that the Federal Reserve controls and has the responsibility for the management of total spending and aggregate demand as well as inflation. In carrying out its monetary policy management (via manipulating reserves), the Federal Reserve influences interest rates – especially short-term rates – as well as foreign exchange rates and other financial market prices. And in times of financial crisis, the Federal Reserve's lender-of-last-resort function stabilizes the entire financial system. The significance of these important considerations is briefly summarized as follows:[18]

1. **Management of aggregate demand** Monetary policy dominates fiscal policy:[19] "Most economists recognize that total spending or aggregate demand is determined more by monetary policy than by fiscal policy. In other words, if Congress passes tax or spending legislation intended to affect total spending or aggregate demand, these effects can be fully offset or outweighed by changes in monetary policy. Indeed, accurate counter-cyclical fiscal policy – altering budget deficits to manage economic activity or aggregate demand – is now seen as neither possible nor desirable. Economists no longer agree even on the direction of the economic effects of changing budget deficits, yet all agree that changes in monetary policy do have predictable and potent effects on aggregate demand and economic activity."[20] This implies

that changes in monetary policy are often a major factor in movements of the business cycle: "... many booms and recessions are directly related to changes in monetary policy". Conversely, stable economic activity is often the result of appropriate, stable monetary policy.

2. **Inflation is determined by monetary policy** Inflation negatively impacts savings, distorts investment decisions and can be used by government to enhance its tax revenue and reduce its real debt. Inflation works to distort the signals of the price system and the signaling mechanism of a free market economy. Studies have demonstrated that higher inflation is associated with lower economic growth. Therefore, the monetary policy can take steps toward fostering long-term economic growth in order to promote price stability.

3. **Interest rates are influenced by the Federal Reserve** The interest rates affect fundamental segments of the economy such as housing, autos, and investment. It is projected that the Federal Reserve influences interest rates by manipulating reserves.

   For instance, short-term rates are more directly influenced by Federal policy because its reserve operations involve purchases and sales of short-term government securities which influence bank reserves. However, long-term rates are also influenced by monetary policy. Among other influences, long-term rates are affected by changes in inflationary expectations as well as expectations of Federal policy. Nonetheless, the easiest way monetary policy can sustain lower long-term rates is by promoting price stability, thereby removing the influence of both inflationary expectations as well as uncertainty premiums.

4. **The Federal Reserve is the lender of last resort** The Central Bank, being the ultimate supplier of system-wide reserves, can satisfy sharp increases in reserve or liquidity demand, thereby preventing systemic liquidity shortages and stabilizing the financial system. Failure to provide this function, as, for example, during the Great Depression of the 1930s, proves disastrous. On the other hand, liquidity provision prevented any serious financial system fallout from the sharp 1987 stock market crash and 1989 stock market decline. The Federal Reserve (and by inference the US Congress) has responsibility to ensure that lender-of-last-resort safeguards are adequate and in place in case of unforeseen financial shocks.[21]

5. **Through their discount and credit operations** Reserve banks provide liquidity to banks to meet short-term needs stemming from seasonal fluctuations in deposits or unexpected withdrawals. Longer-term liquidity could also be provided in exceptional circumstances. The rate the Fed charges banks for these loans is the discount rate (officially the primary credit rate).[22]

6. **By making these loans** the Fed serves as a buffer against unexpected day-to-day fluctuations in reserve demand and supply. This contributes to

the effective functioning of the banking system, alleviates pressure in the reserves market and reduces the extent of unexpected movements in interest rates. For example, on September 16, 2008, the Federal Reserve Board authorized an $85 billion loan to stave off the bankruptcy of international insurance giant American International Group (AIG). The Federal Reserve System's role as lender of last resort was criticized for shifting risk and responsibility away from lenders and borrowers and placing them on others in the form of taxes and/or inflation.[23]

The current functions of the Federal Reserve System are:[24]

- To address the problem of banking panics
- To serve as the central bank for the United States
- To strike a balance between private interests of banks and the centralized responsibility of government
- To supervise and regulate banking institutions
- To protect the credit rights of consumers
- To manage the nation's money supply through monetary policy to achieve sometimes-conflicting goals
- Maximum employment
- Stable prices, including prevention of either inflation or deflation
- Moderate long-term interest rates
- To maintain the stability of the financial system and contain systemic risk in financial markets
- To provide financial services to depository institutions, the US Government, and foreign official institutions, including playing a major role in operating the nation's payments system
- To facilitate the exchange of payments among regions
- To respond to local liquidity needs
- To strengthen US standing in the world economy
- To address the problem of bank panics
- Elastic currency

1.5   Activities and Responsibilities of the Federal Reserve

In conjunction with the FOMC and the 12 Reserve Banks, the Board of Governors' main concern is the development of monetary policy, which it carries out through:

1. **The establishment of reserve-level rates** This determines the amount that member banks must set aside to be reserved against deposits. These amounts are heavily dependent on "… the nation's economic activity status, with

emphasis placed on price levels and the volume of business and consumer expenditures. By lowering the required reserve-level rate, banks can increase the proportion of funds they are able to lend to customers. When the economic activity is flat or low as it now [in 2012], the reserve level rates is one of the tools the Federal Reserve could consider in order to boost the economic activity.

To the contrary, by raising the required reserve-level rate, the Federal Reserve will reduce the amount of liquidity available and thus contract the economic activity. Thus, the Fed can influence such factors as economic activities, the money supply, interest rates, credit availability, and prices. However, a change in a reserve-level rate usually causes banks to change their strategic plans. In addition, a reserve-level rate increase is costly to banks. Consequently, changes in reserve-level rates are uncommon."[25]

2. **The approval of discount rates** (or interest rates at which member banks can borrow short-term funds from their Reserve Bank). During inflation, a discount-rate increase tends to reduce the economic activity because then banks charge higher interest rates to borrowers. On the other hand, a discount-rate decrease is designed to stimulate business activity. The term "discount window" is often used when describing a Reserve Bank facility that extends credit to a member bank.

3. **The federal funds rate** is an important tool affecting day-to-day bank operations. This is the rate charged by one depository institution to another for the overnight loan of funds. This occurs when one bank is short of funds while another has a surplus. The rate is not fixed; it can change from day to day and from bank to bank.

4. **Open market operations** These activities, commonly referred to as "quantitative easing" are conducted by the FOMC. The Fed buys and sells US government securities such as Treasury bills from and to banks and other financial institutions several times a week. As a result, the amounts banks have available to lend to borrowers are affected. For example, when the Fed buys securities, banks have more funds, so interest rates tend to drop. The opposite occurs when the Fed sells its securities. By and large, open-market operations comprise the most powerful tool the Fed has to influence monetary policy.

Other activities and responsibilities of the Federal Reserve System include the following:

1. **Supervision of the 12 Reserve Banks and their branches** With regard to the latter, the Board of Governors, through the Reserve Banks, uses both on- and off-site examinations to maintain awareness of each member

bank's activities. These activities include the quality of loans, capital levels, and the availability of cash.

2. **Cooperative efforts of the US Treasury and the Fed** The Fed acts as the Treasury's fiscal agent by putting par per money and coins into circulation, handling Treasury securities, and maintaining a checking account for the Treasury's receipts and payments.
3. **Oversight of banking organizations** such as bank holding companies (companies that own or control one or more banks).
4. **Provision of an efficient payments system** such as check collections and electronic transactions. With billions of checks in circulation each year, the Fed plays a major role in assuring their efficient processing. By arrangements among the Reserve Banks, member banks and non-member banks, checks are credited (added to) or debited (subtracted from) to depositors' accounts speedily and accurately.
5. **Enforcement of consumer credit protection laws** These laws include: the Community Reinvestment Act, which promotes community credit needs; the Equal Credit Opportunity Act, which prohibits discrimination in credit transactions on the basis of marital status, race, sex, and so forth; the Fair Credit Reporting Act, which allows consumers access to their credit records for the purpose of correcting errors; and the Truth in Lending Act, which enables consumers to determine the true amount they are paying for credit.
6. **Establishment of banking rules and regulations**.
7. **Determination of margin requirements** (the amount of credit granted to investors for the purchase of securities, such as shares of stock). The borrowed funds are usually secured from a bank or a brokerage firm (a company that sells stocks and/or bonds). Liberal margin requirements often damage the stock market and the economy.
8. **Approval or disapproval of applications for bank mergers** The Fed also acts if the new bank is to become a state Member Bank of the Federal Reserve System.
9. **Approval and supervision of the Edge Act** and "agreement corporations". Both cases involve corporations that are chartered to engage in international banking. Edge Act corporations are chartered by the Fed, while "agreement corporations" secure their charters from the states. The latter are so named because they must agree to conform to activities permitted to Edge Act corporations. The Fed is also responsible for approving and regulating foreign branches of member banks and for developing policies regarding foreign lending by member banks.
10. **Issuance and redemption of US savings bonds** Regardless of how the bonds are purchased – for example, through an employer savings plan or a bank – it is the Fed that processes the applications and sends the bonds.

1.5.1 Monetary Commission

In framing its bill, the Monetary Commission seems to have been guided by two principles generally wise in legislation – the scope of the measure was limited to the single purpose of removing purely banking defects in our banking system, and no greater departure from existing arrangements was proposed than was essential for the purpose in sight. The Federal Reserve Act certainly runs counter to the first of these principles. Its primary purpose is similar to that of the bill of the Monetary Commission; but a secondary purpose was to decentralize credits by lessening the concentration of banking funds in a few large banks in the chief financial centers and especially in New York.[26]

The Reserve Banks are permitted to engage in three kinds of open market operations: (1) dealing in government securities, and also in obligations of the states and local bodies, maturing within six months and issues in anticipation of taxes; (2) dealings in foreign exchange; and (3) dealings in domestic bills of exchange. In European countries, many purchasers who pay at once often draw a bill of exchange on their own bank and, after it has been accepted, discount it in the open market. In the US, under the Act banks are to be allowed to accept only bills drawn in connection with merchandize exports and imports.[27]

1.5.2 Policy Operations

The Federal Reserve conducts monetary policy principally using open market operations to alter bank reserves and influence short-term interest rates, but it also can employ the discount rate and changes in reserve requirements as policy tools. The Federal Reserve utilizes the "fed fund rates" as the main policy tool. There have been numerous movements that influence financial market instruments such as interest rates, foreign exchange rates, commodity prices, and yield spreads, monetary and credit aggregates, measures of economic and business activity, and eventually broad measures of inflation. Since there is a long time lag between adjustments to Federal Reserve instruments and ultimate policy goals, monetary policymakers look for those variables that are both reliably influenced by the Fed policy moves and in turn predictably related to subsequent movements in policy goals (i.e., they look for reliable intermediate guides to policy).

Currently, there are numerous debates among economists and scholars over the controversies about monetary policy and which components best serve as intermediate policy guides or targets. In the past, "Keynesian economists" prescribed target variables such as unemployment or interest rates whereas monetarist economists prescribed monetary aggregates as targets. However, none of these targets has been reliable.

Currently, the Federal Reserve has no explicit or preferential policy target. Rather, it uses an eclectic approach, but undoubtedly has paid more attention to movements in financial market variables than in the past. That pragmatic approach has led some scholars to question whether the Federal Reserve itself understands the steps it is taking to fix the economy. Of course, the Federal Reserve is being challenged as never before since its inception. The Federal Reserve policies of today are commanded by the effects of the crisis as they unfold.

1.5.3 Congressional Oversight of Monetary Policy

Congress oversees and establishes objectives for the Federal Reserve and makes certain that the Central Bank is accomplishing this goal. This can be fostered by establishing appropriate incentives for monetary policymakers as well as mandating enhanced reporting and disclosure requirements related to progress in achieving stated objectives. Supervision, therefore, should promote policy transparency which can help to promote the credibility of a given monetary policy.[28] Further, it would be more efficient if Congress itself could rely upon sound experts rather than Washington DC lobbyists.

1.5.4 Open Market Operations

Open market operations put money in and take money out of the banking system. This is done through the sale and purchase of US Government treasury securities. When the US Government sells securities, it gets money from the banks and the banks get a piece of paper (IOU) that says the US Government owes the bank money. This drains money from the banks. When the US government buys securities, it gives money to the banks and the banks give the IOU back to the US Government. This puts money back into the banks. The Federal Reserve education website describes open market operations as follows:[29] "Open market operations involve the buying and selling of US government securities (federal agency and mortgage-backed). The term 'open market' means that the Fed doesn't decide on its own which securities dealers it will do business with on a particular day. Rather, the choice emerges from an 'open market' in which the various securities dealers that the Fed does business with—the primary dealers—compete on the basis of price. Open market operations are flexible and thus, the most frequently used tool of monetary policy".[30] The open market operations control the supply of bank reserves. They typically purchase the "securities issued by the U.S. Treasury, Federal agencies and government-sponsored enterprises. Open market operations are carried out by the Domestic Trading Desk of the Federal Reserve Bank of New York under the direction of the FOMC. The transactions are undertaken with primary dealers."[31] The principal objective in trading securities is to "... affect the federal funds rate, the rate at which banks borrow reserves from each other. When the Fed wants to increase reserves, it buys securities and pays for them by making a deposit to the account maintained at the Fed by the primary dealer's bank. When the Fed wants to reduce reserves, it sells securities and collects from those accounts. Most days, the Fed does not want to increase or decrease reserves permanently so it usually engages in transactions reversed within a day or two. That means that a reserve injection today could be withdrawn tomorrow morning, only to be renewed at some level several hours later. These short-term transactions are called repurchase agreements (repos) – the dealer sells the Fed a security and agrees to buy it back at a later date."[32]

1.6   Independence of the Federal Reserve

Whether the Federal Reserve is independent or not is still a moot point. According to a study conducted by Mehta,[33] the Federal Bank system of the US cannot be independent, mainly because of the following reasons.

It is stated that at the Federal Bank there is a tremendous concentration of power in the hands of a select few, who make decisions for the entire country. Furthermore, any error of judgment by the Fed has dire consequences on the overall economy: "Although the President has the power to appoint the members into Fed's Board of Governors, the bulk of the Fed is elected by members of the Board of Governors, Federal Reserve Bank branches, commercial banks, and financial institutions".[34] Those institutions have the tendency to co-opt their own members, regardless of their qualifications and expertise in the monetary and tax policies required. Given the crucial nature of its objectives, it is imperative that the Federal Reserve attract talented civil servants who would bring knowledge and independence of spirit into the debates.

If the Fed were independent, as Mehta points out, it can run "monetary policies more smoothly and effectively". In addition, the Fed's independence could give it power to immediately avert any crisis without having to delay or wait upon Congress's side-line political show. Having an ability to make self-regulating decisions can work on behalf of the government and give lasting benefits to the US.

Even though the Federal Reserve is perceived as an independent entity, it is not truly so. It is still liable and accountable to Congress and comes under government audit and review. The Federal Reserve officials report regularly to Congress on monetary policy, regulatory policy, and a variety of other issues, and they meet with senior Administration officials to discuss the Federal Reserve's and the Federal Government's economic programs. The Fed also reports to Congress on its finances.[35] This ensures that the Federal Reserve is constantly being checked and supervised by Congress which maintains equilibrium between checks and balances. While all these interactions, checks, and balances could lead to a higher-quality delivery, the result is just the opposite. The doctrine of central bank independence is meaningless when, as in the United States, those to whom the Federal Reserve officers report are not well-equipped to understand the premises of the Federal Reserve monetary policy, or become complacent in monitoring the activities reported before them. Independence in a vacuum provides no benefits.

In contrast, as pointed out by Professor Stiglitz: "Brazil and India, neither of which have fully independent central banks, are among the good performers; the European Central Bank and the Fed are among the poor performers."[36]

1.7   Reforming the Federal Reserve

Over the years there have been numerous proposals pursuant to the Federal Reserve reforms. In a commentary, Otho Smith,[37] professor at the University of Mississippi, asserts that to make sure the Federal Reserve Bank is performing its job effectively, there must be some changes which should be mandated in its systems and policies. There has been debate about reducing the number of regional banks from 12 to five, to be more efficient and ensure the Fed can carry out its supervisory responsibilities efficiently. Another proposal requires that the Federal Reserve be more transparent in its activities so that the general public can better understand the institution.

The Fed functions in almost an opaque manner, under its mistaken assumption that the Freedom of Information Act did not extend to it, at least in key respects.[38] Transparency would certainly assist the Fed in its mission, given the significance of its mandate and its impact on American life. The recent decision by the Federal District Court of District of Columbia Washington against the institution constitutes a step in the right direction, as long as the Circuit Court of Appeals and finally the US Supreme Court are still looking at the best interests of the United States and even the world. The Fed decision affects not only the US financial markets, but also other financial markets across the world. Ultimately, the proposed reforms are intended to (a) make the Fed more accountable to the public; (b) give the responsible people greater incentives to participate in their assigned activities; and (c) define the Fed's goals more specifically.[39] As time passes, the demands of the people vary and the rules and regulations that were written almost a century ago cannot be followed today since they have become almost obsolete. It is vital for the Federal Reserve to be at par with current times so that the laws are more practical and sensible. All the aforementioned proposed reforms by the respective parties are justified. The Federal Reserve should take a new outlook on the way it has been functioning and see whether there are any reforms that will make its policies and processes contemporary and more proficient. The Federal Bank should definitely adopt those so that it works more effectively and efficiently.

Finally, the Federal Reserve needs to focus more on "the issue of U.S. national debt and asset prices instead of a narrow measure of inflation", said Marc Sumerlin.[40] The Federal Reserve should take more account of asset prices in its assessment of overall financial stability. As seen from the European Central

Bank experience, it is clear that a constant monitoring of asset prices helps to identify shocks that might hit the economy. Prior to the Wall Street and Consumer Protection Act of 2010, the Fed did not incorporate asset prices of the banks and other financial institutions into its scrutiny of its monetary analysis. A clear monitoring of asset prices could prevent, or at least mitigate, the sub-prime mortgage scenario. That is, the Fed would have to broaden its view on inflation to add or consider commodity prices and keep credit growth in check.[41] Monetary policies should not be limited to a single variable – the consumer index price – but rather take into account a series of variables such as the price of assets and the exchange rates.[42]

1.8   Conclusion

Finally, the United States' Federal Reserve policy needs to be more transparent to the public. As discussed above, the argument that a lot of the decisions that take place in the Federal Reserve are made by a select few is justified; however, the government must take the necessary measures to ensure that the decisions made by the Fed are the best options for the benefit of the country. It would also be recommended for Congress to step in and include other sectors of the government to take part in the decision-making process of the Federal government. With more people advising the Federal Reserve, it would be easier for the government to have better checks and balances and be an efficient control on the Federal Reserve.

2
The European Central Bank System

2.1 Introduction

On May 3, 1998, European Union (EU) leaders took the most significant step toward European integration since the signing of the Treaty of Rome in 1957. They agreed, in substance, that monetary policy within the Union was no longer under the exclusive control of EU member states' central banks, but was transferred to the Economic Monetary Union (EMU) of the European Union. The substance of monetary union is that most countries within the EMU no longer have distinct national currencies. A new currency – the euro (€) – has replaced nearly all national currencies. To qualify under the European System of Central Banks (ESCB), a member state should meet specific requirements: a high degree of price stability, sound public finances, a stable exchange rate, and stable long-term interest rates. The ESCB commenced operations on June 1, 1998, and assumed responsibility for the conduct of monetary policy for the euro area on January 1, 1999. The ESCB is headquartered in Frankfurt, Germany; and its present is Dr Mario Draghi,[43] the former Governor of the Italian Central Bank. National central banks are the ESCB shareholders. Shares are based on the GDP and population of each member state. However, all states of the ESCB have the same powers of decision, regardless of their size and GDP, and best decisions are made to benefit all the states that use the euro.

The Eurosystem is composed of the ESCB and the national central banks of the 16 member states that adopted the euro out of the 27 EU states, listed in Table 2.1.

When the ESCB was created, it covered a Eurozone of 11 member states, which included Austria, Belgium, Finland, France, Germany, Ireland, Italy, Luxembourg, the Netherlands, Portugal, and Spain. Greece joined the Eurozone in January 2001, Slovenia in January 2007, Cyprus and Malta in January 2008, and Slovakia in January 2009, enlarging the bank's scope and the

Table 2.1 Member states of the ECB
that adopted the euro.

Nation	Joined Date
Austria	Jan. 01. 1999
Belgium	Jan. 01. 1999
Finland	Jan. 01. 1999
France	Jan. 01. 1999
Germany	Jan. 01. 1999
Ireland	Jan. 01. 1999
Italy	Jan. 01. 1999
Luxemburg	Jan. 01. 1999
Holland	Jan. 01. 1999
Portugal	Jan. 01. 1999
Spain	Jan. 01. 1999
Greece	Jan. 01. 2000
Slovenia	Jan. 01. 2007
Cyprus	Jan. 01. 2008
Malta	Jan. 01. 2008
Slovakia	Jan. 01. 2009

Source: ECB.

membership of its Governing Council. The other member states that are a part of the EU but do not use the euro are: Bulgaria, the Czech Republic, Denmark, Estonia, Hungary, Latvia, Lithuania, Poland, Romania, Sweden, and the United Kingdom.

The European Central Bank (ECB) was established in June 1998 alongside the ESCB. However, the foundations which led to the creation of the ECB and the EMU started in January 1958, in the aftermath of the Treaty of Rome even though none of the members had the vision of a single currency in mind.

In January 1999, the euro became the single currency of the Euro area. Conversion rates are fixed irrevocably for the former national currencies of the participating member states and a single monetary policy is created for the Euro area. Thus, having adopted the euro as their single currency, the EU member states that are part of the Euro area have relinquished their monetary sovereignty. The euro currency was designed to bind EU nations into a tighter economic union so that weaker members draw strength from the prosperous members and close the gap in growth and productivity. The ECB, as the core of the newly-established ESCB, has taken on responsibility for the monetary policy in the Euro area. Basically, the ESCB is made up of the ECB and the national central banks (NCBs) of the 27 member states. However, unlike the ECB and the NCBs, the ESCB has no legal personality or capacity to act. Instead, the components of the ECB, the NCBs and the ESCB carry out the tasks assigned to the latter. It also should be noted that the ESCB includes the NCBs of all the

EU member states, including the countries which do not wish to give up the sovereignty of their currency for the euro.

Thus, the respective central banks of the member states, although within the Euro zone, are not obligated to carry out the ESCB's core systems. This is the reason why, in 1998, the Governing Council decided to add in its lexicon the term "euro system" in order to make the public grasp the complexity of the structure of the system. "Euro system" basically refers to the composition of the ECB and the NCB of the member states that have adopted the euro. Three main (political and economic) reasons explain the rationale for the establishment of such a system of central banks:

1. The establishment of a single central bank for the whole Euro area (possibly concentrating central bank business in one single place) would not have been acceptable on political grounds.
2. The Euro system approach builds on the experience of the NCBs, and preserves their institutional set-up, infrastructure, and operational capabilities and expertise. Moreover, NCBs continue to perform some non-Euro system-related tasks.
3. Given the geographic scope of the Euro area, and the cultural differences among the participants, it was deemed appropriate, and even acceptable to have built a system of ESBS that rely upon national banks put under the authority of a unique central bank.[44]

2.2   Organization of the European Central Bank

The ECB has been designed as a network of national central banks plus the ECB itself as a central institution. The ECB is composed of three decision-making bodies: (a) the Executive Board, (b) the Governing Council, and (c) the General Council.

2.2.1   The Executive Board

The Executive Board is made up of the President of the ECB, the Vice-President and four other members, all appointed by common agreement of the presidents or prime ministers of the Euro area countries. In addition to the six, the Executive Board includes governors of the national central banks of the 16 Euro area countries. The Executive Board members are appointed for a non-renewable term of eight years.

The Executive Board is responsible for implementing monetary policy, as defined by the Governing Council, and for giving instructions to the national central banks. It also prepares the Governing Council meetings and is responsible for the day-to-day management of the ECB.

2.2.2   The Governing Council

The Governing Council is the European Central Bank's highest decision-making body. It comprises the six members of the Executive Board and the governors of the 15 central banks of the Euro zone. It is chaired by the President of the ECB. Its primary mission is to define the monetary policy of the Euro zone and, in particular, to fix the interest rates at which the commercial banks can obtain money from the Central Bank.

2.2.3   The General Council

The General Council is the ECB's third decision-making body. It comprises the ECB's President and the Vice-President and the governors of the national central banks of all 27 EU member states. The General Council's role consists of adopting guidelines and making decisions which ensure the continued performance of the tasks of the Euro system. In addition, the General Council

Figure 2.1   EU member states within the Eurozone.
Source: ECB.

formulates monetary policy related to key ECB interest rates and liquidity. Finally, it contributes to the ECB's advisory and coordination work and helps prepare for the future enlargement of the Eurozone. Figure 2.1 shows the EU member states participating in the euro.

2.3   Objectives of the European Central Bank

The objectives of the European Central Bank are defined by the Maastricht Treaty that established it. Under Article 105 of the Maastricht Treaty, the primary objective of the ECB is to maintain price stability and, without prejudice to the objective of price stability, to support the general economic policies in the EU. In contrast to the US Federal Reserve which pursues price stability and full employment simultaneously, the objectives of the ECB have been prioritized.

The Governing Council defined price stability as a year-on-year increase in the Harmonized Index of Consumer Prices (HICP) for the Euro area below 2%. In 2003, the Governing Council clarified that it aims to maintain inflation rates below, but close to, 2% over the medium-term horizon. However, the ECB has never defined the "medium term" with reference to a predetermined horizon, but deliberately retains some flexibility with regard to that time frame. Besides price stability, the ECB is also responsible for or must ensure financial stability with the Eurozone. Recently, or since the 2007–2009 financial crisis, the ECB has performed like a lender of last record to EU central banks in distress, such as Greece, Ireland, Portugal, Spain, and Italy.

2.3.1   The European Central Bank and Price Stability

Under the Governing Council, price stability is based upon two pillars: economic analysis and monetary analysis. The Governing Council often cross-checks the results under the two pillars and makes needed adjustments in order to maintain price stability.

Economic Analysis

Economic analysis aims to assess the short- to medium-term determinants of price developments, with a focus on real activity and cost factors driving prices over those horizons. Put differently, economic analysis focuses on the interplay between the small to medium risks to price stability, taking into consideration several economic and financial macroeconomic variables including, inter alia, overall output, aggregate demand, fiscal policy, foreign exchange conditions, the balance of payment, and the global economic outlook. It relies upon real economic indicators and the financial market development. Further, as the ECB has to be more accurate in its assessment, the economic analysis anticipates series of disturbances or shocks that might hit the economy as well as their overall effect. Such disturbances include, for example, a temporary rise in the oil price, perturbation on other foreign markets, strikes, and so on.

In 2009, the EU Commission endorsed a recommendation from the De Larosière Report and proposed the establishment of the European Systemic Risk Board (ESRB), responsible for macro-prudential supervision in the European Union.[45]

Monetary Analysis

The prime function of monetary analysis is to serve "as a means of cross-checking, from a medium- to long-term perspective, the short- to medium-term indications coming from economic analysis".[46] Monetary analysis, contrary to the economic analysis, gives more weight to the role of money in controlling price stability. The ECB keeps a watch on the rate of money to ensure that growth is consistent with price stability. Any deviation from the threshold would be adjusted by the use of specific tools, mainly interest rates.

2.3.2   The European Central Bank and Financial Stability

The pursuit of financial stability is considered as a contribution to the main objective of price stability. Put differently, financial stability helps the ECB to foster price stability. In the long run, financial stability and price stability reinforce each other.

Financial stability consists of liquidity management with the primary goal to mitigate as much as possible the risk that protracted liquidity shortages turn into bank solvency problems.[47] In 2008, when EU banks became reluctant to lend to each other, the ECB stepped in and provided enhanced credit support in various ways, including: the extension of the maturity of long-term refinancing operations from six to 12 months; the purchase of covered bonds; liquidity provision in foreign currencies; and unlimited provision of liquidity through fixed rate tenders with full allotment. The ECB provided short-term funds to deficit banks and absorbed funds from surplus banks as lender of last resort despite its limited mandate from the Maastricht Treaty.

2.4   Implementation of Monetary Policy

To conduct its monetary policy, the ECB uses several instruments and procedures to steer interest rates, manage liquidity in the money market, and signal monetary policy intentions. To that end, the ECB conducts open market operations.

2.4.1   Open Market Operations

The ECB conducts open market operations either as an expansionary monetary policy[48] or a contractionary monetary policy.[49] The ECB open market operations can be divided into four categories: Main Refinancing Operations (MROs); Long-term Refinancing Operations (LTROs); Fine Tuning Operations (FTOs); and Structural Operations (SOs).

All these operations are executed in a decentralized manner by the national central banks.

Main Refinancing Operations

Main Refinancing Operations (MROs) constitute the most important open market operations and stand as the key monetary policy instrument of the Euro system. Through its MROs, the Euro system lends funds to financially-sound credit institutions subject to the Euro system's minimum reserve, and under the supervision of at least one national banking authority. MROs are conducted on a weekly basis, and have a maturity of one week. Any financial or credit institution that meets the stated eligibility criteria can have access to the MROs under the NCB tenders' requirements. To protect the Euro system against financial risks, borrowers (credit institutions) are required to provide adequate collateral. This collateral is composed of two distinct classes of assets: (a) marketable assets and (b) non-marketable assets.[50] To protect the Euro system against financial risks, all eligible assets are subject to specific risk-control measures. The Euro system MRO tenders come under two distinct forms: the fixed rate MRO tender and the variable rate MRO tender. In both procedures, the ECB determines the amount of liquidity to be provided.

- **Fixed interest rate MRO tender** In a fixed rate MRO tender, participating counterparties bid the amount of money they are willing to transact under the specified interest rate fixed by the ECB. A fixed rate tender implies a pro rata allotment among the participating banks, based upon the ratio between the total bid and the total liquidity to be allotted. A participant can only make one bid for the period.
- **Variable interest rate MRO tender** In a variable interest rate MRO tender, the counterparties bid both the amount of money they are willing to transact and the acceptable interest rates. Participants can make more than one bid. The bids with the highest interest rates are allotted first, followed by bids with lower interest rates until the total amount of liquidity is exhausted.

Long-term Refinancing Operations

Long-term Refinancing Operations (LTROs) aim to provide longer-term liquidity to the banking system. As opposed to MROs, LTROs have a maturity of at least one month but it is possible to find LTROs with maturity of 6–12 months and above. All qualified participants satisfying the eligible criteria can participate under the ECB standard tenders. In general, LTROs are executed in the form of pure variable rate tenders, based upon a specified volume of money fixed by the Governing Council.

Fine-tuning Operations

Fine-tuning Operations (FTOs) aim to manage the Euro system liquidity situation in order to keep the interest rates within the appropriate range. Put differently, FTOs aim to smooth the effects on interest rates caused by unexpected liquidity fluctuations. FTOs are quick tenders, that is, they take one hour from the announcement to the final allotments.

Structural Operations

Structural operations are executed whenever the ECB wishes to adjust the structural position of the Euro system vis-à-vis the financial sector. Structural operations can be conducted either in the form of reverse transactions[51] or issuance of debt instruments.

2.4.2 The Inadequate Implementation of Policy

The Eurozone system lacks institutions, rules, and tools to adequately manage its monetary policy. This is because of one of the main characteristics of the Euro system, which is the coexistence of a single monetary policy and fiscal policies considered to be the responsibility of participant member states. Though some member states' central banks are involved in the management of their public debt, they do so independently from their Euro system responsibilities. Further, various Articles from the Euro System Treaty prohibit or limit the authority of the ECB:

- Article 101 of the Treaty prohibits the ECB or national central banks from providing overdraft facilities or any other type of credit facility as well as from purchasing government debt in the primary market.
- Article 102 prohibits public entities' privileged access to financial institutions.
- Article 103 explicitly stipulates that neither the Union nor any member state is liable for or can assume the commitments of any other member state.

Those prohibitions and limitations were premised upon the assumption that member states would, by themselves, live up to the Treaty's requirements. They did not.

The sharp drop in interest rates in several Eurozone countries, the excessive dependence on external funding, the inadequate risk management at the levels of both the member states and their banks have created the current Eurozone sovereign debt crisis. Sovereign debt crises have revealed the congenital defects of the Euro System Treaty. As the crises unfolded within the group of countries known as "the P.I.I.G.S",[52] the ECB appeared unprepared to tackle the issue as no adequate tool was available. It was then compelled to walk away from the Treaty prohibitions already mentioned and reinvent its mission. The ECB initiated bail-out rescue programs despite the prohibition under Article 103 of the Maastricht Treaty.

On May 9, 2011, the ECB agreed to buy bonds from distressed Eurozone members (Spain and Italy), and suspend the minimum rating threshold for Greek collateral.

In October 2011, the ECB agreed to provide a second bail-out package to Greece in exchange for the Greek government restructuring its debt and conforming with the Stability and Growth Pact. The bail-out of any delinquent Eurozone member state is, at most, a palliative solution. The Eurozone sovereign debt crisis provides a unique opportunity for the Eurozone member states to strengthen their fiscal integration on the one hand and set adequate rules in term of Euro-bank equity capital on the other.

Strengthening Fiscal Integration

An adequate cure for the Eurozone sovereign debt crises would require that member states relinquish the core of their fiscal sovereignty to the ECB or another institution that must have the authority to supervise and oversee national budgets and achieve greater fiscal integration than is currently the case. Several proposals have emerged in the midst of the sovereign debt crises. Wolfgang Schaeuble, the German Finance Minister, has called for the creation of a "European Monetary Fund" and new financing facilities. Though enticing, the institution of a European Monetary Fund, modeled under the IMF, is not a panacea. At best, it is a utopia. A new EU body which copies the flaws of the IMF would deliver as little as the IMF itself. Rather, the search or compromise toward greater Eurozone fiscal integration seems the proper route to pursue.

Adequate Capitalization of Euro System Banks

Capital positions of European banks need to be reinforced to provide additional safety margins and thus reduce uncertainty. Eurozone banks are among the world's most leveraged and remain in need of protection from counterparty risks. Banks' equity capital levels should be significantly increased. Michel Barnier, the EU's Internal Market Commissioner, has proposed a plan to that end. In short, the Barnier draft goes beyond the global Basel III Accord, and would compel the 8200 Euro-banks to hold more and better quality capital over the six years from 2013. The draft insists also on improving EU banks' corporate governance, and introduces whistle-blowing programs.

Though enticing, the draft would not be adopted soon, given the amount of inertia in the EU.

2.5   Monetary Growth and Inflation

The ECB's monetary analysis relies on the fact that monetary growth and inflation are closely related in the medium to long term. Therefore, by assigning money a prominent role through taking policy decisions not only on the basis of the short- to medium-term indications stemming from economic analysis but also on the basis of money and liquidity considerations, the ECB is able to see beyond the impact of the various shocks and avoids any temptation to take an overly activist course. To signal its commitment to monetary analysis and provide a benchmark for the assessment of monetary developments, the ECB has announced a reference value for the growth of the broad monetary aggregate M3. This reference value refers to the rate of M3 growth that is deemed to be compatible with price stability over the medium term.

In December 1998, the Governing Council set this reference value at 4½% per annum and confirmed it in subsequent reviews. The reference value is based on the definition of price stability and on the medium-term assumptions of potential real GDP growth of 2–2½% and a decline in the velocity of circulation of money of between ½% and 1%. The reference value is not a monetary target but a benchmark for analyzing the information content of monetary developments in the Euro area. Owing to the medium- to long-term nature of the monetary perspective, there is no direct link between short-term monetary developments and monetary policy decisions. Monetary policy does not react in a mechanical way to deviations of M3 growth from the reference value. The ECB's monetary analysis is not limited to the assessment of M3 growth in relation to its reference value. Many other monetary and financial variables are closely analyzed on a regular basis.

For example, developments in the components of M3 (cash in circulation, time deposits among others) are studied because they can offer an insight into the overall changes in M3. In this respect, narrower aggregates such as M1 might contain some information about real activity. Similarly, changes in credit extended to the private sector can be informative about financial conditions and, through the monetary financial institutions (MFI), balance sheets can provide additional information about money. Such analysis helps provide both a better insight into the behavior of M3 in relation to the reference value and a broad picture of the liquidity conditions in the economy and their consequences in terms of risks to price stability.[53] Thus, monetary policies adopted by the ECB since 1999 have been mainly dominated by its preoccupation with inflation. The ECB officials often argue that they have succeeded in maintaining inflation at low levels. I personally think that they have every right to be proud of themselves, the reason being that the ECB is relatively new compared to other central banks and the financial environment has not been at its best since two years after the ECB was put in place. However, the 2011 global market turbulence has challenged the ECB Board as never before. The current crisis in Spain and Italy has compelled the ECB to raise economic stability on to the same footing as price stability. The ECB intervened in the markets to buy Spain and Italy bonds in order to cool off the markets.

From this, one can definitely say the ECB engaged in extraordinary measures because the times were calling for such measures. However, one has to agree that even though they manipulated the policy rate more than once just to keep banks afloat, refacilitate credit and ease the growing concerns of a global financial collapse, they stayed true to their number one priority which is price stability.

The ECB monetary policy is blind-sided as it relies only on the consumer price index as the US Federal Reserve, and ignores fluctuations in financial asset prices and the effect of the exchange. To be more effective, the ECB needs also to coordinate, through specific EU mechanisms, the economic situation of its member states. The recent crisis in Portugal, Italy, Ireland, Greece, and Spain could challenge the ECB to rethink its mandate and broaden the scope of its monetary policy.

2.6   Independence of the European Central Bank

The European Central Bank is an independent central bank in the sense that no EU institution has any formal control over it. Further, the independence of the ECB is spelled out in the Treaty that set up the institution. Articles 130 and 282 of the EU Treaty and Article 7 of the European System of Central Banks confirm without ambiguity the independence of the ECB. Furthermore, members of the decision-making bodies of the ESCB cannot be dismissed for reasons other than the reasons stipulated in the ESCB statute. The ECB has its own capital, with an independent budget from other EU institutions.

2.7   Comparing the Fed and the European Central Bank

This section expounds the similarities and the differences between the two banks' monetary policies which have been implemented over the last ten years. The purpose behind the establishment of the Federal Reserve System was to provide the nation with a sound and stable financial system after the nation was plagued with financial crises in the early 19th century. Over the years, the functions of the Federal Reserve have evolved into four main areas: (a) the conduct of the nation's monetary policy by influencing monetary and credit conditions; (b) the pursuit of maximum employment; (c) the stabilization of prices and moderate long-term interest rates; and (d) the supervision or and regulation of the banking institutions to ensure the safety of the nation's economy. The way the European Central Bank and the Federal Reserve Bank analyze monetary strategy in order to make monetary policy is quite different.

The ECB focuses on two strategies. One is the economic analysis that focuses on shorter-term economic and price developments and the second is the monetary analysis that focuses on longer-term inflation. Meanwhile, the Fed focuses mainly on economic forecasts in order to make decisions about monetary policy operations.

Monetary aggregates and asset prices both play a role in the ECB's monetary policy while neither of these conditions play an important role on their effects on growth or inflation for the Fed's monetary policy. One last difference noted by the ECB itself is that, in the Euro area, more than 70% of corporate financing is provided by banks, while this share is about 20% in the US.[54] This means that the transmission of the monetary policy in the Euro area relies mostly on banks, unlike in the United States where financial markets are more important. This is the reason why the Federal Reserve had to engage in many schemes to save several key financial markets when the crisis hit home while the ECB had only to preoccupy itself with providing credit support for the banks.

3
The Central Bank of Japan

3.1 Introduction

Established in June 1882, under the Bank of Japan Act, the Bank of Japan (BoJ) has been operational since October 10, 1882. The Bank of Japan, which is the central bank of Japan, was established in response to (a) the 1868 Meiji Restoration which led towards the country's industrialization; and (b) the failure of the existing banking system, which mirrored the United States' banking system.[55]

Today, the BoJ is one of the most important banks in the international finance arena as a result of its long-term role as a source of the cheapest funding available. It plays a significant role in the global financial markets. Since its establishment, the BoJ has been reorganized several times, in 1942, 1997, and 1998.

Article 1 of the 1942 Law requires that the BoJ conducts policy so "... that the general economic activities of the nation might adequately be enhanced". It has as its objective regulation of the currency, control and facilitation of credit and finance, and the maintenance and fostering of the credit system, pursuant to national policy, in order that the general economic activities of the nation might be enhanced adequately.

The 1997 Law also restricts the monetary policy of the BoJ to two core objectives: price stability and maintenance of an orderly financial system. The 1998 Law provides the BoJ with more independence in the conduct or the pursuit of these two objectives.

Whilst, in general, ownership of central banks is limited to governments and institutions' members, the capital structure of the BoJ did not adhere to this principle. The BoJ is capitalized at 100 million yen in accordance with the Act, which states:

> The amount of stated capital set forth in the preceding paragraph, the amount of contribution by the government shall be no less than fifty-five million yen.

Therefore, the current holding is as follows:

- 55% of the capital is held by the Japanese government;
- 45% of the capital is held by the private sector, mainly individuals.

The BoJ subscription certificates (stocks) are listed on the Japanese stock exchanges (i.e., Tokyo, Osaka, and Nagoya).

3.2   The Organizational Structure of the Bank of Japan

The Bank of Japan's organizational structure is made up of (a) the Governor, (b) two deputy Governors, (c) six Executive Directors, and (d) 16 head offices. The BoJ structure also includes a Management Committee, a Compliance Committee, the office of Auditors, and the office of Counselors.

In order to aid implementation, the BoJ has created:

- 32 branches, which conduct operations relating to currency issue and banking operations, and carry out research on the economic and financial situation in their respective areas;
- 14 local offices in Japan, which handle some of the operations of the head office or branches; and
- seven overseas representatives offices, which perform a liaison function, gather information, and conduct research.

The BoJ is neither a government agency nor a private corporation. It operates with a capital of 100 million yen out of which 55% is subscribed by the Japanese government.

3.2.1   The Bank of Japan Policy Board

The Policy Board of the BoJ is composed of nine individuals: the Governor, the two Deputy Governors, and the six Executive Directors. The nine members are appointed by the Cabinet, with the approval of the Diet, for a five-year term.[56] The Policy Board of the BoJ is the highest decision-making body; it determines the guidelines for currency and monetary control, sets the basic principles for carrying out the Bank's operations, oversees the fulfillment of the duties of the Bank's officers, excepting the Auditors and the Counselors. Contrary to the US Federal Reserve or the European System of Central Banks, the BoJ Policy Board elects its own President, making its decision by a majority vote.

Amongst other things, the duties of the Policy Board include:

- setting the discount and loans rates;
- setting out the reserve requirements for banks;
- conducting open market operations;
- making loans to financial institutions;

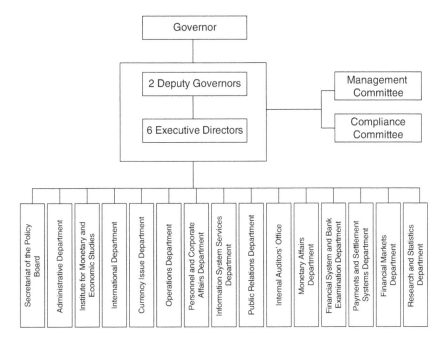

Figure 3.1 Structure of the Board of the Bank of Japan.

- initiating transactions with other central banks; and
- buying and selling foreign exchange in the forex market.

3.2.2 The Officers of the Bank of Japan

The BoJ Officers' body is composed of the Governor, two Deputy Governors, six Executive Directors, six members of the Policy Board, the Auditors,[57] and the Councellors.[58] Figure 3.1 describes the BoJ's board.

3.3 Core Functions of the Bank of Japan

The BoJ pursues multiple objectives: price stability and maintenance of the financial system stability. The 1998 Law sets price stability objectives in qualitative terms. However, the Policy Board has determined a range of 0–2% as the target medium term.

3.4 The Monetary Policy of the Bank of Japan

The BoJ monetary policy is aimed at maintaining price stability. The 1998 Act states that:

> BoJ monetary policy should be aimed at achieving price stability, thereby contributing to the sound development of the national economy.

The Policy Board meets once or twice a month at gatherings known as the Monetary Policy Meetings (MPMs) to discuss and decide the right step in furtherance of the monetary policy goals. The monetary policy decisions are made by a majority vote of the nine members of the Policy Board.

3.5   Implementation of the Monetary Policy

To implement its monetary policy, the Policy Board holds regular scheduled Monetary Policy Meetings, through which several tools are discussed and used to ensure price stability and overall economic growth. Monetary market operations and lendings are the two most used tools. The Policy Board manages its money market operations by either purchasing or selling Japanese Government Securities (JGS) and bills, or by granting loans to financial institutions. Through market operations, the Policy Board controls and influences the volume of money in the economy and the level of interest rates. Money market operations encompass direct loans to commercial and financial institutions. Besides money market operations, the Bank of Japan is also engaged in foreign exchange intervention in the foreign exchange market.

3.5.1   Money Market Operations

There are two types of money market operations: (a) fund-supplying operations, and (b) fund-absorbing operations. Participants in money market transactions are required to provide eligible collateral and their transfer of funds and delivery of JGS stemming from money market operations are processed through the Bank of Japan's financial network system.[59]

Fund-supplying Operations

Through fund-supplying operations, the Bank of Japan supplies funds to financial institutions which, in exchange, provide collateral to back up the transactions. Fund-supplying operations consist of (a) purchases of Treasury bills (T-Bills) and financing bills, (b) borrowing of Japanese Government Bonds, (c) purchase of commercial papers, (d) purchase of bills, and (e) purchase of Japanese Government Bonds.

Purchases of Treasury bills and financing bills Treasury bills are either purchased outright or bought under a repurchase agreement (Repo). The BoJ conducts repo purchases of Treasury bills and financing bills in two steps: (a) it purchases the securities through an auction with the promise to then (b) sell them back on a specified date (within six months), receiving interest for the holding period of these securities. Securities repurchased shall be resold within one year from the next day of the purchase date. The Policy Board takes into consideration the condition of the overall financial markets in order to determine the amount of Treasury bills and financing bills to be purchased, as well as the eligible counterparties.

Borrowings of Japanese Government Bonds (JGBs) Borrowings of JGBs is somehow different, in that the Bank of Japan borrows interest-bearing government bonds against cash collateral, for a specified period of time (usually less than six months). At maturity, the Bank of Japan returns the government bonds to the lender and receives interest.

Purchases of commercial papers Since 1998, the BoJ has operated a commercial paper (CP) purchase facility. The BoJ purchases, through an auction, eligible commercial papers from selected bidders under the condition that the commercial papers are resold on a specified date (usually less than three months). At maturity, the BoJ sells back the commercial paper at a price equivalent to the purchase price plus interest.[60] Purchasable commercial papers include: dematerialized commercial paper issued by domestic corporations; dematerialized commercial paper issued by foreign corporations with guarantees; government-dematerialized commercial paper; dematerialized asset-backed commercial paper; and dematerialized commercial paper issued by real estate investment corporations accepted as eligible collateral by the BoJ. CPs purchased shall be resold within three months from the next date of purchase. CPs shall be purchased and resold through a discount method.

Purchase of bills There are two types of bill-purchasing transactions: (a) outright purchases of bills, and (b) outright purchases of bills collateralized by corporate debt obligations.

Purchases of Japanese Government Bonds Purchases of JGBs consist of outright purchases of interest-bearing government bonds, through an auction, by the Bank of Japan without any repurchase commitment.

Fund-absorbing Operations

Through fund-absorbing operations, the Bank of Japan absorbs funds by issuing and selling bills to financial institutions.

Fund-absorbing operations consist of (a) sales of Treasury bills or financing bills, and (b) sales of bills.

Sales of Treasury bills and financing bills There are two types of sales: (a) outright sales, and (b) sales under REPOs. The transactions are the opposite of the purchases of T-bills and financing bills already discussed.

Sales of bills Sales of bills consist of outright sale. The Bank of Japan drew bills to operation counterparties at face value minus an amount of interest.

3.5.2 Foreign Exchange Interventions

Very often the Bank of Japan, in collaboration with the Minister of Finance, engages in foreign exchange intervention during Tokyo market hours (between

7:00 pm and 3:00 am, NY time). However, if the target goal is not achieved, the BoJ stretches its foreign exchange intervention through the intermediation of the European System of Central Bank in the early hours of the morning. Since 2000, the BoJ has shown some restraints on its foreign exchange intervention.

3.6   The Independence of the Bank of Japan

The 1998 Act states that:

> The Bank of Japan's autonomy regarding currency and monetary control shall be respected.

However, the Act goes on to add that:

> The Bank of Japan shall always maintain close contact with the government and exchange views sufficiently.

In practice, the BoJ has expressed its independent status in such a way that it has been criticized, or even vilified, by many Japanese politicians. For the Japanese public, the people really affected by its monetary policy decisions, the BoJ is one of the most transparent central banks in modern history. The BoJ always clarifies its monetary policy stances, as well as its decision-making processes. The Governor, the Chairman of the Policy Board, holds regular press conferences to discuss monetary policy decisions in more detail. Moreover, twice a year, the BoJ submits a Semiannual Report on Currency and Monetary Control to the Diet. Furthermore, the Governor and other members of the Policy Board appear before committees on both houses of the Diet, the House of Representatives and the House of Councelors, to answer any concerns the bodies might have.

3.7   Reforming the Bank of Japan

The Bank of Japan needs to focus its fight against deflation by using all monetary tools available, and get prices rising again. The quantitative easing steps taken so far are merely palliative and will not boost the money base forever. Japan's economic problems are structural, and the BoJ, in conjunction with the Central Government need to recognize them as such. That is because, though the BoJ is independent, the limits on its authority are set by politicians. The new Governor, Massaki Shirakawa, acknowledges that there are limits to what the monetary policy can achieve.

4
The Bank of England

4.1 Introduction

Established in 1684, the Bank of England (BoE) is the central bank of the United Kingdom. The BoE is an independent public organization, wholly owned by the Treasury Solicitor on behalf of the government. The BoE's conduct of monetary policy is seen by many as a model for the rest of the central banks.[61] The BoE is the sole issuer of bank notes in England and Wales, and regulates the issue of bank notes by commercial banks in Scotland and Northern Ireland. The BoE also manages the United Kingdom's gold reserve and its foreign exchange reserve. Monetary policy is conducted by the Monetary Policy Committee, a talented group of experts.

4.2 The Organizational Structure of the Bank of England

The Bank of England is managed by its Board of Directors, and relies upon its several departments. The BoE board of directors is composed of the Governor and 16 other persons appointed by the UK government for three years. Four directors are employees of the bank and the other 12 are the managers of big companies. The government appoints the Governor of the bank for the period of five years. All practical issues are discussed by the Monetary Policy Committee (MPC) consisting of the Governor, his deputy and five directors.

4.3 The Monetary Policy Committee

The monetary policy of the Bank of England is conducted by both the Chancellor of the Exchequer who sets out the interest rate target, and the MPC, which manages the money aggregate to meet the set up interest rate. The MPC meets at least once a month over two consecutive days. Decisions

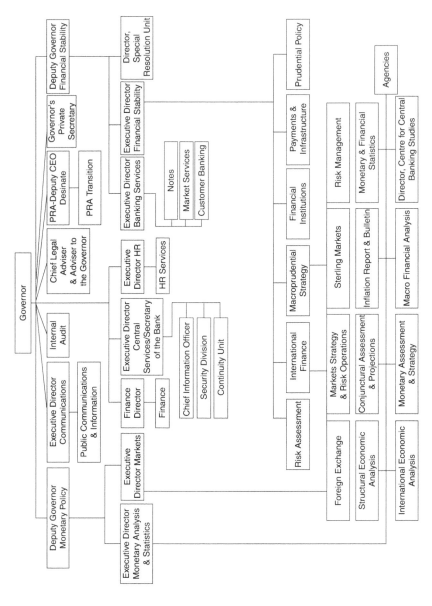

Figure 4.1 The Bank of England divisional structure.

of the MPC are made on a one-person-one-vote basis. The decision is announced the second day (Thursday), by noon. Each member of the MPC is an expert in the field of economics and monetary policy. Members do not represent individual groups or areas; they are independent. Each member of the Committee has a vote to set the interest rate at the level they believe is consistent with meeting the inflation target. The MPC's decision is not a consensus of opinion; it reflects the votes of each individual member of the Committee.

4.4   The Core Functions of the Bank of England

The primary objective of the BoE consists of maintaining monetary stability. Its inflation target is about 2% +/– 1%. Besides the inflation target goal, the BoE pursues a wider economic goal of sustainable growth and employment. The BoE is also tasked with watching for possible risks to the financial system arising from domestic and external factors. Price stability is achieved when inflation remains low and stable for a long period of time. The focus on price stability has raised questions of whether the objective is enough by itself.[62]

4.5   The Bank of England Monetary Policy Framework

The present monetary policy framework is dependent on the 1998 Bank of England Act. It is set by the Government, and carried out by the MPC, which is responsible for setting an interest rate suitable to meet the inflation target as defined by the Chancellor of the Exchequer. Since 1997, the inflation target has been set to 2% with 1% tolerance, based upon the Harmonized Inflation Consumer Index (HICP). The MPC bases its monetary policy decisions upon its forecast of inflation pressures in the economy.[63] Inflation expectations, which derive from the difference in yield between nominal and inflation-indexed bonds, are anchored at around 2.5%. The optimal forecast horizon under inflation targeting depends on two factors: (a) the length of the monetary transmission lags, and (b) the policymaker's output and inflation preferences. The MPC reviews a wide variety of official statistics, survey indicators and financial market data and, through the use of macroeconomic models, forecasts the quarterly interest rates. Further, the MPC considers the relative volatility of real activity when setting interest rates, and does not use monetary rules in setting the policy rate. The MPC monetary policy framework combines a statutory commitment to low inflation and a discretionary power to respond to any shock that could affect the projections.

4.6   Implementation of the Monetary Policy

Though the BoE's monetary policy has multiple objectives, price stability seems to be its main tool. Any deviations from the target inflation above or below 1% would require the MPC (the Governor) to release an "Open Letter Procedure" to the Chancellor of the Exchequer (see Appendix 2), which explains, among other things:

- the causes of the deviations;
- the course of actions contemplated by the MPC in order to correct the deviation and bring it back to the targeted inflation rate;
- the expected time by which the deviation is to be mended;
- the known and unknown effects of the deviation on the overall economy and other pursued goals.

To that end, the BoE, through the Sterling Monetary Framework,[64] uses different monetary tools such as (a) reserve averaging; (b) operational standing facilities; (c) quantitative easing; (d) discount window facilities; (e) the extended collateral term Repo facility; and (f) operational contingencies.

4.6.1   Reserve Averaging

The reserve averaging framework is the BoE's preferred method of implementing monetary policy defined solely in relation to the level of the bank rate. Commercial banks are required to hold an average level of reserve over the maintenance period between MPC gatherings. Usually, the MPC determines an aggregate demand for banks (the collective target) and each participant bank sets its own target within the collective target. A participant bank which cannot meet its target is exposed to charges. However, a participant bank can avoid that charge by making use of the BoE's operating standing facilities. Sterling Monetary Framework members borrow from or lend to each other via their reserve accounts held in the BoE. A participant bank with excess reserves lends through the interbank market to those commercial banks short of liquidity, at market rate.

4.6.2   Operational Standing Facilities

Operational standing facilities (OSF) have two roles: (a) to provide an arbitrage mechanism in normal market conditions to prevent money market rates from moving too far away from the BoE rate; and (b) to provide a means for participating banks to manage unexpected payment shocks.[65]

Through OSF, participant banks borrow reserves directly from the BoE, on a bilateral basis, each business day, which takes the form of overnight Repo against high-quality collateral. OSF also comes with a cost, as commercial banks are required to pay a premium over the bank rate.

4.6.3   Quantitative Easing

Quantitative easing refers to a monetary policy that consists of boosting the money supply through large-scale asset purchases in order to meet the inflation target in the medium term. The MPC uses quantitative easing at any time it considers that, in the medium term, inflation would be more likely to undershoot the target. Quantitative easing does not imply the creation of additional bank notes. Rather, the BoE creates, electronically, new money and uses it to purchase Treasury bonds, notes and the like. The MPC sets a target for the stock of asset purchases financed by the creation of reserves, which is achieved by either purchasing or selling assets through the Bank's Asset Purchase Facility.

4.6.4   Discount Window Facilities

A discount window facility (DWF) is a bilateral facility designed to be able to address short-term liquidity shocks (Figure 4.2). A DWF offers liquidity insurance for idiosyncratic as well as system-wide shocks, and is available throughout each business day. Through the DWF, participants can, for a fee, borrow cash against a wider range of potentially less liquid eligible collateral. DWFs are used as a back-stop rather than a regular source of liquidity. At its discretion, the BoE could agree to lend sterling cash rather than gilts. DWF drawings are intended to be for a maximum of 30 days, although they can be rolled over at the Bank's discretion. For an additional fee, the Bank currently also permits drawings with a maximum term of 364 days. Eligible collaterals are classified in four categories, from the liquid to the least liquid. The fees charged to participants depend on the type of collateral provided, and the size of the drawing relative to the size of the participant group. Participants are called to transfer DWF-eligible collateral into the BoE custody, but still retain legal ownership.

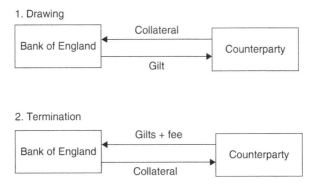

Figure 4.2   Discount window facility structure.

4.6.5   The Extended Collateral Term Repo Facility

An extended collateral term Repo (ECTR) facility is a contingency liquidity facility that the BoE activates in response to actual and prospective market-wide stress of an exceptional nature.[66] Its maturity is 30 days. Introduced on December 6, 2011 to relieve the financial market from exceptional stress, the ECTR is designed to mitigate risks to financial stability arising from a market-wide shortage of short-term sterling liquidity. It is expected that the new facility will provide the Bank of England with an extra layer of flexibility to offer sterling liquidity in an auction format against the widest range of collateral.

In conjunction with the Indexed Long-Term Repo (ILTR) operations, and the permanent availability of the DWF for bilateral transactions, the ECTR facility will give the Bank the ability to ensure that the banking sector has sufficient access to sterling liquidity to mitigate any risks that could arise from unexpected shocks. At its discretion, the BoE would announce ECTR operations to respond to actual or prospective market-wide stress. The operations would offer sterling for 30 days against collateral pre-positioned for use in the Bank's DWF. Participants registered for access to the Bank's DWF would be eligible for ECTR operations. The size of any ECTR operation would be announced the day prior to the operation.

4.6.6   Operational Contingencies

In the event of major operational or financial disruption to the sterling money market or other supporting infrastructure, the BoE can display liquidity facility and provide exceptional contingency liquidity afloat.[67] The BoE makes and publishes recommendations in its report to help improve business continuity planning at financial institutions, and be the coordinating point in the event of a disaster. Its reports suggest that market infrastructures should have specific powers to deal with operational disruptions, that the financial authorities should contribute to international efforts to develop best practices, and that they should promote international cooperation and coordination in handling major operational disruptions. The BoE has contributed to the creation of a high-level committee to ensure coordination across financial markets in the event of a disruption.

4.7   The Independence of the Bank of England

The BoE became a truly independent institution in May 1997. However, the MPC is accountable to both Houses of the UK Parliament: the House of Commons Treasury Select Committee and the House of Lords Select Committee on Economic Affairs.

4.8   Reforming the Bank of England

Recent events, particularly the 2008–2010 financial crisis, have challenged the corporate governance structure of the Board of the MPC. The United Kingdom Parliament is considering adding a supervisory board in addition to the current board of the MPC, which would require that the members of the Supervisory Board be external to the BoE. The proposal also requires that the core missions of the BoE be expanded beyond price stability and financial stability. While the proposal is enticing from a corporate governance viewpoint, it fails to untie the link between the Chancellor of the Exchequer and the MPC. Sound reform would strengthen both the independence of the MPC and its accountability.

5
The People's Bank of China

5.1 Introduction

The People's Bank of China (PBoC) was created in 1948 through the consolidation of China's former banks: Huabei Bank, Beihai Bank, and Xibei Farmer Bank. From 1950 to 1978, the PBoC served the entire Chinese financial system as a central bank as well as a commercial bank. In 1978, the PBoC parted from the Ministry of Finance and ceased to perform as a commercial bank. The commercial bank duties were divided among four state-owned banks: the Bank of China (BoC), the Construction Bank of China (CBC), the Agricultural Bank of China (ABC), and the Industrial and Commercial Bank of China (ICBC). These state-owned commercial banks, though heavily regulated by the government, are becoming more commercially oriented.[68] The PBoC became a central bank in 1983, when its status was changed by the Chinese State Council. Meanwhile, the China Banking Regulatory Commission was established to monitor and supervise China's financial industry.

Article 12 of the People Republic of China's constitution provides:

> The PBoC is to establish a monetary policy committee, whose responsibilities, composition, and working procedures shall be prescribed by the State Council and shall be filed to the Standing Committee of the National People's Congress. The monetary policy committee shall play an important role in macroeconomic management and in the making and adjustment of monetary policy.

The Monetary Policy Committee is a consultative body that advises the PBoC on the formulation and adjustment of monetary policy, application of monetary policy instruments, and coordination between monetary policy and other macroeconomic policies.

The Monetary Policy Committee is composed of 13 members, including the Governor of the PBoC. Despite the Monetary Policy Committee's advisory function, the PBoC is still under the leadership of the State Council, and any decision pursuant to monetary policy must be approved by the State Council before it is implemented. China's reality is even more complicated than that: its monetary policy is the consequence of compromise and negotiation among a variety of bureaucratic agencies and the Communist Party.

5.2   The Status of the People's Bank of China

The Law of the People's Republic of China on the People's Bank of China adopted on March 18, 1995 by the 3rd Plenum of the 8th National People's Congress has since legally confirmed the PBoC as having central bank status. With the improvement of the socialist market economic system, the PBoC, as a central bank, will play an even more important role in China's macroeconomic management. The amended law of the People's Republic of China and the People's Bank of China, adopted by the 6th meeting of the standing committee of the 10th national people's congress on December 27, 2003 provides that the PBC performs the following major functions:

1. Drafting policy related to fulfilling its functions.
2. Formulating and implementing monetary policy in accordance with law.
3. Issuing the renminbi and administering its circulation.
4. Regulating financial markets, including the inter-bank lending markets, the inter-bank bond markets, foreign exchange market and gold markets, etc.

The PBoC is the central bank for China. Its function includes developing and implementing an independent monetary policy to stabilize the currency and promote economic growth. It also supervises all the financial markets and institutions. For many westerners, the PBoC is merely a government department which functions directly under the authority of the State Council, with a relatively independent legal status. Its status of independence should be further strengthened as the society and economy develop.

The China Banking Regulatory Commission is separated from the central bank's financial system which has a great impact on the traditional system of the Central Bank of China. The PBoC and the China Banking Regulatory Commission need to strengthen their connection and communication in order to promote each other, so as to ensure the operation of Chinese financial institutions under a robust, efficient and safe environment. The PBoC is posted in the leading position of a country's financial system, it is responsible for the issuing the currency, controlling its circulation and other national financial policies.

China began to form a modern central bank system from September 1983, and gradually established a combined financial macro-control system which now consists of direct control and indirect regulation. However, the financial macro-control of China has not achieved its goals completely. The results are unsatisfactory; there still exist many institutional and operational problems.

5.3   The Organizational Structure of the People's Bank of China

The PBoC is composed of the Governor and a number of deputy governors. The Governor is appointed into or removed from office by the president of the People's Republic of China, and approved by the National People's Congress. The deputy governors are also appointed into or removed from office by the Premier of the State Council. The PBoC is headquartered in Beijing, and has eight functional departments:

- the Monetary Policy Department;
- the Financial Market Department;
- the Financial Stability Bureau;
- the Credit Information System Bureau;
- the Anti-Money Laundering Bureau;
- the Legal Affairs Department;
- the Graduate School of the PBoC;
- the PBoC Trading Center.

5.4   The Monetary Policy of the People's Bank of China

The objective of the PBoC's monetary policy consists of maintaining stability and promoting economic growth.[69] As summarized by Geiger (2006), the authorities use various monetary policy instruments to achieve that objective.

Since 1998, the PBoC has officially changed the intermediate targets of the monetary policy from total credit quotas and currency in circulation (M0) to money supply. There are two measurements of broad money in China: M1 and M2. Since 1995, the movements of M1 and M2 have displayed divergent patterns. The PBoC nevertheless has never explicitly specified which measure of broad money is to be the intermediate target. According to the PBoC's criteria for its selection, an intermediate target for monetary policy should be measurable, controllable, and have close correlations with the ultimate policy goals (i.e., controlling, inflation and the promotion of economic growth).

China's monetary policy affords a prominent role to money supply. According to the People's Bank, an appropriate supply of money would promote "economic growth positively and contribute to preventing both inflation and deflation" (PBoC, 2005). Moreover, the monetary authority specifies annual targets for money growth, most prominently for the broad money supply (M2). China's monetary policy contrasts with monetary policy models followed by its counterparts (i.e., European Union, United States) which combine money supply and interest rates.

China's monetary authorities have been rather reluctant to use interest rates as a major operating target. Instead, they set annual intermediate targets for money supply growth (M1 and M2). For some years, the central bank also announced a target for credit growth. They have then controlled the money supply by setting the reserve requirement ratio and deciding upon the central bank lending which used to form a significant part of commercial banks' financing. The PBoC has also controlled market liquidity through open market operations with treasury bonds and, since 2003, by selling central bank bills to the commercial banks.

The authorities have also used administrative policy tools to guide financial sector development in China. Until the start of 1998, credit plans basically formed the basis for bank lending. This policy, which means direct guidelines and orders from the authorities to the commercial banks, was intensified due to rapid credit growth in 2003 and again in 2007.

The PBoC uses several monetary policy tools to perform its duties. The key tools are: (a) interest rates, (b) the reserve requirement, (c) open market operations, (d) the exchange rate, and (e) the administrative monetary policy.

5.4.1 Interest Rates

Through its monitoring of lending rates, deposit rates, relending rates, and the rediscount rate, the PBoC controls the supply and demand of circulating money within China's economy. In theory, the PBoC is in charge of fixing the interest rates, but in reality it has little leverage. Twice in 2008,[70] the PBoC cut the one-year lending and deposit rates by 27 and 108 basis points, respectively. Since the beginning of 2011, the PBoC has already twice raised the benchmark one-year borrowing and lending rates. Interest rates and changes thereon are divisible by nine, instead of the increments of 25 used by most other central banks.[71]

5.4.2 The Reserve Requirement

The reserve requirement seems to be one of the most used tools in China's monetary policy, just behind the exchange rate. The PBoC has increased the bank reserve requirement ratio three times in 2011, as it is stumbling to crackdown inflation. The PBoC commits itself to utilizing the reserve requirement ratio in order to withdraw liquidity from the banking system.

5.4.3 Open-market Operations

As with other central banks, the PBoC also conducts open market operations to control the flow of money supply in the economy. To that end, the PBoC issues bonds to the market or buys back its own issued bonds when it desires to increase money supply. In so doing, it manages liquidity to an appropriate level and promotes moderate credit expansion.

5.4.4   Foreign Exchange Rates

In 2005 and 2008, China allowed its currency to appreciate by 21%; the value of the Yuan, which had been fixed at 8.28 Yuan to a US dollar since 1996, was changed to the current fixed rate of 6.83 to protect exporters from slumping demand. The trade-weighted value of the Yuan has been dragged down during the last year by the weakening dollar, while currencies of several other countries have witnessed unprecedented appreciation; the Brazilian real and the Korean won, for instance, have gained 42% and 36%, respectively, against the Yuan, making severe inroads into these countries' export prospects. The exchange rate is key to China's monetary policy and will remain so for a while.

In 2005, the PBoC adopted the so-called "managed" floating foreign-exchange system, which allows the Yuan to trade against a basket of selected currencies. The daily fluctuation limit is set out, as the Yuan was, or is pegged to the US dollar. Therefore, through its "sterilization" monetary policy (see below), China manages to keep its Yuan below the market valuation. The PBoC artificially maintains a fixed exchange rate between the Yuan and the US dollar. With its trade surplus and foreign capital flows coming into the country, the PBoC steps in and buys all these excess dollars at a fixed rate, and accumulates this excess as official reserves. Thereafter, the PBoC issues Yuan in an amount corresponding to the excess to expand its domestic money supply. In a final step, the PBoC takes back the Yuan injected in the preceding step by compelling banks to hold higher reserves than necessary or by selling them special government bonds. The process is referred to as "monetary sterilization", and allows the PBoC to maintain the Yuan at a fixed but lower exchange rate vis-à -vis the US dollar.

The PBoC has recently acknowledged that its sterilization of the foreign exchange excess is becoming increasingly difficult. Now that China is battling to crack down on its rising inflation (above 5%), the PBoC is combining the foreign exchange tool with the reserve requirement tool to cool down its economy.

Having explained the sterilization process, the explanation of China's foreign exchange becomes obvious. China has learned from previous financial crises, mainly the Asian crises in the 1990s, and is afraid that appreciating the Yuan or letting her currency appreciate or depreciate under the market conditions will affect her monetary policy (or its economy) if the US moves unilaterally to depreciate the dollar. If that occurs, China will have no other choice than to intervene in the financial market, and that could jeopardize its export model economy. Further, given that despite its economic size China has not yet been allowed to voice its opinion within the Bretton-Woods institutions, the authorities in China are suspicious of Western economists' argument that the appreciation of the Yuan is the panacea to its inflation disease. Such a suspicion has been reinforced by the fact that some of the US think-tank institutions have been criticized as "intellectual manufacturing" by major Wall Street players.[72]

In a press conference at Beijing on November 18, 2012, the IMF chief observed that the Yuan could in future be added to the basket of currencies that set the value of Special Drawing Rights (SDRs), the IMF monetary unit. At a forum in Beijing, former IMF Managing Director, Michel Camdessus, also supported the addition of the Yuan to the SDR basket. The government has allowed companies in Shanghai and four other cities in the southern province of Guangdong to take part in a pilot program, which started July 2, 2012, the settlement initially limited to trade with Hong Kong, Macau, and the Association of Southeast Asian Nations (Asean). These developments underline the expanding role for the currency of the world's fastest-growing major economy at a time when certain countries, including Russia and China, have challenged the dollar's dominant position as the world's reserve currency.

5.4.5 The Administrative Monetary Policy

Its administrative monetary policy tool allows the PBoC to almost dictate the conduct of the commercial banks within its jurisdiction. In China, the banking sector dominates the financial industry, and the big four commercial banks, with assets over $1 trillion, remain state-owned. Therefore, through its administrative monetary tool, the PBoC can compel commercial banks to restrict loans any time it wants to tighten its monetary policy, or command them to increase loans when it wants to ease monetary policy.

5.5   The Independence of the People's Bank of China

China's economic role in the banking system has been greatly increased by its economic reforms. The banks offer loans to any enterprises or individuals around the country, the state-owned enterprises providing almost 70% of state bank loans. Even though, according to the state plan, banks provide most of the investment capital, the various state-directed financial institutions have accepted some related policy which has been established since the start of the reform. For economic and commercial purposes, the amounts of available funds that are available through the banks have been increased. This action also increased the foreign capital sources. The World Bank and several United Nations programs provided loans to China. Hong Kong was the main place from which to collect this investment, but this investment also could be a source itself. The Shenzhen Stock Exchange and Shanghai Stock Exchange are China's two stock exchanges; in January 2008, these two mainland stock markets had a market value of $1.8 trillion. After Japan and Hong Kong,

China has became the third largest stock market in Asia. Some economists have estimated that China will soon be the third largest stock market in the world.

Note: China's currency was called the "renminbi", which means "people's currency". It was also called the "Yuan". The PBoC is the only monetary authority of China to issue renminbi. The renminbi is abbreviated as CNY, but sometimes also abbreviated as RMB.

6
The Reserve Bank of India

6.1 Introduction

The origin of the Reserve Bank of India (RBI) can be traced back to 1926, when the Royal Commission on Indian Currency and Finance – commonly referred to as the Hilton Young Commission – recommended the institution of a central bank to separate the control of currency and credit from the government and to increase banking facilities over the country.[73] The Reserve Bank of India, the central bank of India, is entrusted with monetary stability, the management of currency, and the supervision of the financial and payments system. The RBI bank also operates the credit systems and the currency and thus plays a critical role in the Indian economy. However, its functions have evolved in response to the country's changing economic environment, and the increasingly globalized economy. At its origin, the RBI was a private institution before it was nationalized by The Banking Regulation Act of 1940. At first, the RBI headquarters were located in Kolkata, Bengal, but since 1937 its headquarters have been permanently moved to Mumbai, Maharashtra. Beside its headquarters, the RBI has 26 regional offices and branches in India.

In 2006, the RBI inaugurated a new department for customer services in order to provide best quality of service to their customers and to reduce the number of customer complaints.

6.2 The Organizational Structure of the Reserve Bank of India

6.2.1 Management

The organizational structure of the RBI can be divided into two parts: (a) the Central Board of Directors, and (b) the Local Boards.

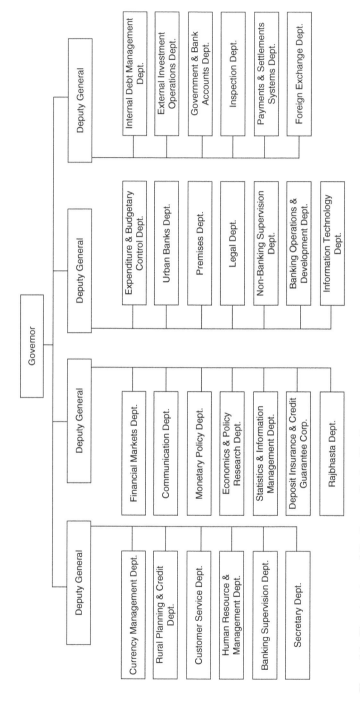

Figure 6.1 The structure of the Reserve Bank of India.

The Central Board of Directors

The Central Board is entrusted with the management of the RBI. It consists of 20 members:

- The Governor is appointed by the central government of India for a five-year term, but can be reappointed for another term. The Governor is the Chief Executive Officer and the Chairman of the Central Board.
- The four Deputy-Governors are nominated by the central government for a five-year term.
- Fifteen Directors are appointed by the Government of India, under the RBI Act, for a four-year term.
- The Governor, the Deputy-Governors, and the Directors can be removed from office by the central government.

The Local Boards

The Local Boards consist of five members appointed by the central government for a four-year term, which can be renewed. Each Local Board elects its own Chairman from among its members. The powers of the Local Boards are limited.

6.2.2 Structure

The RBI is organized into 26 departments that focus on policy issues in their respective areas. Besides these departments, there are 26 regional offices and branches that operate as the RBI interfaces to the public, training centers that provide formation, training and update, research institutes, and subsidiaries. Figure 6.1 describes the structure of the RBI as of the time of writing.

6.3 Core Functions of the Reserve Bank of India

The core functions of the RBI as stated in the Preamble of the RBI Act of 1934 consist of regulating the issue of banknotes and the keeping of reserves in order to secure monetary stability and operate the currency and credit system of the country.[74]

Besides its main function as the Indian Central Bank, the RBI provides additional services, all related to the nation's financial sector.

6.3.1 The RBI as Monetary Authority

The RBI's basic function includes: (a) the regulation of the issue of banknotes, and keeping sufficient reserves in order to secure monetary stability; and (b) the maintenance of the currency and credit system of the country.

The key objectives of the RBI's monetary policy are:

- to maintain price stability;
- to ensure an adequate flow of credit to the productive sectors of the economy to support economic growth; and
- to assure financial stability.

To that end, the RBI monitors and analyzes the movement of a number of indicators including interest rates, inflation rate, money supply, credit, exchange rate, trade, capital flows, and fiscal position.

The Reserve Bank's Monetary Policy Department (MPD) formulates monetary policy; and the Financial Markets Development (FMD) department manages the daily liquidity operations. The RBI uses direct and indirect instruments in monitoring the nation monetary policy.[75]

6.3.2   The RBI as Issuer of Currency

The RBI is the nation's sole issuing authority. It makes sure that the country has an adequate supply of coins, and addresses security issues. The Department of Currency Management is located in Mumbai, and works closely with the regional offices. The RBI acts as a government agent for the distribution, issue and handling of coins.

6.3.3   The RBI as Banker and Debt Manager of the Government

As a banker to the central government, the RBI provides several services, such as:

- undertaking banking transactions for the central government and state governments to facilitate receipts and payments and maintaining their accounts;
- managing the government's domestic debt with the objective of raising the required amount of public debt in a cost-effective and timely manner;
- developing the market for government securities to enable the government to raise debt at a reasonable cost, provide benchmarks for raising resources by other entities and facilitate transmission of monetary policy actions.

6.3.4   The RBI as Banker to Banks

In its capacity as banker to banks, the RBI: enables smooth, swift and seamless clearing and settlement of inter-bank obligations; provides efficient means of funds transfer for banks; and enables banks to maintain their accounts for the purpose of maintaining statutory reserves.

The RBI also operates as a lender of last resort, that is, it provides liquidity to banks in need of liquidity; and extends short-term loans and advances to banks and other financial institutions to facilitate lending for specified purposes.

6.3.5   The RBI as Regulator of the Banking System

The RBI regulates and supervises the nation's financial system. In that capacity, it is in charge of (a) licensing the activities and operations of both domestic and foreign banks within its jurisdiction; (b) prescribing capital requirements; (c) monitoring governance; (d) setting prudential regulations to ensure solvency and liquidity of the banks; (e) prescribing lending to certain priority sectors of the economy; (f) regulating interest rates in specific areas; and (g) initiating new regulation.

6.3.6   The RBI as Foreign Exchange Manager

The RBI assumes three broad roles relating to foreign exchange: (a) regulating transactions related to the external sector and facilitating the development of the foreign exchange market; (b) ensuring smooth conduct and orderly conditions in the domestic foreign exchange market; and (c) managing the foreign currency assets and gold reserves of the country. The stated objective of the RBI's exchange rate policy is to reduce volatility and speculation in the foreign exchange market and to keep the rate in line with economic fundamentals.[76]

The Indian exchange rate became fully "market determined" in January 1993, which means that the exchange rate is not administratively determined. But, in fact, the rupee is pegged to the US dollar through the intervention of the RBI in foreign exchange markets, with very low volatility. The RBI favors exchange rate depreciation in order to boost its export-oriented economic model. India, like China, uses the so-called "sterilization" concept as a means to manipulate her foreign exchange rate. In that regard, the difference between India and China is of degree, not of the nature of the transaction. However, unlike China, the RBI is not allowed by statute to issue bonds. The RBI can only sell bonds as an agent of the Indian Ministry of Finance.

6.3.7   The RBI as Regulator and Supervisor of Payment and Settlement Systems

The Payment and Settlement Systems Act of 2007 gives the RBI power to oversee the payment and settlement systems in the country. This includes transfer of money, currency, paper instruments such as cheques, and other electronic channels of payments.

6.3.8   The RBI's Developmental Role

In this capacity, the RBI performs as an agent of the government to ensure that credit is available to the productive sectors of the economy.

6.4   The Reserve Bank of India's Monetary Policy Framework

India's monetary policy framework has evolved as the country embarks on the development and globalization processes. The framework includes monetary operations and foreign exchange intervention.

6.4.1   Monetary Policy Instruments

The RBI relies on both direct and indirect instruments to conduct its monetary policy.

Direct Monetary Policy Instruments

Direct monetary policy instruments consist of the cash reserve ratio (CRR) and the statutory liquidity ratio (SLR). The CRR refers to the amount of cash that commercial banks must hold with the RBI as a proportion of their net demand and time liabilities. The SLR refers to the sum of money that banks and financial institutions must invest in securities issued by the RBI.

Indirect Monetary Policy Instruments

Indirect monetary policy instruments consist of (a) open market operations (OMO); (b) liquidity adjustment facility (LAF); (c) market stabilization scheme (MSS); and (d) other prudential tools.

Open market operations consist of the outright purchase or sale of government securities. The RBI carries out its OMO in the secondary market on the electronic Negotiated Dealing System – Order Matching (NDS-OM) platform.[77]

Liquidity adjustment facility operations allow the RBI to monitor the overall liquidity conditions and make sure that the volume of liquidity is within the admissible range. The RBI conducts its LAF electronically once or twice a day with participating banks and financial institutions.

Market stabilization scheme operations are another means by which the RBI monitors the volume of the liquidity. Through MSS, the RBI issues securities and government bills in order to absorb any liquidity surplus.

The RBI uses various prudential tools in order to modulate the flow of liquidity. It can do so either by encouraging or restricting credits to specific sectors of the economy to ensure financial stability.

6.4.2   Foreign Exchange Intervention

The RBI has adopted a flexible/managed exchange rate system. It monitors closely the development of both the international and domestic foreign exchange markets and makes adjustments or interventions to keep the rate within the admissible range. Besides the foreign exchange spot market, the RBI is very active in foreign exchange derivatives (i.e., forwards, futures, options, and swap contracts).

7
The Central Bank of Russia

7.1 Introduction

Founded on July 13, 1990, the Central Bank of Russia (CBR) traces its history back to the State Bank of the Russian Empire. The CBR enjoys special status under Article 75 of the Constitution of the Russian Federation. The CBR is not a body of state power; rather, it is a special public and legal institution with the exclusive right to issue currency.

Article 75 of the Russian Federation Constitution provides:

> The monetary unit of the Russian Federation shall be the ruble. The monetary emission shall be the exclusive responsibility of the Central Bank of the Russian Federation. No other currencies may be issued in the Russian Federation.
>
> The protection and stability of the ruble is the main function of the Central Bank of the Russian Federation which it shall exercise independently from other bodies of state power.

According to Article 3 of the Bank of Russia Law, the aims of the Bank of Russia are to: (a) protect the ruble and ensure its stability; (b) promote the development of the Russian banking system; and (c) ensure an efficient and uninterrupted functioning of the payment system.

7.2 The Organizational Structure of the Central Bank of Russia

The organizational structure of the CBR comprises the central apparatus, 60 regional branches, 19 national banks, 1325 cash settlement centers, 13 banking schools, a center of training methods in Tver, a personnel training centre at Klyazma, and 20 organizations accountable to the CBR. The CBR is made up of 26 departments. It is managed by a Board of 11 directors appointed for

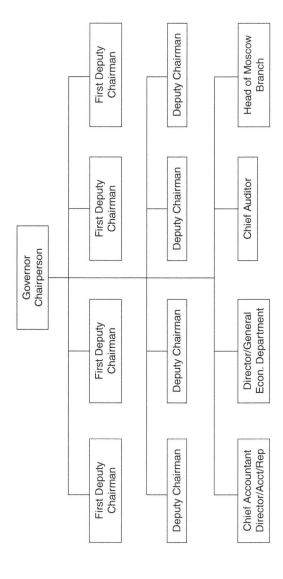

Figure 7.1 The structure of the Central Bank of Russia.

a four-year term. Its current Chairman is Sergey Ignatiew who has been in this position since the 1990s, appointed by President Vladimir Putin. The daily activities of the CBR are conducted by the Board of Directors, appointed by the Federal Assembly of the Russian Federation (State Duma). Figure 7.1 shows the current structure of the Board of Directors.

7.3   Key Functions of the Central Bank of Russia

According to Article 75-2 of the Russian Constitution, the protection and stability of the ruble is the main function of the CBR which it exercises independently from other bodies of state power.

The main tasks of the CBR consist of: (a) maintaining the money supply; (b) pursuing a uniform monetary and credit policy; and (c) preserving the value of the Russian currency. Beside these core tasks, the CBR is entrusted with other missions pursuant to Article 4 of the Bank of Russia Law, inter alia, to:

- regulate the banking industry;
- ensure an efficient and uninterrupted functioning of the payment system;
- issue cash and organize cash circulation;
- organize and exercise foreign exchange regulation and control this pursuant to federal legislation;
- set up procedures for effecting settlements with international organizations, foreign states, legal entities, and natural persons.

7.4   The Monetary Policy of the Central Bank of Russia

The Russian monetary policy consists of targeting money aggregates by using the interest rates and a managed floating exchange rate. Through the interest rates policy, the CBR is able to narrow the volume of circulating money and correct or absorb any excess liquidity. Besides the interest rates, the CBR uses a bi-currency basket as a benchmark to intervene whenever needed. However, the CBR 2009 Guidelines announced that the CBR is considering a monetary policy shift from the money aggregates to an inflation-targeting strategy. Though the shift would provide the CBR with some leeway as to the monetary policy tools to use, the language used in the 2009 Guidelines casts some doubt as to the willingness of the CBR to really move ahead in the direction of an inflation-targeting strategy. Indeed, the 2009 Guidelines went on to add:

> The monetary policy will retain many of the elements formed in recent years: the managed floating exchange rate of the ruble will remain in place, the monetary program will continue to be used to ensure that monetary

indicators match the inflations targets, and the bi-currency basket will be utilized as before as the operational exchange rate policy target.[78]

Whether these monetary policies – inflation targeting and managed foreign exchange floating rate – can be used simultaneously remains to be seen.

7.5   Implementation of the Monetary Policy

In implementing its monetary policy, the CBR uses a quantitative method, which consists of targeting the money growth. It (a) imposes reserve ratios on all commercial banks within its jurisdiction as a means of controlling liquidity flow within the overall banking system, and (b) intervenes regularly in the foreign exchange market to correct any perceived imbalance in the country's balance of payment. To regulate exchange rate dynamics and liquidity flow, and the flow of money supply, the CBR uses simultaneously two main monetary tools: intervention on foreign exchange and sterilization arrangements of excess liquidity with banks and other financial institutions. To maintain an adequate volume of liquidity in the market, the CBR uses either a liquidity absorption or a liquidity supply approach.

7.5.1   Liquidity Absorption

As liquidity absorption instruments, the CBR uses: (a) the inter-bank interest rate; (b) the reserve requirement; (c) the issuance of bonds; (d) deposit operations; (e) the reserve modified repos operations; and (f) other open market operations tools.

The Inter-bank Interest Rate

The inter-bank interest rate is of limited interest in Russia due to the country's underdevelopment of the banking and financial markets. Also, the interest rate is subject to more volatility as a result of the CBR's intervention in the foreign exchange market. The inter-bank market in Russia is small and highly segmented with 15 banks carrying out the major part of the transactions.[79] Moscow banks account for approximately 50% of the loan market participants.

The Reserve Requirement

The reserve requirement is a steering monetary policy tool in Russia. The CBR has divided reserve requirements into three groups:

- reserve requirements for banks' liabilities to foreign banks in both ruble and foreign currencies;
- reserve requirements for ruble liabilities to domestic households; and
- reserve requirements for all other liabilities.

The CBR requests the highest reserve requirements for liabilities to foreign banks as a means to limit or absorb the inflow of foreign capital into Russia.

Bond Sales

The CBR uses bond sales as another tool to absorb excess liquidity and help sterilize foreign currency intervention. Bond sales involve the sale of short-term securities. Through the issuance of bonds, the CBR offers commercial banks an opportunity to invest their excess reserves in a smooth fashion, while keeping the money supply demand at the targeted level.

Deposit Operations

The CBR conducts deposit operations at fixed interest rates daily or weekly at interest rates set by deposit auctions.

Reserved Modified Repos Operations

Since 2002, reserved modified Repos (OMR) operations have allowed the BBR to use long-term loan bonds that it would not otherwise use in direct opera-tion as well as non-market (non-collateralized) coupon interest rates. However, since 2005, the CBR has refrained from using OMR for the purposes of its monetary policy.

Open Market Operations

The CBR conducts its open market operations by issuing Bank of Russia bonds (DBR), short-term government securities (GKO), and federal loans bonds (OFZ). These operations allow the CBR and the market participants to temporarily invest free funds or sell bonds.

7.5.2 Liquidity Supply

Through its liquidity supply approach, the CBR grants two types of credits to commercial banks: (a) marketable papers (or collateralized lendings), and (b) non-marketable papers (or non-collateralized lendings).[80] Besides these two types, the CBR also offers standing facility fixed rate credits to commercial banks (i.e., one day currency swap, one day Repo).[81]

However, in its Guidelines for the Single State Monetary Policy in 2011 and for 2012 and 2013, the CBR is shifting its monetary policy from quantitative methods to money market operations, with inflation target caps.

7.6 The Independence of the Central Bank of Russia

Under Article 75 of the Russian Constitution, the CBR is an independent body distinct from the federal bodies of the state power, regional authorities, and local governments. It is a legal entity with its own authorized capital and properties. The CBR exercises its own power to own, use and manage its property in accordance with the powers entrusted to it by the Constitution and the Federal Bank of Russia Law. Its properties may not be seized or encumbered without its consent or wilful commitment. However, the CBR reports to the State Duma, which holds several committee meetings and hearings on its activities. The Central Bank also publishes an annual report of its core activities. Despite its independent status guaranteed by the Federal Constitution, the CBR is under intense pressure from the Executive and specifically the President of the Republic.[82] The CBR is often seen as the platform where both the Executive and the Legislative (the Supreme Soviet) fight to expand their prerogatives and economic views.

7.7   Towards a Modern Central Bank of Russia

Due to its structural money growth surplus, the CBR needs to shift from its exchange rate targeting towards an inflation target system. Such a shift would enable the CBR to use several monetary tools at the same time and maintain the stability of the ruble. Further, the CBR would have to have multiple simultaneous objectives to alleviate the burden of all and each money tool available in its toolkit. The CBR plan for 2012–1014 has announced positive steps in that direction, provided that the Executive does not interfere much with its implementation of the targeted goals.

8
The Central Bank of Brazil

8.1 Introduction

The Central Bank of Brazil (Banco Central Do Brazil; CBB) was established in 1964 as an autonomous federal institution and part of the Brazil National Financial System (SFN).[83] But it was not until the 1988 Constitution that the CBB could perform the core functions of a modern central bank.

8.2 The Organizational Structure of the Central Bank of Brazil

The CBB is made up of the Board of Directors and several departments, each specializing in a specific banking area (Figure 8.1). These departments are the:

(a) International Department (Derin);
(b) Executive Office for Corporate Risks & Benchmarks (Geris);
(c) Accounting and Financial Department (Deafi);
(d) Information Technology Department (Deinf);
(e) Infrastructure Department (Demap);
(f) Human Resources (HR);
(g) Planning, Budget, and Management Department (Deseg); and
(h) Security (Deseg).

The CBB Board is composed of the following members (Figure 8.2):

(a) Governor;
(b) Deputy Governor for the Administration;
(c) Deputy Governor for International Affairs;
(d) Deputy Governor for Supervision;

64

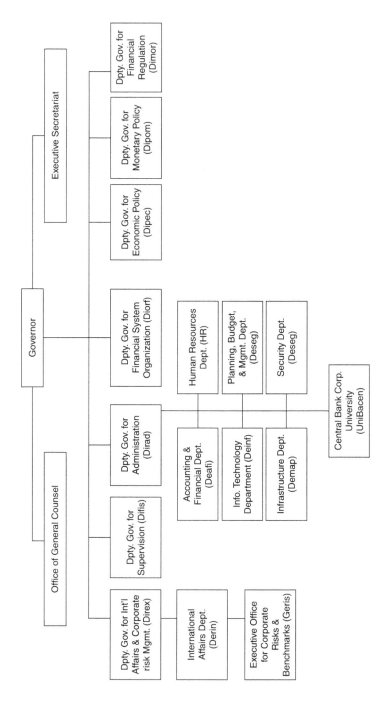

Figure 8.1 The structure of the Central Bank of Brazil.

(e) Deputy Governor for Financial System Organization;
(f) Deputy Governor for Economic Policy;
(g) Deputy Governor for Monetary Policy; and
(h) Deputy Governor for Financial Regulations.

8.3   The Core Functions of the Central Bank of Brazil

The CBB is entrusted with the following functions or missions:

- To ensure the stability of Brazil's currency purchasing power, and the soundness of the country's financial system.
- To regulate and supervise the financial system. Brazil's strong financial markets infrastructure and strong regulation and supervision constitute an important factor in maintaining the country's financial stability. Banking supervision is risk based and robust, which is reflected in a high degree of compliance with the Basel Core Principles for Effective Banking Supervision. Brazil's capital markets operate in transparency, and disclosure standards have been raised and risk-based supervision implemented.
- To oversee payments, securities, and derivatives settlement systems: the CBB oversees and regulates the country's four clearinghouses, including their risk management.

8.4   The Monetary Policy of the Central Bank of Brazil

The CBB monetary policy is carried out by the Monetary Policy Committee (COPOM), created on June 20, 1996. Brazil's monetary policy follows an inflation-targeted aim as with many other modern central banks, but lets the

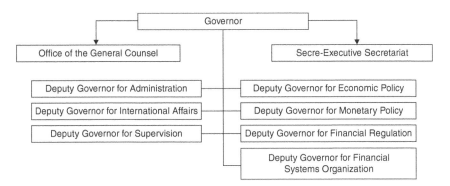

Figure 8.2   The Board of the Central Bank of Brazil.

exchange rate float. The COPOM uses interest rates as an instrument to control inflation. It evaluates constantly the future of inflation's trends and analyzes the reasons for any discrepancies between the inflation projection and the targets set by the government. In the event of discrepancies, the COPOM makes adjustments in a settled-timing fashion. The COPOM is composed of the members of the Central Bank's Board of Directors: the Governors, and the Deputy Governors of Monetary Policy, Economic Policy, Special Studies, International Affairs, Financial System Regulation, Financial Supervision, Bank Privatization, and Administration.

The COPOM holds regular monthly meetings, or at least eight meetings per year, to discuss monetary policy matters. Each meeting lasts two days starting on a Tuesday. Given the weight of monetary policy over macroeconomic policies, the COPOM customarily invites the heads of six of the Central Bank's departments for the first day of each meeting,:

- the Economic Department (DEPEC);
- the International Reserves Operations Department (DEPIN);
- the Banking Operations and Payments System Department (DEBAN);
- the Open Market Operations Department (DEMAB);
- the Investor Relations Group (GERIN); and
- the Research Department (DEPEP).

Besides the heads of the aforementioned departments, the COPOM also invites three senior advisors – the executive secretary of the Board of Directors, the special advisor to the Governor, and the press officer – and any head of department it desires to bring into the gatherings. However, participation during the second day (Wednesday) is limited to members of the COPOM and the heads of the six departments. During the first day of the meeting, each head of department expounds a review of the economic environment, covering, inter alia, the inflation trend, level of economic activity, monetary indicators, fiscal accounts, the balance of payments, external developments, the foreign exchange market, international reserve operations, and so on.[84] COPOM decisions are reached by consensus, and the Governor holds the deciding vote in cases where the COPOM is evenly split. Eight days after each meeting, the COPOM releases the interest target. If, for any reason, the target misses the interest set by the National Monetary Council (NMC), the Governor of COPOM is required to write an "open letter" to the Minister of Finance, in which he explains the reasons why the target interest rate was not achieved, and the measures the COPOM has put in place to meet the target interest rate, and the schedule thereof. The process is similar to the British Monetary Policy Committee discussed in Chapter 5.

The COPOM should make sure that the monetary policy target contributes to the consolidation of a favorable longer-term macroeconomic environment.

8.5   Implementation of the Monetary Policy

To implement its monetary policy, the CBB uses different monetary tools including: (a) the interest rate, (b) the reserve requirement, and (c) the open market operations.

8.5.1   Interest Rates on Overnight Inter-bank Loans

The CBB inter-bank loans have always been among the highest in the world. The official interest rate is the Special System of Clearance and Custody (SELIC) rate. From 1999 to 2010, Brazil's interest rate average was around 17.22%. The CBB lowered the basic interest rate from 13.75% to 12.75% in January 2009 and to 10.25% in April 2010.

8.5.2   Reserve Requirements

The COPOM sets the reserve requirement ratio, that is, the amount commercial banks must hold in the account within the central bank. Different ratios are applicable: 42% on demand deposits, 55% on time deposits, 15–20% on saving accounts. Additional requirements are also possible. The COPOM can and often does rebate the reserve requirements for small- and medium-size banks.

8.5.3   Market Operations

Market operations aim to adjust market liquidity in order to maintain the effective overnight interest rate near to the target. The COPOM does so mainly through two types of operations: (a) repurchase agreements, using the Treasury securities as collateral, and (b) outright operations. In general, Repos agreements are short-term operations (1 to 30 days), the longest operations lasting five to seven months. For its open market operations, the CBB accepts only federal debt securities as collateral.

8.6   The Independence of the Central Bank of Brazil

In practice, the CBB enjoys an independent status vis-à-vis the Federal government. The central government determines the target rate, and the COPOM implements and explains the context. Nonetheless, the COPOM remains independent from the central government as to the choice of monetary instruments it uses in order to attain the assigned goals.

8.7   Reforming the Central Bank of Brazil

The Brazilian government should enshrine the Central Bank's autonomy in legislation as observed in other Latin American countries (i.e., Columbia, Chile, and Peru). Such a legal independent status would assist the Central Bank in the way it conducts monetary policy. For instance, in both 2006 and 2007, the CBB was able to manage the inflation target below the target range. Also, the CBB could consider easing bank reserve requirements over the medium term in accordance with its monetary policy core functions: price stability and growth.

9

The Saudi Arabia Monetary Agency

9.1   Introduction

The Saudi Arabia Monetary Agency (SAMA), the central bank of the Kingdom, became official and effective on October 4, 1952.[85] Given Saudi Arabia's position as a prominent non-G-10 member of both the International Monetary Fund and the World Bank, and as a shareholder of the Bank for International Settlements (BIS), the SAMA is one of the biggest players in the international banking system. The SAMA is also a member of the Core Principles Liaison Group of the Basel Committee on Banking Supervision. The SAMA regulates and supervises the Kingdom's banking system (commercial banks), and the Saudi stock market. In terms of monetary policy debate, the SAMA plays a significant role in the Gulf Cooperation Council (GCC) and is seen as a liaison between the West and the Middle East. Pursuant to its charter, the SAMA must conform and comply with Islamic Law, i.e., it cannot charge or pay interest, accept private deposits, or make advances to the government or to the private sector. To circumvent these prohibitions, new regulations were introduced in the 1980s based on a system of service charges instead of interest. The SAMA publishes audited balance sheets, which include a summary of profit and loss accounts.

9.2   The Organizational Structure of the Saudi Arabia Monetary Agency

Contrary to the organizational structure of many central banks, the SAMA is straightforward and transparent. It is administered and managed by a Board of Directors composed of the:

- Governor, who is the Chairman and the Chief Executive Officer;
- Vice-Governor, who is the Vice Chairman; and
- three members, who are non-governmental officers.

The Governor and the Vice-Governor are proposed by the Minister of Finance and approved by the Council of Ministers before being appointed by royal decree for a four-year term. The three members are appointed for five years. The SAMA's Board members are removed from their office by royal decree, after a recommendation from the Minister of Finance and the approval of the Council of Ministers.

The Board is responsible for the daily operations and the management of the SAMA. The SAMA has no capital, but it is allowed to cover its expenses by charging a fee to the government. Besides the Board of Directors, the organizational structure of the SAMA includes several departments, each pursuing assigned and specific tasks (Figure 9.1).

As of today, the SAMA employs about 2500 agents out of which 50% are employed at its head office in Riyadh and the remainder are spread within the ten branches of the SAMA all over the Kingdom.

9.3   The Core Functions of the Saudi Arabia Monetary Agency

Pursuant to Article 3 of the SAMA's charter, its core objectives and functions consist of:

- issuing and stabilizing the internal and external value of the Saudi currency;
- dealing with the banking affairs of the Kingdom: the Banking Control law of 1966 has vested the SAMA with broad supervisory powers, which include, inter alia, the powers to issue regulations, rules and other guidelines in accordance with international and domestic laws;
- regulating commercial and sharia banks and exchange dealers: the SAMA is vested with the power to examine new applications for granting banking licenses and to grant authorization for the acquisition of ownership or interest in an existing bank. Its supervisory function is conducted through a combination of offsite monitoring and full- and limited-scope onsite monitoring;
- foreign exchange management.

9.4   The Monetary Policy of the Saudi Arabia Monetary Agency

The SAMA is entrusted with the conduct of the monetary policy of the Kingdom. To that end, it pursues both an intermediate objective, which consists of maintaining the US$/ Riyal exchange rate, and an ultimate goal of maintaining price and financial stability, as well as the promotion of economic growth. The Saudi Arabia currency, the Saudi Riyal (SR) is officially pegged to the US dollar at the rate of 3.75/$1. The Riyal peg has not moved since 1986.[86]

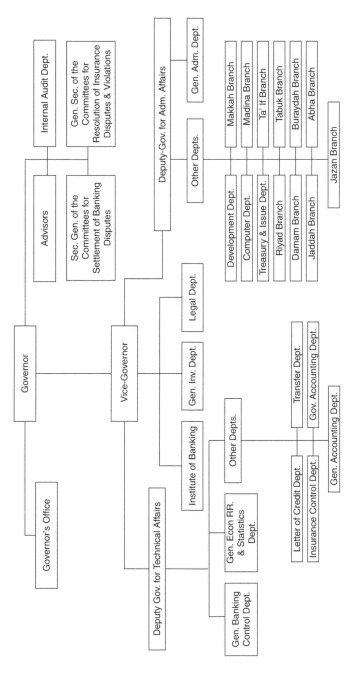

Figure 9.1 Structure of the Saudi Arabia Monetary Agency.

9.5   Implementing the Saudi Arabia Monetary Agency's Monetary Policy

In conducting its monetary policy, the SAMA selects and determines its operating procedures and/or its choice of instruments as it sees fit. That is, there is no direct credit control, foreign exchange, or interest rate control.

The SAMA uses three main tools: minimum reserve requirement; open market operations; and foreign exchange swaps.

9.5.1   Minimum Reserve Requirements

According to Article 7 of the Banking Control Law, commercial banks are required to maintain a percentage of their customers' deposits with SAMA as prescribed cash reserves. The current minimum reserve requirement (MRR) is 7%.

Reserve requirements are imposed on liabilities to non-banks and financial institutions.[87] The role of the MRR has been diluted in the SAMA management of liquidity due to the rise of other liquidity instruments such as open market operations and foreign exchange. Related to MRR, commercial banks are also required to maintain a 20% statutory liquidity ratio based upon their liquid assets such as cash, gold, inter-bank deposits of less than 30 days, and Saudi government bonds.

9.5.2   Open Market Operations

Through open market operations, the SAMA uses the Repo window to fine-tune system liquidity and sell government debt bonds. As commercial banks use Repo to meet their short-term liquidity shortages, the SAMA, through its Repo window, allows banks to have quick access to liquidity in order to conduct their secondary market-making operations. The allocation of Repos is linked to a bank's holding of eligible securities. This tool is used with the aim of either injecting liquidity into the banking system or absorbing liquidity from it. A further liberalization of Repos intermediation to non-bank institutions would increase and diversify demand for government securities and their trading.[88] Besides the Repo window, the SAMA, acting as the Saudi government's banker, places the government institutions' deposit funds with the commercial banks in order to increase their liquidity.

9.5.3   Foreign Exchange Swaps

Foreign exchange swaps are used to provide emergency liquidity to banks in times of higher speculation against the Riyal. Foreign exchange swap transactions are used as one of the main tools to monitor capital flows, particularly disturbances emanating from the foreign exchange market. Foreign exchange swap transactions are considered more flexible in terms of maturities and volume.

9.6   The Independence of the Saudi Arabia Monetary Agency

Though the statute recognizes the SAMA to be independent from the government of the Kingdom of Saudi Arabia, it is somehow difficult to assess how this is so in practice. The SAMA performs as an extension of the Saudi Arabia government to whom it is accountable. Practical independence would require the SAMA to be the sole agency in charge of monetary policy, accountable to either the Parliament or any institutional body representing Saudi Arabia's people.

10
The Bank for International Settlements

10.1 Introduction

Established in 1930 by the Hague Agreement among the ten founding central banks,[89] the Bank for International Settlements (BIS) is an intergovernmental body. The BIS is the world's oldest international financial institution and remains the principal center for international central bank cooperation. In July 1944, the United Nations Bretton Woods Conference adopted a resolution calling for the liquidation of the BIS, on the grounds of its supposed domination by the Axis Powers during the war and because its traditional field of activity would henceforth be largely covered by the soon-to-be-created International Monetary Fund (IMF) and the International Bank for Reconstruction and Development (IBRD). However, in 1946 European bank governors started to reconvene at Basel, and in 1948 the liquidation resolution was officially revoked.[90] While the US Congress, still suspicious, forbade the US Federal Reserve from formally joining the BIS, the NY Federal Reserve and its allied Morgan interests were able to work closely with the BIS, and the BIS treated the NY Federal Reserve as if it were the central bank of the United States.[91]

With the collapse of the Bretton Woods system in the 1970s, the role of the BIS has become even more prominent. It aims to foster international monetary and financial cooperation and to serve as a bank for central banks. The BIS offers a framework for discussion and decision making among central banks. It is a limited liability company, incorporated under Swiss law, with an issued share capital; its shares are traded on stock markets, and it is held by private shareholders. As of March 2007, the BIS had a total asset of $409.15 billion, including 150 tons of fine gold. The BIS is administered by a Board of Directors, which appoints a general manager to be responsible for its operations. The BIS carries out its work through its annual General Meeting of all members.

10.2   Organizational Structure of the Bank for International Settlements

The organizational structure of the BIS has undergone considerable change since its creation in 1930. The BIS is governed by three decision-making bodies: (a) the Governors; (b) the Board of Directors; and (c) the Bank Management.

10.2.1   The Governors

This is the first decision-making body composed of representatives or Governors of the 55 member central banks. These representatives meet every two months to discuss and vote on key banking regulatory issues.

10.2.2   The Board of Directors

The Board of Directors determines and conducts the strategic direction of the bank. The board is composed of the Governors of the central banks of Belgium, France, Germany, Italy, and the United Kingdom, and the Chairman of the Board of Governors of the US Federal Reserve System. The Board elects its Chairman and Vice Chairman and meets at least six times a year.

10.2.3   The Bank Management

The Bank Management carries out the policies determined by the Board and oversees the bank's daily operations. The Management consists of a General Manager, who acts as the bank's chief executive officer, the departmental heads, other senior officials, and chief representatives from two representative offices.

The three main departments are: (a) the Banking Department; (b) the Monetary and Economic Department (MED); and (c) the General Secretariat.

The Banking Department The Banking Department is responsible for carrying out banking transactions on behalf of central bank customers, including the investment of central bank foreign exchange on the market.

The Monetary and Economic Department (MED) While their own monetary policy is determined by each member state, the MED conducts economic and monetary research, and compiles and shares relevant statistics with both its members and non-members. The MED produces the BIS Annual Report, and liaises with member central banks. It prepares and hosts many of the central bank expert meetings which take place at the BIS.

The General Secretariat The General Secretariat provides administrative support and is responsible for the BIS's internal administration.

10.3   The Functions of the Bank for International Settlements

10.3.1   Central Bank Functions

The BIS acts as the central bank for central banks. It organizes regular meetings of the governors and officials of central banks to debate on international banking issues. The BIS extends loans and receives deposits from central banks, and assists their members in their management of external reserves. In support of this cooperation, the BIS has developed its own research into financial and monetary economics and makes an important contribution to the collection, compilation, and dissemination of economic and financial statistics. Besides monetary policy cooperation, the BIS performs "traditional" banking functions for the central bank community (e.g., gold and foreign exchange transactions), as well as carrying out trustee and agency functions. Finally, the BIS also provides or organizes emergency financing to support the international monetary system whenever needed. More recently, the BIS has provided finance in the context of IMF-led stabilization programs (e.g., for Mexico in 1982 and Brazil in 1998).

The BIS operations thereon must be conducted in compliance with Article 19 of its statutes, which states:

> The operations of the Bank shall be in conformity with the monetary policy of the central banks of the countries concerned.

Central banks make deposits to the BIS, which invests the money in high-quality short-term government securities and highly-rated commercial banks.[92] Further, the BIS extends credit facilities to central banks as short-term advances. The BIS also holds international positions as illustrated in Table 10.1.

10.3.2   Investment Advisory Services

The BIS assists central banks in managing their liquidity positions on their foreign assets. It also offers investment instruments with maturities up to five years for central banks in need of long-term reserve management.[93]

10.3.3   Gold Keeping Services

The BIS takes deposits of gold from central banks as their safekeeper and also acts as intermediary seller/purchaser to put the gold into the market, as illustrated in Table 10.2.

10.3.4   Insurance Supervisor

Given the fact that insurance has become part of international banking services, the BIS is more involved in developing standards for global supervision of insurance.[94] In the United States, for instance, since the repeal of the

Table 10.1 BIS: Summary of international positions.

BIS reporting banks
Summary of international positions
In billions of US dollars
Amounts outstanding Estimated exchange rate adjusted changes Preliminary International Banking Statistics. third quarter 2011 January 2012

Positions	Dec 2009	Dec 2010	Jun 2011	Sep 2011	2009	2010	Q4 2010	Q1 2011	Q2 2011	Q3 2011
A. Total assets	33,841.4	33,989.1	35,632.9	35,878.2	-2,341.2	1,051.8	-366.6	528.0	-115.5	804.6
claims on banks	21,086.9	21,027.7	21,786.4	22,460.6	-1,729.8	570.1	-328.6	248.4	-244.7	1,025.1
claims on non-banks	12,754.6	12,961.1	13,846.5	13,417.5	-611.4	481.7	-37.9	279.6	129.3	-220.4
B. External assets	30,081.9	30,187.4	31,591.8	31,682.5	-1,954.7	945.5	-329.4	480.9	-185.8	623.8
claims on banks	19,253.2	19,204.3	19,812.7	20,308.2	-1,528.6	524.6	-323.5	211.3	-299.7	830.1
claims on non-banks	10,828.7	10,983.1	11,779.1	11,374.3	-426.1	420.9	-6.0	269.6	113.9	-206.3
1. Loans and deposits	21,664.1	22,083.6	23,016.4	23,303.2	-1,714.6	975.8	-37.1	411.7	-187.2	535.9
claims on banks	15,667.3	15,742.0	16,109.4	16,466.1	-1,251.9	611.2	-103.8	183.5	-330.5	522.3
claims on non-banks	5,996.8	6,341.6	6,907.1	6,837.1	-462.8	364.6	66.7	228.2	143.3	13.6
2. Holdings of securities and other assets	8,417.8	8,103.8	8,575.3	8,379.2	-240.1	-30.2	-292.3	69.3	1.4	87.9
claims on banks	3,585.8	3,462.3	3,703.2	3,842.1	-276.7	-86.5	-219.7	28.1	30.8	307.8
claims on non-banks	4,831.9	4,641.5	4,872.0	4,537.1	36.6	56.3	-72.7	41.2	-29.4	-219.9
C. Local assets in foreign currency	3,759.6	3,801.7	4,041.1	4,195.7	-386.5	106.3	-37.2	47.1	70.3	180.9
claims on banks	1,833.7	1,823.4	1,973.7	2,152.5	-201.2	45.5	-5.2	37.1	55.0	195.0
claims on non-banks	1,925.8	1,978.3	2,067.4	2,043.2	-185.3	60.8	-32.0	10.0	15.3	-14.2

(continued)

Table 10.1 Continued

Positions	Dec 2009	Dec 2010	Jun 2011	Sep 2011	2009	2010	Q4 2010	Q1 2011	Q2 2011	Q3 2011
D. Total liabilities	**32,338.9**	**32,807.5**	**34,459.6**	**34,878.9**	**-2.505.7**	**1,203.2**	**-157.3**	**713.5**	**-129.8**	**1,039.7**
liabilities to banks	23,175.6	23,172.7	24,189.0	24,703.4	-1,945.4	592.5	-264.2	407.1	-175.2	971.2
liabilities to non-banks	9,163.3	9,634.8	10,270.6	10,175.5	-560.3	610.7	106.9	306.4	45.4	68.4
E. External liabilities	**28,132.0**	**28,532.2**	**29,865.9**	**30,069.2**	**-1,812.0**	**1,041.0**	**-127.2**	**564.6**	**-185.0**	**850.1**
liabilities to banks	20,849.4	20,875.8	21,709.7	22,022.9	-1,342.4	580.9	-194.0	331.7	-210.3	795.5
liabilities to non-banks	7,282.6	7,656.4	8,156.2	8,046.3	-469.6	460.1	66.7	232.9	25.3	54.7
1. Loans and deposits	**23,114.0**	**23,319.4**	**24,184.5**	**24,394.7**	**-1,880.7**	**855.1**	**95.1**	**406.7**	**-246.0**	**657.5**
liabilities to banks	16,523.1	16,316.1	16,785.5	17,076.2	-1,401.7	356.7	-24.4	202.3	-241.1	583.2
liabilities to non-banks	6,590.9	7,003.4	7,399.0	7,318.5	-479.0	498.4	119.5	204.4	-4.9	74.3
2. Own Issues of securities and other liabilities	**5,018.0**	**5,212.7**	**5,681.4**	**5,674.5**	**68.7**	**185.7**	**-222.4**	**157.7**	**61.2**	**192.7**
liabilities to banks	4,326.3	4,559.7	4,924.2	4,946.6	59.3	224.1	-169.6	129.3	31.0	212.3
liabilities to non-banks	691.7	653.0	757.2	727.8	9.4	-38.4	-52.8	28.4	30.2	-19.6
F. Local liabilities in foreign currency	**4,206.9**	**4,275.3**	**4,593.6**	**4,809.7**	**-693.7**	**162.2**	**-30.1**	**148.9**	**55.2**	**189.5**
liabilities to banks	2,326.2	2,296.9	2,479.3	2,680.6	-603.0	11.6	-70.3	75.4	35.1	175.8
liabilities to non-banks	1,880.7	1,978.4	2,114.3	2,129.1	-90.7	150.6	40.2	73.5	20.1	13.7

Table 10.2 BIS: Gold safekeeping services (as of 31 March 2010).

As at 31 March SDR millions	2010	2009
Gold bars held at central banks	41,596.9	22,616.5
Total gold loans	1,442.9	2,799.7
Total gold and gold loan assets	43,039.8	25,416.2
Comprising:		
Gold investment assets	2,811.2	2,358.1
Gold and gold loan banking assets	40,228.6	23,058.1

Glass-Steagall Act, banks are allowed to offer insurance products and services. The Financial Services Modernization Act of 1999 allows banks, through their holdings, to engage in insurance and real estate. While the international banking sector operates under strict rules and regulations, the international insurance industry still operates in a vacuum.

The BIS has stepped in to provide adequate standards in the insurance arena in order to harmonize practice within the banking industry.

10.4   The Bank for International Settlements' Monetary and Banking Policies

In the 1970s and 1980s, the BIS's monetary policy was focused on managing cross-border capital flows following the oil crises and the international debt crisis. The 1970s' crises drove the BIS to consider the issue of regulatory supervision of internationally active banks. Since then, the promotion of international financial stability has become one of its primary concerns.[95]

Further, the BIS has been really effective in the banking system through the Basel 1, 2, and 3 Accords. However, the Basel system is geared towards the stability of individual financial institutions, and does little to take account of their interaction with their environment and its stability. On the other hand, the IMF has developed a set of "Financial Soundness Indicators" (FSIs) as a key tool for macro-prudential surveillance. A consolidation of the two institutions (BIS and IMF) would provide a comprehensive monitoring system, including both the macro- and the microeconomic indicators.

10.5   Conclusion

The benefits of services rendered by the BIS are quite obvious. Since the 2007–2009 financial crises, many have come to consider the BIS as a substitute for the IMF, or at least have advocated the merger of the two institutions. The expertise of the BIS is unparalleled relative to the IMF. Whether such a vital reform would occur is not certain. IMF reforms are more important than the succession of its disgraced managing director, Dominique Strauss-Khan. As Xia Bin, China's Foreign Minister and an adviser to the People's Bank of China, said:[96]

> unless the United States reduces its dominant voting share in the International Monetary Fund, and re-negotiates the EU monopoly, any serious reform would head toward giving emerging economies more of a say in deciding who should take the helm of the IMF.

He went on to add: "The International Monetary Fund leadership should be based on 'merit, transparency, and fairness'."

The replacement of Dominique Strauss-Khan by Christine Lagarde, with the support of the EU, the US, and Japan, is intellectually immoral, in that it was assumed to be better to have a less-qualified Western candidate on job training rather than a well-qualified candidate from an emerging country. Though quite important, the BIS needs to improve its corporate governance, particularly its board of directors in the hand of a handful of developed countries. Some critics view the BIS as an elitist organization through which the wealthy control the world. With the world's wealth shifting eastward, some argue that the BIS should have formal representation from developing countries which have experienced growing importance in the global economy (i.e., China, India).

Another major criticism of the BIS is its obscurity and secrecy. For an international financial institution of its level, the BIS should take a greater leadership role in increasing transparency in other financial and banking transactions across the world. The BIS, with its affiliations with other multilateral financial institutions such as the International Monetary Fund (IMF), the World Bank (WB), and the Organization for Economic Cooperation and Development (ECD) can set an enhanced example of corporate governance.

Part II
Capital Adequacy and Main Operations

Overview of Part II

Central banks and/or regulators need to make sure that banks within their respective jurisdictions are well capitalized to conduct their activities. The Bank for International Settlements has formulated recommendations, known as the "Basels", to assist central banks in their assessment of capital adequacy. Those recommendations set up the minimal capital and bumpers required. Capital requirements of central banks such as the Saudi Arabia Monetary Authority far exceed the minima required under the Basel agreements. Properly capitalized, banks can conduct various activities: foreign exchange markets, derivatives, underwriting and related ancillary activities, mergers and acquisitions, advisory services, private equity deals, and many more.

Part II goes on to analyze in more detail the core banking activities as we know them to date. It does not pretend to encompass all banking activities, rather it focuses on the key activities of both commercial and investment banks. Though different banking activities are analyzed separately in specific chapters, the reality is somehow different. Bank activities are interrelated. For instance, when a mortgage department of a bank extends a mortgage to a customer, it will often pack up all the granted mortgages and pass them to the securitization department, which works closely with the investment bank department. That is to say, an error by one department or service could have a cascade effect and jeopardize the safety and soundness of all the bank's organization.

Central banks acting as regulators should be able to understand each and every one of the business aspects of the banks and financial institutions they oversee. For example, the US Federal Reserve's decision to pay the full-payment demands from the French banks' regulator and two of the largest creditors of the American International Group (AIG), Société Générale and Calyon Securities, illustrates a lack of understanding of the basic concept of the haircut practice pursuant to derivatives. Billions of US dollars were paid without any legal constraint to foreign banks which outmaneuvered the Federal Reserve with an overstated argument. It is therefore an imperative that central banks mastermind all lines of business of the institutions under their regulatory supervision.

11
Internationalization of Banking Business

11.1 Introduction

Despite global banks facing fears and resentment in the past, the banking industry is today one of the most globalized and integrated of businesses. It has become a key player in the world economy as its success or failure impacts the overall economy, not only the international finance sector. Its expansion drew stern criticisms in the midst of the 2008–2010 financial meltdown. The lack of coordination among banks' regulators, the short-sighted monetary policy initiated in the United States and blindly followed by the rest of the world, the absence of sound corporate governance, and the greed of a few have eroded trust in the industry. Nevertheless, the industry is showing signs of recovery, and business tends to expand as usual.

11.2 Representative Officers versus Correspondent Banks

International banks as opposed to domestic banks seek to have a presence in several jurisdictions, often accompanying their clients or stretching for their own business. When an international bank plans to penetrate a market where it has few customers, it often deals with a correspondent bank or financial institution. If the business prospers, the international bank might then add a representative officer but more often separates from the corresponding bank in order to reduce or limit costs. However, the choice of whether to operate through a correspondent bank or a representative has significant tax consequences.

11.2.1 Correspondent Banks

International banks accompany their clients wherever they conduct business. In the case where a bank's client is conducting trade or business in a country or jurisdiction where the bank has no presence, the international bank can still serve its client by entering into a correspondent agreement with a bank located in that country or jurisdiction as the bank sees fit. Correspondent bank agreements are reciprocal accounts that each bank opens in the counterpart bank. They charge commission to each other and net their accounts on an agreed-upon term, not exceeding a taxable year.

11.2.2 Representative Officers

An international bank providing a range of services to a client must need to go further than setting up reciprocal accounts in a specific foreign country or jurisdiction. When the business of the client so requires, banks can send in its officers on short-term secondment to represent their interests or the interests of their clients.

11.3 Subsidiaries versus Branches or Joint Ventures

The decision to operate through a subsidiary or a branch depends on numerous business and tax factors. Establishing a branch requires a pre-existing corporation (or affiliate) to which the branch has to attach for both accounting and tax considerations.

11.3.1 The Subsidiary

A subsidiary is a newly-formed entity in a country or jurisdiction in which the entity is registered. That is, the subsidiary is a local entity for the country of registration and must comply with all the laws of the "host" country or jurisdiction. As a local entity, a subsidiary of an international bank is, in general, allowed to do or enter into all activities domestic banks are allowed, free of any discrimination.

11.3.2 The Branch

A branch is not, per se, a distinct entity from its parent but is a continuation of the parent business. While a subsidiary bank is mainly under the supervision and the laws of the country of its registration, a branch could be compelled to observe both the laws of the parent and the laws of the host country. US branch banks operating overseas remain under the watch of the US Federal Reserve Act. However, US branch banks are not subject to US reserve requirements on deposits and are not required to comply with the FDIC requirements. Nonetheless, the US Federal Reserve Act applies to US branches of foreign banks to the same extent as US banks.

11.3.3 Joint Ventures

Joint ventures are legally independent entities incorporated in the country where their principal operations are conducted and controlled by two or more parent institutions, most of which are usually foreign and not all of which are necessarily banks.[97]

11.3.4   Tax Considerations

US branches of foreign parent banks are not only subject to US corporate income tax for their effectively connected income with the US trade or business, but also to the branch profit tax (BPT) under IRC section 884. The US Congress enacted the BPT as a means to correct the perceived difference in treatment for foreign banks operating in the US through a subsidiary and those operating through a branch. The profit of a foreign bank (and, by extension, a foreign corporation) operating in the US through a branch is subject to tax at a marginal rate of 35% when it is earned, plus an additional 30% branch profits tax when the income is repatriated because it not reinvested in the United States' assets. The 30% BPT is levied on the dividend equivalent amount (DEA) in lieu of a secondary withholding tax on dividends paid by the foreign corporation.[98]

11.4   The Edge Act Banks

Prior to 1913, US national banks were not allowed to finance foreign trade through banker's acceptances, nor to establish overseas branches. In 1916, section 25 of the Federal Reserve Act was amended to allow, under specific conditions, national banks with a capital and surplus of $1 million to invest, either singly or jointly, up to 10% of their capital or surplus in a corporation chartered under the federal or state law, to conduct "international or foreign banking" activities, subject to the approval of the Federal Reserve Board.[99] These corporations were called Edge Act banks. The introduced change was not deemed attractive until 1933 when the Federal Reserve Act was again amended to allow state banks and members of the Federal Reserve to extend overseas. The Edge Act regime was later amended in 1978[100] in order to improve the competitive position of Edge banks relative to foreign banks. The International Banking Act of 1978 eliminated restrictions upon Edge banks' ownership and fostered the ownership of Edge Act corporations by regional and smaller banks throughout the United States.[101] The Edge Act and corporation agreement provided to the parent bank to make equity investment in foreign corporations.

11.4.1   The Edge Act and its ad hoc Federal Jurisdiction

The Edge Act enables "national banks" to assert federal jurisdiction in cases pursuant to international banking or financial operation.

Section 632 of the Edge Act, incorporated in the Glass-Steagall Act in 1933, provides:

> ... notwithstanding any other provision of law, all suits of a civil nature at common law or in equity to which any corporation organized under

the laws of the United States shall be a party, arising out of transactions involving international or foreign banking ... or out of international or foreign financial operations, either directly or through the agency, owner-ship, or control of branches or local institutions in dependencies or insular possessions of the United States or in foreign countries, shall be deemed to arise under the laws of the United States, shall have original jurisdiction of all such suits; and any defendant in any such suit may, at any time before the trial thereof, remove such suits from a State court into the district court of the United States for the proper district by following the procedure for the removal of causes otherwise provided by law.

Put differently, section 632 of the Edge Act provides original federal jurisdiction when a federally chartered bank is a party; and the suit arises out of transac-tions involving international banking or international financial operations. The federal jurisdiction under section 632 is sui generis in that (a) the interna-tional banking or financial activities do not need to be central to the dispute; (b) the foreign party need not be named in the claim; and (c) section 632 is actionable even when the plaintiff alleges only state law claims.

The idea was to grant US national banks access to the US federal courts, which provide a greater sense of legal security than state courts.

11.5   Offshore Banking Centers

An offshore bank is a bank located outside the country of residence of the depositor, mainly in a low tax jurisdiction or tax haven which provides financial and legal incentives. The term "offshore bank center" originated in the United Kingdom with the innovative banking and financial services offered by the banks in the Channel Islands of Jersey and Guernsey. That started as a reaction by the banking industry to excessively high taxes in both the United Kingdom and France, and many regulations were denounced as invasive to individual investors' right to privacy. Today, "offshore banking centers" include other onshore popular banking jurisdictions such as Switzerland, Austria, Liechtenstein, Luxembourg, Singapore, and Hong Kong.

From an ethical point of view, the mere existence of offshore banking cent-ers constitutes a negation to the mission purportedly conferred on the bank-ing system. Offshore banks, located as they are in tax havens or jurisdictions which do not have a double tax treaty, are thus under no obligation to pro-vide or exchange information and pose a threat to the international banking system. The advantages of offshore banking centers are often overstated by their proponents. Offshore bank accounts are less financially secure com-pared with accounts in a regular, onshore tax regime. The bankruptcy of the Iceland banks such as Kaupthing & Friedlander clearly supports the argument.

Individuals and corporations that deposited their saving in Iceland lost almost all their savings.

In 2000, the OECD published a list of tax havens and offshore financial centers. The list was comprehensive and covered countries or jurisdictions such as Switzerland, Luxembourg, and Singapore, as well as well-known ones such as Bermuda, the Bahamas, the British Virgin Islands, etc. In 2008, the OECD revisited its list[102] to exclude jurisdictions such as Switzerland, Luxembourg, and others on the grounds that they were in compliance with the OECD requirement regarding international cooperation. The recent financial and the banking crisis revealed that there was no such compliance. Indeed, the OECD gave into pressure groups and it is expected that the OECD, for its own credibility would have to blacklist some of these countries holding offshore financial centers, such as Switzerland.

It is feared that offshore banking centers serve as safe havens for corrupt officials, corrupt dictators, and their financial advisors.[103]

11.5.1   Weight of Offshore Banking Centers

Offshore banking centers constitute an important component of the international banking system, with some people believing that they manage half of the world's capital flows. The banking activities of offshore banking centers escape all supervision. According to the *World Wealth Report* for 2000, one third of the wealth of the world's high-net worth individuals – nearly $6 trillion out of $17.5 trillion – could now be held offshore. A tiny tax haven island such as the Cayman Islands manages more than $2 trillion within its banking centers.[104]

11.5.2   Efforts to Crack Down on Offshore Banking Centers

Efforts to crack down on offshore banking centers have increased during the last decade, both in the United States and within the European Union.

- In the US, following the terrorist attacks on US soil, many have pointed to offshore banking centers as associated with the underground economy, organized crime, and money laundering.
- Within the EU, a concerted effort has been made through the EU Saving Tax Directive of 2005.[105] EU resident savers depositing money in any country other than the one in which they are resident should be subject to withholding tax in the payer country state, and/or accept that the other state provides relevant information to his home state. Under the withholding tax regime retained by the EU Commission, banks would have to automatically deduct tax from interest and other savings income earned and pass it to their local tax authority, indicating the portion of the income that relates to customers in each member state. The withholding tax rate has risen to 35% as from July 2011.

11.5.3 Pitfalls for Investors using Offshore Banking Centers

US investors depositing in offshore banking centers need to be aware of (a) the tax implications of their investments, and (b) the effects of some money laundering provisions.

- **Tax implications** US citizens and residents are subject to tax on their world-wide income. That is, they have to report and include their earnings from all around the world, including income that derives from tax haven jurisdictions, where most of these offshore banking centers are located. Through their investments in these offshore banking centers, US taxpayers receive mainly passive income: interest, dividends, and royalties. Under IRC sections 861 through 863, the payer would be compelled to hold withholding tax.
- **Money laundering and anti-corruption considerations** Bank managers must conform their business to money laundering laws to avoid recycling illegal money. In the United States, the Money Laundering Control Act of 1986 as amended and completed by the USA Patriot Act requires banks to verify the origins of their international operations to make sure that no dirty money gets laundered.

The US Department of Justice has become more aggressive in enforcing anti-bribery laws, and regulatory scrutiny is spreading to financial firms.

11.6 International Banking Facilities

International banking facilities (IBFs) manage, in a legal capacity, a significant portion of the global money flow. IBFs, which started their operations in the US in December 1981,[106] have grown considerably to become great players in the international banking system. The IBF regime has been designed to catch up with offshore banking centers (e.g., the Bahamas, Cayman Islands), which developed in the 1960s and 1970s. From their inception, IBFs aimed to offer to US banks the advantages of offshore banking centers without the need to locate physically offshore. To do so, in 1981 the Federal Reserve Board amended its regulations to allow US "national" banks to set out IBFs in the United States. IBFs enable depository institutions in the United States to offer deposit and loan services to foreign residents and institutions free of Federal Reserve System reserve requirements (FDIC), and some states' corporate tax exemptions. US commercial banks, Edge Act corporations, foreign commercial banks, savings and loan associations, and mutual saving banks are allowed to establish an IBF in the United States.

11.6.1 Activities of International Banking Facilities

International banking facilities are only allowed to receive deposits and extend loans to non-residents of the United States, other IBFs, and their parent or establishing entities. US banks established IBFs within the Federal Reserve regulations as a means of having access to business overseas. However, funds borrowed by a parent from its own IBFs remain subject to Eurocurrency reserve similar to borrowing from an offshore branch.

The minimum transaction with an IBF by a non-bank customer is $100,000, except for withdrawal or account closing. As of April 2007, there were 232 IBFs in existence, 137 in New York State.

11.7 Bank Holding Companies

Bank holding companies (BHCs) and financial holding companies (FHCs), which are corporations in control of two or more banks and/or financial institutions, are subject to the Bank Holding Company Act of 1956. They are under the supervision of the Federal Reserve, the SEC, and other government agencies.

In the US, most banks are owned by BHCs – about 84% of commercial banks form part of a BHC structure. In 1999, the Gramm-Leach-Bliley Act allowed a BHC to declare itself as an FHC and thereby engage in financial activities, including securities underwriting and dealing, insurance agency and underwriting, and merchant banking.

A company that proposes to acquire control of a bank must apply to the Federal Reserve for approval prior to making the investment. Likewise, an investment by a BHC exceeding 5% of the target bank's outstanding voting shares requires Federal Reserve approval. Moreover, a BHC can engage directly in – or establish or acquire subsidiaries that engage in – non-banking activities closely related to the banking activities. Examples include: mortgage banking, leasing, collection agency, asset management, trust company activities, real estate appraisal, investment advisory activities, management consulting, and certain insurance-related activities. However, for non-related banking activities, the BHC can still engage provided its investment does not exceed 5% of the target company's outstanding voting shares.

On September 22, 2008, Morgan Stanley and Goldman Sachs applied to the Federal Reserve to operate under its umbrella as BHCs. The move allowed these two giants to raise capital more easily than investment banks, assume debt of shareholders on a tax-free basis, acquire other banks and non-banking institutions, and issue stock with relative ease.

By the end of 2009, the top five BHCs had 28 commercial bank subsidiaries, which accounted for 52% of total commercial bank assets. The US top 50 BHCs are listed, with their locations and total assets, in Table 11.1.

11.7.1 Recent Changes under the Volcker Rule

Named after its author, Paul Volcker, the former Federal Reserve Chairman, this rule aims to put in specific restrictions and exceptions, and prohibit certain

Table 11.1   The top 50 bank holding companies (as of December 2009).

Rank	Institution name (RSSD ID)	Location	Total assets
1	BANK OF AMERICA CORPORATION (1073757)	Charlotte, NC	$2,268,347,377
2	JPMORGAN CHASE & CO. (1039502)	New York, NY	$2,117,605,000
3	CITIGROUP INC. (1951350)	New York, NY	$1,913,902,000
4	WELLS FARGO & COMPANY (1120754)	San Francisco, CA	$1,258,128,000
5	GOLDMAN SACHS GROUP, INC., THE (2380443)	New York, NY	$911,330,000
6	MORGAN STANLEY (2162966)	New York, NY	$807,698,000
7	METLIFE, INC. (2945824)	New York, NY	$730,905,863
8	TAUNUS CORPORATION (2816906)	New York, NY	$372,556,000
9	HSBC NORTH AMERICA HOLDINGS INC. (3232316)	New York, NY	$343,699,907
10	U.S. BANCORP (1119794)	Minneapolis, MN	$307,786,000
11	PNC FINANCIAL SERVICES GROUP, INC., THE (1069778)	Pittsburgh, PA	$264,414,112
12	BANK OF NEW YORK MELLON CORPORATION, THE (3587146)	New York, NY	$247,222,000
13	CAPITAL ONE FINANCIAL CORPORATION (2277860)	McClean, VA	$197,503,411
14	TD BANK US HOLDING COMPANY (1249196)	Portland, ME	$176,972,361
15	SUNTRUST BANKS, INC. (1131787)	Atlanta, GA	$172,875,298
16	ALLY FINANCIAL INC. (1562859)	Detroit, MI	$172,011,000
17	STATE STREET CORPORATION (1111435)	Boston, MA	$158,890,975
18	BB&T CORPORATION (1074156)	Winston-Salem, NC	$157,081,396
19	AMERICAN EXPRESS COMPANY (1275216)	New York, NY	$146,005,718
20	REGIONS FINANCIAL CORPORATION (3242838)	Birmingham, AL	$132,399,290
21	CITIZENS FINANCIAL GROUP, INC. (1132449)	Providence, RI	$129,969,527
22	FIFTH THIRD BANCORP (1070345)	Cincinnati, OH	$111,006,778
23	RBC USA HOLDCO CORPORATION (3226762)	New York, NY	$99,178,629
24	KEYCORP (1068025)	Cleveland, OH	$91,718,216
25	NORTHERN TRUST CORPORATION (1199611)	Chicago, IL	$83,843,874
26	UNIONBANCAL CORPORATION (1378434)	San Francisco, CA	$79,097,834
27	BANCWEST CORPORATION (1025608)	Honolulu, HI	$72,770,154
28	HARRIS FINANCIAL CORP. (1245415)	Wilmington, DE	$70,186,838
29	M&T BANK CORPORATION (1037003)	Buffalo, NY	$68,021,263
30	DISCOVER FINANCIAL SERVICES (3846375)	Riverwoods, IL	$63,894,877
31	BBVA USA BANCSHARES, INC. (1078529)	Houston, TX	$63,345,381
32	COMERICA INCORPORATED (1199844)	Dallas, TX	$54,001,083

(continued)

Table 11.1   Continued

Rank	Institution name (RSSD ID)	Location	Total assets
33	HUNTINGTON BANCSHARES INCORPORATED (1068191)	Columbus, OH	$53,801,954
34	ZIONS BANCORPORATION (1027004)	Salt Lake City, UT	$51,035,696
35	CIT GROUP INC. (1036967)	Livingston, NJ	$50,958,218
36	MARSHALL & ILSLEY CORPORATION (3594612)	Milwaukee, WI	$50,900,228
37	UTRECHT-AMERICA HOLDINGS, INC. (2307280)	New York, NY	$42,844,353
38	NEW YORK COMMUNITY BANCORP, INC. (2132932)	Westbury, NY	$41,160,281
39	POPULAR, INC. (1129382)	San Juan, PR	$38,723,000
40	SYNOVUS FINANCIAL CORP. (1078846)	Columbus, GA	$30,093,148
41	FIRST HORIZON NATIONAL CORPORATION (1094640)	Memphis, TN	$24,699,608
42	BOK FINANCIAL CORPORATION (1883693)	Tulsa, OK	$23,889,868
43	ASSOCIATED BANC-CORP (1199563)	Green Bay, WI	$21,785,596
44	CITY NATIONAL CORPORATION (1027518)	Los Angeles, CA	$21,356,479
45	FIRST NIAGARA FINANCIAL GROUP, INC. (2648693)	Buffalo, NY	$21,101,945
46	FIRST CITIZENS BANCSHARES, INC. (1075612)	Raleigh, NC	$20,806,659
47	EAST WEST BANCORP, INC. (2734233)	Pasadena, CA	$20,700,642
48	COMMERCE BANCSHARES, INC. (1049341)	Kansas City, MO	$18,520,044
49	TCF FINANCIAL CORPORATION (2389941)	Wayzata, MN	$18,490,648
50	WEBSTER FINANCIAL CORPORATION (1145476)	Waterbury, CT	$18,042,391

activities of banks and related institutions ("Covered Funds") in investing in and sponsoring private funds. The Volcker Rule has become the new section 13 of the Bank Holding Company Act.

- **Investing in private funds** Covered banks would be permitted to invest in "covered funds" if (a) the bank organizes the fund, and (b) provides sufficient equity capital to permit the fund to attract unaffiliated investors. A year after the bank has put a private fund in place, it should reduce its investment through redemption, sale, or dilution of shares.
- **Sponsoring private funds** Covered banks should not sponsor a hedge fund or a private fund (covered fund) including: (a) acting as general partner, managing member, or trustee of the fund; (b) selecting or controlling a majority

of the employees, officers, or directors of the fund; or (c) sharing the same or similar name with the fund for marketing, promotion, or other purposes.

Though the Volcker Rule has been described as a "private fund industry killer" by its opponents, the rule permits a covered bank to engage in (a) some private equity and hedge fund activities, and (b) proprietary trading activities.

Permitted Private Equity and Hedge Fund Activities

Certain private equity and hedge fund activities of a covered bank would be permitted despite the prohibition under the Volcker Rule, provided the covered bank acts only for its customers, and under the following conditions:

- the banking entity (or covered bank) provides bona fide trust, fiduciary, or advisory services;
- the fund is organized and offered only in connection with such bona fide trust, fiduciary, or advisory services and only to persons who are customers of such services;
- the covered bank does not acquire or maintain more than a de minimis ownership interest in the fund;
- the covered bank does not assume, guarantee, or otherwise insure the obligations or performance of the fund;
- the covered bank and the fund do not share the same name;
- no director or employee of the covered bank has ownership interest in the fund, except for persons who are directly engaged in providing advisory or other services to the fund;
- the covered bank discloses to investors that any losses of the fund are borne solely by the investors and not by the banking entity; and
- the fund complies with any additional rules of the federal banking agencies, the SEC, or the CFTC, designed to ensure that losses in such funds are borne solely by investors in the fund and not by the banking entity.

Permitted Proprietary Trading Activities

Covered banks can engage in some sort of proprietary trading activities, to the extent these activities do not conflict with other provisions under the federal or state laws. Such activities include:

- the purchase or sale of federal, state, and other government obligations;
- the purchase or sale of securities in connection with underwriting or market-making activities on behalf of their customers;
- the purchase or sale of securities by a regulated insurance company;
- hedging activities designed to reduce risk in connection with individuals or aggregate positions, contracts, or other holdings;

- investments in small business investment companies; and
- proprietary trading conducted by a foreign banking entity as long as the trading occurs solely outside the United States and the banking entity is not controlled by a banking entity organized within the United States.

The provisions of the Volcker Rule would enter into effect on the earlier of 12 months after the issuance of final rules, or two years after the date of enactment.

12
Capital Adequacy: The Basels

12.1 Introduction

Established in 1974 by the central-bank governors of ten countries, the Basel Committee on Banking Supervision ("the Committee") meets four times a year to discuss banking supervision and related matters. The Basel Committee formulates broad supervisory standards, and provides guidelines and recommendations for the prudential supervision of banking business. Commonly – but mistakenly – referred to as the central bank of the central banks, the BIS and its committee does not constitute a supra-national supervisory authority. Rather, it provides a forum where central bank governors and/or supervisory bodies in charge of regulating and supervising the banking industry meet to exchange their experiences and discuss directives or actions needed to improve the transparency and efficiency of the banking industry. The Basel Committee reports to the governors of central banks and heads of supervision of its member countries. In 1988, the Committee introduced a capital measurement system commonly referred to as the Basel Capital Accord.

In June 1999, the Committee revised its 1988 framework; then, following the aftermath of the 2008–2010 financial meltdown, it revisited the standards agreed upon, the capital adequacy and liquidity of banking institutions to face unattended issue or issues resulting from lax implementation of the "Core Principles for Effective Banking Supervision" developed in 2006. These Cores Principles are used by the IMF and countries' banking supervision systems and practices.

12.2 The Core Principles

The Core Principles constitute a framework of minimum standards for sound supervisory practices that, if properly implemented, would improve financial stability domestically and internationally. The Basel Core Principles define

25 principles needed for an effective supervisory system. The Principles are classified in seven categories: (1) objectives, independence, powers, transparency, and cooperation; (2)–(5) cover licensing and structure; (6)–(18) cover prudential regulation and requirements; (19)–(21) cover methods of ongoing banking supervision; (22) deals with accounting and disclosure; (23) deals with corrective and remedial powers of supervisors; (24) and (25) cover consolidated and cross-border supervision. These principles are summarized in Table 12.1.

12.3　The Basel I Accord

Under Principle 6, referred to as "capital adequacy", supervisors are required to set out prudent and appropriate minimum capital adequacy for their banks. Capital adequacy management benefits the owners of a bank by making their investment safe. Such adequate capital should be the reflection of the risk undertaken and provide a geography of the capital, as well as the ability to absorb losses. The framework was followed not only by country members but by almost all banking supervisory authorities in both developed and developing countries. Basel I required banks to set aside reserves calculated on the basis of risk-weighted assets. It provided for the implementation of a credit risk measurement framework with a minimum capital standard of 8% of risk-weighted assets for an internationally active bank, by the end of 1992. The Accord divided a bank's capital into two categories: Tier 1, which consists of shareholder equity and retained earnings; and Tier 2,[107] made of internationally-recognized non-equity items and subordinated bonds.

Risk-weighted assets are divided into four different categories, each receiving a specific rate:

- government obligations are weighted at 0%;
- short-term inter-bank assets are weighted at 20%;
- residential mortgages are weighted at 50%;
- other assets are weighted at 100%.

Tables 12.2 and 12.3 provide respectively: an illustration of risk-weighted capital and the JP Morgan Chase risk-weighted capital compliance.

Tier 2 or supplemental capital should count for no more than 50% of the total capital of the bank, and no more than 4% of risk-weighted assets.

Any bank below the Basel Accord capital adequacy standard should decide whether to raise new capital, shrink its assets and liabilities, or reduce its net risk exposure. The Basel Accord would not be efficient without taking into account banks' off-balance sheet items. These are items not reported in either the balance sheet or the statement of income, such as loan commitments, guarantees, swaps, and hedging transactions using derivatives securitization

Table 12.1   The Basel Core Principles.

Principle 1 Objectives, independence, powers, transparency and cooperation	• Clear responsibilities and objectives • Operational independence • Transparent processes • Sharing of information between supervisors
Principle 2 Permissive activities	• Must be clearly defined
Principle 3 Licensing criteria	• An assessment of the ownership structure and governance
Principle 4 Transfer of significant ownership	• Review of any proposal pursuant to significant transfer change
Principle 5 Major acquisitions	• Includes cross-border transactions
Principle 6 Capital adequacy	• Compliance with prudent and adequate capital minimum and reserves
Principle 7 Risk management process	• Identification • Evaluation • Monitoring • Control of risk profile
Principle 8 Credit risk	• Assessment of credit risk under the criteria defined under Principle 7
Principle 9 Problems, assets, provisions and reserves	• Asset management • Evaluation of provisions and reserves
Principle 10 Large exposure limits	• Identification and management of portfolios' concentrations
Principle 11 Exposures to related parties	• Assessment of exposures to related parties
Principle 12 Country and transfer risk	• Identification, measurement, monitoring and controlling of country risk exposures
Principle 13 Market risks	• Identification, measurement, monitoring and controlling of market risk exposures
Principle 14 Liquidity risk	• Liquidity management strategy • Daily management of liquidity
Principle 15 Operational risk	• Identification, measurement, monitoring and controlling of operational risk exposures
Principle 16 Interest rate risk in the banking book	• Identification, measurement, monitoring and controlling of interest risk in the book
Principle 17 Internal control and audit	• Clear and transparent delegation of authority • Separation of functions • Internal independent audit and compliance process
Principle 18 Abuse of financial services	• Promotion of high ethical standards in finance • Detection of fraudulent and criminal activities

(continued)

Table 12.1   Continued

Principle 19 Supervisory approach	• Sound understanding of the banking activities by supervisors
Principle 20 Supervisory techniques	• On- and off-site supervision and regular contacts with management team
Principle 21 Supervisory reporting	• Collection, review and analysis of prudential reports and statistics • Verification of the reports and statistics
Principle 22 Accounting and disclosure	• Compliance with internationally-accepted accounting principles
Principle 23 Corrective and remedial powers of supervisors	• Timely corrective actions to fix an issue or a departure from any principle
Principle 24 Consolidated supervision	• Supervision on a consolidated basis
Principle 25 Home–host relationships	• Cooperation and information exchange between the home supervisors and host-related parties

Source: BIS.

Table 12.2   Example of risk-weighted capital requirements.

Assets	Amount $	Risk weight %	Weighted assets $
Cash	10,000,000	0	0
T-bills	190,000,000	0	0
Municipal bonds	50,000,000	20	10,000,000
Mortgages	300,000,000	50	150,000,000
Home equity loans	40,000,000	100	40,000,000
Total	590,000,000		200,000,000

vehicles. Banks have used securitization as a means to manipulate the Basel primary capital ratios. The Basel provides four different conversion factors in order to convert these items into risk needing capital support. These conversion factors are:[108]

1. 100% conversion factors for: direct credit substitutes, risk participation in banker's acceptances and direct credit substitutes, and securities loans for which the bank is at risk;
2. 50% conversion factor for: transaction-related contingencies, unused portions of commitments with original maturity, and revolving underwriting facilities and note issuance facilities;

3. 20% conversion factor for: short-term, self-liquidating trade-related contingencies, including commercial letters of credit;
4. 0% conversion factor for: unused portions of commitments with original maturity of one year or less or which can be cancelled at any time.

Banks and other financial institutions present their risk-based capital in a more detailed fashion as described in Table 12.3.

12.4 The Basel II Accord

Basel II, available to banks since 2006, elaborated more on capital elements. The capital is divided into three Tiers, 1, 2, and 3 and the total regulatory capital is composed of all three Tiers.

1. Tier 1 capital consists primarily of common equity (excluding intangible assets such as goodwill and net unrealized gains on investment account securities classified as available for sale) and certain perpetual preferred stock.
2. Tier 2 consists primarily of subordinated debt, preferred stock (not included in Tier 1), and loan loss reserves up to a cap of 1.25% of risk-weighted assets.
3. Tier 3 consists of short-term subordinated debt with certain restrictions on repayment provisions. Tier 3 is limited to approximately 70% of a bank's measure for market risk.

Basel II was based on three pillars: (a) minimum capital requirement; (b) a supervisory review process; and (c) the effective use of market discipline.

12.4.1 Minimum Capital Requirement

Basel II maintains the 8% requirement, calculated as the sum of the bank's credit, market, and operational risks. Though Basel II sets out the capital requirement, banks are encouraged to have greater capital than the minimum required. Recognizing the specificities of each banking jurisdiction, the Basel Committee laid out areas of particular interest on which supervisors needed to focus: interest rate, concentration risk, residual risk. Basel II also has made operational risk, market risk, and credit risk major concerns, but provided some leeway to members' regulatory authorities in managing such risks.

Operational Risk

Basel II defines operational risk as loss that results from inadequate or failed internal processes, people and system errors, and external events. The Basel II Committee requires that, based on their size and complexity, banks put in place a system to identify, assess, measure, monitor, and control their operations.

Table 12.3 JP Morgan Chase risk-based capital components.

Risk-based capital components and assets		
December 31, (in millions)	2009	2008
Tier 1 capital		
Tier 1 common capital:		
Total stockholders' equity	$165,365	$166,884
Less: Preferred stock	8,152	31,939
Common stockholders' equity	157,213	134,945
Effect of certain items in accumulated other comprehensive income/(loss) excluded from Tier 1 common equity	75	5,084
Less: Goodwill[a]	46,630	46,417
Fair value DVA on derivative and structured note liabilities related to the Firm's credit quality	912	2,358
Investments in certain subsidiaries	802	679
Other intangible assets	3,660	3,667
Tier 1 common capital	105,284	86,908
Preferred stock	8,152	31,939
Qualifying hybrid securities and noncontrolling interests[b]	19,535	17,257
Total Tier 1 capital	132,971	136,104
Tier 2 capital		
Long-term debt and other instruments qualifying as Tier 2 capital	28,977	31,659
Qualifying allowance for credit losses	15,296	17,187
Adjustment for investments in certain subsidiaries and other	(171)	(230)
Total Tier 2 capital	44,102	48,616
Total qualifying capital	$177,073	$184,720
Risk-weighted assets[c]	$1,198,006	$1,244,659
Total adjusted average assets[d]	$1,933,767	$1,966,895

(a) Goodwill is net of any associated deferred tax liabilities.
(b) Primarily includes trust preferred capital debt securities of certain business trusts.
(c) Indudes off-balance sheet risk-weighted assets at December 31, 2009 and 2008, of $367.4 billion and $357.5 billion, respectively. Risk-weighted assets are calculated in accordance with US federal regulatory capital standards.
(d) Adjusted average assets, for purposes of calculating the leverage ratio, include total average assets adjusted for unrealized gains/(losses) on securities, less deductions for disallowed goodwill and other intangible assets, investments in certain subsidiaries, and the total adjusted carrying value of nonfinancial equity investments that are subject to deductions from Tier 1 capital.

Banks are allowed to use one of three approaches in calculating their operational risk capital: (a) the basic indicator approach (BIA); (b) the standardized approach (SA); and (c) the advanced measurement approach (AMA).

The basic indicator approach Under the basic indicator approach, banks compute their operational capital from a fixed percentage of the average of the annual gross income of the last three years. The Basel II Committee requires that the operational capital be 15% of the predetermined annual gross income average. The basic indicator approach is not used very much, and is less accurate as more banks are involved in various lines of banking activities, each coming with its own level of operational risk. Ignoring that reality would undermine banks' profitability deriving from excessive operational capital.

The standardized approach The standardized approach is deemed to avoid the over-generalized calculation of the operational capital under the basic indicator approach. It divides the activities of a bank into eight business lines, and then applies the beta factors for each business line based on the positive gross income of the three-year average (Table 12.4).

The advanced measurement approach (AMA) Due to its level of sophistication, the use of AMA is subject to strict regulatory requirements. First and foremost, the Basel II Committee did not provide a model, leaving the matter to the authority of each banking institution. Banks are allowed to use the AMA if they can establish and convince their regulatory authorities that they have in place a model that captures almost every high-loss event that could occur.

Credit Risk

Credit risk is embodied under Principle 8 of the Core Principles. It requires that banks put in place a credit risk management process, which takes into

Table 12.4 Beta factors under the standardized approach.

Business unit	Fixed percentage (beta factors) %
Corporate finance	18
Payment and settlement	18
Trading and sales	18
Agency services	15
Commercial banking	15
Asset management	12
Retail banking	12
Retail brokerage	12
Total	100

account the risk profile of the institution. Remember, banks are in the business of collecting deposits from their customers on the one hand, and extending loans to other customers on the other. The assessment of credit risk is the essence of the banking business. Therefore, banks should elaborate a prudent policy thereon and provide a process to identify, measure, monitor, and control their credit risk. To calculate regulatory capital for credit risk, Basel II provides three different approaches: (a) the standardized approach; (b) the internal ratings-based approach; and (c) the advanced internal ratings-based approach.

The standardized approach (SA) Under the standardized approach, the risk weighting is determined by the external credit rating assigned to a borrower. The Basel II Committee departed from the asset-weight approach under Basel I, recognizing that risk-asset weighting related to loans made to a sovereign or a large corporation needed to be more flexible. Wherever a country or jurisdiction has independent and credible rating agencies, banks could rely upon the rating assigned to the borrower by such institutions. However, banks need to update their assessment of a borrower's credit rating to reflect any change that could affect the accuracy of the credit risk capital in their books.

The internal ratings-based approach (IRB) Instead of relying upon independent credit rating agencies (i.e., S&P, Moody's), Basel II allows banks to determine their minimum credit risk capital by referring to their internally-generated credit rating. In so doing, banks provide evidence that their internal rating systems have been put in place under sound financial analysis, and that the assigned rating is proper to a specific borrower. The difficulty with this approach is that banks rely upon their own information to develop their credit risk models. Given the suspicion surrounding banking activities, the Basel II Committee granted such an authorization under specific conditions: internal rating credit risk factors must be developed under common risk factors such as the probability of default (PD),[109] the loss given default (LGD),[110] the exposure at default (EAD),[111] and the expected loss (EL).[112] The Basel II Committee recommends that banks develop a rating system with a minimum of eight probability of default rating grades. Once a rating system is in place, banks should monitor it closely based upon information pursuant to the borrower in order to keep their minimum capital credit risk accurate.

The advanced internal ratings-based approach (AIRB) Under AIRB, banks are required to calculate the rating credit risk based upon seven years' of historical data. Further, contrary to the IRB where banks are required to estimate only the PD, the AIRB approach requires that banks estimate all credit risk components (PD, LGD, EAD, and EL).

Market Risk

As banks increasingly operate worldwide, market risk increases. Understanding the market in which the bank (subsidiary/branch) operates could help anticipate certain events. Broadly speaking, market risk refers mainly to the risk that the market as a whole will fall in value. Put differently, market risk refers to risk of losses due to the financial market variable and adverse prices fluctuations. Market risk also includes foreign exchange (FX) risks that derive from currency fluctuations in international FX markets. International bank managers would have to conduct specific studies and stress tests per sectors of investment businesses as well as define the macroeconomic factors that sustain the overall economic activity of the region. In July 2005, the Basel Committee on Banking Supervision reached an agreement that requires banks to measure and hold default risk not captured under the value-at-risk (VaR), inter alia, the market risk. In March 2008, the Committee decided to expand the scope of the capital charge to improve the internal VaR models for market risk and to update the prudent valuation guidance for positions accounted for a fair value.[113] According to the proposed changes, the trading book capital charge for a bank using the internal models approach for market risk will be subject to a general market risk charge, measured using a ten-day VaR at the 99% confidence level and a stressed VaR. The Committee decided also that the incremental risk capital charge should capture not only default risk but also migration risk.[114] Banks should have complied with the new requirements from December 31, 2010. The use of an internal method should be approved by the bank supervisor in accordance with the Committee guidelines.

An important part of a bank's internal market risk measurement system is the specification of an appropriate set of market risk factors.[115] The Committee allows banks some discretion in specifying their risk factors, the number of which should ultimately be driven by the nature of the bank's trading strategies. However, factors that are deemed relevant for pricing should be included as risk factors in the VaR model. Further, the VaR model should capture non-linearities for options and other relevant products, such as mortgage-backed securities, and the correlation risk and basis.

While banks have some leeway in devising their models, the following minimum standards should apply for the purpose of determining their capital charge:

(a) value-at-risk must be computed on a daily basis, at 99% confidence level;
(b) the minimum holding period will be ten trading days;
(c) the choice of historical observation period for calculating VaR will be constrained to a minimum length of one year;
(d) banks must update their data sets often and reassess them whenever the market prices are subject to material changes;
(e) banks must meet their capital requirement on a daily basis.

12.4.2 Supervisory Review Process

Under Basel II, the supervisory review process is an active dialogue between banks and their supervisors. Supervisors are allowed to make on-site visits, off-site reviews, meet with bank management, and review and monitor periodic reports.

Four principles are the core of Pillar 2:

1. Banks should have a process to assess their overall capital adequacy in relation to their risk profile as well as a strategy to maintain their capital levels.
2. Supervisors should review and evaluate banks' internal capital adequacy assessments and strategies, as well as their ability to monitor and ensure their compliance with regulatory capital ratios. Supervisors should take appropriate supervisory action if they are not satisfied with the result of the process.
3. Supervisors should expect banks to operate above the minimum regulatory capital ratios and they should be able to require banks to hold capital in excess of the minimum.
4. Supervisors should seek to intervene at an early stage to prevent capital from falling below the minimum levels required to support the risk characteristics of a particular bank and should require rapid remedial actions if capital is not maintained or restored.

Recognizing the specificities of each banking jurisdiction, the Basel Committee laid out areas of particular interest on which supervisors need to focus: interest rate, concentration risk, and residual risk. Basel II also has made operational risk a major concern, but lets members' regulatory authorities manage such risk more closely. Basel II defines operational risk as loss that results from inadequate or failed internal process, people and system errors, and external events. The Basel II Committee requires that banks put in place a system, based on their size and complexity, to identify, assess, measure, monitor, and control their operations. Banks are allowed to use one of the three approaches in calculating their operational risk capital: (a) the basic indicator approach (BIA); (b) the standardized approach (SA); and (c) the advanced measurement approach (AMA). These approaches have been described in the section on Minimum Capital Requirement.

12.4.3 Effective Use of Market Discipline

The effective use of market discipline under Pillar 3 requires banks to disclose material information as to capital structure, risk exposures, and capital adequacy. The Basel II Accord considers information as material if its omission or misstatement could change or influence the assessment or decision of the user of that information.

12.5   The Basel III Accord

Both Basel I and Basel II failed to deal with market risk. Banks were allowed to create their own in-house models to assess or measure their market risk exposure. Regulators would then determine the amount of capital required based upon the banks' estimates. The Basel III framework, described as a landmark achievement to protect financial stability and promote sustainable economic growth, was adopted and published by the Committee on December 20, 2010. The framework sets out higher and better-quality capital, better risk coverage, and introduces (a) the leverage ratio as a second layer of protection to the risk-based requirement and (b) two global liquidity standards.

- The leverage ratio, considered as a backstop to the risk-based requirement, will promote the build-up of the capital that can be drawn in periods of stress.
- The two global liquidity standards are the liquidity coverage ratio (LCR) and the net stable funding ratio (NSFR).

Most importantly, Basel III has enhanced the minimum standards for common equity, also known as core Tier 1 capital. Such standards did exist in the past, but they were set extremely low, at 2%, and so were generally ignored. As of now, common equity is the main element that matters. The new standards for common equity are significantly tougher than the old standards for Tier 1 capital in total. The absolute bare minimum for core Tier 1 capital is 4.5%, and the new minimum for Tier 1 capital in general has now been raised to 6%. The minimum for Tier 2 remains at 8%.

Besides the Tiers 1 and 2 capital, Basel III has set up a "conservation buffer" of another 2.5% points. It is expected that most banks would go outside that buffer if they want to be more appealing to customers and be able to pay out dividends. If there is some kind of crisis and they are forced to write down a lot of bad loans, they can eat into the buffer – but that will bring extra regulatory oversight and they won't be able to pay dividends. Adding the conservation buffer into the overall equation, banks need 7% common equity, 8.5% Tier 1 capital, and 10.5% Tier 2 capital.

The countercyclical buffer won't be set by the BIS in Basel; it is left up to national regulators. In the US, for instance, the FDIC Chairwoman has made it clear that enhancing the core equity of the banks is welcome. Biggest banks are going to need significantly more capital than what they have in their balance sheets. The implementation of the requirements under Basel III has been timetabled as described in Table 12.5 and, in a nutshell, in Table 12.6.

Meanwhile, various dubious things which currently count as Tier 1 or Tier 2 capital but shouldn't will be phased out even more slowly, over a period of ten years beginning in 2013. Banks have until 2015 to meet the LCR standard and until 2018 to meet the NSFR standard.

Table 12.5 The implementation schedule for Basel III.

Annex 2: Phase-in arrangements (shading indicates transition periods) (all dates are as of 1 January)

	2011	2012	2013	2014	2015	2016	2017	2018	As of 1 January 2019
Leverage Ratio	Supervisory monitoring		Parallel run 1 Jan 2013–1 Jan 2017 Disclosure starts 1 Jan 2015					Migration to Pillar 1	
Minimum Common Equity Capital Ratio			3.5%	4.0%	4.5%	4.5%	4.5%	4.5%	4.5%
Capital Conservation Buffer						0.625%	1.25%	1.875%	2.50%
Minimum common equity plus capital conservation buffer			3.5%	4.0%	4.5%	5.125%	5.75%	6.375%	7.0%
Phase-in of deductions from CET 1 (including amounts exceeding the limit for DTAs, MSRs and financials)				20%	40%	60%	80%	100%	100%
Minimum Tier 1 Capital			4.5%	5.5%	6.0%	6.0%	6.0%	6.0%	6.0%
Minimum Total Capital			8.0%	8.0%	8.0%	8.0%	8.0%	8.0%	8.0%
Minimum Total Capital plus conservation buffer			8.0%	8.0%	8.0%	8.625%	9.125%	9.875%	10.5%
Capital instruments that no longer qualify as non-core Tier 1 capital or Tier 2 capital			Phased out over 10 year horizon beginning 2013						

Table 12.6 Basel III implementation in a nutshell.

1 January 2013	Core Tier 1 capital requirement will be 3.5%
1 January 2015	Core Tier 1 requirement will be raised to 4.5%
1 January 2019	Full implementation

12.6 Criticisms of the System

Despite progress made over the decades, the BIS is under intense pressure to reorganize itself and reach out to the emerging markets as well as the developing countries. As financial operations/and markets tend be more global, mismanagement or ignorance of the norms pursuant to capital adequacy and risk management could compromise the overall international banking system.

13
Banking and Foreign Exchange Transactions

13.1   Introduction

It is generally believed that the first exchange of international currencies took place in the Middle Ages at the time of the Crusades. At that time, the use of bills of exchange and international debt papers had become commonplace. The foreign exchange market as we know it today, developed in the 19th century while the United Kingdom was at the height of its powers, expanding its economic and trade strenghths over the globe.

The foreign exchange (FX) market is vital to the overall economy in that it:

- facilitates the conversion of one country's currency into another through the buying and selling of currencies, and allows global firms to move in and out of foreign currency to meet their business goals;
- sets and quotes the exchange rates, that is, the ratio of one currency to another;
- offers contracts to manage foreign exchange exposure.

The foreign exchange market is the biggest financial market in the world, with an average daily turnover of US $4 trillion.[116] It is a 24/7 over- the-counter market; that is, there is no central trading location and trade is carried out through an international network of computer and telephone connections. Foreign exchange market activity has become more global, with cross-border transactions representing 65% of trading activity in April 2010, while local transactions accounted for only 35%.[117] Banks located in the United Kingdom accounted for 37% of all FX market turnover, followed by the United States (18%), Japan (6%), Singapore (5%), Switzerland (5%), Hong Kong SAR (5%), and Australia (4%).[118]

Figures 13.1, 13.2, 13.3, 13.4, 13.5, and 13.6 respectively represent the geographical distribution of FX market turnover, the market turnover by

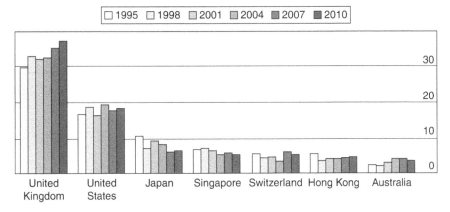

Figure 13.1 Geographical distribution of FX market turnover, 2011.
Source: BIS (2011).

instrument, the average daily turnover, the market participants, and the market turnover by currency.

The foreign exchange industry is more concentrated with the top 13 global FX centers covering 90% of the overall turnover. The market has increased by up to 20% since 2007, where the average estimate was $3.3 trillion. Its size is far more than 35 times the average daily turnover of the NYSE, and ten times the average daily turnover of the global equity markets. The increase registered in 2010 is due to the enlarged trading activity of other financial institutions – a category that includes non-reporting banks, hedge funds, pension funds, mutual funds, insurance companies, and central banks.[119]

The FX market is the most liquid market in the world. Trades occur seven days a week, 24 hours a day, without disruption. This market follows the same course as the sun: starting from Wellington, Sydney, Hong Kong, and Japan in Asia, it continues with London, Frankfurt, and Paris. At the close of the European markets, it pursues its course to the New world: New York, Chicago, Philadelphia, and the like. Among the participants are international commercial banks, non-commercial banks, central governments, and retail traders. Non-commercial banks intervene in the FX market in order to speculate and earn significant spreads. This group includes large institutional investors, hedge funds, and other entities. Hedge funds are not the biggest players within FX markets, but their trading has exponentially increased recently, causing some concern. Hedge funds investing in FX markets, commonly referred to as "Forex funds", are in many respects different from the "traditional" hedge funds characterized as illiquid. They have more liquidity to invest or to trade with, and the transaction costs are lower.

Hedge funds are gaining wider access to FX markets through prime brokerage, a service offered to them by some banks. Prime brokerage allows hedge funds to trade with other banks in the name of their broking banks, using the banks'

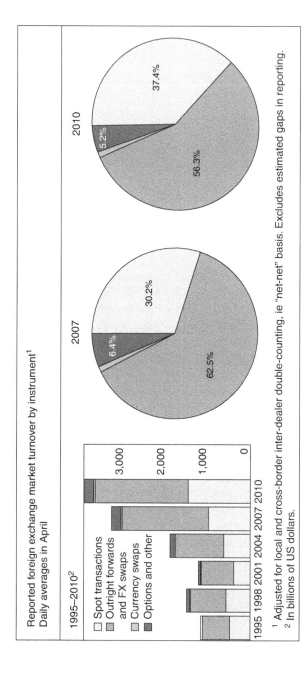

Figure 13.2 FX market turnover by instrument, 2011.
Source: BIS (2011).

lines of credit. Furthermore, many prime brokers are using their clients' assets for their own purposes, thus placing substantial assets at risk. The unorthodox service hedge funds are receiving from prime brokers has raised concern among central banks and regulators, who fear that hedge funds could exploit such a leeway in the system in order to manipulate FX prices.

Emerging FX markets are gradually increasing their share in the global market place:

- the Russian ruble has increased its share in total turnover to 0.9% of 200% FX from 0.7% three years ago;[120]
- the Brazilian real rose to 0.7% of 200% from 0.4%; and
- the Indian rupee's share rose to 0.9% of 200% from 0.7%.

Figure 13.3 represents the FX average daily turnover.

13.2   Foreign Exchange Markets

Commercial and investment banks are trading in almost all the foreign exchange markets: (a) the spot FX market; (b) the forward FX market; (c) the futures FX market; (d) the options FX market; and (e) the swaps FX market.

13.2.1   The Spot FX Market

The spot market involves the immediate purchase or sale of foreign exchange. The spot rate currency quotation can be stated either in direct (American) or indirect (European) terms:

- the American term expresses the exchange rate as the number of US dollars per one unit of a given foreign currency;

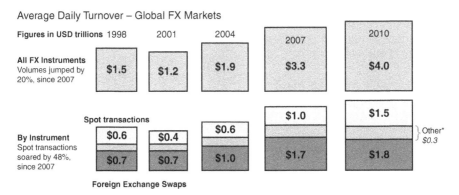

Average Daily Turnover – Global FX Markets

Figure 13.3   FX average daily turnover.
Source: BTS Triennial Central Bank Survey.

- the European term expresses the exchange rate as the number of foreign currency units per one US dollar.

Within the spot market, bank managers purchase an amount of currency using another currency as payment, thereby facilitating the trading of one currency for another. Besides making profit or spread from buying currency for inventory at the "bid price" and selling from that inventory at the higher offer or "ask price", bank managers trading in the spot FX markets are more and more involved in "triangular arbitrage", which consists of trading out of the US dollar into a second currency, then trading it for a third currency, which in turn is traded for US dollars. The spot transaction takes usually two days to be settled.

13.2.2   The Forward FX Market

The forward FX contract allows the buyer to lock in today the future price of a currency to be traded, but the payment is scheduled for an agreed-upon date. The buyer pays the agreed-upon price at the settlement date, regardless of the spot price. The seller delivers the currency on the settlement date as well. Therefore, no cash changes hands prior to the settlement date. Forward exchange rates are set at either a premium or discount of their spot rates. That is, if a currency forward rate is higher in value than its spot rate, the currency would be then quoted at a forward premium; and if a currency's forward rate is lower in value than its spot rate, the currency would be quoted at a forward discount.

13.2.3   The Swaps FX Market

In a swaps FX market, the counterparties agree to exchange the cash flows of two different currencies over the lifetime of the contract. A currency swap agreement requires the principal to be specified in each of the two currencies. The principal amounts are usually exchanged at the beginning and the end of the life of the swaps.[121]

13.2.4   The Futures FX Market

The futures FX markets are different from the forwards FX markets in that an intermediary, the "clearinghouse", stands between the counterparties, which performs as a third party to provide security to the market. That is, in the event of default by one or either of the counterparties, the clearinghouse agent enters into play to seek a refund from the defaulting counterparty. A counterparty willing to enter into a futures FX contract is required to post an initial performance bond, and the futures FX contract is marked-to-market. Bank managers who trade in the FX futures markets communicate their positions to their broker, who then conveys the position to the futures FX trade spit.

13.3   Foreign Exchange Market Participants

There are various participants within the foreign exchange markets: (a) commercial and investment banks; (b) multinationals or big corporations; (c) brokers; (d) non-commercial banks (e.g., hedge funds, private equity firms); and (e) central banks.

13.3.1   Commercial and Investment Banks

Global commercial and investment banks are the foremost big players in FX markets. Most of them get involved to serve their clients by conducting business worldwide. In so doing, commercial and investment banks perform or act in a broker capacity at the request of their clients (i.e., multinational firms, exporters, and importers). Besides serving their clients, commercial and investment banks trade in interbanks FX for their own sake, as a distinct sector of activity. They speculate or make arbitrages in FX seeking for spread, as dealers.

The market maker function of any global bank involves two primary foreign exchange activities: (a) commercial and investment banks quote a two-way price and (b) they buy currency as inventory at bid price, with the expectation to sell the currency later at ask price, and realize a spread. As all foreign currencies are assigned an International Standard Organization (ISO) abbreviation, the market maker expresses the relationship using the two currencies' ISO designations. (e.g., USD/JPY).[122]

Hundreds of international commercial and investment banks are actively involved in the FX markets through their FX desks. Deals are conducted by telephone with brokers or via electronic dealing terminal connection to their counterparty. The standard dollar parcels vary between 5 and 10 million. Sometimes, higher dollar parcels from 100 to 500 million are also quoted.

The ten top currency traders in 2007 are listed in Table 13.1.

13.3.2   Multinationals and Big Corporations

Multinationals and big corporations operating worldwide have to make or receive payment in foreign currencies. Besides performing through their commercial or investment banks, most international managers play directly in the FX markets in order to hedge their risks or offset FX receivables or payables that might jeopardize the firm's financial strength.

13.3.3   Brokers

Brokers perform mainly as intermediaries in the FX markets, matching dealers' orders to buy and sell currencies. They earn fees for the involvement. The broker industry in FX is dominated by two players: Reuters and the European Broking Services (EBS).

Table 13.1   Top currency traders in 2007.

Top 10 currency traders % of overall volume (2007)	Institution	% of volume
1	Deutsche Bank	19.30
2	UBS AG	14.85
3	Citi	9.00
4	Royal Bank of Scotland	8.90
5	Barclays Capital	8.80
6	Bank of America	5.29
7	HSBC	4.36
8	Goldman Sachs	4.14
9	JP Morgan	3.33
10	Morgan Stanley	2.86

13.3.4   Non-commercial Banks

Non-commercial banks include hedge funds, private equity firms, large institutional investors, and other participants in the FX markets. They are mainly speculators on the watch for opportunities in those markets. Hedge funds particularly are increasing their market share, stirring fears that the markets could destabilize.

13.3.5   Central Banks

Central banks hold official or international currency reserves to assist their governments in international trade. Whenever their balances of payments are under deficits and/or surpluses, central banks intervene in the FX to buy and/or sell foreign currencies. The intervention of central banks is often closely watched because it can provide some indication as to the financial wealth of a nation.

Figure 13.4 shows the FX market participants.

13.4   Strategies of Forex Hedge Funds

Bank managers trading in FX markets use various strategies known as: (a) macro; (b) carry trade; (c) momentum; and (d) volatility.

13.4.1   Macro

This strategy applies in both developed and emerging markets. Bank managers take positions in various assets betting on the movement of several currencies. Bank managers are always on the watch for opportunities in FX markets. They study macroeconomic indicators of countries where they plan to trade, seeking and analyzing strengths and weaknesses.

Figure 13.4   FX market participants.
Source: http://www.fxstreet.com/education/forex-basics/the-six-forces-of-forex/2006-06-29.html.

13.4.2 Carry Trade

The carry trade strategy consists of taking advantage of the interest rate dispar-
ity between currencies by buying a currency with a high interest rate while
selling a currency with a low rate. Bank managers will simultaneously take
cross-positions in different currencies betting on interest rate differentials.
These positions ensure that, each trading day, rollover interest will be posted to
the funds' accounts. If conducted carefully, the carry trade increases the banks'
returns significantly. The carry trade strategy has been recently facilitated
with the "Harvest Index" developed by Deutsche Bank, which comes in three
variants: Balanced Index, G10 Index, and Emerging Markets Index. The most
important is the G10 Index, composed of the ten most liquid currencies:

- US dollar
- European Union euro
- Japanese yen
- Canadian dollar
- Swiss franc
- British pound
- Australian dollar
- New Zealand dollar
- Norwegian krone
- Swedish krona

These currencies are sometimes split between major and minor currencies. Major currencies include the US dollar, British pound, Japanese yen, Swiss franc, and the European Union euro. Minor currencies are composed of the remaining. Figure 13.5 shows the FX market turnover by currency.

Bank managers have to follow a five-step procedure in order to implement a carry trade:

1. They select a futures contract used by the Index and re-evaluate interest rates quarterly. While using a futures contract, the manager does not have to incorporate the daily interest rate's credit/debit factor, rather he depends on the interest-rich currencies.
2. They utilize certain related FX trading technical analyses and longer time-frame charts to assess the risk and reward associated with the currency pair in order to determine the trading strategy.
3. They buy currency with a high interest rate and sell currency with a lower interest rate.
4. They monitor the interest rate fluctuations, which could change at any time.
5. They buy based on the moving average cross-over when the exponential moving average (EMA), which moves quickly, intersects the simple moving average (SMA), which moves slowly from the bottom and indicates an upward trend. Conversely, managers should not sell if the EMA, which moves quickly, intersects the SMA, which moves slowly from the top and indicates a downward trend, staying focused on interest with positive rates.

13.4.3 Momentum

In momentum trading strategy, bank managers focus on currencies that are moving significantly in one direction, in high volumes. Positions in momentum trading are not held for a short period of time depending on the way the currencies move and their position changes. The bank manager transacts only when he sees an acceleration in a currency. He takes either a long or short position in the currency with the expectation that the momentum continues, whether upward or downward. Momentum trading strategy relies more on short-term movements in currency price rather than fundamental information about the currency. Like managers in carry trades, momentum traders have to proceed methodically, following different steps:

- define and select the MACD segment;
- measure the value of the highest bar within that segment to record the momentum reference point;[123]
- focus on the prior high (or low) in the preceding segment, and use that value to create a model.

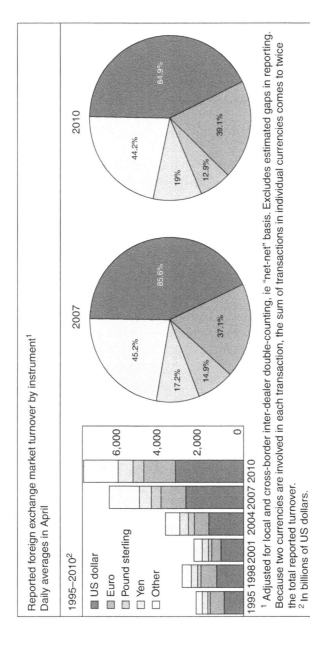

Figure 13.5 The FX market turnover by currency.
Source: BIS (2011).

13.4.4   Volatility

Volatility trading is mostly measuring risk rather than being a trading strategy. Volatility is a statistical measure of how the prices of currencies are moving. Traders usually speculate on changes in the volatility of the market rather than on the direction of the market itself. The opportunity for a higher spread is much higher with volatile positions or portfolios, but an excessive exposure remains risky. Usually, bank managers follow four steps while pursuing the volatility trading strategy:

- they consider the extent to which their leverage would affect their trading positions;
- they use tighter stops in time of high volatility;
- they are selective with trades, despite the higher volatility temptation to engage in bigger positions;
- they engage only when it is safe.

Three different ratios are used to measure volatility: (a) the sharp ratio; (b) the sorting ratio; and (c) the sterling ratio.

The Sharp Ratio

The sharp ratio measures risk-adjusted performance. In terms of risk, the standard deviation of portfolio returns is used as a measure. The return is then adjusted for a known risk-free asset, such as T-bills or some other assets with guaranteed return.

The Sorting Ratio

The sorting ratio measures the amount of incremental return that can be obtained per level of risk. The sorting ratio uses the downside deviation to measure volatility. Under this method, an acceptable rate of return must be assigned – typically, this is set at 0% for hedge funds, but that is not always the case.

The Sterling Ratio

The sterling ratio divides the annualized return of the portfolio by the average yearly maximum drawdown, minus a certain percentage. The drawdown is a measure of loss over time.

13.5   Modern FX Trading

In 1992, George Soros, manager of the Quantum hedge fund, took advantage of the United Kingdom's weaker economy. He bet $10 billion against the UK pound in the midst of the country's economic recession. Soros' personal knowledge of the UK's economic system and the European Monetary System (with the European Currency Unit) led him to consider that the exchange rate of £1/2.95 marks was surrealistic. The UK central bank fought back in an effort to protect the pound from being pushed out of the European Monetary System, but Soros won the party, making a record spread of 1 billion. Emboldened by his UK experience, Soros repeated his macro strategy in 1997, betting on the Thai Baht and various Southeast Asian unstructured capital markets to provoke one of the world's worst financial crises. He bet against the Thailand Baht after observing major inconsistencies in that country's macroeconomic conditions, loose financial regulations, and economic cronyism. He proceeded with the bet despite the efforts of the Thailand central bank to intervene and inject currencies into its international reserves. The bet created contagious effects in four other Asian countries: Indonesia, Korea, Malaysia, and the Philippines.

13.6   Foreign Exchange Risk

As multinational firms, international banks are exposed to foreign exchange risk. Foreign exchange risk represents exposure to changes in the values of current holdings and future cash flows denominated in other currencies. Investments by international banks into a foreign subsidiary, a foreign currency-denominated loan, or future cash flows in foreign currencies are among the transactions which are the most exposed to foreign exchange risk.

International banks that derive large profits from their foreign exchange investment are those who carefully engineer cross-border arbitrages and perform basic brokerage functions in the FX market.[124] To mitigate their foreign exchange risks, banks use various instruments such as currency swaps, foreign exchange options, futures, forwards, and others.[125] The measurement of foreign exchange risk has two main aspects: (a) measurement of traditional currency mismatches by the maturity of the mismatch, and (b) assessment of volatility risk of change of individual currencies versus the domestic currency.

13.7   Measuring Foreign Exchange Risk

The most used techniques in measuring FX risk are: (a) hedging; (b) FX gap analysis; (c) FX rate duration analysis; (d) FX rate simulation analysis; and (e) FX rate volatility analysis.

13.7.1   Hedging

The purpose of foreign exchange hedging consists of minimizing the bank's exposure to changes in foreign exchange rates. There are several hedging techniques, each bearing its own particular features. Some banks use foreign exchange options to hedge currency risk, while others use "delta hedging" to hedge options-type risk or to synthetically create foreign exchange options.[126] If the appropriate measure of risk is related to deviations between actual and predicted exchange rates, a bank could use the forward rate as a prediction of the future spot rate. However, even so, the use of the forward rate does not completely eliminate the volatility risk for a couple of reasons: (a) the forward rate is not a good indicator of future exchange rates; and (b) quotations are available only for major currencies.

13.7.2   Foreign Exchange Gap Analysis

Gap trading allows the bank to take advantage in the gap price of a specific currency from one day to the next. Knowledge of the gap and other relevant information can boost the bank's FX profits in the short term. A bank's FX department would have to determine its own gap for each currency traded between the close and the next day. International banks with offices around the world have advantages relative to domestic banks, as they can trade around the clock.

13.7.3   Foreign Exchange Rate Duration Analysis

Banks and other investors use two methods when purchasing and selling foreign exchange markets: fundamental analysis[127] and technical duration analysis. Foreign exchange rate duration analysis is a variant of technical duration analysis. In the context of foreign exchange, duration means three things:

- the change in the value of a foreign currency bond with respect to foreign currency interest rates;
- the change in the value of a foreign currency bond with respect to domestic currency interest rates;
- the change in the value of a foreign currency bond with respect to the spot rate interest.

Exchange rate duration analysis focuses on the interest rate sensitivity of a given currency.

13.7.4   Foreign Exchange Rate Simulation Analysis

An international bank with open positions in many currencies can manage its foreign exchange risk through simulation models (i.e., Monte Carlo) to simulate various risk scenarios. However, the model should be properly conceived to take any deviation into account.

13.7.5   Foreign Exchange Rate Volatility Analysis

Since the collapse of the Bretton Woods system in March 1973, there has been a high degree of volatility of most exchange rates. Volatility is related, in the most part, to macroeconomic fundamentals (i.e., inflation, real GDP growth, current account deficit). It could also depend on external developments. However, despite the voluminous literature on the topic, there is no generally accepted model of bank behavior subject to risk arising from fluctuations in exchange rates.

13.8 Taxation of Foreign Exchange Transactions

Taxation of forex is not uniform. The taxing regimes are different for (a) spot forex; (b) forward forex; and (c) futures forex.

13.8.1 Taxation of Spot Forex

The taxation of spot forex is one of the opaque areas in the taxation of financial products. From the IRC, only section 988 explicitly provides the taxing regime of spot forex. Under this section, gains or losses resulting from spot forex trades are treated as ordinary gains or losses. That is, a forex trader with excess ordinary losses would not be allowed to carry back or carry forward its losses, unless it has the status of professional trader. Spot trading appeared in the 2000s, just after the collapse of online securities trading in the 1990s. Small securities traders turned on to the spot forex, taking advantage of the inter-banks' openness with the retail forex platforms. Thus, the spot forex market as we know it today developed after the Internal Revenue Service's 1982 and 1984 amendments to the overall foreign exchange taxation.

To some extent, the 1982 and 1984 amendments arose from the situation where banks created an unofficial market referred to as "the inter-banks' market", in which they started advertising to the general public as being willing to purchase, sell, or enter into foreign currency contract with retailers. Banks participating in the FX market generally trade the forward forex, whereas individual traders usually enter into spot forex. Pressed by the banking lobbyists, in 1982 Congress added section 1256(b)(2) in the IRC, allowing banks to opt for the IRC section 1256 contract, if they satisfied three requirements: (1) the contract must require delivery of a foreign currency; (2) the foreign currency should be the one traded through the RFCs; (3) the contract must provide a settlement date. If these three requirements were met, banks trading in forwards forex were fiscally aligned under the preferential regime under section 1256, then recognized only for futures forex contracts. But nothing in the 1982 and 1984[128] amendments explicitly mentioned spot forex trading. Therefore, forex traders have repeatedly argued that, based upon the rationale behind the 1982 and 1984 amendments, spot forex traders should also be allowed to opt for the preferential regime under IRC section 1256(g). In the absence of clear guidance from either the IRS or the courts, they have come to believe that spot forex traders can also opt for

IRC section 1256(g). They rely upon some relevant analogies between the spot and the forwards: (a) both the spot and the forward are bilateral contracts; and (b) both the spot and the forward require delivery of the foreign currency or settlement at the expiration date. Therefore, they argue that an option is also available to the spot under the same requirements set up in 1982 and 1984.

But proponents of the option under IRC section 1256 went on to question the second requirement, which demanded that the spot forex qualify only if the foreign currency was traded in a Regulated Futures Contract (RFC). They argue that such a requirement is outdated, because only a handful of currencies are traded through RFCs. That said, the spot forex trader as well as the forward forex trader should be allowed to opt out of IRC section 988 and elect to be treated under IRC section 1256(g). Besides the straight analogies with the forward forex, proponents of the IRC section 988 opt-out have found in IRS Notice 2007-1, and the recent Tax Court holding in the Summit case a second analogy in support of their arguments. Indeed, neither the IRS Notice nor the Summit case mentions spot forex trading directly, as they dealt with OTC options forex.

13.8.2 Taxation of Forward Forex

In general, forward forex contracts are subject to IRC section 988. However, the taxpayer can make an election to opt out of section 988 and elect for section 1256. Moreover, the section 1256 option is available only if the forward forex is in a major currency, for which RFCs are traded. Forward forex, like futures forex, are "foreign currency contract", under IRC section 1256. The term "foreign currency contract" means a contract that:

- requires delivery of, or the settlement of (which depends on the value) a foreign currency which is a currency in which positions are also traded through regulated futures contracts (RFCs);
- is traded in the inter-bank market; and
- is entered into at arm's length at a price determined by reference to the price in the inter-bank market.

13.8.3 Taxation of Futures Forex

Futures forex is different from the forward in that it is traded in an organized market with a clearing mechanism, is standardized, and offers a mark-to-market option. Futures forex contracts are recognized foreign currency contracts subject to the preferential 60/40 rules under IRC section 1256. Futures forex meet all the three requirements: (a) they are bilateral and not unilateral contracts; (b) they are traded in organized markets; and (c) they always come with settlement dates.

13.8.4 Taxation of Options Forex

In contrast to spot or forward forex, an option forex is a unilateral contract, at the discretion of the option holder, which does not require delivery or settlement unless and until the option holder chooses to exercise the option. An options forex does not qualify as a foreign currency contract and thus is outside the scope of IRC section 1256(g). Thus, option forex tax treatment is different from the taxing regime of the spot, forward and futures forex. That is, the parties to an option have no income, gain, or loss at the time they entered into an option. The tax regime of an option forex becomes a relevant question whenever the option is exercised or lapsed. The exercise of an option forex is treated as a sale of the underlying currency in exchange for the strike price. If the option forex lapses, the paid premium becomes an income for the writer and an expense for the holder. In the recent Summit case,[129] the Tax Court was called to hold whether a major foreign currency call option, a non-exchange traded contract, comes within the meaning of "foreign currency contract" so as to qualify for IRC section 1256 treatment.

The facts of the case can be summarized as follows:

- Summit entered into agreements with Beckenham ("Beckenham") Trading Co., Inc. to engage in cross-currency transactions.
- Beckenham was designated the calculation agent for the transactions to determine all amounts due to or from each party in accordance with terms specified in the agreements with Summit.
- On September 21, 2002, Summit authorized Multinational to purchase two 180-day major currency options, and to sell on behalf of Summit two 180-day written minor foreign currency options.
- On September 23, 2002, Summit purchased from Beckenham two major currency options, each pegged to the US dollar and the European Union euro.
- As the purchaser and holder of the major currency call option, Summit, by exercising its option, could require Beckenham to deliver the euro at a price of USD 0.9788/euro.
- As the purchaser and holder of the put option, Summit, by exercising its option, could require Beckenham to take delivery of the euro at a future date or dates at a price of USD 0.9788/euro.
- On the same day that Summit purchased the major currency options, Summit wrote and sold to Beckenham two minor currency options, each pegged to the USD and the Danish Krone (DKK). The written minor options moved inversely in value to one another over the 180-day period, thus ensuring that Summit would hold a gain position in one of the two minor currency options.
- On September 25, 2002, Summit assigned the major foreign currency call option and the minor foreign currency call option to a charity pursuant

to an assignment agreement in which the charity was substituted for Summit with respect to all obligations under the minor foreign currency call option.

- Summit recognized loss upon its assignment to charity of a major foreign currency call option, but did not include any income upon its assignment to charity of a minor foreign currency call option. Summit relied upon section 1256 of the IRC.
- In March 2007, the CIR issued a notice of deficiency to petitioners for 2002 which disallowed a $1767 flow-through loss from Summit's foreign currency option transactions.
- The Tax Court ruled that IRC section 1256 applies only to futures and options contracts that are traded on a qualified exchange, as well as forex contracts entered into by commercial banks within their "informal market", but not to non-exchange-traded contracts.
- The Tax Court went on to explain that section 1256 requires delivery of the foreign currency, not to a contract in which delivery was left to the discretion of the holder. A foreign currency option is a unilateral contract that does not require delivery or settlement unless and until the option is exercised by the option holder. An obligation to settle might never arise if the holder does not exercise its rights under the option.

14
Banking and Derivatives Transactions

14.1 Introduction

The derivative securities markets have blossomed over the last two decades, with the United States and Canada trading more than half of the $96.67 trillion contracts outstanding in 2007.[130] Among the players are commercial banks, investment banks, and hedge funds. The US banks' total exposure to foreign economies through derivatives increased in 2009, as two investment banks with large foreign exposures became Bank Holding Companies (BHCs) and were added to the Federal Financial Institutions Examination Council's Country Exposure Lending Survey.[131]

Derivative instruments enable banks to mitigate their market and credit risks. Banks transact in a variety of derivatives in their trading portfolios in order to meet the needs of their customers and sometimes for their own sake. Derivatives improve the efficiency of financial markets and, by permitting more financial risks to be hedged, could permit some borrowers more access to sources of funds.[132] Derivatives are a double-edged sword in that (a) they can be used to manage risk, and (b) they can become financial weapons of mass destruction if used solely for speculative purposes.[133] Managing derivatives positions has been shown to be tricky since only a small amount (the margin) is needed to establish a position. That could hide the full extent of a firm's or bank's financial obligations.

Derivative securities (forwards, futures, options, and swaps) are securities whose values depend on the value of an underlying asset but whose payoff is not guaranteed with cash flows from these assets. The underlying asset could be a single security, commodity or currency, interest rate, or other asset. Banks and other market participants have seen in the derivative market the opportunity of overall distribution of risks among various participants. Moreover, banks see the derivative market as a means to increase liquidity and access to capital. That is because credit derivative swaps, for instance, allow banks and other financial institutions to pass on risks from making loans.

The term "credit derivative" encompasses an array of transactions whose value is determined by the creditworthiness of an underlying entity, the most common of which is the credit default swap (CDS). The total notional amount of CDS in the market was about $34.4 trillion at the end of 2006. To quote an example from among many Wall Street derivative players, from 2006 to 2009 Goldman Sachs' trading in derivatives generated between $11.3 billion and $15.9 billion of its $45.17 billion in net revenue. Credit derivative swaps, equity swaps, and interest rates swaps were among the most traded.

Prior to the Wall Street Reform and Consumer Protection Act of 2010, the swap market was not standardized. Market fundamentalists, among them the former head of the Federal Reserve Alan Greenspan, preached that the swap market was able to self-regulate. With the failure and bail-out of main Wall Street swaps players (e.g., AIG), Congress has, through the aforementioned Act, framed and shaped the swap market. The Wall Street Reform and Consumer Protection Act of 2010 significantly amends the over-the-counter (OTC) derivatives. However, the full extent or scope of the new law will be revealed later, after completion of the mandated rulemaking by the government agencies involved. The swap market jurisdiction, for instance, is still split between the Securities and Exchange Commission (SEC) and the Commodity Futures Trading Commission (CFTC). The SEC has jurisdiction over a portion of an equity swap and a portion of a credit default swap, whereas the CFTC's jurisdiction covers commodity swaps, foreign exchange swaps, interest rate swaps, CDS index swaps, and equity index swaps.

Under the new law, most of the regulatory and prudential efforts target two classes of entities: (a) swap dealers and security-based swap dealers; and (b) major swap participants and major security-based swap participants, which are both required to clear most of their standardized swaps with a central counterparty. However, the new law provides an exemption from the mandatory clearance for derivatives end users. Another big change that affects the derivatives' market is the mandatory reporting: swap dealers and major swap participants are required to disclose to the SEC or the CFTC information concerning: (a) the terms and conditions of their swaps; (ii) their swap trading operations; and (c) what measures they have put in place to protect their financial integrity. Furthermore, all non-cleared swaps agreements must be reported to a Swap Data Repository.

Beside their disclosure and reporting obligations, swap dealers and major swap participants have to keep and maintain their daily trading record for each transaction for audit purposes. When entering into a swap agreement with a layperson or a counterparty which is not a swap dealer, swap dealers and major swap participants must disclose in clear and understandable language: (a) the material risks and characteristic of each swap agreement; (b) the source and amount of any compensation; (c) any incentives or conflicts of interest; (d) the clearinghouse for cleared swaps; and (e) the daily mark of the swap dealer or major swap participant, for non-cleared swaps. Swap dealers and major swap participants will be subject to prudential capital and margin requirements to be determined by either the SEC or the CFTC under their specific jurisdictions.

14.2   Forward Contracts

A forward contract is an agreement between financial or banking institutions and their corporate clients to buy and sell an asset at a certain future time, for a certain price. The parties enter into a forward because the future (spot) price or interest on the underlying asset is uncertain. Fearing that the future spot price will fluctuate against them in the future, they pay a financial institution to arrange a forward contract for them. The underlying assets are often non-standardized, that is, each forward contract seems to be different from the next. However, with the development of a secondary market of forward contracts, an effort has been made to standardize the basic or the most commonly-used forward contracts entered into by traders. The existence of such a secondary market has enticed many bank managers to invest and trade in forward contracts. Very often, a bank manager will trade on securities that provide a predictable cash income, such as stock indexes.

The execution of a forward contract in respect to an underlying stock has no tax consequences. If a forward contract is settled by delivery of the underlying asset, the taxpayer delivering the asset must recognize a gain or loss based upon the difference between the price received and the taxpayer's basis in the asset. The gain or loss bears the same character as the underlying asset. Usually, a forward contract is settled by cash payment. However, if a forward contract is sold prior to the pre-agreed date, any gain or loss is deemed a capital asset in the hands of the selling taxpayer. If the character of the income recognized by a party to a forward contract is a capital gain or loss, the income is normally sourced based upon the residence of the taxpayer.

14.3   Futures Contracts

A futures contract is an agreement between two parties to buy and sell (at time 0) a standardized asset for cash in the future, for a certain price. A futures contract is different from the forward contract in that (a) the delivery date is usually not specified as the contract's price is adjusted daily based upon the price of the underlying asset; (b) futures contracts are traded on an organized market (e.g., NYFE, CBT); (c) a futures contract is by default risk free in that if a counterparty defaults on a futures, the Exchange steps in and assumes the defaulting party's position and payment obligation; (d) the terms of a futures contract are set out by the market organization. Some authors define a futures contract merely as a forward contract that is standardized and traded on an organized futures exchange. That is because, under the futures contract, buyers and sellers do not complete the trade on their own. The process is supervised by a clearinghouse department of the Exchange, which ensures that each party has met its obligations under the contract. Bank managers trade on these markets as either speculators or hedgers based upon their strategies and studies of the underlying assets.

A futures contract traded on domestic and some foreign futures exchanges are generally treated as "Section 1265 Contract" in the hand of the investors. Under IRC section 1256(b), the term "Section 1256 Contract" means:

- any regulated futures contract;
- any foreign currency contract;
- any non-equity option;
- any dealer equity option; and
- any dealer securities futures contracts.

The term "Section 1256 Contract" shall not include any securities or option on such a contract unless such contract or option is a dealer securities futures contract. A section 1256 contract held by the taxpayer at the end of the taxable year shall be treated as sold for its fair market value on the last business day of such taxable year (and any gain or loss shall be taken into account for the taxable year). Put differently, section 1265 requires taxpayers to treat each section 1265 contract as if it were sold (and repurchased) for its fair market value on the last day of the year. Furthermore, it imposes a mark-to-market timing regime on instruments within its scope. Any gain or loss with respect to a section 1256 contract is treated as short-term capital gain or loss – to the extent of 40% of the gain or loss – and the remaining 60% is treated as long-term gain or loss. This special "60/40" rule does not apply to certain transactions: (a) hedging transactions; (b) a section 1256 contract that is part of a mixed straddle if the taxpayer makes the selection; (c) a section 1256 contract held by a dealer in commodities or by a trader in commodities that makes the mark-to-market election under IRC section 475(d)(1).

14.4   Options Contracts

An option contract is a contract that gives the holder of the option the right, but not the obligation, to buy or sell an underlying asset, at a pre-agreed price, within a pre-agreed period of time. There are two basic types of options, a call option and a put option:

- A call option is the option that gives the holder (purchaser) the right to buy the underlying security or asset from the option writer or the seller by a certain date referred to as the expiration date or the exercise date or the maturity, for a certain price called the exercise or strike price. A warrant is a call option that is written by a corporation on its own stock.

- A put option gives the holder of the option the right to sell the underlying security or asset to the option writer (or seller) by a certain date, for a pre-specified price.

Option contracts are different from both the forward contract and the futures contract. First, the option holder has the right either to exercise the option or not to exercise it at all. He is not compelled to buy or sell unlike with forward and futures contracts. Second, the option holder must pay to the option writer or the seller an up-front fee referred to as the call premium, whereas parties in a forward or futures contract enter into these contracts free of any premium.

Option contracts are traded as future contracts on an organized exchange. There are three types of options trade: stock options, stock index options, and options on futures contract. The SEC is the main regulator of the option contracts. The CFTC regulates only options on futures contracts. In the 1990s, banks and other financial institutions developed a new form of option contracts known as "exotic options". These options were written for the purpose of hedging very specific risks and were traded over-the-counter (OTC).

14.4.1 Stock Options

The underlying asset on a stock option contract is the stock of a publicly traded company. One option generally involves 100 shares of the company's underlying stock. The US Exchange's trading stock options are:

- Chicago Board Options Exchange (CBOE);
- Philadelphia Exchange (PHLX);
- American Stock Exchange (AMEX);
- Pacific Stock Exchange (PSE); and
- New York Stock Exchange (NYSE).

The most used contract is the "incentive stock option", which is an option granted by a corporation to an individual to purchase stock of the corporation. IRC section 422(b) has specific conditions about this contract: (a) the grant of a stock option must be related to or connected to employment; (b) the employee must remain an employee of the corporation or its affiliates from the time of the issuance until three months prior to the exercise of the option. The option holder would have to report income only when the stock is disposed of.

14.4.2 Stock Index Options

The underlying asset on a stock index option contract is the value of a major stock market index. The three best known indexes are the Dow Jones Industrial

Average (DJIA), the S&P 500 for European options, and the S&P 100 for US options. Stock index options are different from stock options in that, at settlement, the stock index holder receives cash rather than a delivery of portfolio underlying the index. The value of each stock index is determined by using a given multiplier.

14.4.3   Options on Futures Contracts

The underlying asset in a futures contract option is a futures contract. Most of the futures contracts traded are the US Treasury bonds futures.

14.4.4   Exotic Options

Exotic options are OTC derivatives traded by major banks or financial institutions. Exotic options include a variety of financial instruments such as: barrier option, digital option, quantity adjusting option (or quanto), differential option (or Diff option), rainbow option, etc. These options allow the writer to manage only the specific risks they intend to hedge against.

- **Barrier option** A barrier option is an option contract that can only be exercised when the underlying asset reaches some barrier price. There are four basic types of barrier options that each have slightly different payoff structures.[134] Barrier options sometimes come with a rebate paid at the time of the event or at the expiration date.
- **Digital option** A digital option is an option where the payout is characterized as having only two potential values: (a) a fixed payout when the underlying price is above the strike price); or (b) zero payout otherwise.
- **Quantity adjusting option (quanto)** This option has an underlier denominated in one foreign currency, but settles in another domestic currency, at a fixed exchange rate. Quanto options have both the strike price and the underlier denominated in a foreign currency, but the value of the option is determined as the option's intrinsic value in a foreign currency. That intrinsic value is then converted to the domestic currency at the fixed exchange rate.
- **Differential option** Differential options are a variant of quanto options with a fixed-floating or floating-floating interest rate. One of the floating rates is a foreign interest rate, but it is applied to a notional amount in the domestic currency.
- **Rainbow option** The value of this is dependent on two or more underlying securities or events. The option holder is allowed to exercise the option based on the change in the two or more securities used as underlying assets. The price of the rainbow option is dependent on the correlation of the underlying events or assets. One form of rainbow option is the outperforming option,

the value of which is determined by the differential in performance of two securities or assets.

Bank managers use various strategies with the aforementioned options. They might take positions in two or more options of the same type or combined strategies such as straddles, strips & straps, or strangles with options of different types. Gain or loss recognized by the purchaser of an option is considered to have the same character as the underlying asset that the option relates to. In the case of a purchaser of an option on publicly traded stock as an investment, gain or loss will be capital. However, if the purchaser were a dealer in securities, or a taxpayer using the option as a hedging contract, gain or loss will be treated as ordinary income under section 1221(a)(7) of the IRS Code.

A qualified hedging transaction is defined as a transaction that a taxpayer enters into during the normal course of its business to manage primarily: (a) the risk of price changes or currency fluctuations with respect to ordinary property that is held or to be held by the taxpayer, or (b) the risk of interest rate or price changes or currency fluctuations with respect to borrowings made or to be made, or ordinary obligations incurred or to be incurred, by the taxpayer. In the case of termination of an option other than through delivery of the underlying asset, the writer's gain or loss is deemed short-term capital gain or loss, regardless of the terms of the contract. The character of the income recognized by the holder of an option on a publicly traded asset is capital gain or loss; the income is normally sourced based on the residence of the taxpayer.

14.5   Swaps

Swaps are private agreements between parties to exchange cash flows at specified intervals. The first known swap contracts were negotiated in the 1980s. Swap markets were developed in order to meet the needs of corporations, financial institutions, and portfolio managers to modify their exposure to a substantial increase in currency and interest-rate volatility that followed the demise of the Brettons Woods fixed exchange rate system. Since then, the swap market has sprung exponentially to reach the amount of $347.09 trillion in 2007. The United States' commercial banks, investment banks and insurance companies are the biggest players in the swap market, with an overall total of $95.39 trillion in 2007. Swap market participants include swap facilitators and their clients and customers.

By and large, there are five generic types of swaps:

- interest rate swaps;
- currency swaps;
- credit risk swaps;

- commodity swaps; and
- equity swaps.

Of the five types, interest rate swaps are the most commonly used. Usually, bank managers enter into swaps agreements in order to eliminate or mitigate interest rates inherent to their global positions.

14.5.1   Interest Rate Swaps

Interest rate swaps are contracts whereby one party agrees to pay the other party interest at a fixed rate on a notional principal for a number of years, in exchange for a floating interest rate on the same notional principal for the same period of time. The most used is a fixed/floating one in which the payment made by a counterparty is based on a variable or floating rate of interest, and the return payment is based on a variable at floating rate, which is reset periodically according to a benchmark. Counterparties can also enter into a cross-currency swap whereby payments are made in two different currencies, based on fixed or floating interest rates. In a fixed/floating interest rate swap, the notional is never exchanged; rather, it is used to calculate the payment flows. Once a floating payment is made, the rate is reset to establish the next floating payment based upon the benchmark reference rate agreed on (e.g., Libor). This makes a fixed/floating interest rate swap different from a cross-currency swap where the principal amounts are generally exchanged at the spot foreign exchange rate from the outset and then re-exchanged at the maturity, at the same rate. The floating interest rate is usually pegged to some short-term interest rate, such as Libor, and is referred to as the "reference rate". The fixed interest rate is made of two components: (a) a risk-free yield for the maturity of the swap, and (b) a swap spread over the risk-free yield which is the basis for pricing the swap. Interest rate swaps are often entered into by counterparties seeking to improve the cost of funding or to hedge interest rate risks. Banks invest in fixed/floating interest rate swaps in anticipation of future interest rate increases, in order to grab some spreads.

14.5.2   Currency Swaps

Currency swaps are essentially forward contracts between two parties, tailored to meet their specific needs. Currency swaps consist of exchanging principal and fixed-rate interest payments on a loan in one currency for principal and fixed-rate interest payments on an approximately equivalent loan in another currency (Figure 14.1). A currency swap agreement requires the principal be specified in each of the two currencies. The principal amounts are usually exchanged at the beginning and the end of the life of the swaps.

On each settlement date through to maturity, the US party pays interest to the foreign counterparty. That interest is based upon a fixed interest rate and

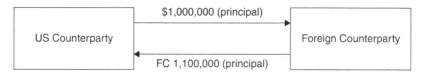

Figure 14.1   Basic currency swap.

is denominated in the foreign currency that was delivered on the date of origination to the US party. At maturity, the US party repays the foreign currency principal to the counterparty, along with the last interest payments, and the foreign counterparty repays the US dollar principal including the last interest payment: this is known as a synthetic fixed/fixed currency swap. Currency swaps can also be created with both counterparties receiving a fixed interest rate. A currency swap can be used to either align assets or liabilities with market expectations or to exploit mispricings among markets, through arbitrage.

14.5.3   Credit Swaps

There are four types of credit swaps: (a) the credit default swap (CDS); (b) the first-to-default CDS; (c) the total return swap; and (d) the asset-backed credit-linked note.

The Credit Default Swap

A credit default swap (CDS) is an agreement between two counterparties (the buyer of the protection and the seller of the protection) against default on a loan or a bond. The borrower (or issuer), also called the referenced credit, pays a premium to the seller of the protection in exchange for contingent payment depending on agreed credit events, which may occur during the lifetime of the agreement. Put differently, a CDS consists of transferring risks that a party is not willing to bear to another party with a desired risk profile.

Credit default swaps have been often criticized. Some have argued that they operate as shock absorbers during corporate crises, cushioning against the worst possible losses. The notional amount of CDSs outstanding by the end of 2007 was estimated to exceed $60 trillion. It declined sharply to just over $30 trillion during the first half of 2010. Market participants include commercial banks, broker-dealers, insurance companies, hedge funds, and special purpose vehicles (SPV). Bank managers enter into CDS in order to reduce the level of credit risk on their various portfolios. Hedge funds enter the CDS market both as credit protection buyers and credit protection sellers in order to manage their risks, speculate, or acquire synthetic exposure.

Prior to the Wall Street reform and Consumer Protection Act of 2010, CDSs were traded in over-the-counter markets. The 2010 Act has moved to include the CDS deals in an organized market to be defined by regulations.

The original trade and the clearing processes are summarized in Figure 14.2.

First-to-Default CDS

The first-to-default CDS allows the insurer to reduce its risk exposure of the loan portfolio to the first loan default. It is an agreement by which a protection seller would have to compensate the counterparty (the buyer of the protection) by paying it a par and receive the defaulted loan.

Total return swaps

A total return swap (TRS) is an agreement whereby the buyer of the risk receives from the seller of the risk a specified economic value for the reference credit rather than a lump sum notional payment in the event of default. A total return swap is often used as a means to transfer the market risk of an asset off-balance sheet to lower regulatory charges. A total return swap is different from a CDS in that (a) the market and credit risks are transferred from the seller to the buyer; and (b) no exchange of the principal, no legal change of ownership, and no voting rights are passed from the seller to the buyer. The buyer of a TRS receives the cash flow or benefit (or pays the losses) if the value of the underlying asset rises (or falls). To hedge against the credit/or market risks, the seller of the TRS often buys the underlying asset.

Asset-backed Credit-linked Notes

An asset-backed credit-liked note (CLN) is an actual security with a credit derivative (a credit default swap) embedded in its structure. A CLN is a debt obligation with a coupon and redemption tied to the performance of the loan. An investment bank manager enters into a CLN if he wants to take a liability out the balance sheet. A CLN is different from a TRS in that the principal exchanges hands, though there is no legal change of ownership of the underlying asset.

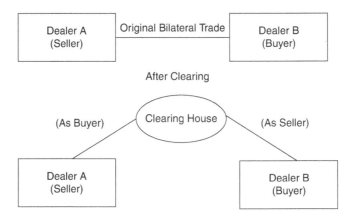

Figure 14.2   CDS clearing.

Tax Regime

Despite their financial importance and recognition, the tax treatment of credit swaps – and particularly CDSs – has remained a mystery. US tax laws provide no clues as to how CDSs should be taxed.

14.5.4   Commodity Swaps

The character of gains or losses realized by a US person selling or exchanging a commodity is largely a function of the taxpayer's status as either an investor or a trader or dealer.

14.5.5   Equity Swaps

An equity swap is a contractual agreement between two counterparties to exchange cash flows from specific assets over a defined period. Put differently, an equity swap is an agreement between counterparties to exchange payments, one of which depends on the value of a selected share or an index. A variant of an equity swap is a total return swap, whereby the exchange payments reflect the dividends on the share or index. The notional principal of the swap is not exchanged; instead, it is used to calculate the periodic payments. Equity swaps give investors such as investment banks the benefits of stock ownership, without the investor actually owning the stocks.

The exact size of the equity swap market is unknown, but according to the Bank of International Settlement, the notional value of all equity swaps and forwards approximated $1.7 trillion in 2009. Banks enter into equity swaps any time they need to trade on a basket of foreign shares but face certain restrictions on ownership or, when there is no such restriction, in order to avoid paying withholding tax on dividends to receive from their equity investments. Well-advised investment bank managers often enter into an equity swap with a specific dealer who is not subject to any withholding tax (or capital gains) prior to making their equity investments. The dealer will borrow money to acquire the shares, and enter into a swap agreement whereby he agrees to pay the total return on the shares to the bank manager. The IRS is currently investigating whether banks, hedge funds, and other financial institutions are using the equity swap as a device to collect dividends without owning the instruments, and at the same time escape the withholding tax payments. The basic swap structure is illustrated in Figure 14.3.

The different types of equity swaps include: (a) contracts for difference; and (b) debt-for equity swaps.

Contracts for Differences

Contracts for differences (CFDs), also referred to as synthetic swaps, allow investors to participate in stock price, stock indexes, or exchange without buying or selling the shares themselves. Investment bank managers derive their spread from the difference of the opening and the closing value for the contract.

Figure 14.3   Basic swap structure.

Debt-for-Equity Swap

Debt-for-equity swaps consist of exchanging debt for a predetermined amount of equity (stock).The value of the swap is determined usually at current market value rates. However, a management could still offer a higher exchange value to entice share and debt holders to participate in a swap. Debt-for-equity swaps were a fairly common means of acquiring a distressed business in the 1980s and 1990s. It is performed when the debtor needs positive net equity or needs to improve its financial condition by reducing interest-bearing debts. Debt-for-equity swap is, or has been, considered a route by which a company can avoid imminent insolvent liquidation due to persistent negative cash flows or balance sheet insolvency.

Tax Regime

A swap with respect to publicly traded equity is taxed as a "notional principal contract" under IRC section 446, which requires that the parties to a notional contract classify all payments thereto as (a) a "periodic payment", (b) a "non-periodic payment", or (c) a "termination payment".

The characterization of payments as "periodic", "non-periodic", or "termination" is important in that the tax treatments are not the same.

For periodic and non-periodic payments, taxpayers must recognize the ratable daily portions for the taxable year, whereas for termination payments, the taxpayer recognizes income in the year the notional principal contract is either extinguished, assigned, or terminated. Income from a swap contract is generally sourced by reference to the residence of the taxpayer, except for income earned through a US branch. Equity swaps also deviate from the main source rule in that the dividend equivalent payment is treated as non-US source income, not subject to US withholding tax.

15
Banking and Underwriting Transactions

15.1 Introduction

Underwriting consists of raising money for clients through issuance of securities – stock and/or bonds to be sold. Prior to 1999, underwriting was the province of investment banks. That was a result of the Glass-Steagall Act of 1933, which organized the banking industry after the Great Depression created a Chinese wall between commercial and investment banks. The exclusion of commercial banks from the underwriting services was deemed necessary to avoid any conflict of interests when the same bank extended a loan to a corporation and then underwrote for the same corporation as a means of getting back its loan. The bank could then hide its risk and shift it on to the investors.

In November 1999, the Clinton administration, through the so-called "Financial Services Modernization Act" repealed this cornerstone of the banking industry in the United States. The deregulation process in the US had actually started decades before the 1999 Act, when the Federal Reserve Board allowed commercial banks to enter the underwriting and security trading markets.

- In the 1980s, the American Bankers Association and its lobbyists began to challenge the wisdom of the Glass-Steagall Act. They claimed that it had become obsolete and prevented commercial banks and thrift institutions from engaging in more profitable activities.
- From 1987, commercial banks were allowed to underwrite municipal revenue bonds, mortgage and asset-backed securities, and commercial paper, provided (a) these activities were organized under Section 20 affiliates of the commercial banks, and (b) the revenue thereof did not exceed 5% of the total revenues of the affiliate.
- From 1989, commercial banks were allowed to underwrite and trade corporate debt and equity, provided (a) these activities were organized under

Section 20 affiliates, and (b) the revenue thereof did not exceed 10% (later 25%) of the total revenues of the affiliate.

- The Financial Services Modernization Act of 1999 (the "Gramm-Leach-Bliley Act") simply ratified what was by then the reality in the banking industry. Prior to its enactment, most US banks, and foreign commercial banks operating in the US, were already actively engaged in the underwriting market. They did so either by establishing a Section 20 affiliate or by acquiring midsize security firms.

15.2   Role and Functions of an Underwriter

The role of investment banks has faced increased scrutiny since the Merrill Lynch scandal in 2008. Merrill Lynch paid a record settlement of $100 million with the New York Attorney General's Office, and agreed to sever all links between analysts' pay and investment banking revenues. Commercial and investment banks engaged in the underwriting business (the "underwriters") raise money for governments through the sale of marketable securities: stock or bonds. Underwriters perform as intermediaries, bringing together in a deal both issuers and investors. When new securities are sold by an issuer, the transaction is referred to as a "primary sale", and the raised money goes to the issuer. When the security holder sells securities, the transaction is referred to as a "secondary market". Rather than raising money through a public sale of securities, underwriters sometimes obtain money directly through a private placement. If and when this option is not possible, underwriters organize a public sale of the underlying securities. In a private placement, the underwriters raise money mainly from institutional investors willing to partake in the deal. Under the Securities and Exchange Commission (SEC) Rule 144, private placements and issuers of privately-placed securities are not required to register with the SEC since the placements are made to large or institutional investors. When securities are offered to the public at large, investment banks can perform either as an agent of the issuer or as a principal. Investment banks performing in best efforts underwriting act as agents for a fee related to the success of the transaction. Alternatively, investment banks performing in firm commitment underwriting act as a principal. That is, they buy all the issuance from the issuer at an agreed price and then put all the issuance in the market with the expectation of making some spread. Whether investment banks act as agent or principal depends mainly on the rating of the issuer by a rating agency.

The Securities Act of 1933 requires the filing of a detailed disclosure statement for any company raising money from the public at large. This is done through the registration form under either Form S-1 or Form SB-2. The issuer must provide information about: (a) the company's business, its officers, directors, and their compensation; (b) the size of the offering, the price range, and the intended use of the funds; (c) its audited financial statements, the management analysis and discussion, and its risk factors; and (d) the underwriter (or a syndicate of underwriters), the type of underwriting, the dividend policy, dilution, capitalization, and related party transactions.

15.2.1   Participants in the Transactions

Many professionals get involved, in various capacities, during the underwriting process from the day the company (the board) makes the decision to go public or raise capital to the completion of the project.

The Underwriter or Syndicate of Underwriters

The underwriter or the syndicate is responsible for selling the securities. It performs a preliminary study of the issuer to determine the soundness of its business. If the company is financially strong, the underwriter will enter into a letter of intent with the issuer to formalize the arrangement.

The Accountant

The SEC requires that the issuer's financial statements be audited by an independent auditor which must certify the accuracy of the statements and the information provided in the registration form, to its best knowledge.

The Advisor

Given the complexity of the process, the issuer often brings in an advisor or professional consultant. Advisors are usually professionals able to round up multiple aspects of the transaction, taking into account the financial, legal, and tax considerations.

Lawyers

Lawyers advise the issuer by conducting due diligence and compliance with the securities laws. A team of in-house lawyers often works together with a law firm all through the process to make sure that the issuer complies with all the related legal side of the process.

The Financial Printer

A financial printer will print the prospectus and the registration forms in compliance with the SEC format and guidelines.

The Public Relations Firm

A public relations firm will assist the issuer prepare the materials for the road-show or the marketing event that gathers business press and releases the information pursuant to the issuance.

15.2.2   The Underwriter's Compensation

An underwriter's compensation is made up of three components: (a) management fees; (b) underwriting fees; and (c) selling fees. The market practice standard rule is known as a "20-20-60", but underwriters are not bound by the rule.[135] When a syndicate rather than a sole underwriter is involved, the compensation is determined by the leader of the syndicate based upon the terms and conditions of the syndicate's agreement.

15.2.3   Quick Underwriting under Alleviated Securities Laws Regulation

An equity underwriting can be burdensome and time-consuming for the issuer. From the initial registration to the public sale, the issuer and the parties involved in the process can wait at least four months, if not more. The SEC has taken significant steps to alleviate the process through specific regulations.

Regulation A Under the slightest requirements of Regulation A, an issuer is allowed to raise up to $5 million within a period of 12 months, through an initial public offering (IPO).

Regulation D Two specific rules under Regulation D allow an issuer to sell securities to non-accredited investors. Rule 504 allows the sale of up to $1 million over a timeframe of 12 months; while Rule 505 goes up to $5 million, provided fewer than 35 investors are non-accredited investors. The values of the world stock and bond markets are provided in Table 15.1.

Commercial bank underwriters are deemed to have a specific advantage relative to security firms from their corporate business exposure. However, such an advantage is not absolute in the absence of development of underwriting skills and qualified personnel.

In 2010, international banks raised capital for their various clients, increasing the volume of IPO by 110% to reach a total of $269.4 billion. The increase has been bolstered by the Asia-Pacific region.

Eight out of the ten largest IPOs in 2010 were from the Pan-Asia expanse. China, Hong Kong, Japan, and India comprised approximately 65% of the total raised capital globally. The average IPO performance in the region (unweighted, issue to year-end) was above 30%.

Figure 15.1 shows the top ten underwriters in 2011.

15.3   International Equity Markets

International banks are more and more involved in the issuance of American Deposit Receipts (ADRs). ADRs provide many international investment opportunities, and allow international banks to reach out to distant markets worldwide. A few statistics highlight the opinion: (a) more than 37,000

Table 15.1 Values of the world stock and bond markets, 2010.

	Stocks		Bonds	
US	16,690	32.2%	32,081	35.1%
Eurozone	5,951	11.5%	24,869	27.2%
China (including Hong Kong, excluding Taiwan)	6,660	12.9%	3,023	3.3%
Japan	3,542	6.8%	12,872	14.1%
UK	2,830	5.5%	4,744	5.2%
Canada	2,002	3.9%	1,957	2.1%
India	1,540	3.0%	699	0.8%
Brazil	1,447	2.8%	1,353	1.5%
Australia	1,309	2.5%	1,432	1.6%
Switzerland	1,122	2.2%	732	0.8%
Norway, Sweden, Denmark, Iceland	1,183	2.3%	1,905	2.1%
South Korea	992	1.9%	1,189	1.3%
South Africa	821	1.6%	189	0.2%
Taiwan	723	1.4%	10	0.0%
Singapore	611	1.2%	115	0.1%
Russia	816	1.6%	146	0.2%
Mexico	431	0.8%	513	0.6%
Malaysia	386	0.7%	246	0.3%
Other	2,697	5.2%	3,224	3.5%
Total	51,753	100.0%	91,300	100.0%
Percent of total stocks & bonds	36.2%		63.8%	
Total stock & bond markets			143,052	

In equivalent US dollars, numbers in billions.
Source: Bloomberg.

companies are listed worldwide, compared to about 5000 companies listed on US exchanges; (b) about 71% of the world GDP is generated in the US; (c) only about a quarter of the world's largest companies are American.

An ADR is a negotiable certificate or "receipt", issued in the United States, which represents ownership of securities of a non-US-based company, issued in a foreign market. The stock of many non-US companies is traded on US stock exchanges through the use of ADRs. That is because ADRs are considered US domestic securities under US law, and offer the benefits of the protection and transparency offered under US securities regulations. ADRs enable US investors to buy shares in foreign companies without undertaking cross-border transactions. ADRs carry prices in US dollars, pay dividends in US dollars, and can be traded like the shares of US-based companies.

There are two types of ADR: sponsored and unsponsored. Sponsored ADRs are initiated by a bank at the request of a foreign company issuer. Each ADR is issued by a US depositary bank and can represent a fraction of a share, a single share, or multiple shares of the foreign stock. An owner of an ADR has

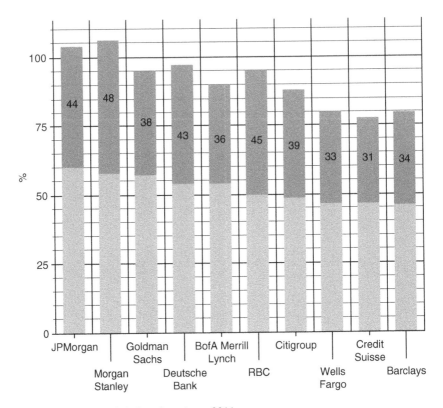

Figure 15.1   Top ten global underwriters, 2011.

the right to obtain the foreign stock it represents, but US investors usually find it more convenient simply to own the ADR. ADRs (except Rule 144A issues) are registered securities that provide for the protection of ownership rights, whereas most underlying stocks are bearer securities. It's a negotiable certificate issued by a US bank representing a specified number of shares (or one share) in a foreign stock that is traded on a US exchange. ADRs are denominated in US dollars, with the underlying security held by a US financial institution overseas. ADRs help reduce administration and duty costs that would otherwise be levied on each transaction.

15.3.1   Depository Agreement

A depository agreement is an agreement entered into between the local custodian and the depository bank. An issuer assigns a bank as depository for its sponsored Depositary Receipt (DR) program. The depositary issues and cancels ADRs and operates as a registrar, transfer agent, and paying agent for

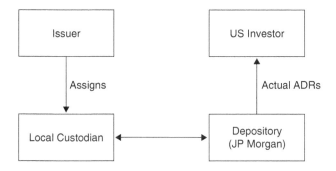

Figure 15.2   ADR scheme.

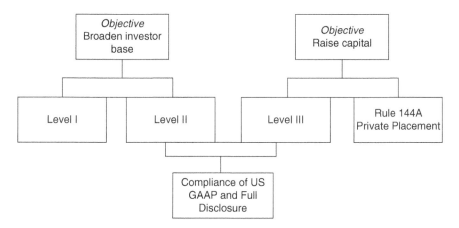

Figure 15.3   ADR structures.

the DR program. Investors can use either the services of a broker or the depositary's direct investment plan as intermediary to the issuer. JP Morgan Chase, Citibank, Deutsche Bank and Bank of New York Mellon are among the biggest players in ADRs. An investor can purchase ADRs through a broker (traditional or online broker). ADRs are listed on the NYSE, AMEX or NASDAQ.

Figure 15.2 illustrates the ADR scheme.

15.3.2   Structure of ADRs

The structure of an ADR depends on the objectives pursued. An ADR issuer could either seek to broaden its investor base or to raise capital. ADRs come under three different levels, each with its specific requirements (Figure 15.3).

Level 1 This is the most basic type of ADR where foreign companies either don't qualify or don't wish to have their ADR listed on an exchange. Level 1 ADRs are found in the over-the-counter market and are an easy and inexpensive way for a company to gauge interest for its securities in North America. Level 1 ADRs also have the loosest requirements from the SEC.

Level 2 This type of ADR is listed on an exchange or quoted on NASDAQ. Level 2 ADRs have slightly more requirements from the SEC, but they also get higher visibility trading volume.

Level 3 The most prestigious of the three, this is when an issuer floats a public offering of ADRs on a US exchange. Level 3 ADRs are able to raise capital and gain substantial visibility in the US financial markets.

15.3.3   Benefits and Weaknesses of ADRs

Benefits

- ADRs are an easy and cost-effective way to buy shares in a foreign company;
- ADRs are convenient;
- they are quoted and traded in US dollars;
- they save money by reducing administration costs and avoiding foreign taxes on each transaction;
- foreign entities like ADRs because they get more US exposure, allowing them to tap into the wealthy North American equities markets;
- they are traded, cleared and settled in accordance with US regulations;
- there is easy access to markets that have some of the world's best companies and/or better valuation than home market;
- opportunity to diversify the portfolio while using $US;
- ADRs tend to outperform their home markets;
- they tend to offer lower trading and custody costs;
- they are often more tax efficient.

Weaknesses

As they are backed by non-US securities, risks specific to ADRs could include the following:

- ADRs are prone to **inflationary risk**, which is an extension of exchange rate risk. Inflation is the rate at which the general level of prices for goods and services rises and, subsequently, purchasing power falls.
- Although ADRs are US dollar-denominated securities and pay dividends in US dollars, they do not eliminate the **currency risk** associated with an investment in a non-US company. This can result in a big loss, even if the company has been performing well;
- **Country risk** – political, economic, and social conditions in the home market could impact the stock price.

Other weaknesses include:

- US GAAP vs. non-US GAAP (IFRS);
- ADR-listed companies have to file Form 20F each year in which they reconcile all their numbers under US GAAP;
- most of Europe reports under IFRS, e.g., SAP reports under US GAAP and reconciles to IFRS

15.3.4   Taxation Regime

US investors acquiring ADRs would receive dividends paid in $US, and be subject to tax under the dividend treatment. However, the dividends could be subject to withholding tax in the ADR company's home country. If that is the case, US investors could qualify for foreign tax credit for any withheld tax paid abroad. The withheld tax is reduced whenever a double tax treaty exists between the US and the home country of the ADR company issuer.

15.4   International Bond and Debt Markets

The global bond market is estimated to be over $80 trillion, with the US portion accounting for about $35 trillion. The international bond market is bigger than the equity market. The main reason is the differential tax treatment between equities and bonds. Put differently, dividends are not deductible by the payers, while the interest paid to bondholders is deductible to the issuer.

15.4.1   Markets Participants

Issuers of bonds are mainly sovereign states, municipalities, and corporations. Besides the primary market, bondholders then transact (buy or sale) their holding into a secondary market through brokers.

Sovereign Issuers

The United States is the world's leading issuer of bonds. As of June 2011, the outstanding debt of the federal government stands at over $8 trillion. The US issue, commonly referred to as US Treasury Securities, is composed of four different assets: (a) Treasury bills; (b) Treasury notes; (c) Treasury bonds; and (d) Treasury inflation-protected securities (TIPS). Treasury bills are short-term, Treasury securities with maturity of a year or less from their issue date. Treasury notes are Treasury securities with maturity of more than one year but less than ten years. Treasury bonds are long-term securities with maturity above ten years. TIPS are marketable securities whose principal is adjusted by changes in the Consumer Protection Index (CPI), where interest rates are applied to the adjusted principal. Treasury bills are different from Treasury notes and bonds in that they do not pay interest to bondholders; rather, they are issued at discount.

Since 1985, the US Treasury has issued a new security referred to as STRIPS, which is the acronym for "Separate Trading of Registered Interest and Principal Securities". Treasury bonds and notes with maturity of ten years or over are eligible under the STRIPS status. STRIPS are zero-coupon securities which separate the cash flows of interest and the principal. The principal and the interest are assigned distinct CUSIP numbers as the Treasury creates separate book-entry instruments for each. The STRIPS markets are less liquid relative to Treasury bonds. STRIPS are not issued or sold directly to investors, who purchase or hold them via the financial institutions and government securities brokers and dealers that become the primary market. The secondary market is composed of inter-dealer brokers. The minimum face amount needed to strip a fixed-principal note or bond is $100, and any par amount to be stripped above $100 must be in a multiple of $100. Treasury STRIPS pay no interest. The buyer only gets a promise that the principal will be fully paid at a certain date, backed by the full faith and credit of the US government. Therefore, STRIPS are issued at a reduced purchase price. From the tax viewpoint, STRIPS can pose a challenge to investors as interest earned on them must be reported in the fiscal year in which it is earned. Further, inflation adjustments to principal on TIPS must also be reported as earned. However, STRIPS are considered a good investment for tax-deferred accounts such as individual retirement accounts (IRA), 401(k) plans, or other non-taxable accounts.

Figures 15.4 and 15.5 represent respectively the levels of US Treasuries outstanding, and the holding of US debt.

The geography of the bondholders has changed dramatically over time. Individuals no longer hold the bulk of US debt. With the globalization of the financial markets, individuals are taking advantage of other investment strategies available and becoming more diversified in their portfolios. The ownership of US Treasury debt is illustrated in Table 15.2.

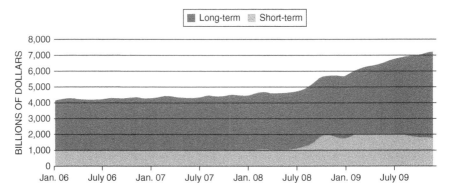

Figure 15.4   Level of US Treasuries outstanding.
Source: Haver.
Note: Monthly Data.

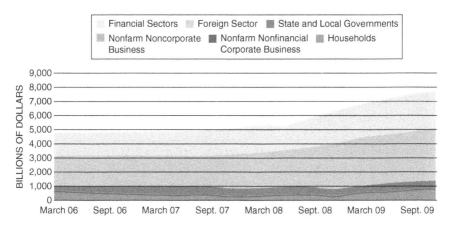

Figure 15.5 Holders of US debt.
Source: Haver.
Note: Quarterly Data.

Table 15.2 Ownership of privately-held US Treasury debt.

	December 1995		March 2010	
	Billions $	**% total**	**Billions $**	**% total**
Deposit institutions	315.4	9.5%	273.7	3.6%
US savings bonds	155.0	4.7%	190.2	2.5%
Private pension funds	142.9	4.3%	462.2	6.2%
S&L govt pension funds	208.2	6.3%	181.6	2.4%
Insurance companies	241.5	7.3%	260.6	3.5%
Mutual funds	225.1	6.8%	648.6	8.6%
State & local governments	289.8	8.8%	534.7	7.1%
Foreign holdings	835.2	25.3%	3,885.0	51.7%
Other (mostly individuals)	864.6	26.1%	1,076.9	14.3%
Total privately held	3,307.7	100.0%	7,513.3	100.0%
Memo:				
Total debt:			12,773.1	
Held by FRS & IG accounts:			5,259.8	41.2%

Source: Treasury Bulletin, September 2010, http://www.fms.treas.gov/bulletin/index.html.

Furthermore, the souring of the United States' debt, which has reached the country debt ceiling of $14.294 trillion, coupled with the Federal government's borrowing of roughly $100 billion per month from the markets to carry out its basic functions, has raised the debate over US dependency on foreign sovereigns such as China, Japan, the United Kingdom, and others. Though both Democrats and Republicans agree that the US should take steps to reduce the burden of the debt, they are still working to reach a common ground outside their ideologies.

States and Municipalities

As of December 2010, the overall states and municipalities bond market was over $3 trillion. The market is in hot trouble as some argue that, due to their current deficits, some states and municipalities would not be able to honor their debts when they become due. In the US, the municipal bond market has dropped to its lowest issuance in more than a decade, to $44 billion. Most states are facing budget deficits (Table 15.3), while a few still have good credit ratings (Table 15.4). Table 15.5 looks at the states' spending.

The state and municipal bond market provides a facility for issuers (both states and local) to raise the money needed to fund their projects. By the end of 2010, long-term municipal issuance volume in the US, including taxable and tax-exempt, was $430.1 billion. State and municipal bonds are often part of an investor's portfolio because interest received is generally not included in the taxpayer's gross income so long as the issuer uses the proceeds for exclusively traditional government purposes. However, interest paid by state or local governments will not be excluded if the proceeds are used to benefit other persons (i.e., private activity bonds), or when the bonds have not been issued in registered form.

Municipal bonds are either general obligation bonds (GOs) or non-general obligation bonds (NGOs). GOs are municipal bonds where payments of the principal and interest are backed by the full faith credit of the issuer. That is, issued with voters' approval, the issuer guarantees to pay all holders of the issue. Alternatively, payments of NGOs derive from the municipality revenue-producing agencies or enterprises.

Corporate Bond Issuers

In 2009, the outstanding amount of corporate bonds increased by 10% to reach over $91 trillion. Out of that amount, 70% came from the domestic market, and the remaining from the international bond markets. Beside corporate bonds, Euro-commercial paper (Euro CP) and Euro-medium-term notes (Euro MTN) have become an important source of funding for corporations as they offer higher rates relative to corporate bonds. Other companies get their financing from banks in the form of a note issuance facility, a credit facility whereby a company obtains a loan underwritten by banks and can issue a series of short-term Eurocurrency notes to replace the expired ones.

15.4.2　Bond and Debt Underwriting

Treasury Bills' Auction

Bond issuance processes vary depending on the issuer. While other sovereign bonds, like corporate and state bonds, are underwritten by an international

Table 15.3 State budget deficits.

States	Mid-Year FY 2009 Budget Gaps	Current Budget Deficit as Percentage of FY2009 General Fund	States	Mid-Year FY 2009 Budget Gaps	Current Budget Deficit as Percentage of FY2009 General Fund
Alabama	$1.1 billion	12.70%	Minnesota	$426 million	2.50%
Alaska	$360 million	6.80%	Mississippi	$175 million	3.40%
Arizona	$1.6 billion	15.90%	Missouri	$342 million	3.80%
California	$13.7 billion	13.60%	Nevada	$536 million	7.30%
Colorado	$604 million	7.70%	New Hampshire	$50 million	1.60%
Connecticut	$1.7 billion	10.10%	New Jersey	$2.1 billion	6.50%
Delaware	$226 million	6.20%	New Mexico	$454 million	7.50%
Florida	$2.3 billion	9.00%	New York	$1.7 billion	3.00%
Georgia	$2.2 billion	10.30%	North Carolina	$800 million	3.70%
Hawaii	$232 million	4.00%	Ohio	$1.2 billion	4.20%
Idaho	$218 million	7.40%	Oregon	$442 million	6.60%
Illinois	$2.0 billion	7.00%	Pennsylvania	$2.3 billion	8.10%
Indiana	$763 million	5.80%	Rhode Island	$372 million	11.40%
Iowa	$134 million	2.10%	South Carolina	$554 million	8.10%
Kansas	$186 million	2.90%	South Dakota	$27 million	2.20%
Kentucky	$456 million	4.90%	Tennessee	$884 million	7.80%
Louisiana	$341 million	3.70%	Utah	$620 million	10.40%
Maine	$140 million	4.60%	Vermont	$66 million	5.40%
Maryland	$691 million	4.60%	Virginia	$1.1 billion	6.70%
Massachusetts	$2.4 billion	8.40%	Washington	$509 million	3.40%
Michigan	$200 million	0.90%	Wisconsin	$346 million	2.50%

Source: Barclays Capital, 2010.

Table 15.4 US states with AAA and AA+ ratings.

The States With the Best Credit Ratings ...

A dozen states get Standard & Poor's top rating, AAA, and 15 get the next-highest, AA-Plus

AAA	Federal Spending As % of State GDP*	Medicaid As % of Outlays	% Change** In Tax Receipts	Tax-Backed Debt As % of State GDP	Funded % of State Pensions	Troubled*** Mortgages	June Unemp Rate %
Delaware	10.6%	14%	4.8%	6.35%	94%	7.2%	8.0%
Florida	20.1	28	4.2	3.93	84	19.0	10.6
Georgia	18.6	20	7.5	2.79	87	8.1	9.9
Indiana	20.7	23	9.9	1.92	67	8.3	8.3
Iowa	17.5	18	8.7	2.24	81	4.8	6.0
Maryland	28.5	20	8.0	3.20	65	8.3	7.0
Minnesota	14.5	22	10.4	6.87	77	5.0	6.7
Missouri	25.5	33	7.2	1.98	79	4.9	8.8
North Carolina	17.6	37	2.7	1.80	97	5.9	9.9
Utah	15.5	14	8.8	6.86	86	6.0	7.4
Virginia	29.8	16	14.7	2.70	80	4.4	6.0
Wyoming AA+	17.1	7	14.6	0.11	89	2.9	5.9
Alaska	19.6	12	16.7	8.88	61	2.2	7.5
Idaho	21.1	21	22.7	3.03	74	5.7	9.4
Kansas	20.4	17	7.1	2.78	64	4.3	6.6

Source: Barrons, August 29, 2011.

Table 15.5 State spending.

AA	Federal Spending As % of Stats GDP*	Medicaid As % of Outlays	% Change** In Tax Receipts	Tax-Backed Debt As % of State GDP	Funded % of State Pensions	Troubled*** Mortgages	June Unemp Rata %
Alabama	28.2%	20%	0.0%	4.76*	74%	5.7%	9.9%
Arkansas	24.4	21	7.2	3.95	78	5.1	8.1
Colorado	15.3	16	13.4	4.03	69	4.5	8.5
Connecticut	18.0	19	11.2	10.80	62	7.7	9.1
Hawaii	23.4	13	−10.1	10.30	69	7.2	6.0
Louisiana	20.0	22	9.8	3.77	60	7.2	7.8
Maine	24.0	29	9.7	10.14	73	8.3	7.8
Massachusetts	19.8	18	6.7	8.65	68	6.9	7.6
Mississippi	33.8	22	7.3	4.55	67	8.0	10.3
Montana	24.4	15	5.5	1.55	74	3.5	7.5
Nevada	13.2	17	4.1	2.44	72	16.0	12.4
New Hampshire	17.2	25	1.7	3.75	58	5.2	4.9
New York	15.2	28	12.3	5.61	101	9.1	8.0
Pennsylvania	22.0	28	11.6	3.11	81	6.3	7.6
Rhode Island	20.9	24	4.3	7.09	59	8.5	10.8
West Virginia	29.0	13	13.7	6.15	56	4.7	8.5
Wisconsin AA−	16.7	16	10.1	4.60	100	6.1	7.6
Arizona	21.8	28	14.0	1.96	78	9.0	9.3
Kentucky	33.5	22	5.1	4.64	58	6.6	9.6
Michigan	21.6	25	20.9	6.03	79	7.9	10.5
New Jersey A+	15.2	21	8.1	7.81	66	11.2	9.5
Illinois A−	15.9	33	13.7	3.97	51	10.5	9.2
California	16.2	22	5.7	5.08	81	8.8	11.8

*FY 2008. **Year over year, as of first quarter, fiscal 2011. ***Includes foreclosed and "seriously delinquent" home loans.
Source: Janney Capital Markets: Evercore: US Census Bureau.

bank or a syndicate, US Treasury bills follow a different path. US Treasury bills are sold by the Treasury Department at scheduled auctions to primary dealers: government securities dealers, financial and non-financial institutions, corporations and individual investors. Bids are submitted via the Treasury Automated Auction Processing System (TAAPS), and are accepted within 30 days prior to the auction. Treasury bills are no longer sold in discrete denominations; they are now issued in denominations of multiples of $1000.

Submitted bids can be either competitive or non-competitive. In a competitive bid, the purchaser specifies the quantity it desires and the bid price, while in a non-competitive bid the purchaser specifies only the quantity it desires to purchase but not the bid price. An investor (dealer) is not allowed to participate in both the competitive bid and the non-competitive bid in the same auction. However, competitive bidders are allowed to submit more than one bid within the same auction. Nonetheless, no single bidder can bid more than 35% of all the T-bills in the auction. All bidders then pay the lowest price of the accepted competitive bidder. All bids submitted through TAAPS are consolidated at the Federal Reserve Bank of New York, the Federal Reserve Bank of Chicago, and the Federal Reserve Bank of San Francisco, then forwarded to the Treasury Department (Washington DC). US Treasury bills are cleared through the Fedwire and transferred to purchasers' accounts.

Bonds Underwriting Process

The underwriting process for US Treasury notes, US Treasury bonds, municipal bonds, and corporate bonds is quite similar to the underwriting process of equities. US Treasury notes and bonds are also rated by independent rating agencies as are other sovereign bonds. US bonds enjoy an automatic triple A rating. However, since the US debt has become a topic of international debate, and the US Congress has become so divided and apparently unable to reach any compromise, rating agencies hesitate to strike until action is taken. The S&P move has rendered the cost of borrowing more expensive for the federal government. Municipal and corporate bonds are automatically rated by independent rating agencies prior to their issuance.

Municipal Bonds Underwriting Process

A state or local government seeking to raise money from the public, either to finance its budget imbalance or to initiate a new project, would have to turn first to an independent rating agency and an investment bank. These would assess the state's creditworthiness, and advise it all along the process. As with the equity underwriting process, the state or local government can, depending on the size of the project, work with a single underwriter or a syndicate of underwriters. Likewise, the issuer and the underwriter will negotiate the costs, terms, fees, and issuance formalities to the best of their respective interests.

Corporate Bonds Underwriting Process

Corporate bonds are classified either as on-shore or off-shore ("Eurobond market") according to the market of their issuance. A Eurobond issue refers to any issuance denominated in a particular currency but sold to investors in national capital markets other than the country which has issued the denominated currency. The on-shore market encompasses both the domestic market and the foreign market. A domestic bond market is when a domestic issuer issues bonds to its home or domestic market. A foreign market refers to bonds issued in any given market by a foreign issuer.

Corporate bonds are relatively easy to price compared to equity issue, because the determination of the price and volume is made by an independent rating agency. A bond price is expressed in terms of credit spread, which is the difference between the interest rate paid and the risk-free rate instrument with the same maturity. A corporation seeking to issue bonds must comply with the requirements of the SEC. The issuer must disclose almost the same information as with an equity issue. However, the SEC provides accommodation to corporate bond issuers through SEC Rule 415, commonly referred to as "shelf registration". Shelf registration allows companies to register, in advance, shares they might want to offer in the upcoming two years. Depending on the credit rating of the borrower, the underwriter or the syndicate of underwriters enter into a private placement agreement or a best-effort agreement.

European Central Bank Debt Certificates

European Central Bank (ECB) debt certificates are debt obligations of the ECB vis-à-vis the holder of the certificate. ECB certificates are issued at discount, that is, they are issued for a nominal below the redemption amount of the certificates.

15.5 Asset Securitization

Banks need to transform some of their more illiquid assets into more liquid assets, and have become more creative in how they create or increase their liquidity. Securitization refers to the repackaging process whereby a bank transforms its flow of illiquid assets, such as mortgages, receivables, and debts, into more liquid bonds sellable or tradable into the market, while using the illiquid assets as collateral to the new debt obligation issue. In the years leading up to the financial crisis, the nearly $10 trillion securitization market provided liquidity to almost every sector of the economy, from residential real estate to student loans to credit card debt.[136]

Modern securitization was developed by certain government-sponsored entities – Fannie Mae, Freddie Mac, and Ginnie Mae – which purchased and securitized first-lien consumer mortgage loans meeting specific requirements. Securitization issuances were then extended to cover various assets beyond the mortgages: credit cards, trade receivables, auto loans, auto leases, student loans, corporate receivables, album collections, and other financial assets. It was not until 1977, when Bank of America issued the first rated non-agency MBS that the door was opened to other forms of securitized financial products. Asset-backed securities issuance grew from $43.6 billion issued in 1990 to $753.9 billion issued in 2006.[137]

15.5.1   Securitization Participants

Many professionals are involved in the securitization process, including, inter alia:

- **The originator** The originator is usually the entity that either generates receivables in its ordinary business or purchases receivables (i.e., factoring).
- **The issuer** Usually, the special purpose entity is created pursuant to an agreement between the originator and the trustee. It is often an owner trust (or a corporation).
- **The underwriter/placement agent** The underwriter is often an investment bank, a broker, or any bank that sells securities in a public offering or private placement. The underwriter plays a vital role such as structuring the transaction, and in various compliance matters with the SEC and other authorities involved.
- **The trustee** The trustee is appointed pursuant to a trust agreement. It holds the receivables, receives payments, and makes payment to security holders.
- **The servicer** The servicer is the entity that deals with the securities on a daily basis, collects receivables, and transfers funds to accounts controlled by the trustee. It is common that the originator serves as servicer.
- **The independent accountant** An independent accountant with tax knowledge assists the parties in all accounting and tax aspects.
- **The legal counsel** The legal counsel assists the parties, raises and solves any legal aspects triggered by the securitization process. It advises on usual opinions concerning the organization, its corporate power, aspects of a true sale, and many other topics.

15.5.2   Securitization Structure

The securitization structure can be complex to design given the great number of participants. The basic securitization structure is illustrated in Figure 15.6.

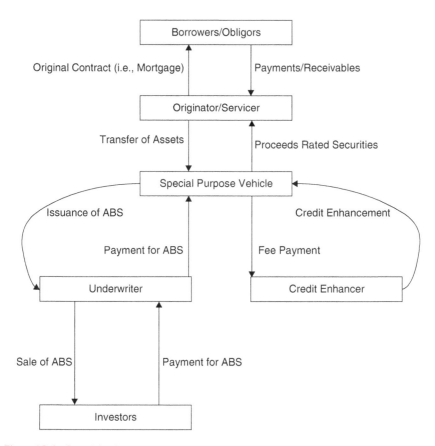

Figure 15.6   Securitization.

Structuring a securitization deal requires several cautious steps in order to comply with a variety of laws: securities laws, contractual laws, tax laws. It is also somewhat of an art form.

Transaction Steps

The first step consists of selecting the assets to securitize. The financial assets are then transferred to a legal entity such as a limited liability corporation, a partnership, or a trust.

- If the transferor or originator is an entity subject to US bankruptcy laws, the transfer must be a "true sale" or a "contribution" of assets to a newly-formed entity.
- If the transferor is an insured depository institution (e.g., bank) under the protection of the Federal Deposit Insurance Corporation (FDIC) in case of

insolvency, the transfer must be made in compliance with the regulations of the supervisory agency.

- The SPE is structured in such as way to be tax-free for tax purposes.
- The SPE can itself issue securities but, in practice, it will transfer in a tax-free manner all the assets to a trust managed by an independent trustee. The aim is to avoid conflict of interest if the SPE also performs as a servicer.
- The selected financial assets are rated by an independent rating agency; depending on the rating, credit enhancement can be added.
- The trust issues securities (ABS) to investors. The securities (bonds) are divided into tranches with different levels of seniority.
- The trust enters into a servicing agreement with the SPE:
  - o the servicer bills the obligors, records collection, addresses delinquencies, conducts foreclosures;
  - o the servicer has contractual rights and obligations with respect to the assets.

Credit Enhancement Mechanisms

Credit enhancement is key to any securitization process as the final aim of the issuer is to get a Triple A rating no matter what its own rating. There are two forms of credit enhancements: (a) external and (b) internal.

- An external credit enhancement involves a third party (i.e., surety bond from an insurance company, or Letter of Credit from a banking institution), which provides a guarantee against losses up to an agreed-upon amount.
- An internal credit enhancement consists of prioritizing the manner in which principal and interest generated by the underlying assets are paid back to investors. No third-party guarantee is needed; instead, the issuer, with the assistance of a rating agency, creates a variety of ABSs with different ratings. Internal enhancement is often achieved through over-collateralization,[138] senior subordinated structure, and reserve funds.[139]

15.5.3 The Wall Street Reform and Consumer Protection Act, 2010

The Wall Street Reform and Consumer Protection Act of July 2010 ("the Act") contains specific provisions pursuant to the securitization process. First, it directs the federal banking agencies as well as the SEC to draft, within 270 days following the publication of the Act, regulations that would require any securitizer to retain an economic interest in a portion of the credit risk for any asset backing the securitization. Second, it requires reporting and disclosures for asset-backed-securities (ABS).

Credit Risk Retention

The SEC is drafting regulations that would require any securitizer to retain not less than 5% of the credit risk for any asset that is not a qualified residential mortgage but is part of a securitization process that includes non-qualified residential mortgages. However, certain issuers could retain less than 5% if they meet the standards to be established by the federal banking agencies. The regulations would have to specify the permissible forms and minimum duration of risk retention. Furthermore, the SEC and the federal banking agencies may exempt, totally or partially, from risk retention requirements any securitization that is deemed appropriate to the public interest or the protection of the investors. Risk retention obligations would be allocated between a securitizer and an originator, if it happened that the securitizer and the originator are different entities. In allocating risk retention, the federal banking agencies must consider whether the assets reflect low credit risk, whether the form or volume of the transactions create incentives for risky origination of the type of loan or asset to be sold, and the potential impact of the risk retention obligations on the access of consumers and businesses to credit on reasonable terms. The Act prohibits a securitizer from directly or indirectly hedging or transferring its credit risk burden to a third party.[140]

Reporting and Disclosures of ABSs

The Act has removed the ability of issuers of publicly-offered asset-backed securities to suspend their reporting obligations under Section 15(d) of the Securities Exchange Act of 1934. Prior to the Act, issuers of publicly-offered securities were allowed to suspend their obligations to file such reports at the end of the first fiscal year in which their securities were offered, if they had fewer than 300 security-holders on record at the beginning of their next fiscal year. The SEC has issued regulations requiring any issuer of a registered ABS to carry out a review of the assets underlying the ABS, to disclose the nature of the review and the review findings and conclusions. The SEC rules implementing this requirement establish a minimum standard of review, which should increase the issuer's accountability for the assets placed in the pool. Further, any time the issuance or sale of ABSs is conditional upon the rating of these ABSs by a rating agency, Items 1103(a)(9) and 1120 of Regulation AB require disclosure of the minimum rating required and the identity of each rating agency issuing the ratings. That is why, as a result of new diligence requirements, Goldman Sachs Group and Citigroup postponed a $1.48 billion commercial mortgage-backed security after receiving information from the rating agency (S&P) that it would not be able to deliver the final rating as scheduled.[141] The SEC is working on establishing new requirements for credit rating agencies registered with the Commission as nationally recognized statistical rating organizations (NRSOs).[142] The proposed regulations aim to provide market participants with information concerning providers and rating agencies in order to improve the quality and timing of the disclosure.

15.5.4   Advantages of Securitization

Securitization provides several advantages to the participants involved because:

- it is a new source of financing as it enables illiquid assets to be changed into liquid securities sellable to multiple investors;
- it transfers the risks of loss related to the portfolio to investors;
- it is used to assist the management in its effort to control balance sheet inflation by the creation of off-balance sheet assets;
- it can be used as an arbitration tool given the fact that any asset producing financial flows can be securitized.

However, there also some disadvantages as the transaction can be costly due to the large number of participants involved.

16
Mortgage Markets

16.1 Introduction

After a decade of continuous boom, since 2007 the mortgage market in the United States and all around the world has entered an economic downturn. The market is organized as a primary market and a secondary market. By 2007, there were $13.98 trillion of primary mortgages outstanding in the United States, and the secondary market was dominated by the federal government, which operated through government-sponsored enterprises (GSEs). After the sub-prime crisis, the US Federal government is considering exiting the secondary market within a period of seven to ten years. In this chapter, I discuss: (a) the primary mortgage market; (b) the secondary mortgage market; (c) mortgage-backed securities; (d) the reform of the GSEs; and (e) the future of the mortgage market after the GSEs exit.

16.2 The Mortgage Primary Market

All around the world, the primary mortgage market – home mortgages, multi-family dwelling mortgages, commercial mortgages, and farm mortgages – is originated by commercial banks and mortgage companies, and government-sponsored enterprises such as the Federal National Mortgage Association (FNMA) and the Government National Mortgage Association (GNMA). The market is divided between prime and sub-prime mortgages. The distinction between the two is crucial. A prime mortgage is a mortgage extended to either an individual or an entity which qualifies under the lender's credit requirements. A sub-prime mortgage, on the other hand, is one extended to a borrower, through a broker, who has been rejected by a prime mortgage initiator. From 1997 to 2006, nominal US housing prices rose by an average of 7.5% per year. Many borrowers acquired their mortgages through the sub-prime market.

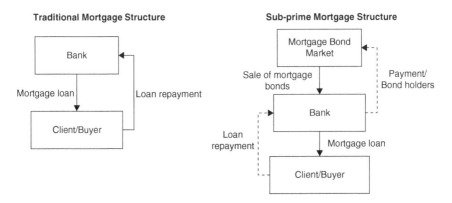

Figure 16.1   The prime and sub-prime mortgage models.

The distinction between the primary mortgage and the sub-prime mortgage is summarized in Figure 16.1.

In the United States, the mortgage origination process has always been driven by private firms (i.e., commercial banks, mortgage companies). That is because the GSEs' charters prohibit them from engaging in mortgage origination. However, as discussed here, the secondary mortgage market in the US has been dominated by GSEs, the Federal Housing Agency (FHA) and Veteran Affairs (VA). By contrast, in the European Union and in other developed countries, the primary and the secondary mortgage markets remain the province of private industry. Therefore, mortgage interest rates in these countries are lower relative to those created in the United States by the GSEs.[143]

Table 16.1 provides a comparison between the EU and the US mortgage markets.

16.2.1   Types of Mortgages

A mortgage is mainly classified as either a "federally insured mortgage" or a "conventional mortgage". Beside this fundamental distinction, the industry has created a variety of mortgages with distinctive financial features.

- Federally-insured mortgages are those issued by commercial banks, financial institutions, and/or other mortgage companies in accordance with the FHA, and the VA specifications. As such their repayments are guaranteed.
- Conventional mortgages, on the other hand, are not insured by the Federal government. The borrower must subscribe to a private insurance any time his down-payment is less than the 20% standard required.

Automatic Rate-reduction Mortgages

An automatic rate-reduction mortgage grants the borrower an option to reduce the loan interest rate at periodic intervals. Such an option is viable when the

Table 16.1   US vs EU mortgage markets.

The Performance of European Mortgage Markets in Comparison with the US[1]

Statistical Measures Computed with annual data by country for the years 1998 to 2008

	(1)	(2)	(3)	(4)	(5)	(6)
	Mortgage To GDP Ratio 2008	Rate of Owner Occupancy 2008	Coefficient of Covariation Housing Starts	Standard Deviation of House Price Inflation	Mortgage Interest Rate Average Level	Mortgage Interest Rate Average Spread[2]
Western Europe						
Austria	25.3%	57.0%	8.3%	2.6%	5.12%	0.66%
Belgium	39.8%	78.0%	16.3%	4.0%	5.87%	1.37%
Denmark	95.3%	54.0%	40.8%	6.1%	5.96%	1.41%
Finland	47.5%	59.0%	11.0%	3.4%	4.50%	0.05%
France	35.9%	57.4%	16.4%	5.5%	4.93%	0.53%
Germany	46.1%	43.2%	30.1%	0.8%	5.27%	0.97%
Iceland	129.0%	82.5%	56.3%	9.8%	5.01%	0.64%
Ireland	80.0%	74.5%	35.8%	11.5%	4.69%	0.22%
Italy	19.8%	80.0%	47.0%	3.1%	5.25%	0.64%
Luxembourg	43.5%	75.0%	19.2%	4.3%	4.33%	–0.16%
Netherlands	99.1%	57.0%	10.2%	5.5%	5.17%	0.77%
Norway	55.7%	77.0%	21.1%	5.0%	6.54%	1.61%
Portugal	63.3%	76.0%	31.5%	5.4%	5.15%	0.61%
Spain	62.0%	84.5%	32.5%	2.5%	4.38%	–0.09%
Sweden	60.6%	52.0%	53.9%	5.1%	4.05%	–0.49%
UK	80.5%	59.0%	10.5%	5.0%	5.32%	0.42%
Euro Average	61.5%	66.6%	27.6%	5.0%	5.10%	0.57%
US	83.6%	67.8%	24.9%	5.5%	6.57%	1.82%
US Rank	4th of 17	9th of 17	9th of 17	4th of 17	1st of 17	1st of 17

Notes:
(1) Unless noted otherwise, the data are all from European Mortgage Federation (2008) an annual fact book that contains comprehensive mortgage and housing market data for the years 1998 to 2008 for the 16 Western European countries and the United States.
(2) The mortgage interest rate spread equals the mortgage interest rate (column 5) relative to the government bond rate of each country derived from the International Financial Statistics to the International Monetary Fund.
Source: Dwight M. Jaffee, 2011.

mortgage rates are declining. Under the automatic rate-reduction mortgage the mortgage rate cannot increase.

Graduated Payment Mortgages

A graduated payment mortgage is a negative amortization loan, that is, the monthly payments do not include all the interest; rather, the remaining interest is added to the principal loan. A graduated payment mortgage starts with a lower interest rate and monthly payment for the first year. The interest increases over subsequent years depending on the borrower, within the range of 7.5% to 12.5%. Graduated payment mortgages are available for 15- or 30-year terms, and the interest rate is locked after year five.

Borrowers must be aware of the fact that they often end up paying more interest over the term of the mortgage relative to a conventional mortgage.

Balloon Mortgages

With a balloon mortgage, the amount of the mortgage is usually amortized over a 30-year period, but the borrower makes payments for only three to five years. The remaining principal (or balloon payment) is due in a large final payment. Such a mortgage is worth while for borrowers with plans to sell their houses within a year after the mortgage contract, with the expectation that the value of the house appreciates quickly.

Growing Equity Mortgages

A growing equity mortgage is a home loan for borrowers seeking to shorten the term of their fixed-rate mortgages and pay less in interest by making larger monthly payments. A growing equity mortgage starts with smaller monthly payments and then gradually increases according to the borrower's increase in earnings over an agreed set schedule. FHA's section 245(a) allows borrowers on a limited income but who expect an appreciable increase in their financial status to acquire a home as their primary residence.

Borrowers must qualify under the specifications of the FHA. A growing equity mortgage plan provides for monthly payments to be increased by a fixed percentage during each year of the loan. The term life of the mortgage should not exceed 22 years and depends on the plan and the interest rate selected. The growing equity mortgage enables the borrower to accumulate equity in their home more quickly. Unlike the graduated payment mortgage where the borrower starts with lower monthly payments and then increases, a borrower with a growing equity mortgages starts with a full payment and adds to that amount.

Second Mortgages

A second mortgage is a loan secured by a property which is already under a first mortgage. In the event of default, the second lender would have to pay off the first lender the gain from the collateral prior to its own satisfaction of the debt. There are two types of second mortgages: (a) the traditional home equity loan; and (b) the home equity lines of credit.

A traditional home equity loan is often used for home improvement and consolidation of other debts. Home equity loans are fixed-rate loans over a longer period of time relative to the home equity line of credit. However, the interest on a second mortgage is usually higher than the interest under the first mortgage for the same home.

- A **home equity line of credit** (HELOC) can be drawn by the borrower as a credit card for all kinds of expense. The interest rate is based on a short-term borrowing and is often lower than the rate under the first mortgage. However, the entire balance payment is due at maturity.

Second mortgages have some drawbacks: they have slightly higher interest rates compared to senior mortgages, and come with second mortgage fees, unless acquired from the initial lender. A variant of the second mortgage is the "wraparound mortgage", whereby the borrower assumes the existing mortgage and adds another. Some lenders may not allow such an arrangement and compel the borrower to pay off the first mortgage immediately.

Participation Mortgages

A participation mortgage is a mortgage whereby the lender has the right to a share in the profits, if any, of an investment as well as the interest charged on the loan. There are two types of participation mortgages, depending upon whether the property financed is income-producing or owner-occupied.

1. **A share appreciation mortgage** (SAM) is used when the homeowner remains in the house, and the only potential profit derives from the appreciation in value between the purchase date and the sale date of the property. By law, the lender's share of appreciation should not exceed 40%, and the maximum loan term is limited to ten years, with an amortization schedule up to 40 years.
2. **An income equity participation mortgage**, on the other hand, is used for property that produces an income. An equity participation mortgage differs from the SAM in that the portion of the profit going to the lender is calculated on the original mortgage amount rather than the purchase price. Furthermore, the lender qualifies for appreciation due to the natural increase in the worth of the property as well as income from operations pursuant to the property. A participation mortgage has some legal drawbacks. Because the lender and the borrower enter into an agreement to share the profit (appreciation), the parties can be legally seen as having created an "implied partnership". Therefore, creditors of the parties or any third party can go after the parties on the basis of an implied partnership and engage their liability for any occurrences related to the property involved.

Reverse Annuity Mortgages

A reverse mortgage is a home equity loan that enables the borrower to convert some of the equity of his house into cash while retaining ownership of the property. Put differently, in a reverse mortgage, the borrower is borrowing money against the amount of equity[144] in his property (home). The borrower retains the ownership of the home and remains liable for payment of property taxes, repairs, and maintenance. Reverse mortgages are "non-recourse" loans, that is, in case of default, the lender cannot be paid upon the borrower's other assets, only by the home itself.

Reverse mortgages are just the opposite of a regular or conventional mortgage in the sense that the lender is making payments to the borrower under the terms and conditions of their agreement. The amount of the mortgage payment depends on the age of the borrower, the value of the home and the current interest rate. By law, the borrower must be the owner of the home; for some reverse mortgages, the borrower must be over 60 years old. The lender must provide a statement prepared by the local or county office (for the elderly). The borrower commits to take good care of the home until the closing date. Reverse mortgages enable borrowers to stay in their house and receive a guaranteed monthly income or a line of credit. However, the interest on a reverse mortgage is compounded.

16.3   Mortgage Amortization Schedule

The amortization schedule is a table that provides a breakdown of the loan payment over its lifetime. It details the fixed monthly payment components of both principal and interest. The mortgage amortization schedule starts from the loan's first payment and ends with the last payment. During the first years of the amortization, the bulk of the fixed monthly payment represents interest on the outstanding principal and a small amount of payoff on the principal.[145] The process repeats each month, but the portion of the fixed monthly payment allocated to interest gradually declines, while the portion allocated to the principal gradually rises. The mortgage amortization schedule is rigid, that is, if the borrower misses one payment, he will accumulate late charges until the arrears are paid off.

Illustration

Suppose that Ms Alexandra purchases a house for $150,000 using a 30-year mortgage obtained from Chase Bank. Suppose that Chase Bank charges 8% for such a mortgage. Assuming that Ms Alexandra has paid a 20% down payment, the mortgage schedule will be as follows:

- Subtract from the loan the amount of the 20% down payment:
  $150,000 – (20% of $150,000)= $120,000.
- The monthly payment of a mortgage being an annuity payment:
  PMT = $120,000/(PVIFA. 6667%, 360)
  PMT = $120,000/136.2835
  PMT = $880.52.

Table 16.2   Example of mortgage amortization.

Months	Loan initial balance	Fixed payment	Interest payment	Principal payment	Loan ending balance
1	120,000.00	880.52	800.00	80.52	119,919.48
2	119,919.48	880.52	799.46	81.06	119.038.96
n	- - -	- - -	- - -	- - -	- - -
36	847.69	880.52	5.83	874.69	0

The monthly payment ($880.52) includes both the interest and the payment on the principal. Table 16.2 provides an example of mortgage amortization.

16.4   Mortgage Secondary Market

As stated in the introduction to this chapter, the mortgage secondary market in the United States was developed by the federal government in the 1930s as a means of boosting the US economy. In 1934, Congress created the National Housing Act,[146] in part to develop the secondary market. In 1938, the National Housing Act of 1934 created the Federal Housing Administration (FHA), which in turn created the Federal National Mortgage Association (FNMA), with the aim of providing liquidity to mortgage primary lenders. The FNMA bought and sold mortgage loans nationwide. In 1968, Congress split the FNMA in two distinct entities: (a) the FNMA (which later became Fannie Mae); and (b) the Government National Mortgage Association (GNMA), a wholly-owned corporation under the US Department of Housing and Urban Development. The GNMA (or Ginnie Mae) was authorized to deal with any mortgages backed up by the FHA and the VA. Two years later, in 1970, the Housing and Urban Development (HUD) created a second GSE, Freddie Mac. Since 1970, both the FNMA and the GNMA have securitized mortgages they purchased from originators. However, only FNMA mortgage-backed securities were officially guaranteed against losses from borrowers' default by the Federal government. Despite appearances, GNMA mortgage-backed securities only obtained official government protection in 2008, in the midst of the sub-prime mortgage crisis. In 1970, the GNMA created the first pass-through mortgage-backed securities by pooling together loans with similar features and sold securities to investors in the market. In 1980, the three GSEs securitized approximately $78 billion of residential mortgage loans. The market boomed, and by mid-2009, the amount was over $1.97 trillion. Figure 16.2 illustrates the FHA securitization structure.

Government Sponsored Enterprises (GSEs: FNMA, GNMA, Freddie Mac) in the secondary market have become more predominant and they purchase and securitize mortgage loans that meet their specifications. In 1977, private market firms followed the path by creating their own mortgage-backed securities,

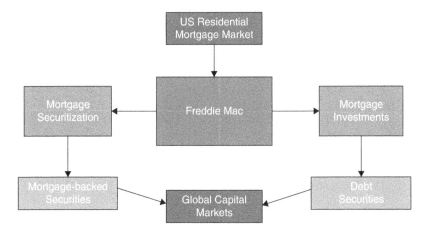

Figure 16.2   The FHA securitization structure.

referred to as private label securities (PLSs). Bank of America issued the first rated mortgage-backed securities. The collateral assets diversified to include auto loans, student loans, equipment loans, leases, credit cards, receivables, etc.

As PLSs have no federal government guarantee, the issuance of securities follows the structure finance model, which consists of tranching the issuance between senior and junior securities. Investors assume the risk that those mortgages are high-quality collateral. Holders of junior securities will be paid only after all senior security holders have been fully paid. Subordinated junior tranches are rewarded with higher interest rates. The ABS market performed perfectly until the 2007 sub-prime mortgage crisis. In an attempt to stabilize the housing industry, the Obama administration increased the role of the three GSEs and, by the middle of 2009, the three GSEs had issued more than $1 trillion in MBS.

16.5   Mortgage Markets' Risk Management

Mortgage activities involve a set of risks that bank managers have to mastermind. Those risks, are not exclusive to the mortgage segment of a bank's activities and are discussed in different sections and chapters of the book: market risk, credit risk and liquidity risk are among the most common. For any bank engaging in primary mortgages, the assessment of the borrower's credit is key to the success of the business. Extending loans to unqualified borrowers jeopardizes the bank's cash inflows and affects its liquidity in the future. Likewise, a bank's activities in the secondary mortgage market, by issuing pass-through securities, collateralized mortgage obligations, and other mortgage-related loans, need to adequately value the underlying assets used as collateral. As the issuance is sold worldwide, bank managers should manage the market risk involved since these instruments are sensitive to interest rate changes. Managers should seek to hedge those risks by entering into options, futures, forwards, and swaps contracts whenever possible.[147]

16.6 Reforming the Mortgage Market

The dominance of the GSEs in the mortgage secondary market became overwhelming. Some have argued that there is no room for the private sector, and some banks began to close their mortgage banking unit. However, in February 2011, the Obama administration submitted to Congress a report that laid out its plan to reform and duck out of the US housing finance market. The report recommends, inter alia, winding down Freddie Mac and Fannie Mae, shrinking the involvement of the GSEs, and bringing back private capital to the mortgage market. However, the FHA and the HUD would still provide services to lower-income families.

16.7 New Opportunities for Private Investors

The configuration of the mortgage market will be different starting from 2014 when the GSEs retreat from the market. That retreat provides unexpected opportunities to banks and other financial institutions to gain and provide a full range of mortgage services as never before. Recent decisions by some mortgage providers (i.e., banks) such as Bank of America to exit the mortgage segment of their business will be soon reversed, as banks would then have to reposition themselves within the mortgage market. Other banks, such JP Morgan Chase & Co, despite the losses incurred, will be able to recoup and position themselves as leaders in the mortgage industry. JP Morgan Chase would need to restructure its mortgage unit, bringing it more in line with its sound banking practice and cut off the "broker" mentality coming from Washington Mutual, acquired in 2009. Meanwhile, the market, and particularly the secondary market, still needs to be redefined. The securitization model as we know it needs to be more regulated, despite the silence under the Wall Street and Consumer Protection Act of 2010. Like the derivatives market, the mortgage secondary market would be better off using a standardized securitization model that can be followed by all participants.

17
Mergers and Acquisitions Advisory Services

17.1 Introduction

Besides underwriting, extending various loans (mortgages, car loans, credit cards, etc.), foreign exchange deals and trading in derivatives, banks are greatly involved in merger and acquisition (M&A) advisory services. The closeness that banks have with their clients provides the opportunity for many to accompany their client in any business endeavors they engage in. M&As constitute an integral part of many organizations' long-range growth strategy. Companies merge or acquire others in order to create or add value to their businesses. The benefits resulting from M&As are referred to as "synergies or efficiencies", that is, the combined value of the businesses involved is greater than the sum of each business' value when operating individually. Revenue enhancement, cost reduction, lowering taxes, and lowering cost of capital are among the most sought-after benefits.

17.2 Mergers and Acquisitions in Perspective

After almost two consecutive years of decline, M&As blossomed in 2010, when the overall volume of M&A rose to $1.1 trillion. The bulk of these transactions occurred overseas, in emerging markets, which accounted for 32% of the total. International banks, mainly United States' banks, are the most involved.

Tables 17.1 and 17.2 illustrate, respectively, the global M&A volume ranking in 2010, and the volume per the top industries.

Energy, finance, telecommunications, and the healthcare sectors are among the industries that saw most regrouping in 2010.

17.3 Supporting M&A Advisory Services

Investment banks assist their clients all through the M&A processes: (a) development; (b) due diligence and negotiations; and (c) post-close integration.

Table 17.1 Global M&A volume ranking, 2010.

Rank	Advisor	Value ($bn)	Deals	Mkt Share (%)*	2009 Rank
1	Morgan Stanley	594.6	356	21.2	2
2	Goldman Sachs	580.6	346	20.7	1
3	Credit Suisse	458.0	296	16.3	6
4	JPMorgan	452.7	308	16.1	3
5	UBS	360.1	281	12.8	7
6	Bank of America Merrill Lynch	358.7	246	12.8	5
7	Citi	354.7	213	12.6	4
8	Deutsche Bank	346.9	300	12.3	9
9	Barclays Capital	319.2	159	11.4	8
10	Lazard	267.2	256	9.5	10
11	Rothschild	263.7	267	9.4	11
12	BNP Paribas	122.7	114	4.4	16
13	Nomura	119.5	170	4.3	14
14	HSBC	90.3	83	3.2	20
15	Evercore Partners Inc	80.3	35	2.9	12
16	Macquarie Group	75.6	129	2.7	13
17	SG Corporate & Investment Banking	73.6	44	2.6	–
18	RBC Capital Markets	63.4	139	2.3	15
19	Perella Weinberg Partners LP	62.4	27	2.2	–
20	Blackstone	60.3	33	2.2	19

Criteria: *Excludes withdrawn deals, buyback programs and carve-outs, includes assumption of debt; Based on full amount credit; Announced deals Jan 1–Dec 31 2010.*
*Due to credit being given to each advisor on a deal, the sum of the Market shares will not equal 100%.

Table 17.2 Global M&A volume by industry.

	Energy	Financials	Telecom	Healthcare	Materials	Utilities
2000	$146.67	$506.91	$526.11	$20.76	$118.69	$97.24
2001	$139.62	$408.24	$140.81	$17.37	$94.75	$108.89
2002	$74.26	$260.77	$91.15	$24.03	$50.50	$95.30
2003	$73.59	$347.89	$105.64	$52.29	$63.81	$47.01
2004	$186.05	$522.14	$220.69	$55.03	$105.19	$68.43
2005	$215.18	$581.61	$269.44	$90.48	$149.37	$123.95
2006	$252.45	$940.56	$281.37	$133.68	$283.92	$249.33
2007	$279.54	$1,016.80	$205.93	$118.66	$296.35	$304.52
2008	$235.33	$724.34	$175.35	$63.53	$184.88	$121.10
2009	$223.14	$422.55	$98.40	$25.96	$81.73	$103.01
2010	$300.10	$328.86	$162.71	$56.05	$134.42	$127.03

Source: Bloomberg, 2010.

Investment banks assist and advise their clients in two ways – effective raid and strategy and effective defensive tactics – depending on the status of the client as raider or target.

17.4   Valuation of the Target

Evaluating the target is key to any merger and acquisition, and consists of determining the market value of the target firm. If not properly conducted, the buyer could end up overpaying the target when the shares of the latter are undervalued. Alternatively, when the target's shares are overvalued, the target could receive less than its fair market value from the acquirer.

Several methods have been worked out to assess the market value of the target. Since the Smith vs van Gorkhom case,[148] a sound, comprehensive valuation analysis conducted by an independent investment bank or valuation firm has become the centerpiece in all M&A. Investment banks are called to deliver a "fairness opinion" whereby they attest that the offered price is fair, based upon the available assumptions. While conducting the valuation, an investment bank uses more than a single method or approach to back up its fairness opinion.

17.4.1   Book Value

Under the book value method, a firm's (target) value is more or less its net asset value, that is, what the shareholders would be entitled to in the event of the liquidation of the firm. The book value method relies on two key elements: (a) the historical cost of assets, and (b) the liabilities and preferred stocks. The problem with this method is that it provides the most conservative value or figure because assets are registered in a corporate balance sheet at their historical costs, a figure that is seen as static, while in reality and in fact, the value of an asset can significantly increase over time. Further, the book value does not take into account certain intangible assets such as the goodwill created by the business.

17.4.2   Liquidation Value

The liquidation value method considers the fair market value to be the amount for which the assets could be sold minus the liabilities owed. This method tends to reflect the market value of the firm's assets at point T (the liquidation period). Given the fact that the liquidation time is almost always a constraint deal, the value of the assets at point T can vary from the value of the same assets in time T1, when a firm has more leeway to dispose of its assets without any constraints.

17.4.3   Discounted Future Cash Flows

Discounted future cash flows determine the value of the target by projecting future cash flows of the target and discounting those projections to the present value, by the use of a discount rate which corresponds to the level of the perceived risks of the same target within its industry. The determination of such a discount rate requires some analysis: for mergers, acquisitions, or restructurings considered without risk, the discount rate will be equal to the rate offered on risk-free Treasury bills. The riskier the investment, the higher the discount rate. For that reason, some investment banks use the target's future earning instead of the future stream of cash flow. Despite its obvious quality, the discounted future cash flow method does have some flaws. Being based solely upon cash flow, it tends to put aside assets not included in the calculation of the cash flow, such as amortization, depreciation or depletion costs. To reach a more precise discounted future cash flow, investment banks add back these costs to the target value. Further, given the options available under the GAAP, the discounted future cash flow method can miss certain specificities of the target firm.

17.4.4   Comparable Multiples

The comparable multiples method encompasses different multiples methods in determining the value of the target firm. The most commonly-used multiples are: (a) price-earnings; (b) price-to-book; (c) enterprise value to EBITDA; and (d) price-to-revenues. The comparable multiples method is conducted in two steps. The first step consists of selecting the correct multiple. The second step consists of applying it to the relevant earnings base. The most commonly-cited multiple is the price–earnings ratio (P/E ratio), which is the ratio of a company's stock price (P) divided by its earnings per share (EPS).

17.5   Advisor on M&A Deals' Protection

At the start of the M&A project or discussion, banks are asked to provide several advisory services pursuant to the course of the events. Often both the buyer and the seller would like to lock-up their ongoing negotiations or talks through a set of clauses such as: no shop clause, option on crown jewels, break-up fees, matching rights, standstill agreement, termination fee, reverse termination fee, or poison pills. As the use of those clauses does not discharge the boards of the entities involved from their fiduciary duties, the boards will work closely with their investment bank and retained counsel. The boards must comply with the Revlon standard,[149] the Unocal standard,[150] or the Paramount standard[151] as developed by the Delaware Chancery and Supreme Courts. Defensive tactics by the target's board are allowed if the board demonstrates that: (a) it had reasonable grounds for believing that a danger to corporate policy and effectiveness existed,[152] and (b) its defensive actions were reasonable in relation to the threat posed.[153]

17.5.1   Classic Defensive Tactics

The Revlon Court summarized both steps in its review of Revlon vs Paramount as follows: (a) when a board implements anti-takeover measures there arises a rebuttable presumption that it could be acting primarily in its own interests rather than those of the corporation and its shareholders; (b) the directors must analyze the nature of the takeover and its effect on the corporation in order to ensure balance.

The Court also held that when the sale of the target becomes inevitable, the board must then work to get the maximum price of the company for the benefit of the shareholders. Applying this principle to the facts, the Court found that the board entered into an auction-ending lock-up agreement with Fortsman on the basis of impermissible considerations at the expense of the shareholders.

In both Revlon and Paramount, the Court held that lock-up clauses are invalid when they favor a Bidder but allowed termination fees. Defendants in the Paramount case contended that they were precluded from negotiating with QVC or seeking an alternative. After considering the merit of the facts, the Court held:

> Such provisions, whether or not they are presumptively valid in the abstract, may not validly define or limit the directors; fiduciary duties under Delaware law or prevent the Paramount directors from carrying out their fiduciary duties under the Delaware law.

In the Unocal case, the Delaware Supreme Court set out a list of elements or factors to consider when assessing the existence of the threat to the target corporation. These factors include, inter alia: the inadequacy of the offered price, the nature and timing of the offer, the impact on constituencies other than shareholders, the risk of non-consumption, and the quality of securities being offered in the exchange process. However, none of these factors alone should be, per se, considered controlling in the examination process.

In Phelps Dodge Corp.,[154] the Court held that a merger agreement that has a "no talk provision" is per se invalid. Phelps Dodge challenged Cyprus Amax's merger agreement with Asarco, Inc., which included a "no talk" provision. After examining the merits of the case, the Delaware Chancery Court found that Cyprus Amax and Asarco should not have completely foreclosed the opportunity to negotiate and that their wilful blindness constituted a breach of a board's duty of care.

In IXC Communications, the Court held that directors need flexibility to lock-up a deal. The Chancery Court was called to overrule the validity of a "no talk" provision that prevented the parties from entertaining other potential deals.

The Court rejected the plaintiff's claim that the board "wilfully blinded" itself by approving the "no talk" provision. The Chancery Court did so because the challenged "no talk" provision emerged later in the process, and that the parties had retracted the provision, permitting the board to hear any proposals it saw fit.

In Mills vs MacMillan,[155] the Court invalidated a lock-up clause when it found the auction to be unfair.

In Omnicare vs NCS,[156] the Court found the lock-up provisions to be preclusive and coercive. The lock-up by Genesis took the form of (a) voting agreement with majority shareholders, (b) no-shop clause, (c) termination fee of $6 million, and (d) shareholder approval of the agreement. The Court found that Omnicare enhanced its bid to shareholders only when it discovered that a competitor was buying NCS. More importantly, the Court found that the voting agreement and the vote requirement used as lock-up were preclusive and coercive.

In all these instances, investment banks or counsels should walk their clients through the technicalities of M&A and explore strategic alternatives with their clients. They must also advise the board of any risk related to the merger agreement or clauses within. Poison pills posed a more serious challenge and need to be analyzed separately.

17.5.2   Poison Pills as a Defensive Tactic

Prior to 1985, private equity firms and other corporate raiders threatened corporate boards with hostile takeovers. Many corporate boards seemed powerless to resist the takeover tornadoes. Things dramatically changed in 1985, when the Delaware Chancery Court ruled for the validity of poison pill[157] as a defensive tactic. In Moran vs Household International Inc.,[158] the Delaware Court, for the very first time, upheld the Household plan as a legitimate exercise of the board's business judgment. Whenever a bidder acquires more than the preset share of the target company's stock, the poison pill will be triggered which allows all the shareholders of the target company, except the hostile bidder, to exercise their right to purchase additional stock at 50% discount. The final aim of a poison pill is to massively dilute the target equity, thus rendering the bid either expensive or difficult.

Poison pills quickly transformed the array of defensive tactics available to corporate boards. However, the use of the device by corporate boards triggered vehement criticisms on behalf of the takeovers. Some have argued that the mere existence of a poison pill violates the essence of corporate governance as it allows the board and not the shareholders to have a final say on the bid. Others have argued that the pill advances shareholders' interests by enabling a board to resist incentive takeover tactics and allowing the corporate board to negotiate on an even level with the raider.

Poison pills as defensive tactics have become a cornerstone of corporate board defensive tactics since 1985. However, neither the Delaware Court nor a federal district court have provided clues as to how long a board can maintain a pill against an inadequate bid. After 25 years, the Delaware Chancery Court has recently, in Air Products and Chemicals, Inc.,[159] shed light by providing specific criteria to look at. While the Court recognized that the board's ability to maintain the pill is not absolute, it highlighted the elements that should be taken into account when making a proper determination of the situation:

- the board is acting in good faith;
- the board relies upon outside independent financial advisors in making its decision;
- the board's determination is supported by the company strategic plan, prepared in the normal course of business;
- the majority of the board is composed of independent directors;
- the raider's offer is final.

Whenever those elements are found in a case, the Delaware Court would approve the maintenance of the board's poison pill deterrent. By and large, poison pills are referred to as either "flip-in" pills or "flip-over" pills. The two are quite different.

Flip-in Pills

With a flip-in pill, shareholders other than the hostile bidder are allowed to acquire, with the approval of the board, additional shares of the target corporation at a significant discount[160] of their current market value. When these shareholders exercise their right, the corporate equity becomes significantly diluted, rendering the takeover more expensive.

Flip-over Pills

A flip-over pill is somehow different from the flip-in in that the acquisition of additional shares by non-bidder shareholders occurs after the bidder has already taken over the target corporation. The flip-over pill, which exists in the target's corporation bylaws, is triggered by the target board reinforcing the position of the pre-existing shareholders in the target equity. The effect is almost the same as with the flip-in pill: the target equity is diluted. The flip-over pill is triggered at the discretion of the target board.

17.6   Mergers and Acquisitions Structuring

Mergers and acquisitions come in various forms. Structuring the deal to comply with all legal, regulatory, and tax aspects requires specific skills for any investment bank retained as advisor. The structuring of a statutory merger is different from the structuring of a consolidation or a triangular merger. Figures

17.1, 17.2, 17.3, and 17.4 illustrate, respectively, the statutory merger, the consolidation, the triangular merger, and the reverse triangular merger.

17.6.1   Statutory Mergers

In a statutory merger or acquisition, one entity will absorb the other entity after the completion of the process (Figure 17.1; Phase 2).

17.6.2   Consolidation

In a pure consolidation, two companies merge into a newly-formed company which survives at the expense of the other two (Figure 17.2).

17.6.3   Regular Triangular

In a regular triangular merger, the acquiring corporation sets up a vehicle for the acquisition, which then merges with the acquired corporation. In the final step, the acquired corporation is liquidated (Figure 17.3). Under IRC section 368(a)(2)(D), a forward triangular qualifies as an M&A (or reorganization) only if substantially all of the assets of the target company are acquired by the set-up acquisition vehicle in consideration of the acquiring company's stock. That is, no stock of the newly-created subsidiary can be used as merger consideration.

17.6.4   Reverse Triangular

In a reverse triangular, the acquired corporation sets up a vehicle to be merged with the acquiring entity. In the final step, the acquiring entity is liquidated (Figure 17.4). A reverse triangular qualifies as tax free under IRC section 368(a)(2)(E) if two conditions are met: (a) the target company's shareholders

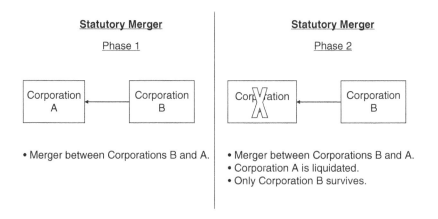

Figure 17.1   The statutory merger.

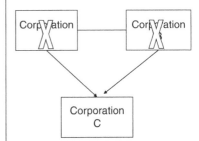

Consolidation

Step 1

Consolidation

Step 2

• Corporations A and B will merge into a newly-created corporation ("Corporation C").

• Corporations A and B will merge into a newly-created corporation ("Corporation C").
• Corporations A and B are liquidated.

Figure 17.2   Consolidation.

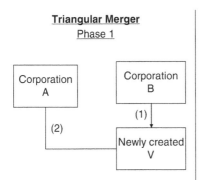

Triangular Merger
Phase 1

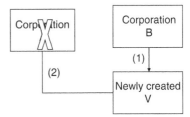

Triangular Merger
Phase 2

• Corporation B sets up a new vehicle for the acquisition of Corporation A.
• The newly-created (V) merges with Corporation A.

• Corporation B sets up a new vehicle for the acquisition of Corporation A.
•The newly-created (V) merges with Corporation A.
• Corporation A is liquidated.

Figure 17.3   Triangular merger.

must exchange at least 80% of their stock for the voting stock of the acquiring company; and (b) after the transaction, the target company must own "substantially" all of the assets of the newly-created vehicle in addition to its own assets.[161]

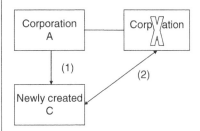

Reverse triangular

Phase 1

- Merger between Corporations A and B.
- Corporation A sets up a newly-created "C"
- The newly-created "C" merges with Corporation B.

Reverse triangular

Phase 2

- Merger between Corporations A and B.
- Corporation A sets up a newly-created "C"
- The newly-created "C" merges with Corporation B
- Corporation B is then liquidated.

Figure 17.4   Reverse triangular merger.

17.7   Different Types of Mergers and Acquisitions

Though by law all mergers and acquisitions must have legitimate business purposes, the choice of the M&A is influenced by tax and accounting considerations. The acquiring corporation would be looking for a type of M&A that allows it to increase the basis of many depreciable assets, with no or less tax carryover loss, in order to reduce its overall tax exposure and not face any reduction of its foreseeable profit after the transaction. Also, depending on the transaction, the acquiring company might prefer to enter into a taxable transaction or a tax-free transaction.

17.7.1   Tax-free Mergers and Acquisitions

Under IRC section 368, certain M&As (reorganization) would qualify for tax-free treatment if specific requirements are met. In addition to statutory requirements, courts have elaborated a series of judicially-created requirements that must also be met for an M&A to benefit from the tax-free treatment. While the statutory requirements vary depending on the type of reorganization involved, the judicially-created requirements apply similarly to all types of M&A type. The three judicially-created requirement for an M&A to qualify under the tax-free regime are: (a) continuity of interest; (b) continuity of business enterprise; and (c) business purpose.

Court-judicially Doctrines

The following court-judicially doctrines apply to all tax-free mergers and acquisitions.

Continuity of interest The continuity of interest doctrine requires that, in any M&A, the shareholders of the acquired corporation retain some significant equity participation in the acquired or combined enterprise after completion of the transaction. The doctrine of continuity of interest looks at the type of consideration the shareholders of the acquired company receive, and requires that they receive a "substantial portion" of equity or equity-like security.[162] Continuity of interest will not be satisfied in an M&A where the shareholders of the target company receive only cash or debt-obligation. Though neither the courts nor the IRS have defined what constitutes a "substantial portion" of equity, it is commonly understood that equity must be considerable in the transaction. The IRS requires for tax ruling purposes that at least 50% of the total value of the target company's equity securities be acquired in consideration of equity security of the acquiring company.[163] While 50% was considered the minimum threshold, in its 2005 regulations the IRS surprisingly admitted to an example where only 40% of the value of the target was in the equity form that satisfied continuity of interest.[164] The IRS goes on to add in another example that 15% of continuity will be deemed insufficient.[165] That is, for any consideration between 40% and 15%, the best practice would be to apply for a Private Letter Ruling with the IRS. The 1995 regulations went on to add that a redemption by the acquiring company of its stock, in connection with an M&A, will be characterized as cash, whether the source of the funding comes from the acquiring or the target company.[166] Likewise, continuity of interest will be compromised by an "extraordinary distribution" made by the acquiring company prior to an M&A.

Continuity of business enterprise Continuity of business enterprise requires that the acquiring company uses a significant portion of the assets of the acquired company in its business, or at least carries on a business line of the acquired company.[167]

Business purpose The business purpose doctrine seeks to deny tax-free treatment to M&A transactions entered into solely for tax purposes, without a genuine business rationale. Under the business purpose doctrine, a transaction will qualify as an M&A only if undertaken for reasons germane to the business of a corporation which is a party to the reorganization.[168]

Analysis of the Different Tax-free Regimes

Once all these court-judicially doctrines are satisfied, the tax-free treatment transaction must qualify and fit in within a specific type or classification under

IRC section 368. The IRC has classified M&A reorganizations as type "A" to "G". This section discusses only types A, B, C, and D.

Type "A" reorganization IRC section 368(a)(1)(A) defines type "A" reorganization as a statutory merger or consolidation. To qualify as a tax-free type "A", the transaction must be carefully structured to fit with all the statutory requirements:

- at least 50% of the consideration must be in the form of stock of the acquiring company (voting or non-voting stock, common or preferred stock, even other securities);
- the acquiring company must be in control of the target (acquired) company just after the transaction.

However, under IRC section 368(a)(1)(A) the concept of control is subject to the continuity of business purpose and the continuity of proprietary interest.[169] As opposed to types "B", "C", and "D", type "A" allows the acquiring company to use and pay a significant amount of cash, notes or other taxable consideration to the shareholders of the target company.

Tax considerations under type "A" M&A are as follows:

1. Shareholders of the target company do not recognize gains, except for considerations which do not qualify as security (boots). However, no loss should be recognized on the exchange of the target stock, unless the target's shareholders have received no stock or security but only boot.
2. Shares that are exchanged for non-equity consideration would be subject to capital gains tax. In that case, the taxable amount is the lesser of the amount of boot or the total gain on the transaction.
3. The target corporation shareholders take carryover bases in the acquiring corporation stock under IRC section 358.
4. The acquiring company basis in the assets acquired will be equal to the target company basis in those assets, increased by the amount of gain (if any) recognized by the target company as a result of the transaction.
5. The acquiring corporation does not recognize gain or loss and takes a carryover basis in the target corporation's assets under IRC section 362.

Type "B" reorganization IRC section 368(a)(1)(B) defines a type "B" M&A as the acquisition by one company, in exchange solely for all or portion of its voting stock … of the stock of another company (target), if immediately following the transaction, the acquiring company has the control of the target company. The acquiring company must buy at least 80% of the target, and the shareholders of the target should have no option for cash.[170]

The observance of the threshold (80%) constitutes a mandatory requirement under type "B" reorganization. However, under the Roosvelt Hotel Co. case,[171] payments by the acquiring corporation of expenses arising in a reorganization such as legal fees, investment banking fees, costs of stock registration under the securities laws, etc., have been held not to represent additional consideration.[172] Cash payments to the target corporation's shareholders in lieu of fractional shares would not violate the solely for voting requirement.[173]

A transaction would still qualify as a type "B" when the acquiring company purchases the stock of the target in several transactions over a period of time not exceeding 12 months, if the transactions are held to be part of a predetermined plan. Likewise, the target company may redeem up to 50% of its stock prior to the merger without destroying the tax-free features of the transaction, provided the cash for the redemption did not come from the acquiring corporation.[174]

Tax considerations under type "B" M&A are as follows:

1. Shareholders of the target company do not recognize gain or loss on the exchange of their target stock for the acquiring corporation voting stock under IRC section 354. Instead, each takes a substituted basis in the acquiring corporation's exchanged stock. Any gain on appreciation in value of the target company stock is deferred until later sale or taxable disposition.
2. The target corporation stockholders take a carryover basis in the acquiring corporation voting stock under IRC section 358. The receipt of a carryover basis preserves the unrecognized gain for later recognition in a taxable sale or other taxable disposition.
3. The acquiring corporation generally does not recognize gain or loss under IRC section 1032.
4. The acquiring company basis in the assets acquired will be equal to the target company basis in those assets, and the acquiring is not allowed to elect to step up the basis under IRC section 338.

Type "C" reorganization IRC section 368(a)(1)(C) defines a type "C" M&A as "the acquisition by one corporation, in exchange solely for all or a part of its voting stock ... of substantially all of the properties of another corporation ... but in determining whether the exchange is solely for stock, the assumption by the acquiring corporation of a liability of the other ... shall be disregarded." Three statutory requirements should be met:

- the acquiring corporation must purchase at least 80% of the fair market value of the target's assets;

- the target corporation should distribute the consideration received and liquidate; and
- immediately after the transfer, the transferor or its stockholders or both must be in control of the transferee (target) corporation or retain the ownership of at least 80% of the voting stock and at least 80% of the total of all classes of stock of the corporation.[175]

Unlike the type "B" reorganization, in type "C" a small amount of boots is permitted so long as the amount does not exceed 20% of the fair market value of the target's assets.

Tax considerations under type "C" M&A are as follows:

1. Shareholders of the target company do not recognize gain or loss on the distribution of the acquiring corporation stock following the liquidation of the target. Instead, each takes a substituted basis in the acquiring corporation's received stock. Any gain on appreciation in value of the target company's stock is deferred until later sale or taxable disposition.
2. The target corporation shareholders that received boot in the liquidation are taxed on the receipt of that boot as either capital gain or a dividend, under IRC section 356. The taxable amount is the lesser of the amount of the boot or the total gain on the transaction.
3. The acquiring company does not recognize any gain or loss, and the basis in the assets acquired will be equal to the target company basis in those assets prior to the exchange.
4. The target (or acquired) corporation tax attributes will be carried over to the acquiring corporation tax attributes, subject to certain limitations under IRC section 383.

Type "D" reorganization Type "D" reorganization covers two different sets: the acquisitive type "D" and the divisive type "D". Divisive type "D" includes spin-offs,[176] split-ups,[177] and split-offs.[178] To benefit for a tax-free spin-off under IRC section 355(b), both the controlling and the distributed corporations must have been engaged in active conduct of trade or business prior to the distribution. A corporation is considered engaged in an active conduct of trade or business when it is not itself (directly or indirectly) under control of any distributee.[179] Treasury Regulation 1. 355-3(b)(3(iii) provides an exception to the five-year mandatory requirement in the case of a corporation engaged in one business purchasing, creating or acquiring another business, in the same line of business. The fact that a trade or business underwent change during the five-year period shall be disregarded if the changes are not of such a character as to constitute the acquisition of a new or different business.[180] IRC section 368(a)(1)(D) requires the target corporation or its shareholders be in control of or possess at least 50% of vote or value of the acquiring corporation. But, contrary to type "C", section 368(a)(1)(D) has not expressed a limitation on the consideration that may be used.[181] If the requirements of an acquisitive type "D" reorganization are met, the parties generally defer current federal taxation on gains (on their stock or assets). Type "D" reorganization, particularly a spin-off, should be carefully structured since the IRS has enacted section 355(e) to challenge prearranged series of transactions that used to qualify for tax-free spin-off. IRC section 355(e) provides:

> Stock or securities in a controlled corporation will not be considered qualifying property for purposes of section 355(C)(2) or section 361(C)(2) if the intended distribution under section 355 is part of a plan (or series of related transactions) in which one or more persons acquire directly or indirectly stock representing a 50% or greater interest in the distributing or any controlled corporation, within the four-year period beginning two years before the spin-off distribution.[182]

17.7.2   Taxable Mergers and Acquisitions

In taxable acquisitions, the acquiring company's tax basis in the stock or assets acquired is equal to the amount paid. The selling company recognizes immediately the entire gain (or loss) which is subject to tax. Taxable mergers occur in two main forms: (a) taxable purchase or sale of stock, and (b) taxable sale or purchase of assets.

Taxable Purchase of Stock

In a taxable purchase of stock transaction, one corporation purchases stock of the target corporation directly through the target's shareholders, in consideration of cash, notes or other. The tax considerations of the transaction are as follows:

1. The target's corporation shareholders recognize gain or loss on the sale, measured by the difference between the basis of the stock and its purchase price.
2. The target corporation itself does not recognize any gain or loss, and its tax attributes remain unchanged.
3. The acquirer corporation takes a new basis in the stock purchased equal to the purchase price.

Under Revenue Ruling 90-95,[183] a liquidation or merger of the target corporation subsequent to a taxable purchase of 80% or more will render the transaction tax-free.

Taxable Sale/Purchase of Assets

In a taxable purchase of assets transaction, one corporation (transferor) transfers substantially all of its assets to another (transferee), in consideration of the payment of cash, notes or other. After the transfer, the transferee becomes the new owner and assumes liabilities. The transferor may or may not remain in existence.

The tax considerations are as follows:

1. The transferor corporation recognizes gain or loss on the sale (or transfer) of its assets. The gain or loss may be capital or ordinary depending on the nature of the assets transferred.
2. The transferor corporation's shareholders do not recognize gain or loss unless the transferor is liquidated.
3. If the assets transferred have been amortized (or depreciated) in the United States, a recapture of depreciation will be subject to tax as ordinary income, under IRC sections 1245 and 1250.
4. The transferor corporation's tax attributes do not carry over to the transferee, which takes the assets at their purchase price as basis.

17.7.3 Tax-free Advisory Considerations

Advising corporations after a taxable or tax-free M&A is of even greater significance than in the midst of any M&A. This is because some tax or corporate aspects of the transaction unfold some time after the deal has been closed.

Section 381 of the United States IRC stipulates that major benefits, privileges, elective right, and obligations of the transferor in a tax-free reorganization can, after some limitations, be carried over to the acquiring corporation: "The successor corporation steps in the tax shoes of its predecessor."[184]

However, only obligations not reflected in the amount of the consideration on the date of the transfer have to be taken into account. Therefore, a mere promise to pay speculative liabilities, such as workforce contingent, would not be taken into account. Two main items are of importance after a restructuring: (a) contingent liabilities, and (b) the net operating losses.

Contingent Liabilities

Liabilities or obligations are considered to be reflected in the amount of the consideration transferred if, on the transfer date, the parties were aware of their existence and adjusted the amount to the extent of them.[185]

Revenue ruling 58-374 has held that no gain or loss should be recognized if the income involved is a mere adjustment of the stock price or property value related to a tax-free reorganization. However, the issue is somewhat tricky when the liabilities paid later are higher than the initial estimation.

In the Illinois case,[186] the tax court considered the overpayment as part of the acquisition price and subsequently required its capitalization.

Furthermore, the IRS is reluctant to allow the deductibility required, when the taxpayer, in determining the basis of the liability, has departed from general principles of tax law under IRC section 1.338-5(b)(2)(ii). Under IRC section 357(b), liabilities are considered as a distribution of money or boots if, after the IRS scrutiny, it appears that the principal purpose of the taxpayer was to avoid federal income tax on the exchange; or was not a bona fide business purpose. The classification of the income related to contingent liability is to be determined by the nature and the basis of the liability involved. Payment of contingent liabilities in connection with a tax-free reorganization is treated as capital (profit or loss) if it constitutes an addition to the basis of the asset conveyed. In contrast, such payment will be treated as ordinary income when it is a mere recovering, through litigation or settlement of an ordinary income owed to the predecessor.

In the Hort case,[187] where the contention between the taxpayer and the Commissioner of Internal Revenue was over the consideration received for cancellation of a lease, the High Court held: "The cancellation of the lease is nothing more than a relinquishment of the right for future rental payment."

The formulation of the principle by the Supreme Court requires some precision. Indeed, the Supreme Court has stated:

> When the origin of the claim is an action to recover a capital asset, the proceeds to the recovery could then be capital in nature. But, when ... the origin of the claim is a right to recover an item of ordinary income, then the proceeds of the recovery necessarily represent ordinary income in the hands of the recipient.

It is worthy to note that for the recovery of a capital asset, the Supreme Court used "could", which excludes all automaticity of the capital nature of the proceeds, whereas, for the proceeds of an item of ordinary income, the Supreme Court established this automaticity by the use of the adverb "necessarily".[188] This is not merely a semantic ju-jitsu, but requires for the investment bank and/or the counsel to conduct a thorough analysis of the transaction in order to cope with the issue rather than jumping to hazardous conclusions departing from the current jurisprudence trend.

Net Operating Loss (NOL)

A tax-free reorganization could be followed by unduly harsh tax consequences for the ongoing business after the restructuring. Therefore, the IRC has supplied privileges – carry over and carry back – to set off lean years against lush years in a single business. Subsequent to a tax-free reorganization, the NOL can be used as a "net operating carry-back" to the two years and, if not exhausted by that carry-back, the remainder can be used as a "net operating carry-over" to the three succeeding years. The NOL is the most sought-after attribute because it can be used to directly reduce the taxable income. Therefore, its management or use must fit with the statutes. Otherwise, the entire carry-over can be disallowed or limited.

Disallowance of the entire carry-over Change in corporate identity and/or ownership can strip the corporate of the use of the privilege. In the New Colonia case,[189] where the continuity of ownership between the two corporations was broken, and neither corporation had any control over the other at the time the privilege was sought, the Supreme Court has held that: "The taxpayer who sustained the loss is the one to whom the deduction be allowed ... the privilege is not transferable to or usable by another."

Likewise, under the Libson Shops case,[190] the privilege has been denied to a taxpayer who had made a sovereign management decision to file separate income tax returns rather than a consolidated one after the merger.

Limitations on NOL carry-overs and carry-backs The NOL's carry-overs are limited if there is a substantial change in the controlling interest in the loss corporation. That occurs often if, within the three years, more than 50% of stock changes hands, or where the losses are created by interest deductions allocatable to corporate equity-reducing transactions. Likewise, carry-backs are limited after the NOL corporation acquires the stock of another corporation, or makes an extraordinary distribution. When generated by interest deductions as a result of a major stock acquisition, the NOL can be unusable.[191] The limited amount equals the product of the value of the corporation loss on the date of the ownership change, multiplied by a statutory rate of return published monthly by the Treasury bill yield.

17.8   International Tax-free Reorganization

IRC section 367(a) provides in general that all outbound transfers of appreciated property, by a U.S. person, in exchange for other property, in transactions described under IRC sections 332, 351, 354, 356, or 361, to a foreign corporation would give rise to gain recognition. That is, because for the purpose of section 367(a), the Tax Reform Act of 1984 treats the foreign corporation as a non-corporation. Section 367 addresses three categories of transactions: (a) the outbound transaction, where assets used in the US are transferred to a foreign taxpayer; (b) inbound transactions, where assets used by a foreign taxpayer are transferred to a US taxpayer; and (c) foreign-to-foreign taxpayer transfer of assets.

IRC section 367(a) requires recognition of built-in gain as if the property was disposed of in a taxable exchange. This section applies only to gain, and losses incurred through the transaction should not be deducted. However, certain international transfers are exempt to the extent specifically provided for in the IRC and the regulations thereof. That is the case, for instance, if the foreign parent continues to operate a US business, or if the distributed property is a US Real Property Interest. However, the exception would not be available if the transferor corporation was owned by individual shareholders or by more than five US corporations.[192] To qualify for non-recognition of gain under IRC sections 367(a) or (d) the taxpayer must satisfy specific notice requirements of the IRC section 6038B.[193] The non-outbound transactions under IRC section 367(b) applies to three transactions: (a) repatriation of foreign assets; (b) certain foreign-to-foreign reorganizations; and (c) certain divisive reorganizations involving a foreign corporation.[194]

18
Private Equity Business and Miscellaneous Services

18.1 Introduction

Private equity consists of professional investors pooling money with the aim of (a) investing and getting actively involved in the management of the target, and (b) exiting after a certain period of time. International banks, particularly their investment units, have become more active in the private equity industry. Besides private equity, international banks offer a litany of services to their clients and sometimes offer them a selection of miscellaneous services.

Private equity constitutes a significant segment of international banking, whether as a specific bank unit or a lucrative activity conducted under the umbrella of a specific bank unit. As Professor Liaw puts it:

> Private equity is of interest to banks because it has several benefits including management fees, capital gains, and contributing to underwriting and merger and acquisition business.[195]

The origin of private equity can be traced back to the 1940s, with the creation of two US venture capital firms in 1946: American Research and Development Corporation (ARDC) and J.H. Whitney & Company. At the beginning, private equity was the domain of wealthy individuals or families. The success of the business has attracted other players such as banks, hedge funds, and even endowments. Table 18.1 shows the ten largest private equity firms as of December 2010.

Private equity business can be classified into two main areas: (a) venture capital, and (b) buy-out, with the latter representing the biggest segment of private equity deals.

18.2 Venture Capital vs Buy-out

Venture capitalists seek companies in which to invest and take part in their management in order to boost its growth and lead a publicly-traded company.

Table 18.1   The ten largest private equity firms, 2010.

Ranking	Name
1	Goldman Sachs Principal Investment Area
2	The Carlyle Group
3	Kohlberg Kravis Roberts
4	TPG
5	Apollo Global Management
6	CVC Capital Partners
7	The Blackstone Group
8	Bain Capital
9	Warburg Pincus
10	Apax Partners

Source: Private Equity International.

Venture capital business can itself be broken down into three areas: (1) early stage; (2) expansion stage; and (3) late stage. Venture capital investments are made for several years – three to seven years on average prior to exiting. Alternatively, buy-out investors seek the control or majority of the target company with the expectation of managing it themselves or with some professionals from their world. Put differently, venture capital funds provide equity capital to privately-owned businesses by investing directly in the target company's newly-issued securities. Buy-out funds invest with the aim of obtaining control of publicly-traded companies. Tables 18.2 and 18.3 respectively describe venture investments by stage and by industry.

Early stage Two types of investment are commonly made during this stage: seed investment and start-up investment. Seed capital is used to finance expenses related to setting up, product testing, and so on. Start-up capital will often be used to support the expansion of the business.

Expansion stage Within the expansion stage, the venture capitalists finance the working capital and other fixed costs of the undertaking.

Late stage During the late stage, the venture capitalists may still finance the business, but over and above this they are seeking the exit to cash out their return.

In 2010, venture capital's share of total private equity declined by 14% compared to 2009, with the yearly investment estimated at around $21.6 billion. The bulk of the investment went to the technology, healthcare, and business industries (Table 18.3). For the same period (2010), buy-out investments reached $53 billion with 138 funds formed.[196]

Table 18.2   Venture investment by stage, 2010.

Development Stage	# Rounds	$ Invested ($ mm)	%
Start-up/Seed	363	1,712	8
Early Stage	1,147	5,304	24
Expansion	1,021	8,492	39
Late Stage	746	6,315	29
2010 Annual Total	3,277	21,823	100

Source: NVCA.

Table 18.3   Venture investment by industry, 2010.

Industry Sector	# Rounds	$ Invested ($ mm)	%
Technology	826	10,482	48
Health Care	1,858	6,275	29
Business/Industrial	437	4,334	20
Consumer/Retail	130	706	3
Other	26	26	0
2010 Annual Total	3,277	21,823	100

Source: NVCA.

18.3   Structuring a Private Equity Deal

A bank is either a sponsor of private equity deals or an investor in a pool of investors. Either way, the structure of the fund should be carefully organized for both business and tax purposes. The structure under our analysis refers to the buy-out fund, as a venture capital fund consists of direct investment without control. The buy-out fund begins by creating a vehicle for its acquisition. That requires a plan for (a) the legal form of the fund, (b) the status of the investors involved, and (c) the tax treatment of the fund as well as the investors.

18.3.1   The Legal Form of the Fund

The fund is organized as a pass-through entity to (a) avoid taxation at the level of the fund, and (b) facilitate the pass-through of capital gain to the sponsor and/or investors. That is, the fund will be structured as either a US limited liability partnership (LLP) or limited liability company (LLC), or a foreign limited liability entity.

As buy-out funds operate globally, the sponsor (bank) or investors should also be aware of the fact that under IRC section 7704(b), a fund can be characterized as a publicly-traded partnership (PTP) if its interests are traded on an established securities markets or readily tradable on a secondary market or the substantial equivalent thereof. However, even when the fund's interests are tradable on the securities markets, the PTP status can still be avoided if the fund earns sufficient qualifying income, which consists of interest, dividends, and capital gains.[197] Funds that raise capital from public markets are more likely to be reclassified as PTP, regardless of the election made by the sponsor or investors.

18.3.2   The Status of the Fund's Investors

When a bank operates a private equity line of business, it can invest solely in selected target companies, or it can join other investors in the deals and be one of a number of players in the project. Operating as a player, the bank will side with other investors, such as institutional investors, wealthy individuals, pension funds, endowments, insurance companies, and others. In that regard, the status of each investor must be carefully examined to avoid legal and tax hurdles.[198]

18.3.3   Structuring a Buy-out Deal

A bank investing in a private equity deal (buy-out) starts by setting up an acquisition vehicle referred to as a fund. The basic structure can be established as shown in Figure 18.1.

But often, a bank joins a consortium of professional investors in a buy-out deal. In that scenario, the structuring of the deal is quite complex, depending whether (a) all the investors are US (Figure 18.2 or (b) a mix of US and foreign investors (Figure 18.3).

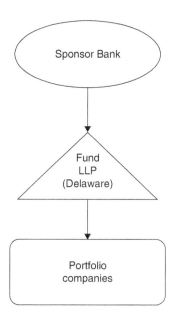

Figure 18.1   Structure of a fund.

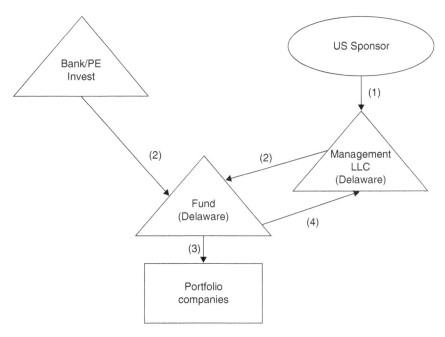

Figure 18.2   Structure A: US investors.

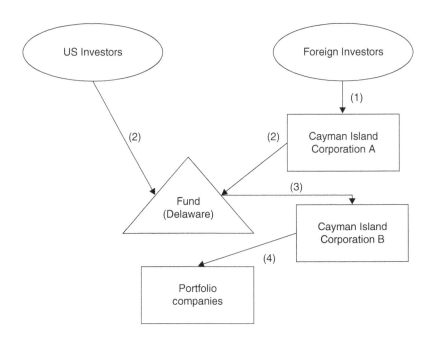

Figure 18.3   Structure B: A mix of US and non-US investors.

Under this structure, various steps have been carefully considered:

- The US sponsors create a management company (LLC/LLP) in Delaware, a US business-friendly state. The management company performs as a general partner (GP) of the fund.
- The US sponsors and bank private equity business invest side-by-side.
- The fund then invests in selected companies, referred to as portfolio companies.
- The fund enters, for fees, into a management agreement with the Delaware management company.

In a more complex cross-border deal, sponsors would have to bring together both US and non-US investors. Here, the structure would be more elaborate to protect the status of all the parties in the deal. That is accomplished by inserting a master fund into the structure (Figure 18.3).

Under this structure, US and non-US investors invest differently:

1. Foreign investors invest in a blocker entity, a Cayman Islands corporation, through which they invest in a US fund.
2. US taxable investors invest directly in the US fund.
3. The US fund sets up a second blocker, a corporation in the Cayman Islands.
4. The Cayman Islands (second blocker) invests in all portfolio companies.

Tables 18.4 and 18.5 describe respectively types of private equity deals and the top takeovers.

Table 18.4   Types of private equity deal.

Deal Type Summary	# Deals	Volume	%
Company Takeover	757	131.84B	62.42
Cross Border	672	109.46B	51.82
Leveraged Buyout	454	92.71B	43.9
Asset sale	217	30.97B	14.66
Minority purchase	618	33.2B	15.72
Real Estate	12	7.22B	3.42
Special Situations/Distressed	12	5.81B	2.75
Venture Capital	270	4.18B	1.98
Co-Investment	30	3.47B	1.64
Mezzanine	6	3.03B	1.43

All Total Value figures in USD Billions.
Data is as of November 30, 2010.
Source: Bloomberg, 2010.

Table 18.5 Top private equity company takeovers.

Deal Type	Announce Date	Target Name & Country	Acquirer Name & Country	Announced Total Value	Target Business Description
Acquisition	11/25/10	Del Monte Foods Company *United States*	Centerview / KKR / Vestar *United States*	$5.10	Private label food & pet product, producer, distributor, & marketer
Acquisition	07/19/10	Thomkins PLC *United Kingdom*	Pinafore Acquisitons Ltd *Canada*	$4.77	Group of manufacturirg co
Acquisition	04/22/10	Burger King Holdings *United States*	3G Capital Inc *United States*	$3.93	Fast-food hamburger chain & franchisor
Divestiture	07/27/10	Extended Stay America Inc *United States*	Blackstone / Centerbridge / Paulson *Russia*	$3.93	Develops, owns, & operates extended long stay facilities
Acquisition	07/15/10	NBTY Inc *United States*	Carlyle Group *United States*	$3.81	Nutritional supplement manufacturer & retailer in US & UK
Divestiture	06/23/10	Cognis Holding GmbH *Germany*	BASF SE *Germany*	$3.80	Chemicals holding co
Acquisition	10/25/10	CommScope Inc *United States*	Carlyle Group *United States*	$3.79	High-performance electronic & fiber optic cable operations
Divestiture	08/11/10	Albertis Infraestructers SA *Spain*	CVC Capital Partners Ltd *United Kingdom*	$3.69	Toll highway & parking garage operations
Divestiture	11/04/10	Eversholt Rail Group *United Kingdom*	Eversholt Investment Group *United States & United Kingdom*	$3.41	Diversified operations
Divestiture	11/05/10	High Speed 1 *United Kingdom*	Ontario Teachers' Pension Plan *Canada*	$3.40	Rail transportation

AS *Total Value figures in USD Billions.*
Data as is for November 30, 2010.
Source: Bloomberg, 2010.

18.4   Financing Structure

Most of the time, private equity finances its buy-out dealings with a mix of (a) senior debt, (b) mezzanine fund, and (c) equity.

Senior debt Senior debt consists of debt secured by liens on particular assets (e.g., land, plant, equipment, receivables, and inventories) of the target company. Senior debt provides protection needed by the lenders, and represents the bulk of the financing. Senior debt is often provided by a bank.

Mezzanine fund A mezzanine fund, which is subordinated to senior debt, is provided by institutional investors. A mezzanine fund is used by private equity investors to reduce the amount of equity capital required to finance a leveraged buyout. In compensation for the increased risk, mezzanine funds come with higher compensation to secure the lenders in case of default.

Equity Equity financing represents the least portion and often the smallest ingredient of the financing package

18.5   Exit Strategy

Almost always, LBO funds and their sponsors plan their exit strategies during the formation and buy-out processes. They analyze different efficient tax planning means for both the fund and the investors. Exit strategies include: (a) distribution of earnings; (b) partial sale of assets; and (c) complete sale of the portfolio group.

18.5.1   Distribution of Earnings

From the US perspective, it is more efficient to structure the distributions as tax-free returns of capital or repayment of principal on notes. If the distributions are treated as dividends, such dividends should qualify for a reduced rate of tax and carry indirect foreign tax credit under IRC sections 902 and 78 for US corporate investors in the fund. Also, the exit strategy should anticipate distributions to be exempt from foreign taxes: (a) by initially financing the fund with hybrid securities such as convertible preferred equity certificates (CPECs); (b) by locating the fund in a jurisdiction that applies or offers a participation-exemption regime; or (c) through a tax-free complete liquidation of the acquisition vehicle.

18.5.2   Partial Sale of Portfolio Operations

From the US perspective, the avoidance of Sub-part F income at the level of vehicle of acquisition ("BuyCo") remains the primary consideration in any partial sale of operating business ("OpCo"). Under IRC section 954(c)(1)(B)(i) a sale of property that gives rise to dividends qualifies as a foreign personal holding company (FPHC). That is, if the operating companies are treated as a corporation for US tax purposes, a sale by "BuyCo" of the stocks of "OpCo" would trigger FPHC income at the level of "BuyCo'" investors.

Assuming that both "BuyCo" and "OpCo" are foreign-controlled corporations as defined under IRC section 951, section 964(e) will re-characterize gain from the sale of "OpCo" as a dividend to the extent of the E&P of "OpCo". The same-country exception does not apply to any amount treated as dividend under IRC section 954(c)(6). Also, depending on the classification of "BuyCo" for US tax purposes, whether as a corporation or a partnership, the effects of IRC section 964(e) are not the same.

1. If "OpCo" is organized as a domestic partnership in the jurisdiction where it is located, these dividends would flow through the domestic fund and be taxed at the hands US investors, regardless of whether or not these US investors meet the definition of a US shareholder under IRC section 951(b). To avoid such a rough tax treatment, it is worthy to elect that "OpCo" be treated as a disregarded entity for US tax purposes.
2. If "OpCo" is a disregarded entity from US tax purposes, the exit from the operating portfolio would be characterized as a sale of assets, provided the underlying assets do not give rise to dividends, interest, royalties, or annuities or do not give rise to any income.

18.5.3   Complete Liquidation of the Acquisition Vehicle

A complete liquidation of the acquisition vehicle is the ideal exit for many buy-outs. This occurs when investors have received a substantial part of or the whole of their return. In almost all cases, both the acquisition vehicle and the operating investment portfolio would be characterized as controlled foreign corporations (CFCs) under IRC section 951. Therefore, gains derived by the fund on the sale of the stock of the operating investment company will be re-characterized as dividends to the extent of the operating investment company's earnings and profits (E&P) attributable to the fund's holding and period of ownership. However, the amount of E&P taxable at the fund level should not exceed the fund's gain on the sale of the operating investment entity.

18.6   Miscellaneous Services

Miscellaneous services offered by international banks include, inter alia, trust services, processing services, and wealth management services.

18.6.1   Trust Services

International banks provide trust services to their clients, whether individuals or corporations. To understand the nature of the services rendered under "trust services", let us first and foremost define the trust institution itself and its function. A trust arises from the expressed intention of the owner of property to create a trust with respect to the property. The trustee holds legal title to specific property under a fiduciary duty to manage, invest, and safeguard the trust assets for the benefice of designated beneficiaries, who hold equitable title. Trust departments within commercial banks perform trust and agency services. Their principal function is to serve as trustee under an indenture or mortgage securing a bond issuance.

Commercial banks understand that though they are the main source of capital for corporations, a significant portion of financing comes from outside the realm. Corporations can raise capital directly from the public by issuing bonds. The trust department of a commercial bank performs as a trustee in the contract between the corporation and its bondholders. During the life of the bond, it acts on behalf of the bondholders to monitor the issuer's performance, serves notice on the issuer as to any material breach of the indenture, and institutes legal actions if no corrective action is taken by the issuer to protect the bondholders. As a trustee, the trust department manages the investment of its clients, keeps the records, prepares court accounting and carries out other similar duties. The trust department provides escrow services or facilities as an intermediary whenever needed. Some banks have created corporate trust services not as a department within the commercial bank but as a separate corporation under their BHC umbrella. Deutsche Bank AG, Wells Fargo, and US Bank are among those institutions with a corporate trust service.

18.6.2   Processing Services

Banks offer various processing services to their clients, such as cash or management services to large corporations. Many banks handle cash collections and payments and receivables for their customers. Banks issue letters of credit as guarantee payment for fee for their clients.

18.6.3   Wealth Management Services

Wealth management is broader than asset management as it covers both sides of the client's balance sheet. Wealth management consists of providing services tailored to clients' needs. Banks offer a full array of wealth management products and services to their clients, such as tax management strategies, retirement, estate planning, asset allocation, and the like. Through their wealth management services, banks are now offering different types of investment products: structured financed products, complex financial engineering products, and others similar to the ones offered by hedge fund managers.[199] Banks are increasing their wealth management services as the income stream for such services is less volatile than income they derive from underlying or trading. Wealth management units of banks are increasing significantly, due to the growth of wealth itself, and clients' demand for broader services beyond regular private banking. Citigroup estimates that, globally, wealth management accounts for 20% of the financial services revenue pool, which is higher than investment banking.[200]

The industry is more fragmented, with rooms to be filled. Wealth managers are called to determine clients' profiles, goals, and tailor investment strategies and proposals that meet clients' expectations. This includes investments in alternative investment vehicles, real estate, structured finance products, low-cost index funds, guaranteed income products, and more. Banks in the US need to exploit their channels and relations with their affluent or soon-to-be affluent customers to offer a full array of services in various fields such as tourism and traveling. Asia-Pacific countries, mainly China, produce an increasing number of individual investors seeking innovative opportunities and financial services beyond the reach of traditional private banks. Servicing "VIP-cards" for selected affluent customers is the 21st century's key banking unit for those banks willing to seize the opportunities ahead of them.

In managing their clients' wealth, investment managers must comply with a variety of laws, including (a) anti-laundering laws and (b) harmful tax practices.

Anti-laundering Laws

Since the terrorist act on September 11, 2001, the US Congress has enacted the US Patriot Act, which has enhanced money laundering legislation already in place to cover both banks and hedge funds and other financial institutions handling significant sums of money (cash or wire-transfer). Section 311 of the US Patriot Act sets out specific measures to identify beneficial owners dealing with prime brokerages. Section 312 of the Act includes, for the first time, in the definition of "financial institution" the privileged hedge fund business, besides commodity trading advisors, commodity pool operators, and futures commission merchants. The Act encourages the US Treasury Department to exercise vigorously the authority it possesses through the Bank Secrecy Act of 1970 and fight any anti-laundering schemes. The Patriot Act, for the first time, combats the financing of terrorism with the scope of its anti-laundering laws.[201]

Recently, the Federal Reserve and the Office of the Comptroller of the Currency have launched a series of cease-and-desist orders against several foreign banks such as HBSC Holding PLC, Barclays PLC, and Royal Bank of Scotland PLC, requiring them to improve the supervision of their operations in the United States, specifically to comply with the US laws relating to money laundering, bank secrecy, financing of terrorism, and US economic sanctions. In 2010, the London-based Barclays paid $298 million and admitted to processing payments to the US from clients in Cuba, Sudan, and other countries blacklisted by the US government. The United Kingdom's Lloyds Banking Group

PLC and Switzerland's Credit Suisse Group A.G. settled with the Federal Reserve for $350 million and $536 million respectively.[202]

Harmful Tax Practice

The harmful tax practice guidance was developed by the OECD in the late 1990s. It is intended to crack down on the avoidance of tax through the use of banks and other financial institutions located in tax havens. However, the definition of "tax haven" is loose, and the OECD approach lacks consistency regarding the set of criteria used to take a country out from the agreed-upon list of tax havens. Despite all the flaws in the OECD approach, wealth managers still need to make sure that their advice would not be characterized as harmful tax gymnastics.

Part III
Risk Management

Overview of Part III

Central banks all around the world are responsible for the supervision and regulation of most domestic and international banks and other financial institutions within their respective jurisdictions. The US Federal Reserve, the European Central Bank, the Bank of Japan, the Bank of England, and other central banks discussed in Part I of the book oversee and regulate their banking and financial institutions. In the US, for instance, the Federal Reserve Board approves member banks' mergers and acquisitions and grants permission for member banks' non-banking activities.

Central banks use banks' financial statements (i.e., balance sheet, statement of income, and statement of cash flows) to assess their overall safety and soundness. Under the Uniform Financial Institution Rating System (UFIRS), each bank member is assigned a CAMELS rating based on (a) **C**apital adequacy, (b) **A**sset quality, (c) **M**anagement, (d) **E**arnings, (e) **L**iquidity, and (f) **S**ensitivity to market risk. CAMELS ratings range from 1 to 5:

Rating 1 is granted to banks considered basically sound in every respect.

Rating 2 is granted to banks which are fundamentally sound, with modest weaknesses correctable in their due business course.

Rating 3 is granted to banks with moderate financial, operational, and compliance weaknesses.

Rating 4 is granted to banks with serious financial, operational, and compliance weaknesses.

Rating 5 is granted to banks with extreme financial, operational, and compliance weaknesses, posing an immediate threat or probability of failure.

Central banks' supervision would be facilitated if member banks operated within sound corporate governance cultures, where risk metrics are clearly defined, monitored and assessed through various available techniques, and the Boards are well-equipped with financial and banking knowledge to analyze and prevent excessive risks, such as liquidity, credit, or operational risks. Therefore, Chapters 19 and 20 focus on both the financial analysis of banking activities, and the management of risk associated with these activities.

19
Analyzing Financial Statements

19.1 Introduction

By and large, financial statements include the: (a) balance sheet; (b) statements of income; (c) shareholder equity; (d) statement of cash flow; and (e) notes to the aforementioned statements. Besides these five key sets of data, the modern financial statements incorporate the Management Discussion and Analysis, the Proxy Statement, the Auditor's Report, and, sometimes, the firm's corporate governance structure.

The analysis here is based upon, but is independent of, the 260-page 2009 consolidated financial statements of JP Morgan Chase.

19.2 JP Morgan Chase Balance Sheet

A balance sheet (BS) shows all the assets, liabilities, and equity of the bank at one particular point in time, whether quarterly or at the end of the fiscal year.

Tables 19.1, 19.2, 19.3, 19.4, 19.4, 19.5, 19.6, 19.7, 19.8, 19.8, 19.9, and 19.10 provide, respectively: JPM Chase Detailed Balance Sheet, JPM Chase Snapshot of BS, JPM Chase Off-BS Statement, JPM Chase Statement of Income, JPM Chase Income by Activity, JPM Chase Statement of Cash Flows, JPM Chase Asset Analysis, JPM Chase Liabilities Analysis, JPM Chase Capital Components, JPM Chase Lines of Business.

Often, the balance sheet does not provide the full picture as corporations can keep out some transactions. The transactions referred to as "Off-balance sheet" include lending-related financial instruments, guarantees, and other commitments, described further.

19.3 JP Morgan Chase Statement of Income

The statement of income is a reflection of the financial transactions carried out by a bank over a specified period of time, such as quarterly or annually. The

Table 19.1 JP Morgan Chase detailed balance sheet.

December 31, (in millions, except share data)	2009	2008
Assets		
Cash and due from banks	$26,206	$26,895
Deposits with banks	63,230	138,139
Federal funds sold and securities purchased under resale agreements (included $20,536 and $20,843 at fair value at December 31, 2009 and 2008, respectively)	195,404	203,115
Securities borrowed (included $7,032 and $3,381 at fair value at December 31, 2009 and 2008, respectively)	119,630	124,000
Trading assets (included assets pledged of $38,315 and $75,063 at December 31, 2009 and 2008, respectively)	411,128	509,983
Securities (included $360,365 and $205,909 at fair value at December 31, 2009 and 2008, respectively, and assets pledged of $100,931 and $25,942 at December 31, 2009 and 2008, respectively)	360,390	205,943
Loans (included $1,364 and $7,696 at fair value at December 31, 2009 and 2008, respectively)	633,458	744,898
Allowance for loan losses	(31,602)	(23,164)
Loans, net of allowance for loan losses	601,856	721,734
Accrued interest and accounts receivable (included $5,012 and $3,099 at fair value at December 31, 2009 and 2008, respectively)	67,427	60,987
Premises and equipment	11,118	10,045
Goodwill	43,357	48,027
Mortgage servicing rights	15,531	9,403
Other intangible assets	4,621	5,581
Other assets (included $19,165 and $29,199 at fair value at December 31, 2009 and 2008, respectively)	107,091	111,200
Total assets	**$2,031,989**	**$2,175,052**
Liabilities		
Deposits (included $4,455 and $5,605 at fair value at December 31, 2009 and 2008, respectively)	$938,367	$1,009,277
Federal funds purchased and securities loaned or sold under repurchase agreements (included $3,396 and $2,993 at fair value at December 31, 2009 and 2008, respectively)	261,413	192,546
Commercial paper	41,794	37,845
Other borrowed funds (included $5,637 and $14,713 at fair value at December 31,2009 and 2008, respectively)	55,740	132,400

(*continued*)

Table 19.1   Continued

December 31, (in millions, except share data)	2009	2008
Trading liabilities	125,071	166,878
Accounts payable and other liabilities (included the allowance for lending-related commitments of $939 and $659 at December 31, 2009 and 2008, respectively, and $357 and zero at fair value at December 31, 2009 and 2008, respectively)	162,696	187,978
Beneficial interests issued by consolidated variable interest entities (included $1,410 and $1,735 at fair value at December 31, 2009 and 2008, respectively)	15,225	10,561
Long-term debt (included $48,972 and $58,214 at fair value at December 31, 2009 and 2008, respectively)	266,318	270,683
Total liabilities	**1,866,624**	2,008,168
Commitments and contingencies (see Note 30 on page 238 of this Annual Report)		
Stockholders' equity		
Preferred stock ($1 par value; authorized 200,000,000 shares at December 31, 2009 and 2008; issued 2,538,107 and 5,038,107 shares at December 31, 2009 and 2008, respectively)	**8,152**	31,939
Common stock ($1 par value; authorized 9,000,000,000 shares at December 31, 2009 and 2008; issued 4,104,933,895 shares and 3,941,633,895 shares at December 31, 2009 and 2008, respectively)	**4,105**	3,942
Capital surplus	**97,982**	92,143
Retained earnings	**62,481**	54,013
Accumulated other comprehensive income/(loss)	**(91)**	(5,687)
Shares held in RSU Trust, at cost (1,526,944 shares and 4,794,723 shares at December 31, 2009 and 2008, respectively)	**(68)**	(217)
Treasury stock, at cost (162,974,783 shares and 208,833,260 shares at December 31, 2009 and 2008, respectively)	**(7,196)**	(9,249)
Total stockholders' equity	165,365	166,884
Total liabilities and stockholders' equity	**$ 2,031,989**	$ 2,175,052

statement of income details the origin of the company's revenue, and the effect of the cost over the overall generated revenue. As more and more banks have become international, this statement provides revenue per line of business, and their relationship to the net income of the bank.

Table 19.2 JP Morgan Chase snapshot balance sheet.

December 31, (in millions)	2009	2008
Assets		
Cash and due from banks	**$26,206**	$26,895
Deposits with banks	**63,230**	138,139
Federal funds sold and securities purchased under resale agreements	**195,404**	203,115
Securities borrowed	**119,630**	124,000
Trading assets:		
Debt and equity instruments	**330,918**	347,357
Derivative receivables	**80,210**	162,626
Securities	**360,390**	205,943
Loans	**633,458**	744,898
Allowance for loan losses	**(31,602)**	(23,164)
Loans, net of allowance for loan losses	**601,856**	721,734
Accrued interest and accounts receivable	**67,427**	60,987
Premises and equipment	**11,118**	10,045
Goodwill	**48,357**	48,027
Mortgage servicing rights	**15,531**	9,403
Other intangible assets	**4,621**	5,581
Other assets	**107,091**	111,200
Total assets	**$2,031,989**	$2,175,052
Liabilities		
Deposits	**$938,367**	$1,009,277
Federal funds purchased and securities loaned or sold under repurchase agreements	**261,413**	192,546
Commercial paper	**41,794**	37,845
Other borrowed funds	**55,740**	132,400
Trading liabilities:		
Debt and equity instruments	**64,946**	45,274
Derivative payables	**60,125**	121,604
Accounts payable and other liabilities	**162,696**	187,978
Beneficial interests issued by consolidated VIEs	**15,225**	10,561
Lonq-term debt	**266,318**	270,683
Total liabilities	**1,866,624**	2,008,168
Stockholders' equity	**165,365**	166,884
Total liabilities and stockholders' equity	**$2,031,989**	$2,175,052

Table 19.3 JP Morgan Chase off-balance sheet statement.

By remaining maturity at December 31, (in millions)	2009					2008
	2010	2011-2012	2013-2014	After 2014	Total	Total
Lending-related						
Consumer:						
Home equity — senior lien	$293	$1,650	$5,603	$11,700	$19,246	$27,998
Home equity—junior lien	647	3,998	12,050	20,536	37,231	67,745
Prime mortgage	1,654	—	—	—	1,654	5,079
Subprime mortgage	—	—	—	—	—	—
Option ARMs	—	—	—	—	—	—
Auto loans	5,380	84	3	—	5,467	4,726
Credit card	569,113	—	—	—	569,113	623,702
All other loans	9,907	207	109	1,006	11,229	12,257
Total consumer	586,94	5,939	17,765	33,242	643,940	741,507
Wholesale:						
Other unfunded commitments to extend credit[a]	71,855	94,977	20,728	4,585	192,145	189,563
Asset purchase agreements	8,659	11,134	2,755	137	22,685	53,729
Standby letters of credit and financial guarantees[a][b][c]	25,568	47,203	16,349	2,365	91,485	95,352
Unused advised lines of credit	31,826	3,569	62	216	35,673	36,300
Other letters of credit[a][b]	3,713	1,183	255	16	5,167	4,927
Total wholesale	141,621	158,066	40,149	7,319	347,155	379,871
Total lending-related	$728,615	$164,005	$57,914	$40,561	$991,095	$1,121,378
Other guarantees						
Securities lending guarantees[d]	$170,777	$ —	$ —	$ —	$170,777	$169,281
Residual value guarantees	670	1	—	—	672	670
Derivatives qualifying as guarantees[e]	20,310	18,608	8,759	39,514	87,191	83,835

Contractual cash obligations

By remaining maturity at December 31, (in millions).

Time deposits	$211,377	$14,479	$4,865	$938	$231,659	$299,101
Advances from the Federal Home Loan Banks	23,597	2,583	741	926	27,847	70,187
Long-term debt	37,075	95,915	42,805	90,523	266,318	270,683
Long-term beneficial interests(f)	3,957	2,515	407	3,559	10,438	10,561
Operating leases(g)	1,652	3,179	2,857	8,264	15,952	16,868
Equity investment commitments(h)	1,477	2	—	895	2,374	2,424
Contractual purchases and capital expenditures	2,005	862	419	488	3,774	2,687
Obligations under affinity and co-brand programs	1,091	2,144	1,604	2,059	6,898	8,138
Other liabilities(i)	906	891	873	2,690	5,360	5,005
Total	**$283,137**	**$122,570**	**$54,571**	**$110,342**	**$570,620**	**$685,654**

(a) Represents the contractual amount net of risk participations totaling $24.6 billion and $26.4 billion for standby letters of credit and other financial guarantees at December 31, 2009 and 2008, respectively, $690 million and $1.1 billion for other letters of credit at December 31, 2009 and 2008, respectively, and $643 million and $789 million for other unfunded commitments to extend credit at December 31, 2009 and 2008, respectively. In regulatory filings with the Federal Reserve Board these commitments are shown gross of risk participations.

(b) JPMorgan Chase held collateral relating to $31.5 billion and $31.0 billion of standby letters of credit, respectively, and $1.3 billion and $1.0 billion of other letters of credit at December 31, 2009 and 2008, respectively.

(c) Includes unissued standby letters-of-credit commitments of $38.4 billion and $39.5 billion at December 31, 2009 and 2008, respectively.

(d) Collateral held by the Firm in support of securities lending indemnification agreements was $173.2 billion and $170.1 billion at December 31, 2009 and 2008, respectively. Securities lending collateral comprises primarily cash, and securities issued by governments that are members of the Organisation for Economic Co-operation and Development ("OECD") and US government agencies.

(e) Represents notional amounts of derivatives qualifying as guarantees. For further discussion of guarantees, see Note 5 on pages 175–183 and Note 31 on pages 238–242 of this Annual Report.

(f) Included on the Consolidated Balance Sheets in beneficial interests issued by consolidated variable interest entities.

(g) Includes noncancelable operating leases for premises and equipment used primarily for banking purposes and for energy-related tolling service agreements. Excludes the benefit of noncancelable sublease rentals of $1.8 billion and $2.3 billion at December 31, 2009 and 2008, respectively.

(h) Includes unfunded commitments to third-party private equity funds of $1.5 billion and $1.4 billion at December 31, 2009 and 2008, respectively. Also includes unfunded commitments for other equity investments of $897 million and $1.0 billion at December 31, 2009 and 2008, respectively. These commitments include $1.5 billion at December 31, 2009, related to investments that are generally fair valued at net asset value as discussed in Note 3 on pages 156–173 of this Annual Report.

(i) Includes deferred annuity contracts. Excluded contributions to the US pension and other postretirement benefits plans, as these contributions are not reasonably estimable at this time. Also excluded are unrecognized tax benefits of $6.6 billion and $5.9 billion at December 31, 2009 and 2008, respectively, as the timing and amount of future cash payments are not determinable at this time.

Table 19.4   JP Morgan Chase statement of income.

Year ended December 31, (in millions, except per share data)	2009	2008	2007
Revenue			
Investment banking fees	**$7,087**	$5,526	$6,635
Principal transactions	**9,796**	(10,699)	9,015
Lending- and deposit-related fees	**7,045**	5,088	3,938
Asset management, administration, and commissions	**12,540**	13,943	14,356
Securities gains[a]	**1,110**	1,560	164
Mortgage fees and related income	**3,678**	3,467	2,118
Credit card income	**7,110**	7,419	6,911
Other income	**916**	2,169	1,829
Noninterest revenue	**49,282**	28,473	44,966
Interest income	**66,350**	73,018	71,387
Interest expense	**15,198**	34,239	44,981
Net interest income	**51,152**	38,779	26,406
Total net revenue	**100,434**	67,252	71,372
Provision for credit losses	**32,015**	20,979	6,864
Noninterest expense			
Compensation expense	**26,928**	22,746	22,689
Occupancy expense	**3,666**	3,038	2,608
Technology, communications, and equipment expense	**4,624**	4,315	3,779
Professional and outside services	**6,232**	6,053	5,140
Marketing	**1,777**	1,913	2,070
Other expense	**7,594**	3,740	3,814
Amortization of intangibles	**1,050**	1,263	1,394
Merger costs	**481**	432	209
Total noninterest expense	**52,352**	43,500	41,703
Income before income tax expense/ (benefit) and extraordinary gain	**16,067**	2,773	22,805
Income tax expense/(benefit)	**4,415**	(926)	7,440
Income before extraordinary gain	**11,652**	3,699	15,365
Extraordinary gain	**76**	1,906	—
Net income	**$11,728**	$5,605	$15,365
Net income applicable to common stockholders	**$8,774**	$4,742	$14,927
Per common share data			
Basic earnings per share			
Income before extraordinary gain	**$2.25**	$0.81	$4.38
Net income	**2.27**	1.35	4.38

(*continued*)

Table 19.4   Continued

Year ended December 31, (in millions, except per share data)	2009	2008	2007
Diluted earnings per share			
Income before extraordinary gain	**2.24**	0.81	4.33
Net income	**2.26**	1.35	4.33
Weighted-average basic shares	**3,863**	3,501	3,404
Weighted-average diluted shares	**3,880**	3,522	3,445
Cash dividends declared per common share	**$0.20**	$1.52	$1.48

(a) Securities gains for the year ended December 31, 2009, included credit losses of $578 million, consisting of $946 million of total other-than-temporary impairment losses, net of $368 million of other-than-temporary impairment losses recorded in other comprehensive income.

Table 19.5   JP Morgan Chase income by activity.

	2005	2006	2007	2008	2009
Investment Bank	$3,673	$3,674	$3,139	$(1,175)	$6,899
Retail Financial Services	3,427	3,213	2,925	880	97
Card Services	1,907	3,206	2,919	780	(2,225)
Commercial Banking	951	1,010	1,134	1,439	1,271
Treasury & Securities Services	863	1,090	1,397	1,767	1,226
Asset Management	1,216	1,409	1,966	1,357	1,430
Corporate*	(3,554)	842	1,885	557	3,030
Total net income	$8,483	$14,444	$15,365	$5,605	$11,728
Return on tangible equity	15%	24%	22%	6%	10%
Earnings per share – diluted	$2.35	$4.00	$4.33	$1.35	$2.26

*Includes extraordinary gains and merger costs.

19.4   JP Morgan Chase Statement of Cash Flow

The statement of cash flow traces the flow of funds for working capital into and out of a bank during a fiscal period. In 1987, the Financial Accounting Standards Board issued Statement No. 95, whereby the statement of cash flow became a requirement for publicly-traded companies such as JP Morgan Chase (19.6). Statement No. 95 requires that the statement be presented or classified as (a) operating activities, (b) investing activities, and (c) financing activities.

19.5   Analysis of the Statements

19.5.1   Overview of the Industry

After one of the worst international economic crises, which began in 2007 and ended in 2009, the banking industry is facing a number of challenges: sluggish

Table 19.6 JP Morgan Chase statement of cash flow.

Year ended December 31, (in millions)	2009	2008	2007
Operating activities			
Net income	**$11,728**	$5,605	$15,365
Adjustments to reconcile net income to			
net cash provided by (used in) operating			
activities:			
Provision for credit losses	32,015	20,979	6,864
Depreciation and amortization	2,783	3,143	2,427
Amortization of intangibles	1,050	1,263	1,394
Deferred tax (benefit) expense	(3,622)	(2,637)	1,307
Investment securities gains	(1,110)	(1,560)	(164)
Proceeds on sale of investment	—	(1,540)	—
Stock-based compensation	3,355	2,637	2,025
Originations and purchases of loans held-for-sale	(22,417)	(34,902)	(116,471)
Proceeds from sales, securitizations, and paydowns of loans held-for-sale	33,902	38,036	107,350
Net change in:			
Trading assets	133,488	(12,787)	(121,240)
Securities borrowed	4,452	15,408	(10,496)
Accrued interest and accounts receivable	(6,312)	10,221	(1,932)
Other assets	32,182	(33,629)	(21,628)
Trading liabilities	(79,314)	24,061	12,681
Accounts payable and other liabilities	(26,450)	1,012	4,284
Other operating adjustments	6,167	(12,212)	7,674
Net cash provided by (used in) operating activities	121,897	23,098	(110,560)
Investing activities			
Net change in:			
Deposits with banks	74,829	(118,929)	2,081
Federal funds sold and securities purchased under resale agreements	7,082	(44,597)	(29,814)
Held-to-maturity securities:			
Proceeds	9	10	14
Available-for-sale securities:			
Proceeds from maturities	87,712	44,414	31,143
Proceeds from sales	114,041	96,806	98,450
Purchases	(346,372)	(248,599)	(122,507)
Proceeds from sales and securitizations of loans held-for-investment	30,434	27,531	34,925
Other changes in loans, net	51,251	(59,123)	(83,437)
Net cash received (used) in business acquisitions or dispositions	(97)	2,128	(70)
Proceeds from assets sale to the FRBNY	—	28,850	—

(*continued*)

Table 19.6 Continued

Year ended December 31, (in millions)	2009	2008	2007
Net maturities (purchases) of asset-backed commercial paper guaranteed by the FRBB	11,228	(11,228)	—
All other investing activities, net	(762)	(934)	(4,973)
Net cash provided by (used in) investing activities	**29,355**	**(283,671)**	**(74,188)**
Financing activities			
Net change in:			
Deposits	(107,700)	177,331	113,512
Federal funds purchased and securities loaned or sold under repurchase agreements	67,785	15,250	(7,833)
Commercial paper and other borrowed funds	(76,727)	9,186	41,412
Beneficial interests issued by consolidated variable interest entities	(7,275)	(2,675)	1,070
Proceeds from issuance of long-term debt and trust preferred capital debt securities	51,324	72,407	95,141
Repayments of long-term debt and trust preferred capital debt securities	(55,713)	(62,691)	(49,410)
Proceeds from issuance of common stock	5,756	11,500	—
Excess tax benefits related to stock-based compensation	17	148	365
Proceeds from issuance of preferred stock and Warrant to the US Treasury	—	25,000	—
Proceeds from issuance of preferred stock	—	7,746	—
Redemption of preferred stock issued to the US Treasury	(25,000)	—	—
Repurchases of treasury stock	—	—	(8,178)
Dividends paid	(3,422)	(5,911)	(5,051)
All other financing activities, net	(1,224)	540	3,028
Net cash (used in) provided by financing activities	**(152,179)**	**247,831**	**184,056**
Effect of exchange rate changes on cash and due from banks	238	(507)	424
Net decrease in cash and due from banks	(689)	(13,249)	(268)
Cash and due from banks at the beginning of the year	26,895	40,144	40,412
Cash and due from banks at the end of the year	**$26,206**	**$26,895**	**$40,144**
Cash interest paid	**$16,875**	**$37,267**	**$43,472**
Cash income taxes paid	**5,434**	**2,280**	**7,472**

Note: In 2008, the fair values of noncash assets acquired and liabilities assumed in: (1) the merger with Bear Stearns were $288.2 billion and $287.7 billion, respectively (approximately 26 million shares of common stock valued at approximately $1.2 billion were issued in connection with the Bear Stearns merger); and (2) the Washington Mutual transaction were $260.3 billion and $260.1 billion, respectively.

economic growth, persistent high unemployment, and the need for federal banking reform. However, opportunities for growth are plentiful. These could occur through expansion in new markets (e.g., China), providing new products and services, and internal restructuring. The banking industry plays a major part in the US and the overall global economy. In 2007, for instance, the industry had over $12 trillion in total assets in the United States, with $5.5 trillion of total domestic deposits in the United States alone.[203]

Given the significance of the industry, banks' financial statements are examined by reviewers from the OCC, the Federal Reserve, the FDIC, and other agencies. The results of the examinations are summarized in a CAMELS rating.[204] Despite the economic situation and the tightened regulatory framework, according to a recent report from Deloitte Research, many of the bankers surveyed felt that their margins would widen over the next several years.

19.5.2   Analysis of JP Morgan Chase Balance Sheets

JP Morgan Chase is a leading global financial services with assets of $2 trillion. The firm is a leader in investment banking, financial services for consumers, small business and commercial banking, financial processing services, and asset management and private equity services.

This analysis encompasses both the regular balance sheet as well as the off-balance sheet statements, bearing in mind that the Board's analysis and explanations are not sufficient to enable one to understand and read behind the numbers.[205]

The Assets

While the total overall assets of US banks contracted by 3.5% in 2009 due to, in large part, a fall in gross loans, JP Morgan Chase's total assets' contraction is below the industry average. A little decrease of ($2,031,989 2,175,052) = $144 million.

Deposits with banks, derivative receivables, and loans have significantly contracted, while securities have increased. The trend is in line with the overall industry considering that, in 2009, commercial and industrial loans on books plummeted by 18.5%, household loans declined by 1.75%, and other loans by 7.25%.[206] Also, while the overall industry decline on derivatives was about 43%, JP Morgan Chase's decline (50%) seems higher relative to the average. A geographical analysis of the markets involved would assist the analyst to understand such a variance.

Finally, JP Morgan Chase's increase of more than 50% in securities holdings is better relative to the overall increase of 20% in the industry. However, analysts still need to comprehend the sense and components of the increase.

The management analysis provides little information to catch up with the differences in each asset line. Therefore, analysts should, besides understanding the overall industry information, dig into the assets of JP Morgan Chase line by

Table 19.7 JP Morgan Chase balance sheet assets analysis.

December 31, (in millions, except share data)	2009	2008
Assets		
Cash and due from banks	**$26,206**	$26,895
Deposits with banks	**63,230**	138,139
Federal funds sold and securities purchased under resale agreements (included $20,536 and $20,843 at fair value at December 31, 2009 and 2008, respectively)	**195,404**	203,115
Securities borrowed (included $7,032 and $3,381 at fair value at December 31, 2009 and 2008, respectively)	**119,630**	124,000
Trading assets (included assets pledged of $38,315 and $75,063 at December 31, 2009 and 2008, respectively)	**411,128**	509,983
Securities (included $360,365 and $205,909 at fair value at December 31, 2009 and 2008, respectively, and assets pledged of $100,931 and $25,942 at December 31, 2009 and 2008, respectively)	**360,390**	205,943
Loans (included $1,364 and $7,696 at fair value at December 31, 2009 and 2008, respectively)	**633,458**	744,898
Allowance for loan losses	**(31,602)**	(23,164)
Loans, net of allowance for loan losses	**601,856**	721,734
Accrued interest and accounts receivable (included $5,012 and $3,099 at fair value at December 31, 2009 and 2008, respectively)	**67,427**	60,987
Premises and equipment	**11,118**	10,045
Goodwill	**48,357**	48,027
Mortgage servicing rights	**15,531**	9,403
Other intangible assets	**4,621**	5,581
Other assets (included $19,165 and $29,199 at fair value at December 31, 2009 and 2008, respectively)	**107,091**	111,200
Total assets	**$ 2,031,989**	$ 2,175,052

line to understand the numbers (Table 19.7). However, given that the balance sheet under consideration is a consolidation, a line-by-line asset analysis would require decrypting the consolidated numbers.

The Liabilities

Banks' liabilities consist of various types of deposit account and other borrowings used to fund the investments and loans on the asset side of the balance sheet, such as federal funds purchased and securities loaned or sold under Repo agreements, commercial paper, and other borrowed funds.

The total liabilities on banks' books have declined by about 5.5%, while the core deposits grew by 8% in 2009.[207] Two liabilities accounts have changed significantly: (a) federal loans and securities loaned or sold under Repo agreements; and (b) derivable payables. However, JP Morgan Chase's core deposits contracted in 2009 by $70,990 million (Table 19.8).

A reduction in core deposits is, per se, not a good indication. The analyst needs to understand the sense of such a contraction which is not in line with the industry trend.

Stockholders' Equity

In 2009, the equity capital of US commercial banks increased by 11.25% compared to 2008. The increase was due largely to substantial infusions of capital from parent BHCs all through the year. The Tier 1 and total risk-based capital ratios, measured relative to risk-weighted assets, each increased substantially from about 9.75% to 11.5% and from about 12.75% to 14.25%, respectively.[208] JP Morgan Chase, Tier 1 and Tier 2, reflect this trend. However, the risk-based capital components and assets remain unchanged in 2009 (Table 19.9).

Moreover, JP Morgan Chase's increase in risk-based equity is across all its lines of business due to diversity and risk profile of each line of business, as shown in Table 19.10.

Off-balance sheet Assets and Liabilities

Off-balance sheet items refer to contingent assets and liabilities not currently reported in the balance sheet, but destined to be reported at the occurrence of some specified events. Those items depend on the activities of the bank. They include, inter alia, loan commitments, lending-related financial instruments (e.g., commitments and guarantees), special purpose entities, contractual cash obligations, letters of credits, and related items. Special purpose entities (SPEs) are an important part of the financial markets as they provide market liquidity. Banks use SPEs as a source of liquidity for themselves or/and their clients.

JP Morgan Chase, for instance, is involved in SPEs in three forms: (a) by using multi-seller conduits; (b) by providing its intermediation; and (c) through loans securitizations. Contractual cash obligations refer to a firm contractual obligation that may require future cash payments in the occurrence of certain events.

19.5.3   Analysis of JP Morgan Statement of Income

First, JP Morgan Chase has six lines of business (Figure 19.1). Second, it provides the income per activity line, relevant to understand the performance of each line of business, besides the overall income generated in fiscal year 2009. Figure 19.2 provides the net revenue by lines of business.

From the snapshot provided in Figures 19.1 and 19.2, one can infer that JP Morgan Chase derives almost a third of its revenue from retail financial services, and near a third from its investment bank activities. The third line of business income comes from card services. The remaining lines of business

Table 19.8 JP Morgan Chase liabilities analysis.

Liabilities		
Deposits (included $4,455 and $5,605 at fair value at December 31, 2009 and 2008, respectively)	**$938,367**	$1,009,277
Federal funds purchased and securities loaned or sold under repurchase agreements (included $3,396 and $2,993 at fair value at December 31, 2009 and 2008, respectively)	**261,413**	192,546
Commercial paper	**41,794**	37,845
Other borrowed funds (included $5,637 and $14,713 at fair value at December 31, 2009 and 2008, respectively)	**55,740**	132,400
Trading liabilities	**125,071**	166,878
Accounts payable and other liabilities (included the allowance for lending-related commitments of $939 and $659 at December 31, 2009 and 2008, respectively, and $357 and zero at fair value at December 31, 2009 and 2008, respectively)	**162,696**	187,978
Beneficial interests issued by consolidated variable interest entities (included $1,410 and $1,735 at fair value at December 31, 2009 and 2008, respectively)	**15,225**	10,561
Long-term debt (included $48,972 and $58,214 at fair value at December 31, 2009 and 2008, respectively)	**266,318**	270,683
Total liabilities	**1,866,624**	2,008,168
Commitments and contingencies (see Note 30 on page 238 of this Annual Report)		
Stockholders' equity		
Preferred stock ($1 par value; authorized 200,000,000 shares at December 31, 2009 and 2008; issued 2,538,107 and 5,038,107 shares at December 31, 2009 and 2008, respectively)	**8,152**	31,939
Common stock ($1 par value; authorized 9,000,000,000 shares at December 31, 2009 and 2008; issued 4,104,933,895 shares and 3,941,633,895 shares at December 31, 2009 and 2008, respectively)	**4,105**	3,942
Capital surplus	**97,982**	92,143
Retained earnings	**62,481**	54,013
Accumulated other comprehensive income/(loss)	**(91)**	(5,687)
Shares held in RSU Trust, at cost (1,526,944 shares and 4,794,723 shares at December 31,2009 and 2008, respectively)	**(68)**	(217)
Treasury stock, at cost (162,974,783 shares and 208,833,260 shares at December 31, 2009 and 2008, respectively)	**(7,196)**	(9,249)
Total stockholders' equity	**165,365**	166,884
Total liabilities and stockholders' equity	**$ 2,031,989**	$ 2,175,052

Table 19.9 JP Morgan Chase capital components.

Risk-based capital components and assets

December 31, (in millions)	2009	2008
Tier 1 capital		
Tier 1 common capital:		
Total stockholders' equity	**$165,365**	$166,884
Less: Preferred stock	**8,152**	31,939
Common stockholders' equity	157,213	134,945
Effect of certain items in accumulated other comprehensive income/(loss) excluded from Tier 1 common equity	75	5,084
Less: Goodwill[a]	**46,630**	46,417
Fair value DVA on derivative and structured note liabilities related to the Firm's credit quality	912	2,358
Investments in certain subsidiaries	802	679
Other intangible assets	3,660	3,667
Tier 1 common capital	105,284	86,908
Preferred stock	**8,152**	31,939
Qualifying hybrid securities and noncontrolling interests[b]	**19,535**	17,257
Total Tier 1 capital	132,971	136,104
Tier 2 capital		
Long-term debt and other instruments qualifying as Tier 2 capital	**28,977**	31,659
Qualifying allowance for credit losses	**15,296**	17,187
Adjustment for investments in certain subsidiaries and other	**(171)**	(230)
Total Tier 2 capital	44,102	48,616
Total qualifying capital	**$177,073**	$184,720
Risk-weighted assets[c]	**$1,198,006**	$1,244,659
Total adjusted average assets[d]	**$1,933,767**	$1,966,895

(a) Goodwill is net of any associated deferred tax liabilities.
(b) Primarily includes trust preferred capital debt securities of certain business trusts.
(c) Includes off-balance sheet risk-weighted assets at December 31, 2009 and 2008, of $367.4 billion and $357.5 billion, respectively. Risk-weighted assets are calculated in accordance with US federal regulatory capital standards.
(d) Adjusted average assets, for purposes of calculating the leverage ratio, include total average assets adjusted for unrealized gains/(losses) on securities, less deductions for disallowed goodwill and other intangible assets, investments in certain subsidiaries, and the total adjusted carrying value of nonfinancial equity investments that are subject to deductions from Tier 1 capital.

Table 19.10   JP Morgan Chase lines of business.

Line of business equity

December 31, (in billions)	2009	2008
Investment Bank	$33.0	$33.0
Retail Financial Services	25.0	25.0
Card Services	15.0	15.0
Commercial Banking	8.0	8.0
Treasury & Securities Services	5.0	4.5
Asset Management	7.0	7.0
Corporate/Private Equity	64.2	42.4
Total common stockholders' equity	**$157.2**	**$134.9**

Line of business equity	Yearly Average	
(in billions)	2009	2008
Investment Bank	$33.0	$26.1
Retail Financial Services	25.0	19.0
Card Services	15.0	14.3
Commercial Banking	8.0	7.3
Treasury & Securities Services	5.0	3.8
Asset Management	7.0	5.6
Corporate/Private Equity	52.9	53.0
Total common stockholders' equity	**$145.9**	**$129.1**

(commercial banking, treasury and securities services, asset management, and corporate) each derive income less than 10%.

Retail Financial Services (RFS)

JP Morgan Chase Retail Financial Services (RFS) is made up of two components: retail banking and consumer lending. The retail banking side provides checking and saving and investment to US consumers and small businesses as well as student, home, business, and auto loans, while consumer lending extends other types of loan to individuals for home and auto loans for consumers. In 2009, the RFS alone reported 30% of the firm's income, or $32,692 billion.

Investment Bank Services

Investment banking services include: (a) advising companies and investors; (b) raising capital; and (c) making markets. JP Morgan Chase is the leading bank in investment banking activities. In 2009, the firm had a net income of $28,109 billion as a result of best activities overseas and record investment banking fees. It raised $620 billion of equity or bonds for both private corporations and public institutions (Figure 19.3).

JPMorgan Chase

Investment Bank	Retail Financial Services	Card Services	Commercial Banking	Treasury & Securities Services	Asset Management
Businesses:	**Businesses:**	**Businesses:**	**Businesses:**	**Businesses:**	**Businesses:**

• Investment Banking
  - Advisory
  - Debt and equity underwriting
• Market-Making and Trading
  - Fixed Income
  - Equities
• Corporate Lending
• Principal Investing
• Prime Services
• Research
	• Retail Banking
	  - Consumer and Business Banking (including Business Banking loans)
	• Consumer Lending:
	  - Loan originations and balances (including home lending, student, auto, and other loans)
	  - Mortgage production and servicing
		• Credit Card
		• Merchant Acquiring
			• Middle Market Banking
			• Commercial Term Lending
			• Mid-Corporate Banking
			• Real Estate Banking
				• Treasury Services
				• Worldwide Securities Services
					• Investment Management:
					  - Institutional
					  - Retail
					• Private Bank
					• Private Wealth Management
					• Bear Stearns Private Client Services[a]

(a) Bear Stearns Private Client Services was renamed to JPMorgan Securities at the beginning of 2010.

Figure 19.1   JP Morgan Chase lines of business.

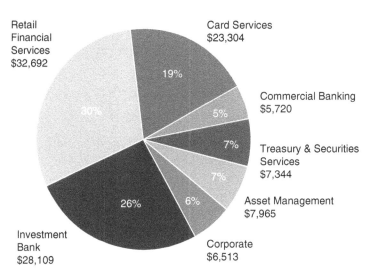

Figure 19.2   JP Morgan chase net revenue by line of business.

Credit Card Services

The credit card service (CCS) provides facility payment for the firm's customers, whether individuals, corporations, non-profit organizations, or government-related services. Despite the firm's effort and creativity in this specific sector,

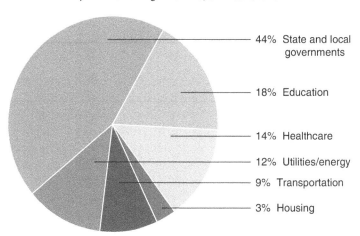

Figure 19.3 JP Morgan Chase public sector activities.

JP Morgan Chase had a loss of $4 billion. That negative performance is due to some regulatory changes – The Wall Street and Consumer Protection Act of 2010 – which restrict banks' ability to change rates and prohibits non-consumer-friendly practice. JP Morgan Chase has embraced all these changes and tried to adjust this particular sector for the year ahead.

Remaining Activities

JP Morgan Chase activities include: commercial banking; treasury and securities services;[209] asset management; and corporate. In 2009, JP Morgan Chase had assets under management of $1.7 trillion, almost the total of all assets under management by the hedge fund industry in 2009. JP Morgan Chase assisted institutions and retail investors to manage their cash, and provided equity, fixed income, and alternative investment strategies.[210]

19.5.4   Analysis of the Cash Flows

Operating Activities

Cash flow from operating activities includes cash inflows and outflows generated from the bank's daily operations. In 2009, JP Morgan Chase's operating assets and liabilities supported the firm's activities – capital markets and lending activities – including the origination or purchase of loans initially designated as held-for-sale. The firm's 2009 cash flow from operating activities declined from $13.2 billion in 2008 to $689 million. The decrease is due to the major acquisitions completed during the fiscal year. JP Morgan Chase's management remains confident that the firm's ability to generate cash through short- and long-term borrowings is still sufficient to fund the firm's operating liquidity needs. Analysts would have to see the firm's cash flow from operating activities in 2010 prior to raising a warning flag.

Investing Activities

Investing activities include buying and selling non-current assets which will be used to generate revenues over a long period of time (exceeding a year), and/ or buying and selling securities not classified as cash equivalent. JP Morgan Chase's investing activities predominantly include originating loans to be held for investment, the AFS securities portfolio and other short-term interest-earning assets. For FY 2009, the firm's net cash for investing activities was $29.4 billion – a significant increase compared to FY 2008, when the net cash was a negative $283.7 billion. The decrease was due to lower demands for inter-bank lending and lower deposits with the Federal Reserve Bank.

Financing Activities

Financing activities include borrowing and repaying money, issuing stock, and paying dividends. JP Morgan Chase's financing activities consist of customer deposits, issuance of long-term debts, and equities (preferred and common stocks). In 2009, the net cash for financing activities declined from $247.8 billion (2008) to $152.2 billion. The decrease is due to a decline in borrowings from the Federal Reserve Bank, the repayment of advances from Federal Home Loan Banks, and the maturity of the non-recourse advances under the Federal Reserve Bank of Boston AML facility.

19.5.5   Relevancy of the Notes

JP Morgan Chase's 2009 Annual Report contains well-detailed "Notes to consolidated financial statements". While all the information provided is relevant for financial analysis, the following discusses some of the key points, vital in order to comprehend the numbers in the financial statements: valuation method, and the valuation's options.

Valuation Methods under Note 3

Note 3 explains both the process whereby certain assets and liabilities are valued and the "fair value" process in order that the reader of the financial assets can understand how the numbers have been determined. First, the fair value is based on quoted market prices, where available. Second, if no market's quoted price is available, the firm proceeds with its internally-developed method, which consists of independently-sourced market parameters. Whenever necessary, the firm makes adjustments to reach out the fair value of certain assets and liabilities. JP Morgan Chase follows the three-level valuation hierarchy established by the US GAAP for disclosure of fair value measurement.[211]

The Valuation's Options under Note 4

JP Morgan Chase had also made some choices in determining the fair value of certain assets and liabilities in order to (a) mitigate income statement volatility, (b) eliminate the complexities of applying certain accounting models, and (c) better reflect those instruments that are managed on a fair value basis.

The areas covered by such elections include:

- securities financing arrangements with an embedded derivative and/or a maturity of greater than one year;
- loans purchased or originated as part of securitization warehousing activity, subject to bifurcation accounting, or managed on a fair value basis;
- structured notes issued as part of investment business client-driven activities;
- certain tax credits and other equity investments acquired as part of the Washington Mutual transaction.

While all the Notes to the financial statements are relevant, the determination of the fair value of assets and liabilities for a bank is crucial. Financial analysts should re-examine the assumptions which JP Morgan Chase relied upon and question their relevancy and their accuracy. The use of independent market input, for instance, can hide "creative accounting" practices. Also, whenever a firm provides internal models as a means of explaining its valuation, blind-sided reliance upon the model can be deceptive, unless the model is well conceived and well explained to a lay person.

19.6   Conclusion

While JP Morgan Chase's Annual Report seems detailed and comprehensive, it does not provide relevant ratios upon which a financial analysis can start over broad comparison. The firm has different lines of business, and for some of them did provide the ratios of return on equity. It did not provide some relevant data such as the return on asset (ROA), the risk-adjusted return on capital (RAROC), and others. These quick measures are necessary to understand the performance beyond the net profit.

20
Corporate Governance, Risk Metrics, Liquidity, and Credit Risks

20.1 Introduction

During the 2008–2010 financial crisis, corporate governance of many international banks was questioned. Some major banks' corporate governance frameworks were poor and bank managements were unfit under the BIS standards.[212] A bank cannot properly monitor its operational, counterparty, liquidity, and credit risks without an adequate and efficient corporate governance mechanism. To that end, a risk metric model must be conceived and used as a key tool by the Board of the bank.

Liquidity risk is embodied under Principle 14 of the "Core Principles for Effective Banking Supervision". It requires that banks put in place a system that assists them in managing their liquidity, in the short, mid, and long term. Liquidity refers to a bank's ability to fund increases in assets and meet obligations as they become due, without incurring unacceptable losses. For a commercial bank, for instance, whose main function consists of collecting deposits from one set of customers and granting loans to another set of customers, the process of transforming the core deposits into loans could make the bank vulnerable to liquidity risk.

Credit risk is embodied under Principle 8 of the "Core Principles for Effective Banking Supervision". It requires that banks put in place a credit risk management process which takes into account the risk profile of the institution. Credit risk refers to a risk of loss due to failure by a counterparty to meet its contractual obligations.[213]

20.2 Corporate Governance

Corporate governance can be defined as the material obligations of a company toward shareholders, employees, customers, suppliers, creditors, tax, and other supervisory authorities.[214] From this definition, we can infer that corporate governance is a set of relationships framed by corporate bylaws, articles of association, charters, and applicable statutory or other legal rules and principles, between the Board of Directors, shareholders, and other stakeholders of an organization that outlines the relationship among these groups, and sets rules as to how the organization should be managed, as well as its operational framework.[215] Concerns over corporate governance emerged in the 1980s, when US pension funds decided to invest the bulk of their stockholdings in index funds. From that time, a series of financial scandals have raised questions pursuant to US and other developed economies' corporate governance ethics. The Chrysler rescue in 1980; the Black Monday stock market crash in 1987; the Long Term Capital Management (LTCM) stock market failure in 1998; the Enron, Tyco, Swissair, Vivendi, Kmart, Parmalat, Siemens, and Worldcom fiascos; the US sub-prime and its series of failures (i.e., Bear Stearns, Lehman Brothers, Meryll Lynch), have all led to corporate governance becoming the predominant debate in academic, business, and even political circles. Almost all around the world, corporate governance has become the topic, the heated debate among unfettered free market proponents and market-ruled advocates. The International Corporate Governance network, a not-for-profit organization, was solicited to lecture on corporate governance in various jurisdictions: 1997, in London, with the sponsorship of the Corporation of the City of London; 1997, in Paris, with the sponsorship of the Paris Bourse; 1998 in San Francisco; 2001 in Tokyo; 2007 in Cape Town, sponsored by the Johannesburg Stock Exchange; 2008 in Seoul. The modern financial ideology of "laissez-faire" that was the modus operandi of businesses and regulators over decades has become obsolete. To attract investors, companies are attaching a brief overview of their corporate governance to their financial statements.

> The corporate governance discussion in public has now departed from how to best organize accountability and responsibility at the helm of the company. It has moved on to a more fundamental debate about corporate roles in society, basic attitudes and behaviours in businesses, which are perceived as more powerful than governments.[216]

Empirical evidence suggests that good corporate governance increases the efficiency of capital allocation within and across firms, reduces the cost of capital for issuers, helps broaden access to capital, reduces vulnerability to crises and makes corrupt practices more difficult to take root. Furthermore, recent research has found a relationship between the state of corporate governance in an economy and the severity of the crises that it suffers.[217]

In the banking industry particularly, besides banks such as JP Morgan Chase, corporate governance was not among the top priorities. Banks are in the business of risk taking. Since the Steagall Act of 1999, most banks have become universal, running both commercial and investing banking activities. For all speculative risks inherent to their activities, banks should manage the risk properly. Due to their role in the overall economy, corporate governance for banking organizations is of great importance to the international financial system. The Basel Committee on Banking Supervision has published specific guidelines to assist banking institutions with their corporate governance. The eight principles developed by the Basel Committee provide guidance pursuant to the role of the Board of Directors and supervision authority. Under the BIS, corporate governance involves the manner in which the business and the affairs of banks are governed by their boards and senior management.[218]

20.2.1 Bank Board Fiduciary Duties

The Board of Directors owes fiduciary duties to the shareholders: duty of care and duty of loyalty. Any breach of these duties can result in shareholders' specific suits and damages stemming from the actions of the Board.

20.2.2 Duty to be Informed

For a bank's Board to live up to its fiduciary duties, the directors must first and foremost be informed of the ongoing concerns of the bank. Principle VI.F of the Basel Committee states that Board members should have access to accurate, relevant, and timely information. Courts in the US, and particularly the Delaware Chancery and Supreme Courts, have developed specific standards to ascertain the Board's actions.

20.2.3 Duty of Care

Directors must discharge their duty in good faith, with such a degree of diligence, care, and skill that an ordinary prudent person would exercise under similar circumstances. Directors would be held responsible for either nonfeasance or misfeasance any time their inaction or action causes harm to the corporation. The duty of care requires directors to take certain responsibilities or actions. In Francis vs United Jersey Bank,[219] the New Jersey Supreme Court held that:

> Directors should have some understanding of the business, keep informed on activities, perform general monitoring including attendance at meetings, and have some familiarity with the financial status of the business as reflected on the financial statements.

However, the company's Certificate of Incorporation could shield the directors from the liability pursuant to their duty of care if the breach and the harm suffered by the corporation did not occur as a result of bad faith or with an intentional misconduct of disregard. To establish that a director has failed to act in good faith, a shareholder must show whether that director's conduct was motivated by an actual intent to do harm, or that the director acted with a conscious disregard as to his (her) fiduciary duties.

In Re Walt Disney Co. Derivative Litigation, the Delaware Court has held:

> Fiduciary action taken solely by reason of gross negligence and without any malevolent intent does not constitute bad faith.[220]

20.2.4   Duty of Loyalty

Directors should perform their duty with loyalty. That is, directors must act (a) in good faith, and (b) with the conscientiousness, fairness, morality, and honesty that the law requires of fiduciaries. The duty of loyalty prevents them from engaging in self-dealing, usurping the corporation opportunity, or making secret profits to the detriment of the corporation. The duty of loyalty is often breached when directors engage in interested transactions. Such transactions are suspicious and set aside, unless the directors (a) establish that the transactions were fair and reasonable at the time they were entered into, or (b) have disclosed the material facts and won the approval of the Board. Likewise, directors should not usurp the corporation's business opportunity. This refers to any business or transaction in which the corporation has a tangible interest or expectancy, or logically related to the corporation's core and auxiliary businesses.

20.3   The BIS Corporate Governance Principles

The BIS has developed eight sound corporate governance principles to assist management in their daily approach to issues that affect the banking industry. These principles are well-explained and detailed here. Table 20.1 shows the eight principles in a nutshell.

20.3.1   Bank Boards' Lack of Financial Skills

Despite the existence of these well-defined duties, the practice within the banking industry falls short of compliance. The reason is two-fold: lack of competence and lack of training.

20.3.2   Lack of Skills

Several of the corporate governance principles set out by the Basel Committee require specific sets of skills needed by directors sitting within bank boards. Principles VI.D.1, VI.D.4, VI.D.7 are among the most telling:

- Principle VI.D.1 states that the Board should fulfil certain key functions including reviewing and guiding corporate strategy, major plans of action, risk policy.

Table 20.1   The eight principles of corporate governance.

Principles	Requirements
Principle I	Board members should be qualified for their positions, have a clear understanding of their role in corporate governance and be able to exercise sound judgment about the affairs of the bank.
Principle II	The Board of Directors should approve and oversee the bank's strategic objectives and corporate values that are communicated throughout the banking organization.
Principle III	The Board of Directors should set and enforce clear lines of responsibility and accountability throughout the organization.
Principle IV	The Board should ensure that there is appropriate oversight by senior management consistent with board policy.
Principle V	The Board and senior management should effectively utilize the work conducted by the internal audit function, external auditors, and internal control functions.
Principle VI	The Board should ensure that compensation policies and practices are consistent with the bank's corporate culture, long-term objectives and strategy, and control environment.
Principle VII	The Board should be governed in a transparent manner.
Principle VIII	The Board and senior management should understand the bank's operational structure, including where the bank operates in jurisdictions, or through structures, that impede transparency.

Source: BIS.

- Principle VI.D.7, which defines key functions, goes on to include, inter alia, risk management, and financial and operational control.

The recent financial crisis has revealed that many major banks lack an adequate risk management structure or, where there was one in place, the directors within this risk management body lacked basic knowledge of sophisticated financial engineering risk and business experience on risk issues.[221]

Such a finding contrasts with the requirements under Principle VI.E of the Basel Committee which states: "the board should be able to exercise objective independent judgment on corporate affairs."

Plenty of studies that looked at directors sitting within bank risk committees have revealed some disturbing findings. Out of eight US major banks and financial institutions studied, two-thirds of directors had no experience in banking and finance.[222] Other banks' risk committees were made up of retirees often not acquainted with new types of risk. For instance, at Lehman Brothers, four out of the ten members of its board were individuals over 75 years of age, and only one had current financial knowledge.[223] The situation does not only affect the US – European Union banks face a similar picture. To bring qualified people within bank Boards, the recruiting committees should focus more on knowledge and skills rather than who knows who. A good location to find expertise is within the academic profession, as is the custom in countries such as France and the United Kingdom. Academics with sound expertise in finance, law, accounting, and tax are more likely to see the issues from different perspectives and round up cogent and practical solutions. They ask questions, are open to adverse opinions, and are not eager to jump to conclusions. Directors having such skills should also be judged through an enhanced standard of care due to their profile.

20.3.3   Lack of Adequate Training

When it is not easy for a Board to bring in qualified directors, the alternative would be to provide continuous training to those directors sitting within the risk and audit committees. The PCAOB, the Federal Reserve, and the SEC can be of great help to that end. St. John's University, located within the heart of these financial institutions, can also work on partnership continuous education programs in risk management to refresh and update directors sitting within these highly-technical risk committees.

20.3.4   Bank Boards and Gatekeepers' Conflicts of Interest

Though the Board of Directors is the main body responsible for managing the institution's risks, it can also delegate or seek outside advice in order to make an informed decision that protects the shareholders' interests. Financial analysts, credit rating agencies, and external auditors are often consulted by banks in the course of their business.

Principle V.F of the Basel Committee provides that:

> The corporate governance framework should be complemented by an effective approach that addresses and promotes the provision of analysis or advice by analysts, brokers, rating agencies and others that is relevant to decisions by investors, free from material conflicts of interest that might compromise the integrity of their analysis or advice.

On paper, external auditors, rating agencies, and analysts are deemed to abide by higher standards of integrity, and not blindly sign fraudulent or reckless statements submitted for their review. In practice, it has always been different. The interests of these gatekeepers become more aligned with those of corporate managers than with investors and shareholders. Both the external auditors and the rating agencies engage in advisory services for the same clients that they audit; rating agencies, for example, advise their client how to structure the deal to meet their own rating benchmark.

When banks delegate, without internal supervision, the rating of some complex financial structured product to the rating agency that has advised how to reach the coveted triple A (AAA) rating, conflict of interest is inevitable.

20.3.5   Reforming the Corporate Governance Structure

Key to the banking industry's corporate governance structure is transparency in both the daily manangement and the compensation practices. Without transparency, it will remain difficult for the shareholders and other stakeholders to assess the performance of the Board and senior management. Depending upon the size of the bank, the complexity of its core businesses, and its risk profile, management needs to properly communicate with the shareholders as to the strategies and short- and long-term objectives. Most of the time, corporate governance challenges arise where a bank operates through an opaque structure. Last but not least, the Board must link compensation policies and practices to the bank's long-term strategy and keep them consistent with the bank's culture, strategy, and long-term objectives. Compensation policies and practices need to be monitored by a body of truly independent directors to avoid any conflict of interest.

With a sound and efficient corporate governance mechanism in place, a bank can better manage its liquidity and credit risks, provided a risk metric system is in place.

20.4   Risk Metrics

Risk management is not about eliminating all potential risks. It is even fair to say that risk is to an undertaking what shadow is to a being. Rather, risk management consists of identifying, measuring, and keeping under control risks inherent to the business.[224] The manager is called to review information about the bank's positions, transactions, orders, and margins to identify and monitor exposures at the individual portfolio level and on an aggregate basis for portfolios pursuant to the retained strategies.[225] Despite all efforts at transparency, risk management remains a subjective process concerning the risk assessment methodologies retained, the interpretations of the measurements and the appropriate corrections thereof.

According to a recent study by McKinsey & Company,[226] a sound risk management consists of:

- ensuring full transparency across all risks and across the organization;
- putting in place vigorous risk governance structures;
- clearly defining the firm's risk appetite;
- instilling a consistent, strong risk culture focused on optimizing well-understood risk return trade-offs within the defined risk strategy.

20.4.1 Categories of Risk

By and large, international banks are exposed to: (a) liquidity risk; (b) leverage risk; (c) market risk; (d) concentration risk; (e) counterparty credit risk; and (f) operational risk. Figure 20.1 illustrates the key risks to be managed.

Liquidity Risk

Liquidity refers to the ability of a bank to fund increases in assets and meet obligations as they become due, without incurring unacceptable losses. For a commercial bank, for instance, where the main function consists of collecting deposits from one set of customers and granting loans to another set of customers, the process of transforming the core deposits into loans could make the bank vulnerable to liquidity risk.

Leverage Risk

Leverage consists of increasing an investment's value or return without increasing the amount invested. Initially, leverage was achieved by purchasing securities with borrowed money. Modern leverage has been expanded to include futures, options, and derivatives. Leverage risk stands as a complement to liquidity risk. Leverage is somehow desirable as it helps achieve the desired risk/ return profile of a defined strategy. The result of misunderstanding leverage is shown by the high level of bankruptcy in the banking and financial industry.

Figure 20.1   Risks per category.

The demise of LTCM in 1997 illustrates the point. At the time of its bailout, LTCM had a leverage ratio of 25:1.

Founded in 1993, Long-Term Capital Management Partners was managed by John Meriwether, a fine bond trader who sat on the board of Salomon Inc. Meriwether teamed up with two Nobel laureates, Robert Merton and Myron Scholes, and with David Mullins, a former Federal Reserve regulator. In its first two years, LTCM posted impressive returns on investment of 43% and 41%. The LTCM managers hedged on derivatives to offset risks with a portfolio containing $125 billion of borrowed funds. As the models upon which the managers based their assumptions failed, LTCM lost 90% of the value of its assets under management. The balance sheet leverage ratio had risen to over 150:1 at the time of the government intervention. Excess leverage hidden under off-balance sheet derivative transactions, and a risk management approach that relied more on models than strict test-retesting gap risk and liquidity risk contributed to the demise of the fund.

Market Risk

As international banks operate worldwide, market risk increases. Understanding the market in which the bank operates could help anticipate certain events. Market risk refers mainly to the risk that the market as a whole will fall in value. Put differently, it refers to risk of losses resulting from the variable adverse prices fluctuations in the financial markets. The bank manager should conduct specific studies per sector of business as well as study the macroeconomic factors that sustain the overall economic activity of the region. Market risk also includes foreign exchange risks that derive from currency fluctuations in international FX markets.

Concentration Risk

It is often tempting for a commercial or investment bank manager to specialize in one or two investment strategies. However, highly concentrated positions bear their own risk and could be counterproductive. The misfortune of LTCM, which had heavily invested in real estate, should be a reminder of concentration risk. It would always be better for a bank manager to consider diversifying their positions, combining short-term positions with long-term positions, based upon overall well-conceived goals and investor expectations. Excessive investment in sub-prime mortgages has bankrupted several banking institutions in the US and around the world.

Counterparty Risk

Counterparty risk, also known as "credit risk", refers to a change in the financial position of a counterpart, whether due to a default or a downgrade of its rating. Credit risk is a main issue when the position is an asset.[227] Counterparty credit risk includes the risks associated with derivatives counterparties, prime brokers, and margin lenders.[228] The bank manager needs to understand and to assess the risks posed by each counterpart business and the effect that their misfortune could have on his various portfolios. A regular assessment of these collateral risks would lead a bank manager to request specific assurances whenever a counterparty presents some immediate risks.

Operational Risk

The success or failure of any bank depends on its ability to attract talent. It is always better to recall the Chinese adage, which says, "It does not matter if a cat is black or white, so long as it catches mice".[229] A manager needs to put in place a talented team of people able to understand the complexity and the technicalities of finance, law, and tax that arise with each deal. Furthermore, an internal control process at every level would help save both time and money.

20.4.2   Techniques to Manage Risk

Like other investors or traders, bank managers need to properly manage their positions in different markets in which they operate. Several methods are available and used to that end. Among the most used are (a) the "Greeks"; (b) the value-at-risk technique (VaR); (c) the conditional value-at-risk (CVaR); (d) stressed value-at-risk; and (e) stress testing.

The Greeks

The Greeks, also known as "risk measures", refer to the quantities representing the sensitivity of the price of derivatives (i.e., options) to a change in the underlying asset upon which the value of the derivative depends. The most common Greeks are Delta, Vega, Gamma, Theta, and Rho.

Delta measures the change in the value of an asset, a financial derivative (e.g., futures, swaps, options) to a given change in value or level of the underlying assets (e.g., interest rate, stock price, FX rate, commodity price). Delta can be calculated either analytically or by changing the value of the given underlying asset by a given amount to measure the effect on the value. Delta is always positive for long (calls) and short (puts) and negative for long puts and short calls. Delta risk can be hedged by purchasing and/or selling quantities of the underlying market.

Gamma measures the rate of change in the Delta with no changes in the underlying price. The higher the Gamma, the more valuable the option is to the holder.

Vega measures the value change of a derivative or portfolio to changes in volatility of the underlying asset. When markets become volatile or decline, traders and banks with positive Vega are likely to reap a profit from their positions.

Theta measures the sensitivity of the value of the derivative or portfolio to the passage of time. Put differently, Theta is an indication of time decay. The total Theta for a portfolio of options can be determined by taking the sum of the Thetas for each individual position.

Rho measures the sensitivity of the value of the derivative or portfolio to the interest rate; more specifically, to a change in the zero-coupon rate of the same maturity. However, changes in interest rate do not create as great risk to position as Delta, Gamma, Vega, and Theta.

Despite their significance, the Greek measurements have some weaknesses: they cannot be aggregated to produce an overall measure of the risk inherent to a specific position or portfolio. Therefore, in order to have a comprehensive measure of risks across the markets, bank supervisors add to their arsenal the value-at-risk technique.

Value-at-Risk

Value-at-risk (VaR) stemmed from a request by JP Morgan's Chairman, Dennis Weatherstone, that a simple report be made available to him every day pursuant to the firm's risk exposure. VaR can be defined as the worst loss that might be expected from holding a security or portfolio over a given period of time, given a specified level of probability, referred to as the confidence level.[230] VaR measures the maximum loss for a given confidence level. VaR was conceived to measure risk over a short period of time and is not a reliable measure for the long run. Therefore, each business day a bank should calculate a comprehensive VaR, including market risk. Most banks use historical simulation, based on a one-day time horizon. The simulation is based on available data from the previous 12 months. A bank's VaR exposure varies over the fiscal year due to positions change, market volatility, and portfolio diversification. Put differently, the VaR of the position or portfolio is simply the maximum loss at this 99% confidence level, measured relative to the expected value of the portfolio at the target horizon.[231]

VaR is the most used measure of market risk for individual assets and portfolios despite its imperfections: its measurement of sensitivities cannot be added up across risk types, nor across markets. Despite this, it has been endorsed by several financial institutions: the Bank of International Settlement, the US Federal Reserve, the International Swaps and Derivatives Association, and the US Securities and Exchange Commission. However, there is no standard method to compute VaR. Several accepted methods have emerged: variance-covariance; historical simulation; and the Monte Carlo simulation method.

Conditional Value-at-Risk

Conditional value-at-risk (CVaR) can be defined as the expected loss exceeding VaR. CVaR measures the maximum expected loss from holding a security or portfolio, considering only the cases in which the loss is greater than the VaR. Conditional VaR was developed as a coherent measure of expected loss given that actual loss exceeds some VaR threshold. CVaR is in many respects superior to VaR.

Stressed Value-at-Risk

In the midst of the 2007–2009 financial meltdown, the Basel Committee on Banking Supervision published an update (in December 2010) to the VaR model, referred to as stressed value-at-risk. The purpose of stressed VaR is to deliver the charge that the banks' current VaR model would generate if the bank was experiencing a period of financial stress relevant to its portfolio. The stressed VaR applies to all risks for which the bank in question has approval from its supervisor to use an internal VaR model. For the sake of efficiency, the Committee recommends that the period covered for the stressed VaR test be constantly reviewed by the supervisor.[232]

Stress Test

Stress testing is an important risk management tool in the sense that it is used by financial institutions as part of their internal risk management. Stress testing refers to a range of techniques used to assess the vulnerability of a portfolio to major changes in the macroeconomic environment or to exceptional but plausible events. Stress tests are meant to find weak spots in the bank's portfolios at an early stage, and to guide preventive action by bank managers or the officer in charge of risk management.

While VaR reflects the risk of loss due to adverse changes in normal markets, stress testing captures the firm's exposures to unlikely but plausible events in abnormal markets. Thus the two tests are often complementary. That is, often banks use stress testing to test the soundness of the VaR or vice versa. Stress testing is often used as a supplementary risk assessment method to simulate extreme changes in the value of a portfofio beyond the market's normal condition. Stress testing attempts to answer the following question: how would the portfolio or position perform under an extreme market move? Bank managers should routinely conduct stress tests to assess the strength of their positions and portfolios by simulating extreme market and operational risks. The EU Alternative Investment Fund Managers Directive, for instance, requires hedge funds operating within the Eurozone to conduct frequent stress testing in order to assess the strength of the positions in whatever market they operate.

Stress testing combines various "stress categories and shocks" across all possible markets for every business. For the purpose of the test, the manager should use adverse macroeconomic variables such as the GDP, interest rates, unemployment, etc., to test the resilience of his positions in various markets. the macro-economic scenario should be translated into reference risk parameters to be applied. These references include the probabilities of default (PD), the loss given default (LGD), and the haircuts whenever the fund holds position in government bonds.

Generally, managers or institutions (e.g., IMF, World Bank, Federal Reserve, EU Commission)[233] applying stress testing use three different approaches: (a) historical; (b) customized; and (c) reverse testing.

Historical stress testing tests the healthiness of a bank's portfolio by analyzing what would occur to the portfolio if particularly adverse and unexpected movements which occurred in the past hit the portfolio in the near future. Some known examples of historical financial crises include the US Great Depression, the Russian crisis, and the sub-prime crisis. Historical stress testing has several weaknesses: it is quite impossible that the same event occurs under the same or similar circumstances. Therefore, a diligent review is needed when selecting historical events (crises) used as benchmarks. In the United States, for instance, where historical financial crises are differently interpreted by scholars and financial commentators, the choice of an event should be carefully considered in order to avoid any complacency.

Customized stress testing is based upon selecting past and perceived areas of vulnerability in various portfolios, such as shocking correlations, stressing a liquidity squeeze, or creating a scenario which is more likely to impact a portfolio. Customized testing has also weaknesses in that the design is made by the manager or the institution based on their own perception of portfolio risks. To be effective, customized testing needs to be conceived and conducted by a body of independent experts, who understand the global markets and have no conflict of interest with the entities involved.

Reverse stress testing aims to simulate a harsh macroeconomic downturn using factors such as the GDP contraction, a higher unemployment rate, a free-fall in the real estate market and the like. The strength or seriousness of the reverse test depends on the macroeconomic aggregates retained and their correlation with the portfolios tested. In 2009, the US Federal Reserve conducted reverse stress testing upon the 19 largest banks, asking them to project estimated losses on loans, mortgage securities, and other structured products, including off-balance sheet positions. The tests measured bank reserves based on what is known as common equity, the value of a company's common stock and profits. Some of the banks have big enough reserves by traditional measures but fall short by this narrower standard. The test was loose and did not take into account sovereign debt, and failed to address the key issues of over-leveraging practices and transparency. Furthermore, the US test was less complex in the sense that it only included three supervisory authorities and was conducted under one jurisdiction. The test could not lead to a sound understanding of US banks, and was perceived more as a marketing tool to calm down the markets. A year later, in 2010, the EU Commission in concert with the Committee on European Banking Systems conducted a reverse stress test over 91 banks across the European Union, with the involvement of the state supervisory authorities. Moreover, the EU reverse test included sovereign crisis.

The EU test was praised by many bank analysts as being more comprehensive and realistic than the US test. However, with the recent crises in Greece, Ireland, and even Portugal and Spain, the quality of the EU stress test is being questioned. The EU Commission and the CEBS came to realize that they need to improve the design of their stress test in order to prevent the emergence of currently unperceived risks within Irish and Greek tested banks.

The European Banking Authority (EBA), which will soon replace the CEBS, is committed to including additional elements in any future test including, inter alia, the banks' liquidity risk. The need has become urgent since the collapse of Dexia bank and its nationalization by both the French and the Belgian governments. In July 2011, Dexia bank passed the EU stress test. Its core Tier 1 ratio was 10.3%. Despite the perceived strengths of Dexia, the bank was ten times leveraged and held significant government and public sector debts. Dexia was among those EU banks more exposed to the Greek government bonds (approximately €20 billion) and other sovereign bonds (approximately €700 billion). Absolute capital ratios can hide absolute levels of leveraged and/or the amount of borrowed money used to generate profit. The gap between Dexia's capital and equity ratios was particularly wide.

For testing to be more rigorous, national regulators would have to accept to work under the supervision of the Bank of International Settlement to devise an accepted model applicable to all alternative investment vehicles.

20.5   Liquidity Risk

Liquidity is crucial to the ongoing viability of any banking organization, and sound liquidity management can reduce the likelihood of serious problems.[234]

Sound liquidity management would require a bank to have in place a strategy to meet its cash flow obligations. In 2008, the Basel Committee on Banking Supervision published a "Liquidity Risk Management and Supervisory Guide" to raise awareness in bank managers. Many bank managers were not able even to anticipate their need to satisfy contingent obligations, whether contractual or non-contractual. They viewed funding of these obligations as highly unlikely.

Managing liquidity risk requires taking the following elements into consideration:[235]

- establishing an adequate liquidity risk tolerance;

- maintaining an adequate level of liquidity, including a cushion of liquid assets;
- allocating liquidity costs, benefits, and risks to all significant business activities;
- identifying and measuring the full range of liquidity risks, including contingent;
- designing and using design and use of severe stress test scenarios;
- implementing a robust and operational contingency funding plan;
- managing intraday liquidity risk and collateral, and promoting market discipline through public disclosure.

The 2007–2009 financial meltdown revealed how unprepared major banks and financial institutions were in managing their liquidity risks. The lesson learned by the end of 2009 was that liquidity and solvency are two twin principles in the banking and financial industry.

20.5.1   The Concept of Liquidity Management

Managing liquidity risk is somehow challenging to bankers because of the nature of the risk itself, that is, because liquidity is an intangible quality of a firm's financial position. There is no simple formula or ratio to assess a definite measurement of liquidity for any specific banking institution. For a bank, liquidity is – more or less – the capacity to obtain enough cash to meet all contractual (and even non-contractual) obligations at any specific time. In the context of the banking industry, liquidity risk is even more complex, due to the very nature of the business. Holding excess liquidity can mitigate or limit the profit potential as a bank would not be able to invest or seize opportunities in the markets. On the other hand, a shortage of liquidity can lead to bankruptcy proceedings. Liquidity management should never be seen as a separate goal for a bank. Rather, it should stand together with other objectives, such as prudent management of lending, investments, deposits, borrowings, and the like. Anything that generates liquidity – inflow – should be part of the equation in assessing the liquidity risk.

20.5.2   Sources of Bank Liquidity

Prior to discussing a bank's sources of liquidity, let us first define the concept itself. In finance, liquidity refers to the capacity to obtain (enough) cash to meet all contractual obligations, whenever required. Banks with relatively strong liquidity have a strong competitive advantage over illiquid banks. Adding this last feature to the definition, liquidity can better be defined as the possibility and the perceived ability to meet known near-term and projected long-term funding commitments, while supporting selective business expansion in accordance with the bank's strategic plan.[236] A bank's main source of liquidity comes from retail deposits (the cash in the till), unsecured short- and long-term instruments (e.g., Fed funds purchased), certificated deposits, banks notes, secured short-term instruments (i.e., Repo), off-balance sheet sources (e.g., contingent financings, securitization), and other forms of liquidity.

The more a bank is able to generate liquidity from diverse sources, the more solvent it is.

Deposits

Deposits constitute an important source of short-term bank liquidity, with maturity raging from overnight to a few weeks. As well as deposits received from bank customers, banks also collect inter-bank deposits from other banks or financial institutions.

Unsecured Short-term Instruments

Banks can borrow for a short term from other banks with surpluses in their Federal Reserve accounts, and from the Federal Reserve discount. These unsecured short-term instruments are not available every time a bank is in need for a quick liquidity fix. When US banks face funding pressure, such as in 2008, the Federal Reserve discount window becomes an alternative to secured borrowings. In the midst of the financial crisis, Goldman Sachs, for instance, was forced to convert to a commercial bank holding company regulated by the Federal Reserve to avoid being acquired. The move allowed Goldman Sachs to have access to the Federal Reserve discount, which is only available to commercial banks.

Repurchase Agreements

Repurchase agreements (Repo) is an agreement whereby one party (i.e., the bank) sells securities or other assets to a counterparty, and simultaneously commits to repurchasing the same or similar assets from the counterparty, at an agreed future date, at a repurchase price equal to the original sale price plus interest. Put differently, Repo is a secured financing effected through a short-term sale of securities to a cash provider with the commitment to repurchase the same or similar securities at an agreed-upon price in the future. The securities delivered to a cash investor are valued at their current market price plus accrued interest to date. The securities are delivered either to the customer or its agent. Upon termination, the securities are returned to the original seller and the cash investor receives back the original plus the financing interest charged by the cash investor. Under the Repo arrangement, the original owner of the securities remains the owner, therefore any coupon paid during the life of the Repo is deemed for the original owner.

There are two types of Repo: the open and the term. An open Repo refers to a Repo without a predetermined end date. That is, the transaction remains open until the dealer moves to close it. With the open Repo, interest accrues daily all through the life of the Repo and is paid at the actual termination date. To cover against interest rate fluctuations in the interim, the agreed-upon interest rate is tied up to the LIBOR rate and, most of the time, roll-over. A term Repo is quite different in many respects: (a) the fixed period for the execution of the trade is longer than one day; and (b) the lifetime of the trade as well as the quantity of the securities are agreed upon from the start.

Repo was initiated by the Federal Reserve Bank of New York in 1918, and then boosted by the Glass-Steagall Act of 1933 when the US investment banks started to fund their inventory. Since then, it has become the main instrument of open market operations for most central banks around the world, and a source of liquidity. In the 1990s, with the Latin American money crisis, Repo rose as a superior investment tool preferred by US and European commercial and investment banks, and was hedged to extend cash to most of the Latin American banks in dire need of liquidity. The emergence of Repo transactions in the 1990s offered a window of opportunity to many bank managers to move into emerging markets by providing leverage consistent with their markets' needs. Figure 20.2 provides an illustration.

Beside regular Repos, banks often enter into "reverse Repo" financing transactions. A reverse Repo is a short-term purchase of securities from a cash borrower with the commitment to resell the same or similar securities at an agreed-upon price in the future. Hedge fund managers enter into reverse Repos in order to borrow specific securities to cover their short positions without having to liquidate their securities inventory.

Securitization

Securitization – the process of creating securities backed by a pool of illiquid assets (i.e., receivables, credit cards, student loans) – has become an important

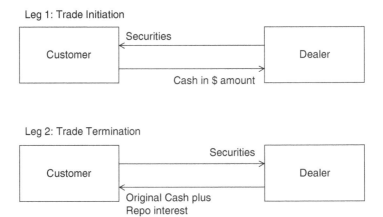

Figure 20.2   Standard Repo.

funding source and a major source of liquidity for many banks. The securitization process allows banks to transfer their illiquid assets into liquid assets sellable in the financial markets. Banks often sell their portfolios of long-term assets, such as mortgages, loans, and corporate bonds into a trust or Special Purpose Vehicle (SPV), generating cash inflows to sustain or meet their liquidity needs.

Derivatives Transactions

Banks enter into some derivative contracts, such a total return swap or options, as means to secure their cash inflows. Put differently, there are two ways a bank can meet its liquidity needs: by holding cash and by having investments that can be converted into cash as soon as it is needed.[237] The assumption is somehow over-generalized, and a bank manager would have to examine the cash equivalent portfolio to identify the assets that can provide true liquidity without any significant loss from the others based upon market realities. In times of market duress, only the highest assets (securities) will be sold without potentially unacceptable losses.

20.5.3 Components of Liquidity Risk

Liquidity risk has three common components: (a) liquidity mismatch; (b) liquidity contingency; and (c) market liquidity.

- Liquidity mismatch risk is based on the mismatch between contractual amounts and dates for inflows and outflows.
- Liquidity contingency risk is the risk that occurs when future events require a materially larger amount of liquidity.
- Market liquidity risk is where there is potential of not being able to offset specific exposures without significant losses.

20.5.4 Approaches to Liquidity Risk Management

Measuring a bank's liquidity is not easy due to the fact that liquidity is fluid. However, several approaches have been proposed or used to assess the liquidity of a bank by looking at its balance sheet components, income statement, and statement of cash flows. In addition, bank managers use haircut and stress tests to back up their assessments. In practice, most banks provide some liquidity ratios in their financial statements as a snapshot of their liquidity strength. Several approaches have been proposed including the financial statement approach, and the cross-transversal approach.

The Financial Statement Approach

The cash flow approach to liquidity relies upon a bank's balance sheet and statement of income. Under the cash flow approach, the bank looks at its cash inflows and outflows to determine its liquidity threshold. The problem with this approach is that cash flows are "point-in-time" estimates of liquidity and do not necessarily reflect the bank's daily liquidity position. The example of Bearn Stearns in 2008 illustrates the difficulty of the cash flow approach. During the week of March 10, 2008, when rumors surfaced that the investment bank would not be able to meet its financial obligations, lenders and counter-parties became reluctant to lend not only unsecured financing but also short-term secured financing. Though Bear Stearns met and exceeded regulatory net capital, capital, and liquidity standards, it did not have access to short-term liquidity. Bear Stearns' appreciation of its liquidity position relied upon its cash flow assessment, but when the investment bank could not borrow quickly from the markets, its $18 billion in liquidity (as of March 10, 2008)[238] declined so badly that it had no choice but to be acquired by JP Morgan Chase.

The Cross-transversal Approach

Broadly, the cross-transversal approach tends to assess a bank's liquidity position through a combination of financial statements, value-at-risk (VaR), and stress tests. The idea is that through various components, bank managers should be able to look at "point-in-time" and daily assessment simultaneously, in order to assess the bank's liquidity position. While the cross-transversal approach provides a better statement of liquidity relative to financial statements alone, the stress test must be based upon relevant criteria for the liquidity position to be accurate. This is far from being the case, as most banks rely heavily upon historical events for their stress test. The efficiency of historical events is often exaggerated and dubious. Professor Nassim Taleb expresses the point as follows:

> The tools we have in quantitative finance do not work in what [I] call the "Black Swan" domain ... People underestimate the impact of infrequent occurrences. Just as it was assumed that all swans were white until the first black species was spotted in Australia during the 17th century, historical analysis is an inadequate way to judge risk.[239]

That said, a cross-transversal approach coupled with (a) liquidity-adjusted value-at-risk (LAVaR), (b) haircut, and (c) stress tests would better assist the bank managers in their management of liquidity risk.

Liquidity-adjusted value-at-risk (LAVaR) is a VaR with an asset-specific sampling horizon and a liquidation period that is synchronized to some exogenously determined trading frequency. Put differently, a LAVaR is a VaR method that takes into account the liquidity characteristics of a portfolio.[240] The LAVaR adds to the conventional VaR either a volatility scaling factor or a time scaling factor. In so doing, the LAVaR divides each portfolio into various sub-portfolios that reflect their liquidity features, and the time horizon assigned to each sub-portfolio.

Haircuts A haircut is a value discount of a portfolio based upon the value and nature of an asset. Haircuts are mostly based on the quality and type of asset and tend to provide the degree to which an asset can be sold or pledged in a relatively short time period in order to raise liquidity. Haircuts are used in relation to financial assets that are marked-to-market. The greater the volatility of an asset, the greater its haircut.[241] Although haircuts are a good supplement to the cross-transversal approach in liquidity management, their use has some limitations. When the asset involved is unique (i.e., derivative contracts), the determination of the appropriate haircut becomes arbitrary, if not impossible to determine with precision.

Stress tests Banks are required to conduct stress tests that identify events that could impact or affect their liquidity positions. The stress test must be broad and comprehensive enough (quantitative and qualitative) to encompass all relevant events that have an impact on the liquidity risk.

20.5.5   Measurement of Liquidity: Ratios

Measuring liquidity positions from one bank to another is as difficult as assessing it in the first place. In practice, most banks provide some liquidity ratios in their financial statements as a snapshot of their liquidity strength. Though financial ratios provide useful information about a bank's financial position, they also have limitations that require sound judgment on behalf of those who analyze the financial statements. That is even more obvious within the banking industry where banks have stretched their business segments to include insurance and real estate. The diversification and over-extension within the industry make it more difficult to construct a meaningful set of industry averages. Furthermore, even assuming that the average ratios one would like to use derive from similar banks, the accounting practices can distort industry comparisons. Creative accounting poses a problem to financial experts and misleads them in their efforts to track the earnings reported by the bank's management. Despite these limitations, liquidity financial ratios give a quick snapshot of a bank, and can be used as a starting point to look at a banking institution's liquidity position. The current and most-used liquidity ratios are: (a) borrowing ratios; (b) loan deposit ratios; (c) cash liquidity ratios; and (d) capital ratios.

Borrowing ratios As opposed to manufacturing companies, a bank's liquidity ratios are different due to the very nature of its business. Trying to provide and understand a bank's liquidity through the working capital ratio, the current ratio (or the quick ratio), liquidity coverage ratio, or operating cash flow coverage ratio would be misleading. However, certain specific ratios, such as the borrowing ratio, could shed some light on a bank's liquidity position. Borrowing ratios measure a bank's need to use volatile borrowings to support business, and the degree to which cash and equivalents can be used to repay "hot money". Borrowing ratios derive from:

- = Total deposits/Borrowed funds;
- = Volatile funds/Liquidity assets; or
- = (Volatile funds, current assets)/Total assets

Loan deposit ratios This ratio measures the degree to which a bank can support its core lending business through deposits. The loan deposit ratio is determined by dividing the total loans by the total deposits.

Cash balances This ratio measures or indicates the number of days that a bank can pay its debts, as they become due, out of current cash.

Capital ratios Capital ratio measures the amount of a bank's capital expressed as a percentage of its risk-weighted credit exposures. Two types of capital ratio are often measured: (a) Tier 1 and (b) Tier 2. Tier 1 capital ratio provides the extent to which a bank can absorb losses without ceasing trading, and Tier 2 measures the extent to which a bank can absorb losses in the event of a winding-up.

20.6   Credit Risk

Remember, banks are in the business of collecting deposits from their customers on the one hand, and extending loans to other customers on the other. The assessment of credit risk is the essence of the banking business. Therefore, banks should put in place a prudent policy and process to identify, assess, measure, mitigate, and monitor their credit risks.[242] The banking industry has developed various methods in order to mastermind their credit processing and ensure their profit. Remember, for big borrowers such as governments and large corporations, the Basel II approach might be sufficient. But as retail banks compete with each other to grab business from individuals and SMEs, the credit risk analysis discussed in this chapter is devoted to examining credit risk processing in the granting of loans to individuals and SMEs.

20.6.1   Credit Risk Processing

The analysis of a customer's credit by a lending bank (or an underwriting bank in the case of new issuance) relies upon a set of features commonly known as the "five Cs". The bank would conduct a study to understand the customer's character, capacity, collateral, conditions, and capital. Of all the "five Cs", capacity is the most important as it refers to the applicant's ability to pay back pursuant to the terms and conditions of the loan. The remaining "four Cs" are also crucial in conducting credit analysis. Whether the application is for an individual's consumption, a mortgage, or a small business, the analysis of the credit follows almost the same path. Small business loans are somewhat complex as the bank has to rely upon a cash flow projection that might not actually be close to the reality of the situation.

Capacity

The assessment of an applicant's capacity by a bank is to some extent a subjective analysis concerning the applicant's ability to repay both the principal and the interest of the loan. The bank would consider the cash flow of the individual or the projected business, as well as the likelihood that the applicant can meet its obligations. Whether the bank is dealing with an individual (i.e., mortgage loan) or a small business, the credit history of the applicant is key. The lending bank has to look at not only the applicant's credit history, but must also check some indicators of future payment performance. Contingent sources of payment will also be considered as the lender is trying to draw a consistent picture of the credit application.

Character

Character refers to the trustworthiness of the applicant to live up to its commitment. At this juncture, the lending bank must assess the ability of the applicant to generate funds from the projected investment or project. To that end, the bank would consider the applicant's background, education, business savvy, knowledge of the industry in which the projected business fits, the quality of the references (if any), and other factors depending on the specificities of the business or project.

Collateral

Collateral, or guarantee, refers to the assets (whether tangible or intangible) that the applicant offers as security to the lending bank. Generally, a lending bank will request the applicant to pledge as collateral an asset upon which he has an ownership right. That is somewhat different from a guarantee that can be provided by a third party (i.e., parents, siblings, friends). If the borrower defaults on the loan, the lending bank has a legal right to look to the pledged asset in order to recoup its loan. The value of the collateral depends upon the size or amount of the credit sought. The higher the risk perceived by the lending bank, the more collateral would be required. Small business applicants often provide guarantees from the Small Business Administration or other institutions. Individual mortgage borrowers used to go after Government Sponsored Enterprises, such as Fannie Mae, Freddie, or the Veteran Affairs for guarantees, under specific requirements.

Capital

Capital refers to the amount the applicant is willing to put up, whether as a down payment (for a mortgage loan) or an equity capital in the business.

Sufficient capitalization is always seen as evidence of the applicant's confidence in the project, whereas thin-capitalization shows the reverse. The higher the undertaking starting capital, the more the lending bank feels confident to partner in the investment. The lending bank often looks after the applicant's financial statements: balance sheet, income statement, and the cash flow statement. For an existing business, some ratios[243] would provide a glance as to the health and the wealth of the undertaking. For a new business, the projected financial statements should be more detailed and contain specific information.

Conditions

Conditions refer to the purpose of the loan, the overall economy, and specific trends within the industry or sector of activities. For a pre-existing business, conditions could include the existence of prior loans, their size, purposes, etc. For a new undertaking, conditions would include the perceived market, the competition, and any related links.

20.6.2   Credit Risk Management

Credit risk is to many commercial banks a daily game. Banks are competing each other to extend credit to borrowers and derive spreads. To win the game, banks must mastermind the credit factors for each borrower by going beyond the zone of credit safety. Banks manage their credit risk through (a) diversification of the loans, and (b) obtaining collateral assets from the borrowers.

Diversification of the Loans

By spreading the credit risk over loan categories, a bank puts itself in a better position to mitigate or reduce its aggregate risks.[244] However, diversification will not eliminate all credit risk as certain risks are inherent to the business' systemic risk. In assessing credit risk pursuant to a portfolio, the bank manager should consider and analyze factors such as the aggregate level of economic activity, inflation, level of interest rates, the vacancy rate for commercial real estate, the market value of the most important types of collateral used, etc.[245] According to Dennis G. Uyemura, the primary responsibilities of a bank manager can be summarized as five principal duties:

- to ensure that the performance of the bank's loan portfolio depends on a balance of independent risk variables;
- to ensure that the portfolio is very highly diversified in four areas: geographical concentration, industrial diversification, maturity, and acceptable types of collateral;
- to ensure that no loans are added to the portfolio unless the risk-adjusted loan is higher;

- to evaluate all lending opportunities with pricing over the risk-adjusted loan rates;
- to adjust the price in accordance with market changes.

Collateral

Depending on the features of the loan extended and the perceived risks, banks often will require that borrowers provide collateral asset that the bank can go after in the event of default. When a borrower applies for a loan, he has to provide a business plan that contains and provides relevant information pursuant to the use of the capital. The projected financial statements, particularly the statement of cash flows, will detail the reimbursement process. Even when the projected cash flows are sufficient, banks can still demand that the borrowers provide a guarantee that backs up the loan.

21
Conclusion

At the end of this broad "tour d'horizon" of the international banking system and its core operations, it is clear the industry landscape is under pressure to change. The change is being driven by consumers seeking – sui generis – services that traditional banks are not used to providing since the last boom after World War Two. The infrastructure of our banking system today has become obsolete. With all these changes come also new opportunities. However, these new opportunities would only benefit banks eager to adapt and to accommodate their business with clients' expectations. That is, the stream of mergers and acquisitions within the industry will increase within the next decade or so. Banks too big to manage would go under or be acquired by more prudent and accommodating banks with new management teams. JP Morgan Chase, Bank of America, and Goldman Sachs are all expected to expand their business lines. Wealth management and private equity are among the business segments to observe in the next two decades. The industry's prospects are bright; however, excessive greed and amateur risk management could jeopardize the future. As with central banks, private banks need to bring in more economists given that economists are more likely to comprehend risk management relative to their counterpart lawyers. Better management of risk is key to success and private banks need to face and live with that reality.

Appendices

Appendix 1: Four Federal Reserve Tabs: (a) Changes in balance sheet items, all U.S. banks, 1999–2008; (b) Changes in notional value and fair value of derivatives, all U.S. banks, 2003–2008; (c) Exposure of U.S. banks to selected economies at year end relative to Tier 1 capital; (iv) Report of income, all U.S. banks, 1999–2008

Appendix 2: Open Letter from the Monetary Policy Committee to the Chancellor of the Exchequer, UK Government

Appendix 3: Credit rating and their interpretations

Appendix 4: Sample of Letter of Comfort

Appendix 5: Sample of Bank Capability Letter (BCL)

Appendix 6: Sample of Engagement Letter

Appendix 7: Sample of a Binding Letter of Intent

Appendix 8: Sample of Merger Agreement

Appendix 9: Sample of Due Diligence

Appendix 10: Sample of Term Sheet

Appendix 11: Sample of Capital Call Notice

Appendix 12: Sample of Certificate of Ownership

Appendix 13: Form 41-103 F1-Securitized Products Prospectus

Appendix 14: Financial Ratios

Appendix 15: Sample Business Plan Outline

Appendix 16: Selected IRC Sections

Appendix 17: NYSE (Corporate Governance)

Appendix 1: Four Federal Reserve Tabs

Table A1 Changes in balance sheet items, all US banks, 1999–2008.

Item	1999	2000	2001	2002	2003	2004	2005	2006	2007	2008	MEMO Dec. 2008 (billions of dollars)
Assets											
Interest earning assets	5.44	8.76	5.11	7.19	7.18	10.78	7.73	12.36	10.81	10.24	12,212
Loans and leases (net)	5.87	8.66	3.96	7.53	7.27	11.29	7.97	12.45	10.11	8.59	10,389
	8.1	9.24	1.82	5.9	6.51	11.21	10.39	11.97	10.57	2.23	6,617
Commercial and industrial	7.88	8.54	−6.73	−7.41	−4.56	4.35	12.53	11.81	20.27	3.49	1,408
Real estate	12.22	10.74	7.94	14.44	9.75	15.41	13.8	14.94	7.04	4.49	3,797
Booked in domestic offices	12.36	11.02	8.02	14.85	9.66	15.09	13.93	15.05	6.77	4.76	3,735
One in four family residential	9.7	9.28	3.7	19.86	10	15.75	11.95	15.11	5.53	3.08	2,056
Other real estate	16.06	13.31	10.95	8.81	9.19	14.2	16.61	14.96	8.39	6.89	1,678
Booked in foreign offices	6.28	−1.62	3.97	−7.41	15.7	35.59	7.19	8.79	22.76	−9.31	63
Consumers	−1.48	8.04	4.16	6.55	9.31	10.16	2.3	6.19	11.67	4.22	9,888
Other loans and leases	7.17	7.01	−2.02	−0.03	8.31	3.57	−0.18	3.17	13.01	−6.26	581
Loan loss reserves and other income	2.37	7.98	13.15	5.73	−2.68	−4.19	−5.75	1.63	27.97	75	158
Securities	5.11	6.36	7.22	16.2	9.44	10.58	2.4	11.53	4.54	0.6	2,208
Investment account	6.68	2.85	8.88	13.53	8.7	6.15	1.19	6.94	−4.42	10.08	1,719
U.S Treasury	−1.89	−32.72	−40.27	41.92	14.1	−15.87	−17.6	−19.3	−26.9	7.96	32
U.S government agency and corporation obligation	1.83	3.75	12.84	18.09	9.68	9.46	−1.83	4.71	−12.2	14.81	1,025
Other	20.9	13.39	12.18	2.72	5.98	3.02	10.12	13.78	10.75	3.57	662
Trading account	−6.93	37.16	−3.72	36.12	14	36.81	7.96	31.32	35.98	−22.78	489
Other	−8.37	10.3	13.09	−2.93	6.76	14.25	5.81	19.31	22.35	73.68	1,565
Non-interest earning assets	2.64	9.45	12.74	5.11	6.64	7.61	6.19	11.79	15.42	20.75	1,823

Liabilities	5.58	8.59	4.45	7.13	7.24	9.56	7.74	12.1	10.79	11.28	11,063
Core deposits	0.23	7.53	10.55	7.58	7.29	8.25	6.4	5.84	5.49	14.47	5,405
Transaction deposits	-8.97	-1.31	10.2	-5.12	2.82	3.2	-1.18	-4.28	-1.22	20.51	838
Savings deposits (including MMI)	6.68	12.51	20.68	18.46	13.7	11.72	6.93	5.53	3.34	10.03	3,295
Small time deposits	-0.76	7.2	-7.23	-4.92	-6.79	1.58	12.88	16.97	18.03	23.29	1,272
Managed liabilities	15.72	8.79	-2.73	5.34	6.96	12.06	12.24	19.45	16.57	6.49	4,845
Large time deposites	14.19	**19.37**	-3.65	5.05	1.42	**21.86**	**22.88**	15.94	1.9	4.75	1,072
Deposits booked in foreign offices	14.6	7.84	-10.96	4.49	12.6	16.84	6.32	29.67	25.86	2.46	1,539
Subcoordinated notes and debentures	**5.07**	13.98	9.56	-0.59	5.08	10.49	11.41	22.6	16.83	4.6	182
Gross federal funds purchased and RPs	1.56	6.49	5.72	12.75	-8.7	8.4	15.62	9.47	7.06	5.76	786
Other managed liabilities	35.27	1.8	-0.28	0.97	22	1.37	6.15	18.89	28.44	14.38	1,265
Revaluation losses held in trading accounts	-13.2	7.47	-17.06	33.44	14	-12.61	-17.9	6.39	42.66	88.6	388
Other	-1.26	14.9	14.9	5.23	5.28	17.19	-1.6	22.33	3.21	-8.45	425
Capital account	3.89	10.65	12.29	**7.54**	6.61	23.14	7.59	14.69	10.94	1.15	1,149
MEMO											
Commercial real estate loans	15.42	12.16	13.1	6.82	8.99	**13.93**	16.87	14.91	9.2	6.77	1,634
Mortgage-backed securities	-3.34	3.29	29.05	15.54	10.1	13.45	2.06	10.22	-1.24	11.37	1,069
Federal Home Loan Bank advances	na	na	na	17.21	3.71	3.73	10	29.8	30.62	15.6	526

Source: Federal Reserve Bulletin, May 2010, p.4.

Table A2 Changes in notional value and fair value of derivatives, all US banks, 2003–2008.

Item	2003	2004	2005	2006	2007	2008	MEMO Dec. 2008 (billions of dollars)
Total derivatives							
Notional amount	26.54	23.69	15.38	29.75	25.68	21.06	201,070
Fair value							
Positive	0.36	13.71	−6.46	−4.5	68.18	250.2	7,100
Negative	1	13.75	−5.78	−4.27	65.77	249.27	6,908
Interest rate derivatives							
Notional amount	27.62	22.07	11.92	27.11	20.54	26.98	164,397
Fair value							
Positive	−5.95	13.14	−5.52	−14.55	56.19	290.51	5,120
Negative	−5.07	12.94	−5.15	−15.06	58.19	286.47	4,989
Exchange rate derivatives							
Notional amount	18.81	21.03	7.69	29.27	36.69	2.03	17,523
Fair value							
Positive	41.81	14.86	−35.84	22.86	43.59	149.12	645
Negative	38.81	12.74	−37.36	21.39	43.4	163.8	661
Credit derivatives							
Notional amount	55.98	134.52	148	54.93	75.87	0.21	15,897
Guarantor	61.82	139.07	137.87	67.69	73.94	−0.12	7,811
Beneficiary	51.13	130.46	157.53	44.03	77.79	0.54	8,086
Fair value							
Guarantor	68.31	69.92	81.43	92.96	295.25	281.97	1,048
Positive	378.09	74.56	−5.62	201.4	−38.79	41.97	44
Negative	−68.87	38.37	827.98	−1.59	1187.41	312.45	1,004
Beneficiary	19.85	51.28	83.5	90.26	301.2	260.81	1,126
Positive	−63.13	2.64	505.51	3.98	1086.95	303.42	1,078
Negative	295.74	66.36	2.79	187.44	−18.95	6.54	48
Other derivatives							
Notional amount	3.77	32.66	29.43	75.17	13.44	−9.31	3,254
Fair value							
Positive	3.16	8.55	58.51	18.99	41.22	33.7	213
Negative	−5.25	19.73	74.29	24.15	15.66	39.27	206

Source: Federal Reserve Bulletin, May 2010, p.16.

Table A3 Exposure of US banks to selected economies at year end relative to Tier 1 capital.

Year	Asia				Latin America and Caribbean			Eastern Europe	G10 and Switzerland	Non G10 Developed Countries	Total
	All	China	India	Korea	All	Mexico	Brazil				
1997	n.a	n.a	n.a	n.a	n.a	n.a	n.a	n.a	n.a	n.a	n.a
1998	28.20	1.00	2.20	7.10	42.90	9.90	11.30	3.50	182.50	37.10	294.30
1999	26.10	0.80	2.40	6.60	39.00	9.50	10.50	2.90	164.20	32.50	**264.60**
2000	24.00	0.80	2.60	6.40	37.90	9.10	11.20	4.40	174.60	32.80	273.70
2001	22.40	0.90	2.50	5.80	54.10	26.00	13.00	4.30	164.80	28.40	274.00
2002	21.90	0.90	2.70	5.80	38.90	20.80	8.40	5.50	172.10	29.80	259.80
2003	22.80	1.30	3.90	**5.50**	32.80	18.00	6.80	5.40	182.00	35.00	278.10
2004	32.20	1.40	4.20	15.00	31.80	16.60	6.50	6.10	198.20	37.20	**305.40**
2005	30.70	2.40	4.90	12.90	31.80	17.40	6.90	5.90	165.20	31.60	265.30
2006	34.70	4.10	6.10	13.60	30.80	16.80	5.70	6.50	174.70	38.50	285.10
2007	44.60	4.50	9.80	14.40	35.60	17.20	8.20	9.00	219.30	48.30	356.60
2008	30.80	3.40	6.10	10.70	25.50	12.90	5.00	5.40	166.30	35.30	263.30
MEMO Total exposure (billions of dollars)											
1997	87.10	3.50	5.10	25.30	101.70	18.80	33.40	11.90	354.90	88.70	644.30
1998	69.10	2.30	5.40	17.30	105.00	24.10	27.60	8.50	446.30	90.80	719.60
1999	67.90	2.00	6.20	17.20	101.60	24.80	27.30	7.40	427.80	84.70	689.50
2000	68.00	2.20	7.50	18.10	107.30	25.70	31.60	12.30	494.60	93.00	775.30
2001	67.20	2.70	7.70	17.50	162.40	78.00	39.00	12.90	495.10	85.40	823.00
2002	69.50	2.70	8.70	18.40	123.50	66.20	26.60	17.50	546.50	94.70	824.70
2003	79.90	4.40	13.60	19.20	115.20	63.00	23.70	19.10	638.50	122.70	975.40
2004	125.80	5.30	16.30	58.70	124.40	65.20	25.50	23.80	775.70	145.50	1,195.40
2005	134.80	10.40	21.60	56.70	139.70	76.10	30.40	25.70	**724.80**	138.60	1,163.50
2006	190.50	22.70	33.60	74.80	168.90	92.50	31.50	35.50	959.10	211.20	1,565.20
2007	249.80	25.50	54.90	80.80	199.30	96.10	46.20	50.20	1,229.00	270.50	1,998.80
2008	217.40	24.30	43.10	75.30	179.70	90.70	35.60	37.90	1,172.90	248.60	1,856.50

Source: Federal Reserve Bulletin, May 2010, p. 26.

Table A4 Report of income, all US banks, 1999–2008.

Millions of Dollars	1999	2000	2001	2002	2003	2004	2005	2006	2007	2008
Gross interest income	367,123	423,345	404,251	349,603	329,218	348,667	426,000	551,059	616,995	566,000
Taxable equivalent	369,758	426,479	406,937	332,131	332,000	351,651	429,556	554,295	620,456	568,685
Loans	279,217	326,804	311,539	269,397	257,697	269,408	328,088	421,879	464,879	426,181
Securities	62,415	67,666	63,061	59,311	53,316	58,577	65,864	78,913	82,710	81,548
Gross federal funds sold and reverse repurchase agreements	12,337	13,546	12,647	6,221	5,015	5,142	11,045	21,288	28,682	16,853
Other	13,157	15,829	17,006	14,672	13,189	15,538	61,602	28,959	40,723	41,418
Gross interest expense	175,397	222,161	188,746	118,741	94,123	98,541	162,501	263,372	310,412	227,066
Deposits	119,969	151,147	132,311	81,701	62,400	63,639	105,922	173,878	212,783	154,812
Gross federal funds purchased and reverse repurchase agreements	21,210	26,860	19,583	9,920	7,590	8,842	19,161	33,775	37,715	19,755
Other	34,215	44,155	36,852	27,122	24,133	26,058	37,418	55,720	59,914	52,499
Net interest income	191,726	201,684	215,505	230,862	235,095	250,126	264,099	287,667	306,583	338,934
Taxable equivalent	194,361	204,318	218,191	233,610	237,877	253,110	267,055	290,923	310,044	341,619
Loss provisions	21,220	29,386	43,084	45,206	32,742	23,894	25,579	25,386	56,746	170,019
Non-interest income	144,800	153,101	160,902	168,236	183,792	188,999	201,768	222,887	218,554	207,880
Service charges on deposits	21,591	23,720	26,872	29,629	31,692	33,454	33,830	36,194	39,187	42,540
Fiduciary activities	20,519	22,202	21,988	21,404	22,453	25,088	26,381	28,312	32,962	32,907
Trading revenue	10,437	12,235	12,382	10,794	11,605	10,308	14,375	19,170	5,289	(2,336)
Other	92,256	94,945	99,638	105,410	118,042	120,154	127,180	139,213	141,115	134,767

Non-interest expense	205,207	216,375	225,979	230,128	243,214	263,304	274,136	294,890	321,406	355,910
Salaries, wages and employee benefits	86,396	89,016	94,196	100,447	108,446	115,254	124,038	135,868	144,700	147,595
Occupancy	25,945	26,762	27,939	29,311	31,314	33,253	35,051	36,393	38,531	40,909
Other	92,867	100,598	103,844	100,368	103,453	114,797	115,048	122,629	138,177	167,406
Net non-interest expense	60,407	63,274	65,077	61,892	59,422	74,305	72,368	72,003	102,852	148,030
Gains on investment account securities	246	(2,280)	4,630	6,411	5,633	3,393	(220)	(1,320)	(649)	(16,186)
Income before taxes	110,345	106,741	111,971	130,176	148,563	155,322	165,933	188,960	146,335	4,698
Taxes	39,315	37,249	37,284	42,816	48,498	50,264	53,368	60,956	44,230	2,199
Extraordinary items, net of income taxes	169	(31)	(324)	(68)	427	59	241	2,647	(1,672)	5,388
Net income	71,199	69,461	74,363	87,291	100,494	105,115	112,604	130,652	100,433	7,887
Cash dividend declared	52,280	52,547	54,844	67,230	77,757	59,523	64,624	82,310	85,265	43,253
Retained income	18,919	16,913	19,519	20,062	22,738	45,591	47,981	48,340	15,168	(35,367)

Source: Federal Reserve Bulletin, May 2010, p.37.

Appendix 2: Open Letter from the Monetary Policy Committee to the Chancellor of the Exchequer, UK Government

13 February 2012

BANK OF ENGLAND
LONDON EC2R 8AH

The Rt Hon George Osborne
Chancellor of the Exchequer
HM Treasury
1 Horse Guards Road
London SW1A2HQ

The Office for National Statistics (ONS) will publish data tomorrow showing that CPI inflation was 3.6% in January. In November, I wrote an open letter to you because CPI inflation had remained more than one percentage point above the 2% target. As it is three months since I last wrote to you, and the rate of inflation is more than one percentage point above the target, I am writing a further open letter on behalf of the Monetary Policy Committee.

In accordance with our remit, this letter explains why inflation has moved away from the target, the period within which we expect inflation to return to the target, the policy action that the Committee is taking to deal with it, and how this approach meets the Government's monetary policy objectives. Following our usual procedure, the Bank of England will publish this open letter at 10.30am tomorrow. The Committee's latest judgments on the outlook for output and inflation will be published in the February *Inflation Report* on Wednesday 15 February.

Why has inflation moved away from the target?

CPI inflation has been above the 2% target since the end of 2009, prompting a series of open letters. As described in those previous letters, and in the Bank's quarterly *Inflation Reports,* inflation was pushed up over that period by increases in VAT, import prices and energy prices that were largely unexpected. In contrast, domestically generated inflation has been subdued.

The effect of the factors that temporarily pushed up inflation is now waning. CPI inflation peaked in September 2011 at 5.2% and has fallen back in each month since then, to 3.6% in January. As expected, the sharp decline in the latest CPI figure largely reflected the impact of the increase in VAT in January 2011 dropping out of the twelve-month comparison. Since September, the contributions of petrol and food prices have also fallen back. Nevertheless CPI inflation remains well above the 2% target.

Over what period does the MPC expect inflation to return to target?

The Committee's best collective judgment is that CPI inflation will continue to fall back to around the target by the end of 2012. In coming months, that further moderation is likely to reflect the declining contributions from petrol prices and any remaining VAT impact, together with recently announced cuts to domestic energy prices. The upward pressure from past rises in energy and import prices should dissipate further over 2012, and the margin of spare capacity that has built up in the economy is likely to continue to bear down on wages and prices beyond that. But the pace and extent of the fall in inflation remain highly uncertain. Key factors include the degree to which slack in the labor market restrains wages, and the rate at which firms rebuild their profit margins. Any further external price shocks, precipitated for example by heightened tensions in oil exporting countries, could also have a material impact on the inflation outlook. The MPC's February *Inflation Report* will set out the Committee's latest projections in more detail.

What policy action are we taking?

Monetary policy affects inflation only with a lag. The key consideration when setting monetary policy is, therefore, the medium-term outlook for inflation, and the balance of risks around it, rather than its current rate. With external price pressures diminishing, and the underlying weakness in domestically generated inflation likely to persist, the Committee's assessment of the inflation outlook at its February meeting was that, in the absence of further policy action, the balance of risks around the inflation target in the medium term lay to the downside. That is why we judged that it was appropriate to increase the size of the asset purchase programme, financed by the issuance of central bank reserves, by £50 billion to a total of £325 billion, while maintaining Bank Rate at 0.5%. Although the Committee expects that programme of asset purchases to take three months to complete, we will re-evaluate the outlook for inflation and our policy stance every month. In the coming months, we will pay particular attention to prospects for the euro area and their implications for the banking system and credit conditions; the degree of spare capacity in the economy and its impact on domestically generated inflation; and measures of inflation expectations and their effect on pay and prices. The MPC stands ready to react as necessary to changes in the balance of risks to the inflation outlook.

How does this approach meet the Government's monetary policy objectives?

The unwelcome combination of sluggish growth and high inflation over the past two years is a reflection of the need for the economy to rebalance following the financial crisis and associated deep recession, together with rises in the costs of energy and imports. Although inflation is now falling broadly as expected, the process of rebalancing still has a long way to go. Growth remains weak and unemployment is high. While the MPC can use Bank Rate or asset purchases to help ease the transition, there is a limit to what monetary policy can achieve when real adjustments are required. The best contribution that monetary policy can make to high and stable levels of growth and employment is to respond flexibly and transparently to bring inflation back to target. The Committee remains determined to set policy to ensure that inflation is on track to meet the target in the medium term.

I am copying this letter to the Chairman of the Treasury Committee, through which we are accountable to Parliament, and will place this letter on the Bank of England's website for public dissemination.

....

(Signature)

Appendix 3: Credit Ratings and their Interpretations

Credit ratings and their interpretations

Grades	Description	Fitch and S&P		Moody's		Explanation
Investment grade	Highest credit quality/lowest risk	AAA		Aaa		Exceptionally strong capacity for the timely payment of financial commitments, which is highly unlikely to be adversely affected by foreseeable events
	Very high credit quality/low risk	AA	AA+ AA AA−	Aa	Aa1 Aa2 Aa3	Very strong capacity for timely payment of financial commitments, which is not significantly vulnerable to changes in circumstances/economic conditions
	High credit quality/low risk	A	A+ A A−	A	A1 A2 A3	Strong capacity for timely payment of financial commitments, which may be more vulnerable to changes in circumstances/economic conditions
	Good credit quality/medium risk	BBB	BBB+ BBB BBB−	Baa	Baa1 Baa2 Baa3	Adequate capacity for timely payment of financial commitments but adverse changes in circumstances/economic conditions are more likely to impair this capacity
Speculative grade	Speculative/high risk	BB	BB+ BB BB−	Ba	Ba1 Ba2 Ba3	Possibility of credit risk developing, particularly due to adverse economic change over time. Business/financial alternatives may be available to allow financial commitments to be met
	Highly speculative/high risk	B	B+ B B−	B	B1 B2 B3	Significant credit risk with a limited margin of safety. Financial commitments are currently being met, however, continued payments are contingent upon a sustained, favorable business or economic development
	High default risk/higher risk	CCC		Caa		Default is a real possibility. Capacity for meeting financial commitments is solely reliant upon sustained, favorable business or economic development

(continued)

Appendix 3 Continued

Grades	Description	Fitch and S&P	Moody's	Explanation
	Probable default/ very high risk	CC	Ca	Default of some kind appears probable and the issue is vulnerable to worsening in the issuer's conditions
	Likely default/ highest risk	C	C	Default imminent and highly vulnerable to any worsening in the issuer's conditions.
Default	Default	D		Defaulted issue. Payment of interest and repayment of principal have not been made on the due date, and it is highly uncertain that such payment will be made, or the issuer enters in bankruptcy, reorganization, or a similar procedure

Source: Felix Lessambo.

Appendix 4: Sample of Letter of Comfort

[Name of Underwriters]
[Address of Underwriters]

Dear Sirs

We have audited the consolidated balance sheets of ABC IPO Company and subsidiaries (the "Company") as of December 31, 2009 and 2008, and the consolidated statements of income, retained earnings, (stockholders' equity), and cash flows for each of the three years in the period ended December 31, 2009 (the "consolidated financial statements"), and the related financial statement schedules, all of which are included in the registration statement (no. 333-[12345]) on Form S-1 filed by the Company under the Securities Act of 1933, as amended (the "Act"); our reports with respect thereto is included in that registration statement. The registration statement, as amended on June 2, 2010, is herein referred to together as the "Registration Statement."

In connection with the Registration Statement—

1. We are independent certified public accountants with respect to the company within the meaning of the Act and the applicable published rules and regulations thereunder adopted by the Securities and Exchange Commission (the "SEC") and as required by the Public Company Accounting Oversight Board (United States) (the "PCAOB").
2. In our opinion, the consolidated financial statements and financial statement schedules audited by us and included in the Registration Statement comply as to form in all material respects with the applicable accounting requirements of the Act and the related published rules and regulations adopted by the SEC.
3. We have not audited any financial statements of the Company as of any date or for any period subsequent to December 31, 2009; although we have conducted an audit for the year ended December 31, 2009, the purpose (and therefore the scope) of the audit was to enable us to express our opinion on the financial statements as of December 31, 2009, and for the year then ended, but not on the financial statements for any interim period within that year. Therefore, we are unable to and do not express any opinion on the unaudited condensed consolidated balance sheet as of March 31, 2010, and the unaudited condensed consolidated statements of income, retained earnings (stockholders' equity), and cash flows for the three-month periods ended March 31, 2010 and 2009, included in the Registration Statement, or on the financial position, results of operations, or cash flows as of any date or for any period subsequent to December 31, 2009.
4. For the purposes of this letter we have read the 2009 and 2010 minutes of the meetings of the stockholders, the board of directors, and audit committee of the Company and its subsidiaries as set forth in the minutes books as of June 2, 2010, officials of the Company having advised us that the minutes of all such meetings through that date were set forth therein; we have carried out other procedures to June 4, 2010, as

follows (our work did not extend to the period from June 4, 2010, to June 5, 2010, inclusive):

a. With respect to the three-month periods ended March 31, 2010 and 2009, we have—
   (i) Performed the procedures specified by the PCAOB applicable to reviews of interim financial information, on the unaudited condensed consolidated balance sheet as of March 31, 2010, and unaudited condensed consolidated statements of income, retained earnings (stockholders' equity), and cash flows for the three-month periods ended March 31, 2010 and 2009, included in the Registration Statement.
   (ii) Inquired of certain officials of the Company who have responsibility for financial and accounting matters whether the unaudited condensed consolidated financial statements referred to in a.(i) comply as to form in all material respects with the applicable accounting requirements of the Act and the related published rules and regulations adopted by the SEC.
b. With respect to the period from April 1, 2010 to May 31, 2010, we have:
   (i) Read the unaudited consolidated financial statements of the Company and subsidiaries for April and May of both 2010 and 2009 furnished us by the company, officials of the company having advised us that no such financial statements as of any date or for any period subsequent to May 31, 2010, were available.
   (ii) Inquired of certain officials of the Company who have responsibility for financial and accounting matters as to whether the unaudited consolidated financial statements referred to in b.(i) are stated on a basis substantially consistent with that of the audited consolidated financial statements included in the Registration Statement.

The foregoing procedures do not constitute an audit conducted in accordance with generally accepted auditing standards. Also, they would not necessarily reveal matters of significance with respect to the comments in the following paragraph. Accordingly, we make no representations as to the sufficiency of the foregoing procedures for your purposes.

5. Nothing came to our attention as a result of the foregoing procedures, however, that caused us to believe that:
   a. Any material modifications should be made to the unaudited condensed consolidated financial statements described in 4a.(i), included in the Registration Statement, for them to be in conformity with generally accepted accounting principles in the United States of America.
   b. The unaudited condensed consolidated financial statements described in 4a.(i) do not comply as to form in all material respects with the applicable accounting requirements of the Act and the related published rules and regulations adopted by the SEC.
   c. (i) At May 31, 2010, there was any change in capital stock, increase in long-term debt or any decrease in consolidated net current assets or stockholders' equity of the Company and its subsidiaries as compared with amounts shown on the March 31, 2010 unaudited condensed consolidated balance sheet included in the Registration Statement, or (ii) for the period from April 1, 2010 to May 31, 2010, there were any decreases, as compared to the corresponding period in the preceding year, in consolidated net sales or in the total or per-share amounts of income before extraordinary items or net income, except in all instances for

changes, increases or decreases that the Registration Statement discloses have occurred or may occur, except as follows: [describe line item changes].

6. As mentioned in 4b., Company officials have advised us that no consolidated financial statements as of any date or for any period subsequent to May 31, 2010, are available; accordingly, the procedures carried out by us with respect to changes in financial statement items after May 31, 2010, have, of necessity, been even more limited than those with respect to the periods referred to in 4. We have inquired of certain officials of the Company who have responsibility for financial and accounting matters whether (a) at June 4, 2010 there was any change in capital stock, increase in long-term debt or any decrease in consolidated net current assets or stockholders' equity of the Company and its subsidiaries as compared with amounts shown in the March 31, 2010 unaudited condensed consolidated balance sheet included in the Registration Statement, or (b) for the period from April 1, 2010, to June 4, 2010, there were any decreases, as compared with the corresponding period in the preceding year, in consolidated net sales or in the total or per-share amounts of income before extraordinary items or of net income. On the basis of these inquiries and our reading of the minutes as described in 4, nothing came to our attention that caused us to believe that there was any such change, increase or decrease, except in all instances for changes, increases or decreases, that the Registration Statement discloses have occurred or may occur, except as follows:

7. For purposes of this letter, we have also read the items identified by you on the attached copy of the Registration Statement and have performed the following procedures, which were applied as indicated with respect to the letters explained below.

   a. Compared or recalculated the amount to or from an amount that appeared in or was derived from the Company's audited financial statements included in the Registration Statement for the period indicated and found them to be in agreement.

   b. Compared or recalculated the amount to or from an amount that appeared in or was derived from the Company's unaudited financial statements included in the Registration Statement for the period indicated and found them to be in agreement.

   c. Compared or recalculated the amount to or from an amount that appeared in or was derived from a schedule prepared by the Company and found the amounts to be in agreement. We traced the amounts shown on the schedule prepared by the Company to the accounting records and found such amounts to be in agreement.

   d. Compared or recalculated the amount to or from an amount that appeared in or was derived from a schedule prepared by the Company and found the amounts to be in agreement.

8. The procedures enumerated in the preceding paragraph do not constitute an audit conducted in accordance with generally accepted auditing standards. Accordingly, we make no representations regarding the sufficiency of the foregoing procedures for your purposes.

9. It should be understood that we make no representations regarding questions of legal interpretation or regarding the sufficiency for your purposes of the procedures enumerated in the preceding paragraphs; also, such procedures would not necessarily reveal any material misstatement of the amounts or percentages listed above. Further, we have addressed ourselves solely to the foregoing data as set forth in the Registration Statement and make no representations regarding the adequacy of disclosure or regarding whether any material facts have been omitted.

10. This letter is solely for the information of the addressees and to assist the underwriters in conducting and documenting its investigation of the affairs of the Company in connection with the offering of the securities covered by the Registration Statement, and it is not to be used, circulated, quoted, or otherwise referred to for any other purpose, including but not limited to the purchase or sale of the securities, nor is it to be filed with or referred to in whole or in part in the Registration Statement or any other document, except that reference may be made to it in the underwriting agreement or in any list of closing documents pertaining to the offering of the securities covered by the Registration Statement.

Regards,

Source: Felix Lessambo.

Appendix 5: Sample of Bank Capability Letter (BCL)

Banker's Letterhead
(BANK MUST BE ONE OF THE TOP 50 PRIME BANKS)

Date
To
Nizoul International Corp.
GULF
London NZ3 4XD United Kingdom

Dear Sirs,

This is to confirm that our mutual clients (namely)...
.... maintain a banking account with us.

At their instructions we, ...
....(full name of the Bank) with full authority and mandate hereby confirm that the said clients are willing and financially able to initiate the
process of purchasing of... tons of..
.........(Product Name) during the next.../months/years. We
understand the total value of imports under the sight irrevocable Documentary Credit
on C & F basis is in the region of US $:

We certify that our clients named above have sufficient funds and/or have credit line
with our bank to complete the proposed transaction within the time period shown
above.

Our clients hereby give authority to the Sellers to procure usual banker's references.

....
Signed

Source: Felix Lessambo.

Appendix 6: Sample of Engagement Letter

Alpha Investment Banking Group
Greedy Financial Center
South Tower
Old World, New York
(212) 999–1999

Strictly Confidential

Bucher Inc.
24, Loyola Street, North Colorado
Colorado 23560
Attn: Mr. McGreedys

May, 2012

ENGAGEMENT LETTER

Dear Mr. McGreedys,

This letter confirms our understanding that Bucher Inc., a Colorado corporation, (the "Issuer") has engaged Alpha Investment Banking Group (the "Advisor") to act as the Issuer's exclusive financial advisor and placement agent in connection with the issuance and sale by the Issuer (the "Private Placement") of Convertible Preferred Stock (the "Securities"). It is currently contemplated that the Securities will be authorized by the Issuer as soon as practicable and will reflect the terms contained in Appendix A.

Section 1: Scope of Engagement

In connection with this engagement, the Advisor shall act as financial advisor to and agent for the Issuer in connection with the Private Placement, which duties will include:

(a) advising as to the specific terms of the Securities and the Private Placement;
(b) developing a list of potential purchasers of the securities;
(c) consulting with the Issuer from time to time as to potential purchasers;
(d) if requested by the Issuer, assisting the Issuer and its counsel in the preparation and distribution of appropriate offering materials; and
(e) attempting to arrange the Private Placement of the Securities at a price and on terms acceptable to the Issuer, it being understood and agreed that the aggregate offering price for the Securities is currently expected to be up to a maximum of approximately $250 million, and that such consideration may take the form of cash and/or exchanges of the Issuer's 5% Delayed Convertible Preferred Stock.

Nothing contained herein constitutes a commitment on the part of the Advisor to purchase any of the Securities or an assurance that the Private Placement will be completed, and the Advisor shall not have the power or authority to bind the Issuer to any sale of the Securities.

Section 2: Cooperation

The Issuer agrees to provide or cause to be provided to Alpha Investment Banking Group such information (the "Information") as Alpha Investment Banking Group believes appropriate to its assignment. The Issuer recognizes and confirms that Alpha Investment Banking Group (a) will use and rely primarily on the Information and on information available from generally recognized public sources in performing the services contemplated by this letter of agreement without having independently verified the same, (b) does not assume responsibility for the accuracy or completeness of the Information and such other information, and (c) will not make an appraisal of any assets or liabilities of the Company. The Issuer represents and warrants that all such information, data and documents, taken in their entirety, shall not contain any untrue statement of a material fact or omit to state a material fact necessary in order to make the statements herein not misleading.

The Issuer will promptly advise Alpha Investment Banking Group, in writing, as soon as the Issuer becomes aware that any Information previously provided has become inaccurate in any material respect or is required to be updated. If requested by the Advisor, the Issuer shall provide to the Advisor a certificate signed by two of its executive officers as to the accuracy of the second sentence of this paragraph at each closing of a sale of the Securities.

Further, it is understood that the Issuer shall involve the Advisor in all discussions between the Issuer and potential purchasers and shall make available to the Advisor all information regarding potential purchasers that it shall receive from any source whatsoever. The Issuer recognizes and confirms that the Advisor in acting pursuant to this authorization will be using information provided by the Issuer and that the Advisor does not assume responsibility for the accuracy or completeness of any such information.

Alpha Investment Banking Group commits to use its best efforts, consistent with the customary practice, to effect the financing as expected in ordinary course of business.

Section 3: Term of the Engagement

This Contract shall have a term of 18 months starting from May 1st 2012.

Either party to this Agreement may terminate this Agreement, with or without cause, by giving 10 days' prior written notice to the other party. The Issuer can terminate this Contract, at any time, with or without cause, provided a written notice be sent, in a timely manner, to Alpha Investment Banking Group. Alpha Investment Banking Group may terminate the Contract whenever it finds the Issuer to be in material violation of the Contract, as defined in Appendix (1) to the Contract. In a case of termination, the Advisor shall be entitled to receive its full compensation under Section 2 hereof if at any time prior to the date twelve months after the termination of this Agreement a transaction is agreed to or consummated by the Issuer involving the sale or issuance of securities of the type contemplated hereby in a private placement to investors contacted by Advisor regarding purchase of Securities in connection with this engagement (the "Libra Investors"). Promptly following termination of this engagement, Advisor shall provide Issuer with a list of Libra Investors.

Section 4: Fee Arrangement

In consideration of the Advisor's agreements hereunder, the Advisor shall be paid an advisory fee of 3.0% of the aggregate gross proceeds from the Securities sold, payable in immediately available funds upon closing of the Private Placement; provided, that such fee shall be reduced to 1.655% of gross proceeds with respect to the first $50,000,000 of Securities purchased by Richardson Capital International, Ltd., Richardson Capital Fund L.P. and other entities managed by Richardson Capital Limited (i.e. such fee shall be reduced by $450,000). In the event that the Private Placement is completed in multiple closings, a pro rata portion of such advisory fee shall be paid to the Advisor at each closing.

No fee payable to any other financial advisor either by the Issuer or any other entity shall reduce or otherwise affect the fees payable hereunder to the Advisor.

Section 5: The Advisor's Expenses

In addition to the compensation payable pursuant to Section 4 of this Agreement, the Issuer shall reimburse the Advisor for all reasonable costs and expenses (including without limitation reasonable fees and disbursements of its legal counsel) incurred in connection with this engagement, whether or not the Private Placement is consummated.

Section 6: Work Product

The Advisor's advice shall be the proprietary work product and intellectual property of the Advisor and such advice may not be disclosed to other parties by the Issuer without the prior written permission of the Advisor unless such disclosure is required by law. Any document or information prepared by the Advisor in connection with this engagement shall not be duplicated by the Issuer and shall be returned by the Issuer to the Advisor upon termination of this Agreement.

Section 7: Confidentiality

The Advisor agrees that all confidential information which it may now possess or may obtain relating to the financial condition, results of operations, business properties, assets, liabilities, or future prospects of the Issuer shall not be published, disclosed or made accessible by it to any other person or any entity at any time or used by it without the written consent of the Issuer; provided, however, that the restrictions of this sentence shall not apply (a) as may otherwise be required by law, (b) as may be necessary or appropriate in connection with this Agreement, or (c) to the extent such information shall be or shall have otherwise become publicly available, including without limitation all information contained in the Issuer's publicly-available reports and filings with the Securities and Exchange Commission, if any.

Section 8: Conflicts

The Issuer acknowledges that the Advisor and its affiliates may have and may continue to have investment banking, broker–dealer, and other relationships with parties other than the Issuer pursuant to which the Advisor may acquire information of interest to the Issuer. The Advisor shall have no obligation to disclose such information to the Issuer (except to the extent such information relates directly to the Issuer or the Securities), or to use such information in connection with its efforts hereunder.

Section 9: Exclusivity

No other financial advisor or other entity is or will be authorized by the Issuer during the term of this Agreement to perform services on its behalf of the type which the Advisor is authorized to perform hereunder.

Section 10: Indemnifications and Contributions

The Issuer agrees to indemnify the Advisor and its affiliates, directors, officers, employees, agents, and controlling persons (each such person being an "Indemnified Party") from and against any and all losses, claims, damages, and liabilities, joint or several, to which such Indemnified Party may become subject under any applicable law, domestic or foreign, or otherwise, and related to or arising out of (i) any untrue statement or alleged untrue statement of a material fact contained in any information (whether oral or written) or documents, including, without limitation, any Information, furnished or made available by the Issuer, directly or through Alpha Investment Banking Group, to any offeree of securities included in any Offering or in the Exchange Offer or any of their representatives or the omission or the alleged omission to state therein a material fact necessary in order to make the statements therein not misleading, in the light of the circumstances under which they were made, or (ii) any matters contemplated hereby or the appointment of the Advisor pursuant to, and the performance by the Advisor of the services contemplated by, this letter agreement and will promptly reimburse any Indemnified Party for all expenses (including reasonable counsel fees and expenses) as they are incurred in connection with the investigation of, preparation for or defense of any pending or threatened claim or any action or proceeding arising therefrom, whether or not such Indemnified Party is a party and whether or not such claim, action or proceeding is initiated or brought by or on behalf of the Issuer except as otherwise provided in the immediately following sentence. The Issuer will not be liable under clause (ii) of the foregoing indemnification provision to any Indemnified Party to the extent that any loss, claim, damage, liability or expense is found in a final, non-appealable judgment by a court to have resulted from the bad faith or gross negligence of such Indemnified Party.

The Issuer also agrees that no Indemnified Party shall have any liability (whether direct or indirect, in contract or tort or otherwise) to the Issuer or the Issuer's respective affiliates or security holders or creditors related to or arising out of the engagement of the

Advisor pursuant to, or the performance by the Advisor of the services contemplated by, this letter agreement except to the extent that any loss, claim, damage, liability, or expense is found in a final, non-appealable judgment by a court to have resulted from the bad faith or gross negligence of such Indemnified Party.

If the indemnification of an Indemnified Party provided for in this letter agreement is for any reason held unenforceable, the Issuer agrees to contribute to the losses, claims, damages and liabilities for which such indemnification is held unenforceable (i) in such proportion as is appropriate to reflect the relative benefits to the Issuer, on the one hand, and Alpha Investment Banking Group, on the other hand, from the Offerings and the Exchange Offer (whether or not such Offerings or the Exchange Offer are consummated) or (ii) if (but only if) the allocation provided for in clause (i) is for any reason held unenforceable, in such proportion as is appropriate to reflect not only the relative benefits referred to in clause (i) but also the relative fault of the Issuer, on the one hand, and Alpha Investment Banking Group, on the other hand, as well as any other relevant equitable considerations.

The Issuer also agrees that for the purposes of this paragraph the relative benefits to the Issuer, on the one hand, and to the Advisor, on the other hand, shall be deemed to be in the same proportion as the anticipated or actual total proceeds from the proposed sale or placement of the securities received or to be received by the Issuer in connection with the Offerings and the Exchange Offer bears to the fees paid or to be paid to the Advisor under this letter agreement; provided, however, that, to the extent permitted by applicable law, in no event shall the Indemnified Parties be required to contribute an aggregate amount in excess of the aggregate fees actually paid to the Advisor under this letter agreement. The foregoing contribution agreement shall be in addition to any rights that any Indemnified Party may have at common law or otherwise. No investigation or failure to investigate by any Indemnified Party shall impair the foregoing indemnification and contribution agreement or any right an Indemnified Party may have.

The Issuer agrees to notify the Advisor promptly of the assertion against the Issuer , the Advisor or any other person of any claim or the commencement of any action or proceeding relating to a transaction contemplated by this letter agreement or the Advisor's engagement hereunder, and the Advisor agrees to notify you promptly after receipt of notice of any claim or the commencement of any action or proceeding with respect to which an Indemnified Party may be entitled to indemnification hereunder. The failure of Alpha Investment Banking Group to so notify the Issuer shall not affect any liability of the Issuer to the Advisor or any other Indemnified Party.

The issuer agrees that, without the Advisor's prior written consent, it will not settle, compromise or consent to the entry of any judgment in any pending or threatened claim, action or proceeding in respect of which indemnification could be sought under the indemnification provision of this letter agreement (whether or not Alpha Investment Banking Group or any other Indemnified Party is an actual or potential party to such claim, action or proceeding), unless such settlement, compromise, or consent includes an unconditional release of each Indemnified Party from all liability arising out of such claim, action or proceeding.

In the event that an Indemnified Party is requested or required to appear as a witness in any action brought by or against the Issuer or any of its affiliates in which such Indemnified Party is not named as a defendant, the Issuer agrees to reimburse Alpha Investment Banking Group for all expenses incurred in connection with such Indemnified Party's appearing and preparing to appear as a witness, including, without limitation, the reasonable fees and disbursements of legal counsel, and to compensate Merrill Lynch in an amount to be mutually agreed upon.

The Issuer acknowledges and agrees that the Advisor has been retained solely to act as financial advisor to the Issue as provided herein and potentially to act as lead placement agent or underwriter in connection with the Offerings and placement.

The issuer, further, acknowledges that the Advisor shall act as an independent contractor, and any duties of Alpha Investment Banking Group arising out of its engagement pursuant to this letter agreement shall be owed solely to the Issuer.

Section 11: Notices

All notices and other communications provided for in this Agreement shall be made by first class mail or telecopier. All notices to the Issuer shall be delivered at the address shown on the first page of this agreement or to telecopier number (212) 999–1999.

Section 13: Applicable Laws

Each of the Advisor and the Issuer (on your own behalf and, to the extent permitted by applicable law, on behalf of your affiliates and your and their respective security holders) waives all right to trial by jury in any action, proceeding or counterclaim (whether based upon contract, tort or otherwise) related to or arising out of the engagement of Alpha Investment Banking Group pursuant to, or the performance by Alpha Investment Banking Group of the services contemplated by, this letter agreement.

The Issuer acknowledges that the Advisor may, at its option, place an announcement in such newspapers and periodicals as it may choose, stating that the Advisor has acted as the placement agent or underwriter for the Company in connection with any Offering or the financial advisor to the Company in connection with the placement Offer.

The Issuer agrees that, except as required by applicable law in the opinion of your counsel or unless the Advisor has otherwise consented in writing, you will not disclose, provide a copy of or circulate this letter to any person or entity or reference Alpha Investment Banking Group or the fees payable to Alpha Investment Banking Group in any offering circular, registration statement or other disclosure document, or in any press release or other document or communication.

No waiver, amendment or other modification of this letter agreement shall be effective unless in writing and signed by each party to be bound thereby.

This letter of agreement shall be governed by, and construed in accordance with, the law of the State of New York.

Please confirm that the foregoing correctly sets forth our agreement by signing and returning to [name of Advisor] the duplicate copy of this letter of agreement enclosed herewith. We look forward to the successful conclusion of this assignment.

Very truly yours,

ALPHA INVESTNMENT BANKING GROUP

By: /s/ Goriila

Name: Funny Gorilla
Title: Managing Director
Alpha Investment Banking Group

Accepted and Agreed:

Bucher INC.

By: /s/ Horrible David

Name: Horrible J. David
Title: Executive Vice President
and Chief Financial Officer

Source: Felix Lessambo.

Appendix 7: Sample of a Binding Letter of Intent

This letter agreement sets forth our agreement and understanding as to the essential terms of the sale to _____ (the "Purchaser") by _____ (the "Seller") of the Seller's business (the "Business"), located in _____ and engaged in _____ _____. The parties intend this letter agreement to be binding and enforceable, and that it will inure to the benefit of the parties and their respective successors and assigns.

1. Purchased Assets. At the closing, the Purchaser will purchase substantially all of the assets associated with the Business, including all inventories, all intellectual property, all accounts and notes receivable, all contracts and agreements, all equipment, all legally assignable government permits, and certain documents, files and records containing technical support and other information pertaining to the operation of the Business.

2. Assumed Liabilities. The Purchaser will assume as of the closing date only those liabilities and obligations (i) arising in connection with the operation of the Business by the Purchaser after the closing date, and (ii) arising after the closing date in connection with the performance by the Purchaser of the contracts and agreements associated with the Business.

3. Purchase Price. The purchase price will be $____, payable in cash in immediately available funds on the closing date.

4. Pre-Closing Covenants. The parties will use their reasonable best efforts to obtain all necessary third-party and government consents (including all certificates, permits and approvals required in connection with the Purchaser's operation of the Business). The Seller will continue to operate the Business consistent with past practice. The parties agree to prepare, negotiate and execute a purchase agreement which will reflect the terms set forth in this letter agreement, and will contain customary representations and warranties.

5. Conditions to Obligation. The Purchaser and the Seller will be obligated to consummate the acquisition of the Business unless the Purchaser has failed to obtain, despite the parties' reasonable best efforts, all certificates, permits and approvals that are required in connection with Purchaser's operation of the Business.

6. Due Diligence. The Seller agrees to cooperate with the Purchaser's due diligence investigation of the Business and to provide the Purchaser and its representatives with prompt and reasonable access to key employees and to books, records, contracts and other information pertaining to the Business (the "Due Diligence Information").

7. Confidentiality; Non-competition. The Purchaser will use the Due Diligence Information solely for the purpose of the Purchaser's due diligence investigation of the Business, and unless and until the parties consummate the acquisition of the Business the Purchaser, its affiliates, directors, officers, employees, advisors, and agents (the Purchaser's "Representatives") will keep the Due Diligence Information strictly confidential. The Purchaser will disclose the Due Diligence Information only to those Representatives of the Purchaser who need to know such information for the purpose of consummating the acquisition of the Business. The Purchaser agrees to be responsible for any breach of this paragraph 7 by any of the Purchaser's Representatives. In the

event the acquisition of the Business is not consummated, the Purchaser will return to the Seller any materials containing Due Diligence Information, or will certify in writing that all such materials or copies of such materials have been destroyed. The Purchaser also will not use any Due Diligence Information to compete with the Seller in the event that the acquisition of the Business is not consummated. The provisions of this paragraph 7 will survive the termination of this letter agreement.

8. Employees of the Business. Until the consummation of the acquisition of the Business, or in the event that the parties do not consummate the acquisition of the Business, the Purchaser will not solicit or recruit the employees of the Business.

9. Exclusive Dealing. Until _____, the Seller will not enter into any agreement, discussion, or negotiation with, or provide information to, or solicit, encourage, entertain or consider any inquiries or proposals from, any other corporation, fire or other person with respect to (a) the possible disposition of a material portion of the Business, or (b) any business combination involving the Business, whether by way of merger, consolidation, share exchange or other transaction. If for any reason the acquisition of the Business is not consummated, and the Seller is unable to enforce the provisions of this letter agreement, the Buyer will pay to the Seller a break-up fee which will equal the sum of 1% of the purchase price, and the Seller's expenses in connection with the negotiation of the acquisition.

10. Public Announcement. All press releases and public announcements relating to the acquisition of the Business will be agreed to and prepared jointly by the Seller and the Purchaser.

11. Expenses. Subject to the provisions in paragraph 9 of this letter agreement, each party will pay all of its expenses, including legal fees, incurred in connection with the acquisition of the Business.

12. Indemnification: The Seller represents and warrants that the Purchaser will not incur any liability in connection with the consummation of the acquisition of the Business to any third party with whom the Seller or its agents have had discussions regarding the disposition of the Business, and the Seller agrees to indemnify, defend and hold harmless the Purchaser, its officers, directors, stockholders, lenders and affiliates from any claims by or liabilities to such third parties, including any legal or other expenses incurred in connection with the defense of such claims. The covenants contained in this paragraph 12 will survive the termination of this letter agreement.

If you are in agreement with the terms of this letter agreement, please sign in the space provided below and return a signed copy to _____ by the close of business on _____. Upon receipt of a signed copy of this letter, we will proceed with our plans for consummating the transaction in a timely manner.

Very truly yours,

XYZ CORPORATION

By:_____
[Name and Title]

_____

ABC CORPORATION
By: _____
[Name and Title]

Source: Ian Giddy.

Appendix 8: Sample of Merger Agreement

This Merger Agreement (the "Agreement") is dated as of _____, _____, and is entered into by and between (legal name of bank) ("Merging Bank"), a _____ banking corporation, and (legal name of bank) ("Surviving Bank"), a [state name] banking corporation. Merging Bank and Surviving Bank are the constituent corporations in this Agreement.

Note: One or both holding companies may in some circumstances also be parties to the Agreement.

RECITALS

Merging Bank is a banking corporation duly organized and existing under the laws of the State of _____ with authorized capital stock of $_____, consisting of _____ _____ shares of common stock, par value $_____ _____ per share (the "Merging Bank Common Stock"), all of which shares are issued and outstanding. Its principal place of business is located in (city, state) .

Surviving Bank is a banking corporation duly organized and existing under the laws of the State of [state name] with authorized capital stock of $_____, consisting of _____ _____ shares of common stock, par value $_____ per share (the "Surviving Bank Common Stock"), all of which shares are issued and outstanding. Its principal place of business is located in _____ _____, [state name].

(Holding Company Name) is a _____ corporation duly organized and existing under and by virtue of the laws of the State of _____ and is a bank holding company owning _____% of the common capital stock of Merging Bank.

(Holding Company Name) is a [state name] corporation duly organized and existing under and by virtue of the laws of [State name] and is a bank holding company owning _____% of the common capital stock of Surviving Bank.

The parties intend by this Agreement to set forth the terms and conditions of a "merger," satisfying the terms and conditions of [state name] Statutes, Sections [ ] to [ ] and other applicable law.

For business reasons, Merging Bank and Surviving Bank desire to have Merging Bank merge into the Charter of Surviving Bank and to have the banking offices of Merging Bank become banking offices of Surviving Bank.

Section 1. MERGER

1.1 <u>Merger</u>. On the Effective Date (as defined in Section 1.11), pursuant to the provisions of this Agreement and pursuant to the provisions of [state name] Statutes Sections

[ ]-[ ], Merging Bank shall be merged with and into Surviving Bank under the charter of Surviving Bank. The separate existence of Merging Bank shall cease and its charter shall be surrendered and returned to the \[state name] Department of Commerce. The existence of Surviving Bank, as the surviving organization ("the Merged Bank"), shall continue with all the rights, privileges, immunities, powers and franchises and subject to all the duties, restrictions and liabilities of a banking corporation organized under the laws of the State name.

1.2   Effect of Merger. All rights, privileges, immunities, powers, franchises and interests of Merging Bank in and to every type of property (real, personal and mixed) and courses in action shall be transferred to and vested in the Merged Bank by virtue of such merger without any deed or other transfer, and the Merged Bank, without any order or other action on the part of any court or otherwise, shall hold and enjoy all rights of property, privileges, immunities, powers, franchises and interests, including, without limitation, appointments, designations and nominations, all other rights and interests as trustee, executor, administrator, registrar of stocks and bonds, guardian of estates, assignee, receiver and committee of estates of incompetence and in every other fiduciary capacity, in the same manner and to the same extent as such rights, privileges, immunities, powers, franchises and interests are held or enjoyed by Merging Bank at the time the merger becomes effective.

The Merged Bank shall be liable for all liabilities of Merging Bank; all deposits, debts, liabilities, obligations and contracts of Merging Bank, matured or un-matured, whether accrued, absolute, contingent or otherwise and whether or not reflected or reserved against on balance sheets, books of account or records of Merging Bank, shall be those of the Merged Bank and shall not be released or impaired by the merger. All rights of creditors and other obligees and all liens on property of Merging Bank shall be preserved unimpaired.

1.3   Name. The name of the Merged Bank shall be:
_____.

1.4   **Principal Place of Business; Detached Facilities. The Merged Bank's principal place of business shall be at** _____
__, **[state name]** _____.

The Merged Bank shall operate detached facilities at (List both continuing pre-merger facilities of Surviving Bank and those facilities which were formerly offices of Merging Bank.). The merged bank shall also continue to operate the following loan production offices, trust service offices, and representative trust offices (List both continuing pre-merger facilities of Surviving Bank and those facilities which were formerly offices of Merging Bank.) .

1.5   **Capital Stock. The Merged Bank shall have authorized capital stock of $_____
_____ divided into** _____ **shares of $_____
par value per share.**

1.6   Certificate of Incorporation. The Certificate of Incorporation of Surviving Bank, as in effect on the Effective Date, shall continue to be the Certificate of Incorporation of the Merged Bank until it is thereafter amended or restated.

Note: If the name or capital stock of the Merged Bank will be different from that of Surviving Bank, this should be addressed: "until it is thereafter amended or restated" should be deleted and replaced by "except as amended herein to reflect the new name as stated in Section 1.3, the new amount of capital stock as noted in Section 1.5," etc. The Certificate of Incorporation may also be amended to address a change in the number of directors if the Merged Bank will have a number of directors which falls outside of the range presently stated in Surviving Bank's Certificate of Incorporation. It is strongly advised that Surviving Bank's certificate of incorporation NOT be appended as an exhibit to the Agreement.

1.7   Bylaws. The Bylaws of Surviving Bank in effect at the Effective date shall be the Bylaws of the Merged Bank until they are duly amended or repealed.

1.8 Directors. On the Effective Date, the following persons shall serve as the initial Board of Directors of the Merged Bank:

Name   Name
Street Address   Street Address
City, State, Zip Code   City, State, Zip Code
Name   Name
Street Address   Street Address
City, State, Zip Code   City, State, Zip Code

Source: Ian Giddy.

Appendix 9: Sample of Due Diligence Checklist

Note: the following due diligence checklist is only a sample, and will differ from the actual list used during your deal process.

A. Organization of the Company

1. Describe the corporate or other structure of the legal entities that comprise the Company. Include any helpful diagrams or charts. Provide a list of the officers and directors of the Company and a brief description of their duties.
2. Long-form certificate of good standing and articles or certificate of incorporation from Secretary of State or other appropriate official in the Company's jurisdiction of incorporation, listing all documents on file with respect to the Company, and a copy of all documents listed therein.
3. Current by-laws of the Company.
4. List of all jurisdictions in which the Company is qualified to do business and list of all other jurisdictions in which the Company owns or leases real property or maintains an office and a description of business in each such jurisdiction. Copies of the certificate of authority, good standing certificates and tax status certificates from all jurisdictions in which the Company is qualified to do business.
5. All minutes for meetings of the Company's board of directors, board committees and stockholders for the last five years, and all written actions or consents in lieu of meetings thereof.
6. List of all subsidiaries and other entities (including partnerships) in which the Company has an equity interest; organizational chart showing ownership of such entities; and any agreements relating to the Company's interest in any such entity.

B. Ownership and Control of the Company

1. Capitalization of the Company, including all outstanding capital stock, convertible securities, options, warrants and similar instruments.
2. List of security holders of the Company (including option and warrant holders), setting forth class and number of securities held.
3. Copies of any voting agreements, stockholder agreements, proxies, transfer restriction agreements, rights of first offer or refusal, preemptive rights, registration agreements or other agreements regarding the ownership or control of the Company.

C. Assets and Operations

1. Annual financial statements with notes thereto for the past three fiscal years of the Company, and the latest interim financial statements since the end of the last fiscal year and product sales and cost of sales (including royalties) analysis for each product which is part of assets to be sold.
2. All current budgets and projections including projections for product sales and cost of sales.

3. Any auditors' (internal and external) letters and reports to management for the past five years (and management's responses thereto).
4. Provide a detailed breakdown of the basis for the allowance for doubtful accounts.
5. Inventory valuation, including turnover rates and statistics, gross profit percentages and obsolescence analyses including inventory of each product which is part of assets to be sold.
6. Letters to auditors from outside counsel.
7. Description of any real estate owned by the Company and copies of related deeds, surveys, title insurance policies (and all documents referred to therein), title opinions, certificates of occupancy, easements, zoning variances, condemnation or eminent domain orders or proceedings, deeds of trust, mortgages and fixture lien filings.
8. Schedule of significant fixed assets, owned or used by the Company, including the identification of the person holding title to such assets and any material liens or restrictions on such assets.
9. Without duplication from Section D below, or separate intellectual property due diligence checklist, schedule of all intangible assets (including customer lists and goodwill) and proprietary or intellectual properties owned or used in the Company, including a statement as to the entity holding title or right to such assets and any material liens or restrictions on such assets. Include on and off balance sheet items.

D. Intellectual Property

List of all patents, trademarks, tradenames, service marks and copyrights owned or used by the Company, all applications therefor and copies thereof, search reports related thereto and information about any liens or other restrictions and agreements on or related to any of the foregoing (without duplication from attached intellectual property due diligence checklist).

E. Reports

1. Copies of any studies, appraisals, reports, analyses or memoranda within the last three years relating to the Company (i.e., competition, products, pricing, technological developments, software developments, etc.).
2. Current descriptions of the Company that may have been prepared for any purpose, including any brochures used in soliciting or advertising.
3. Descriptions of any customer quality awards, plant qualification/certification distinctions, ISO certifications or other awards or certificates viewed by the Company as significant or reflective of superior performance.
4. Copies of any analyst or other market reports concerning the Company known to have been issued within the last three years.
5. Copies of any studies prepared by the Company regarding the Company's insurance currently in effect and self-insurance program (if any), together with information on the claim and loss experience thereunder.
6. Any of the following documents filed by the Company or affiliates of the Company and which contain information concerning the Company: annual reports on SEC Form 10-K; quarterly reports on SEC Form 10-Q; current reports on SEC Form 8-K.

F. Compliance with Laws

1. Copies of all licenses, permits, certificates, authorizations, registrations, concessions, approvals, exemptions and other operating authorities from all governmental

authorities and any applications therefor, and a description of any pending contemplated or threatened changes in the foregoing.

2. A description of any pending or threatened proceedings or investigations before any court or any regulatory authority.

3. Describe any circumstance where the Company has been or may be accused of violating any law or failing to possess any material license, permit or other authorization. (List all citations and notices from governmental or regulatory authorities.)

4. Schedule of the latest dates of inspection of the Company's facilities by each regulatory authority that has inspected such facilities.

5. Description of the potential effect on the Company of any pending or proposed regulatory changes of which the Company is aware.

6. Copies of any information requests from, correspondence with, reports of or to, filings with or other material information with respect to any regulatory bodies which regulate a material portion of the Company's business. Limit response to the last five years unless an older document has a continuing impact on the Company.

7. Copies of all other studies, surveys, memoranda or other data on regulatory compliance including: spill control, environmental clean-up or environmental preventive or remedial matters, employee safety compliance, import or export licenses, common carrier licenses, problems, potential violations, expenditures, etc.

8. State whether any consent is necessary from any governmental authority to embark upon or consummate the proposed transaction.

9. Schedule of any significant U.S. import or export restrictions that relate to the Company's operations.

10. List of any export, import or customs permits or authorizations, certificates, registrations, concessions, exemptions, etc., that are required in order for the Company to conduct its business and copies of all approvals, etc. granted to the Company that are currently in effect or pending renewal.

11. Any correspondence with or complaints from third parties relating to the marketing, sales or promotion practices of the Company.

G. Environmental Matters

1. A list of facilities or other properties currently or formerly owned, leased, or operated by the Company and its predecessors, if any.

2. Reports of environmental audits or site assessments in the possession of the Company, including any Phase I or Phase II assessments or asbestos surveys, relating to any such facilities or properties.

3. Copies of any inspection reports prepared by any governmental agency or insurance carrier in connection with environmental or workplace safety and health regulations relating to any such facilities or properties.

4. Copies of all environmental and workplace safety and health notices of violations, complaints, consent decrees, and other documents indicating noncompliance with environmental or workplace safety and health laws or regulations, received by the Company from local, state, or federal governmental authorities. If available, include documentation indicating how such situations were resolved.

5. Copies of any private party complaints, claims, lawsuits or other documents relating to potential environmental liability of the Company to private parties.

6. Listing of underground storage tanks currently or previously present at the properties and facilities listed in response to Item 1 above, copies of permits, licenses or

registrations relating to such tanks, and documentation of underground storage tank removals and any associated remediation work.

7. Descriptions of any release of hazardous substances or petroleum known by the Company to have occurred at the properties and facilities listed in response to Item 1, if such release has not otherwise been described in the documents provided in response to Items 1-6 above.

8. Copies of any information requests, PRP notices, "106 orders," or other notices received by the Company pursuant to CERCLA or similar state or foreign laws relating to liability for hazardous substance releases at off-site facilities.

9. Copies of any notices or requests described in Item 8 above, relating to potential liability for hazardous substance releases at any properties or facilities described in response to Item 1.

10. Copies of material correspondence or other documents (including any relating to the Company's share of liability) with respect to any matters identified in response to Items 8 and 9.

11. Copies of any written analyses conducted by the Company or an outside consultant relating to future environmental activities (i.e., upgrades to control equipment, improvements in waste disposal practices, materials substitution) for which expenditure of funds greater than $10,000 is either certain or reasonably anticipated within the next five years and an estimate of the costs associated with such activities.

12. Description of the workplace safety and health programs currently in place for the Company's business, with particular emphasis on chemical handling practices.

H. Litigation

1. List of all litigation, arbitration and governmental proceedings relating to the Company to which the Company or any of its directors, officers or employees is or has been a party, or which is threatened against any of them, indicating the name of the court, agency or other body before whom pending, date instituted, amount involved, insurance coverage and current status. Also describe any similar matters which were material to the Company and which were adjudicated or settled in the last ten years.

2. Information as to any past or present governmental investigation of or proceeding involving the Company or the Company's directors, officers or employees.

3. Copies of all attorneys' responses to audit inquiries.

4. Copies of any consent decrees, orders (including applicable injunctions) or similar documents to which the Company is a party, and a brief description of the circumstances surrounding such document.

5. Copies of all letters of counsel to independent public accountants concerning pending or threatened litigation.

6. Any reports or correspondence related to the infringement by the Company or a third party of intellectual property rights.

I. Significant Contracts and Commitments

1. Contracts relating to any completed (during the past 10 years) or proposed reorganization, acquisition, merger, or purchase or sale of substantial assets (including all agreements relating to the sale, proposed acquisition or disposition of any and all divisions, subsidiaries or businesses) of or with respect to the Company.

2. All joint venture and partnership agreements to which the Company is a party.

3. All material agreements encumbering real or personal property owned by the Company including mortgages, pledges, security agreements or financing statements.

4. Copies of all real property leases relating to the Company (whether the Company is lessor or lessee), and all leasehold title insurance policies (if any).

5. Copies of all leases of personal property and fixtures relating to the Company (whether the Company is lessor or lessee), including, without limitation, all equipment rental agreements.

6. Guarantees or similar commitments by or on behalf of the Company, other than endorsements for collection in the ordinary course and consistent with past practice.

7. Indemnification contracts or arrangements insuring or indemnifying any director, officer, employee or agent against any liability incurred in such capacity.

8. Loan agreements, notes, industrial revenue bonds, compensating balance arrangements, lines of credit, lease financing arrangements, installment purchases, etc. relating to the Company or its assets and copies of any security interests or other liens securing such obligations.

9. No-default certificates and similar documents delivered to lenders for the last five (or shorter period, if applicable) years evidencing compliance with financing agreements.

10. Documentation used internally for the last five years (or shorter time period, if applicable) to monitor compliance with financial covenants contained in financing agreements.

11. Any correspondence or documentation for the last five years (or shorter period, if applicable) relating to any defaults or potential defaults under financing agreements.

12. Contracts involving cooperation with other companies or restricting competition.

13. Contracts relating to other material business relationships, including:
    a. any current service, operation or maintenance contracts;
    b. any current contracts with customers;
    c. any current contracts for the purchase of fixed assets; and
    d. any franchise, distributor or agency contracts.

14. Without duplicating Section D above or the intellectual property due diligence schedule hereto, contracts involving licensing, know-how or technical assistance arrangements including contracts relating to any patent, trademark, service mark and copyright registrations or other proprietary rights used by the Company and any other agreement under which royalties are to be paid or received.

15. Description of any circumstances under which the Company may be required to repurchase or repossess assets or properties previously sold.

16. Data processing agreements relating to the Company.

17. Copies of any contract by which any broker or finder is entitled to a fee for facilitating the proposed transaction or any other transactions involving the Company or its properties or assets.

18. Management, service or support agreements relating to the Company, or any power of attorney with respect to any material assets or aspects of the Company.

19. List of significant vendor and service providers (if any) who, for whatever reason, expressly decline to do business with the Company.

20. Samples of all forms, including purchase orders, invoices, supply agreements, etc.

21. Any agreements or arrangements relating to any other transactions between the Company and any director, officer, stockholder or affiliate of the Company (collectively, "Related Persons"), including but not limited to:
    a. Contracts or understandings between the Company and any Related Person regarding the sharing of assets, liabilities, services, employee benefits, insurance, data processing, third-party consulting, professional services or intellectual property.
    b. Contracts or understandings between Related Persons and third parties who supply inventory or services through Related Persons to the Company.

c. Contracts or understandings between the Company and any Related Person that contemplate favorable pricing or terms to such parties.

d. Contracts or understandings between the Company and any Related Person regarding the use of hardware or software.

e. Contracts or understandings regarding the maintenance of equipment of any Related Person that is either sold, rented, leased or used by the Company.

f. Description of the percentage of business done by the Company with Related Persons.

g. Covenants not to compete and confidentiality agreements between the Company and a Related Person.

h. List of all accounts receivable, loans and other obligations owing to or by the Company from or to a Related Person, together with any agreements relating thereto.

22. Copies of all insurance and indemnity policies and coverages carried by the Company including policies or coverages for products, properties, business risk, casualty and workers compensation. A description of any self-insurance or retro-premium plan or policy, together with the costs thereof for the last five years. A summary of all material claims for the last five years as well as aggregate claims experience data and studies.

23. List of any other agreements or group of related agreements with the same party or group of affiliated parties continuing over a period of more than six months from the date or dates thereof, not terminable by the Company on 30 days' notice.

24. Copies of all supply agreements relating to the Company and a description of any supply arrangements.

25. Copies of all contracts relating to marketing and advertising.

26. Copies of all construction agreements and performance guarantees.

27. Copies of all secrecy, confidentiality and nondisclosure agreements.

28. Copies of all agreements related to the development or acquisition of technology.

29. Copies of all agreements outside the ordinary course of business.

30. Copies of all warranties offered by the Company with respect to its product or services.

31. List of all major contracts or understandings not otherwise previously disclosed under this section, indicating the material terms and parties.

32. For any contract listed in this Section I, state whether any party is in default or claimed to be in default.

33. For any contract listed in this Section I, state whether the contract requires the consent of any person to assign such contract or collaterally assign such contract to any lender.

Note: Remember to include all amendments, schedules, exhibits and side letters. Also include brief description of any oral contract listed in this Section I.

J. Employees, Benefits and Contracts

1. Copies of the Company's employee benefit plans as most recently amended, including all pension, profit sharing, thrift, stock bonus, ESOPs, health and welfare plans (including retiree health), bonus, stock option plans, direct or deferred compensation plans and severance plans, together with the following documents:
   a. all applicable trust agreements for the foregoing plans;
   b. copies of all IRS determination letters for the foregoing qualified plans;
   c. latest IRS forms for the foregoing qualified plans, including all annual reports, schedules and attachments;

    d. latest copies of all summary plan descriptions, including modifications, for the foregoing plans;

    e. latest actuarial evaluations with respect to the foregoing defined benefit plans; and

    f. schedule of fund assets and unfunded liabilities under applicable plans.

2. Copies of all employment contracts, consulting agreements, severance agreements, independent contractor agreements, non-disclosure agreements and non-compete agreements relating to any employees of the Company.
3. Copies of any collective bargaining agreements and related plans and trusts relating to the Company (if any). Description of labor disputes relating to the Company within the last three years. List of current organizational efforts and projected schedule of future collective bargaining negotiations (if any).
4. Copies of all employee handbooks and policy manuals (including affirmative action plans).
5. Copies of all OSHA examinations, reports or complaints.
6. The results of any formal employee surveys.

K. Tax Matters

1. Copies of returns for the three prior closed tax years and all open tax years for the Company (including all federal and state consolidated returns) together with a work paper therefor wherein each item is detailed and documented that reconciles net income as specified in the applicable financial statement with taxable income for the related period.
2. Audit and revenue agents reports for the Company; audit adjustments proposed by the Internal Revenue Service for any audited tax year of the Company or by any other taxing authority; or protests filed by the Company.
3. Settlement documents and correspondence for last six years involving the Company.
4. Agreements waiving statute of limitations or extending time involving the Company.
5. Description of accrued federal, state and local withholding taxes and FICA for the Company.
6. List of all state, local and foreign jurisdictions in which the Company pays taxes or collects sales taxes from its retail customers (specifying which taxes are paid or collected in each jurisdiction).

L. Miscellaneous

1. Information regarding any material contingent liabilities and material unasserted claims and information regarding any asserted or unasserted violation of any employee safety and environmental laws and any asserted or unasserted pollution clean-up liability.
2. List of the ten largest customers and suppliers for each product or service of the Company.
3. List of major competitors for each business segment or product line.
4. Any plan or arrangement filed or confirmed under the federal bankruptcy laws, if any.
5. A list of all officers, directors and stockholders of the Company.
6. All annual and interim reports to stockholders and any other communications with securityholders.
7. Description of principal banking and credit relationships (excluding payroll matters), including the names of each bank or other financial institution, the nature, limit

and current status of any outstanding indebtedness, loan or credit commitment and other financing arrangements.

8. Summary and description of all product, property, business risk, employee health, group life and key-man insurance.
9. Copies of any UCC or other lien, judgment or suit searches or filings related to the Company in relevant states conducted in the past three years.
10. Copies of all filings with the Securities and Exchange Commission, state blue sky authorities or foreign security regulators or exchanges.
11. All other information material to the financial condition, businesses, assets, prospects or commercial relations of the Company.

Source: Ian Giddy.

Appendix 10: Sample of Term Sheet

Placement of Series X Preferred Stock

Date

The terms set forth below are solely for the purpose of outlining those terms pursuant to which a definitive agreement may be entered into and do not at this time constitute a binding contract, except that by accepting these terms the company agrees that for a period of 30 days following the date of signature, provided that the parties continue to negotiate to conclude an investment, they will not negotiate or enter into discussion with any other investors or group of investors regarding this "Series X" round of investment. An investment in the company is contingent upon, among other things, completion of due diligence and the negotiation and execution of a satisfactory stock purchase agreement.

I. Issuer: **Richmondson, Inc.**

II. Investor: **Venture Capital Partners, LLC or its affiliates ("VC")**   and other investors acceptable to the Company and VC (collectively the "Investors")

III. Security: Series X Preferred Stock ("Preferred")

IV. Amount of Investment: $[   ]

V. Valuation: The Original Purchase Price is based upon a fully-diluted pre-money valuation of $[_____] and a fully-diluted post-money valuation of $[_____] (including an employee pool representing [__]% of the fully-diluted post-money capitalization).

VI. Post-Investment Ownership:
The company would be capitalized such that post-investment ownership at closing would be as follows:

VC [   ]%
Founders, Management & Other [   ]%
Option Pool [   ]%

VII.   Closing Date:
As soon as practicable following the Company's acceptance of this Term Sheet and satisfaction of the Conditions to Closing (the "Closing").

VIII. Board Representation:

The Board of Directors will include a total of five (5) people. Holders of Series X Convertible Preferred Stock are entitled to two (2) representatives on the Company's Board of Directors. Common Shareholders will have three (3) designees to the board, one of which must be the CEO of the Company. Board of Directors meetings would be scheduled on a monthly basis until such time as the Board of Directors votes to schedule them less frequently.

VC's representative would be appointed to all Board Committees (including the compensation committee), each of which would consist of three (3) members. The Company would reimburse each Director's reasonable expenses incurred in attending the board meetings or any other activities (e.g., meetings, trade shows) which are required and/or requested and that involve expenses.

IX. Proprietary Information and Inventions Agreement:

Each officer, director, and employee of the Company shall have entered into a proprietary information and inventions agreement in a form reasonably acceptable to the Company and the Investors. Each Founder and other key technical employee shall have executed an assignment of inventions acceptable to the Company and Investors.

DESCRIPTION OF SERIES B PREFERRED

X. Dividends:

An [ ]% annual dividend would accrue as of the closing date to holders of the Series X Convertible Preferred. Accrued dividends would be payable (a) if, as and when determined by the Company's Board of Directors, (b) upon the liquidation or winding up of the company, or (c) upon redemption of the Series X Preferred. Upon an automatic conversion, accrued but unpaid dividends would be forfeited. No dividends may be declared and/or paid on the Common Stock until all dividends have been paid in full on the Convertible Preferred Stock. The Convertible Preferred Stock would also participate *pari passu* in any dividends declared on Common Stock. Dividends will cease to accrue in the event that the Investor converts its holdings to Common Stock.

XI. Liquidation Preference:

In the event of any liquidation or winding up of the Company, the Series X Preferred will be entitled to receive in preference to the holders of Common Stock an amount per share equal to their Original Purchase Price plus all accrued but unpaid dividends (if any).

The Series X Preferred will be participating so that after payments of the Original Purchase Price and all accrued dividends to the Preferred, the remaining assets shall be distributed pro-rata to all shareholders on a common equivalent basis.

A merger, acquisition or sale of substantially all of the assets of the Company in which the shareholders of the Company do not own a majority of the outstanding shares of the surviving corporation shall be deemed a liquidation of the Company.

XII. Conversion:

The Preferred will have the right to convert Preferred shares at the option of the holder, at any time, into shares of Common Stock at an initial conversion rate of 1-to-1. The conversion rate shall be subject from time to time to anti-dilution adjustments as described below.

XIII. Automatic Conversion:

The Series X Preferred would be automatically converted into Common Stock, at the then applicable conversion price, upon the sale of the Company's Common Stock in an initial public offering ("Public Offering") at a price equal to or exceeding [ ] times the Series X Preferred original purchase price in an offering which, after deduction for underwriter commissions and expenses related to the gross proceeds, is not less than [ ].

XIV. Antidilution Provisions:

Proportional antidilution protection for stock splits, stock dividends, combinations, recapitalization, etc. The conversion price of the Preferred shall be subject to adjustment to prevent dilution, on a "weighted average" basis, in the event that the Company issues additional shares of Common or Common equivalents (other than reserved employee shares) at a purchase price less than the applicable conversion price.

XV. Voting Rights:

The Preferred will have a right to that number of votes equal to the number of shares of Common Stock issuable upon conversion of the Preferred.

XVI. Restrictions and Limitations:

Consent of the Series X Preferred, voting as a separate class would be required for any actions which:

(i) alter or change the rights, preferences or privileges of the Series X Preferred;
(ii) increase the authorized number of shares of Series X Preferred;
(iii) increase the authorized number of shares of any other class of Preferred Stock;
(iv) create any new class or series of stock, which has preference over or is on parity with the Series X Preferred;
(v) involve a merger, consolidation, reorganization, encumbrance, or sale of all or substantially all of the assets or sale or of more than 50% of the Company's stock;
(vi) involve a repurchase or other acquisition of shares of the Company's stock other than pursuant to redemption provisions described below under "Redemption"; or
(vii) amend the Company's charter or bylaws.

XVII. Redemption:

After five (5) years and at the request of the holders of the Series X Preferred, all or part of the Series X Preferred shares may be redeemed at 110% of the Series X purchase price plus all accrued but unpaid dividends.

XVIII. Conditions Precedent to Investor's Obligation to Invest:

(i) legal documentation satisfactory to the Investor and Investor's counsel;
(ii) satisfactory completion of due diligence;
(iii) if not already in place, the Company would obtain employment agreements with key employees, which would include satisfactory (to Investor) non-compete and non-disclosure language.

XIX. Registration Rights:

1. If, at any time after the Issuer's initial public offering (but not within 6 months of the effective date of a registration), Investors holding at least 51% of the Common issued or issuable upon conversion of the Preferred request that the Issuer file a Registration Statement covering at least 20% of the Common issued or issuable upon conversion of the Preferred (or any lesser percentage if the anticipated aggregate offering price would exceed $[ ]), the Issuer will be obligated to cause such share to be registered. The Issuer will not be obligated to effect more than two registrations (other than on Form S-3 under these demand right provisions.

2. Company Registration: The Preferred shall be entitled to "piggy-back" registration rights on registrations of the Company or on demand registrations of any later round investor subject to the right, however, of the Company and its underwriters to reduce the number of shares proposed to be registered pro rata in view of market conditions. No shareholder of the Company shall be granted piggyback registration rights superior to those of the Series X Preferred without the consent of the holders of at least 50% of the Series X (or Common Stock issued upon conversion of the Series X Preferred or a combination of such Common Stock and Preferred).
3. S-3 Rights: Preferred shall be entitled to an unlimited number of demand registrations on Form S-3 (if available to the Company) so long as such registration offerings are in excess of $500,000, provided, however, that the Company shall only be required to file two Form S-3 Registration Statements on demand of the Preferred every 12 months.
4. Expenses: The Company shall bear registration expenses (exclusive of underwriting discounts and commissions and special counsel of the selling shareholders) of all demands, piggybacks, and S-3 registrations. The expenses in excess of $15,000 of any special audit required in connection with a demand registration shall be borne pro rata by the selling shareholders.
5. Transfer of Rights: The registration rights may be transferred provided that the Company is given written notice thereof and provided that the transfer (a) is in connection with a transfer of at least 20% of the securities of the transferor, (b) involves a transfer of at least 100,000 shares, or (c) is to constituent partners of shareholders who agree to act through a single representative.
6. Other Provisions: Other provisions shall be contained in the Investor Rights Agreement with respect to registration rights as are reasonable, including cross-indemnification, the period of time in which the Registration Statement shall be kept effective, standard standoff provisions, underwriting arrangements and the ability of the Company to delay demand registrations for up to 90 days (S-3 Registrations for up to 60 days).

XX. *Right of First Offer:*

The Preferred shall have the right in the event the Company proposes an equity offering of any amount to any person or entity (other than for a strategic corporate partner, employee stock grant, equipment financing, acquisition of another company, shares offered to the public pursuant to an underwritten public offering, or other conventional exclusion) to purchase up to [ ]% of such shares.

The Company has an obligation to notify the Preferred of any proposed equity offering of any amount.

If the Preferred does not respond within 15 days of being notified of such an offering, or decline to purchase all of such securities, then that portion which is not purchased may be offered to other parties on terms no less favorable to the Company for a period of 120 days. Such right of first offer will terminate upon an underwritten public offering of shares of the Company.

In addition, the Company will grant the Preferred any rights of first refusal or registration rights granted to subsequent purchasers of the Company's equity securities to the extent that such subsequent rights are superior, in good faith judgment of the Board, to those granted in connection with this transaction.

XXI. *Right of Co-Sale:*

The Company, the Preferred and the Founders will enter into a co-sale agreement pursuant to which any Founder who proposes to sell all or a portion of his shares to a third party, will offer the Preferred the right to participate in such sale on a pro rate basis or to exercise a right of first refusal on the same basis (subject to customary exclusions for up to 15% of the stock, gifts, pledges, etc.). The agreement will terminate on the earlier of an IPO or fifteen (15) years from the close of this financing.

XXII. Use of Proceeds:

The proceeds from the sale of the Preferred will be used solely general corporate purposes.

XXIII. Reporting Covenants:

The Company would furnish to the Investor the following:

(i) Monthly reports. Within 20 days following the end of each month, an income state-ment, cash flow and balance sheet for the prior monthly period. Statements would include year-to-date figures compared to budgets, with variances delineated.

(ii) Annual Financial Statements. Within 90 days following the end of the fiscal year, an unqualified audit, together with a copy of the auditor's letter to management, from a Big Five accounting firm or equivalent, which firm would be approved by the Investor.

(iii) Audit. In the event the Company fails to provide monthly reports and/or financial statements in accordance with the foregoing, Investor would have the authority, at the Company's expense, to request an audit by an accounting firm of its choice, such that statements are produced to the satisfaction of the Investor.

(iv) Annual Budget. At least 30 days before the end of each fiscal year, a budget, includ-ing projected income statement, cash flow and balance sheet, on a monthly basis for the ensuing fiscal year, together with underlying assumptions and a brief qualitative description of the company's plan by the Chief Executive Officer in support of that budget.

(v) Non-compliance. Within 10 days after the discovery of any default in the terms of the stock purchase agreement, or of any other material adverse event, a statement outlining such default or event, and management's proposed response.

XXIV. Purchase Agreement:

The purchase of the Company's Series X Preferred Stock would be made pursuant to a Series X Convertible Preferred Stock Purchase Agreement drafted by counsel to the Investor, which would be mutually agreeable to the Company, and the Investor. This agreement would contain, among other things, appropriate representations and warran-ties of the Company, covenants of the Company reflecting the provisions set forth herein and other typical covenants, and appropriate conditions of closing, including among other things, qualification of the shares under applicable Blue Sky laws, the filing of a certificate of amendment to the Company's charter to authorize the Series X Preferred, and an opinion of counsel. Until the Purchase Agreement is signed, there would not exist any binding obligation on the part of either party to consummate the transaction. This Summary of Terms does not constitute a contractual commitment of the Company or the Investor or an obligation of either party to negotiate with the other.

XXV. Other:

The Company would pay legal expenses incurred by the Investor at closing from the pro-ceeds of the investment. The investor would make all reasonable efforts to see that this expense does not exceed $30,000. Once this term sheet is signed, the Company would accept responsibility for legal fees incurred by the Investor if the transaction does not close up to the amount set forth above.

XXVI. Exclusivity:

(i) Upon the acceptance hereof, the Company, its officers and shareholders agree not to discuss the sale of assets or any equity or equity type securities, provide any information to or close any such transaction with any other investor or prospective investor, except to named entities mutually acceptable to Management and Investor.

(ii) The undersigned agree to proceed in good faith to execute and deliver definitive agreements incorporating the terms outlined above and such additional terms as are customary for transactions of the type described herein. This letter expresses the intent of the parties and is not legally binding on any of them unless and until such mutually satisfactory definitive agreements are executed and delivered by the undersigned. This letter of intent may be signed by the parties in counterparts.

If this Summary of Terms is not signed and returned to VC by midnight (EST) [ ], it shall expire without any further action on the part of VC and shall be of no further force or effect.

XXVII. No Shop Provision:

The Company agrees to work in good faith expeditiously towards a closing. The Company and the Founders agree that they will not, for a period of [_____] weeks from the date these terms are accepted, take any action to solicit, initiate, encourage or assist the submission of any proposal, negotiation or offer from any person or entity other than the Investors relating to the sale or issuance, of any of the capital stock of the Company [or the acquisition, sale, lease, license or other disposition of the Company or any material part of the stock or assets of the Company] and shall notify the Investors promptly of any inquiries by any third parties in regards to the foregoing. [In the event that the Company breaches this no-shop obligation and, prior to [_____], closes any of the above-referenced transactions [without providing the Investors the opportunity to invest on the same terms as the other parties to such transaction], then the Company shall pay to the Investors $[_____] upon the closing of any such transaction as liquidated damages.] The Company will not disclose the terms of this Term Sheet to any person other than officers, members of the Board of Directors and the Company's accountants and attorneys and other potential Investors acceptable to [_____], as lead Investor, without the written consent of the Investors.

VENTURE CAPITAL PARTNERS, LLC
Date _____
By: _____
Terms agreed to and accepted by:
NEWCO, INC.
Date _____
By:_____
Source: Compiled by the author based on a review of the literature.

Appendix 11: Sample of Capital Call Notice

Date

Name of the Firm
Address
[City, State and Zip Code]

Capital Call Notice of Richardson Investment group, L.P. (the "Fund")

Dear Investor,

We are writing to notify you that pursuant to Section 2 of the Amended and Restated Limited Partnership Agreement of the Fund, dated May 15, 2012, the Fund is calling capital from you in the amount of $4,000,000 (the Capital Contribution), which represents 15% of your unfunded Capital Commitment.

Your Capital Contribution is due on or before June 30, 2012 and must be wired in immediately available funds to the Fund's account N0. K12986304.
The wire instructions are as follows:

SUN City Bank
SWIFT Code: IN 094432
Account: K12986304
Sub-account: SB 2135

For security sake, please instruct the financial institution handling the wire transfer to include your name, as a Limited Partner of the Fund, on the wire transfer.

Would you have further queries regarding this information, please feel free to contact Ms. Janet Woodruff, the Managing Director Assistant at (212) 212-2121.

Sincerely,

Source: Felix Lessambo.

Appendix 12: Sample of Certificate of Ownership

On 15 of May 2011, MM. Robert Proudy and Gilbert Montquck appear before the State of Bristol Secretary of State and certify that:

1. They are the president and the secretary, respectively, of NIZOUL Corporation, *a Corporation incorporated in the State of Bristol.*
2. NIZOUL Corporation owns 100% of the outstanding shares of Alexandria Corporation, an undertaking incorporated in the State of Illinois.
3. The board of directors of this corporation duly adopted the following resolution:

RESOLVED, that this corporation merges Alexandria corporation, Its wholly-owned subsidiary corporation, into itself and assumes all its obligations pursuant to Bristol Corporations Code section 6348.

We further declare under penalty of perjury under the laws of the State of Bristol that the matters set forth in this certificate are true and correct of our own knowledge.

Date: _____

(Signature of President)
(Typed Name of President), President
(Signature of Secretary)
(Typed Name of Secretary), Secretary

The sample Certificate of Ownership is for use by a parent corporation owning 100 percent of the outstanding shares of the subsidiary. The sample is provided to be used as a guideline only in the preparation of original documents for filing with the Secretary of State.

Ms. Penguin,

(Seal)

Source: Felix Lessambo.

Appendix 13: Form 41-103F1 – Securitized Products Prospectus

Supplementary Information Required in a Securitized Products Prospectus

INSTRUCTIONS

This Form sets out specific disclosure requirements relating to securitized products that are in addition to the general requirement under securities legislation to provide full, true and plain disclosure of all material facts relating to the securities to be distributed. Issuers must comply with the specific instructions or requirements in this Form if the instruction or requirement is applicable. Issuers must also comply with the applicable instructions or requirements in Form 41-101F1 or Form 44-1-01F1 that address areas that are not otherwise covered by the instructions or requirements in this Form.

DEFINITIONS

1. Sponsor

A "sponsor" is a person or company who organizes and initiates a securitized product transaction by selling or transferring assets, either directly or indirectly, to the issuer.

2. Arranger

An "arranger" is a person or company that arranges and structures a securitized product transaction, but does not sell or transfer assets, directly or indirectly, to the issuer of the securitized products, and in the absence of evidence to the contrary, includes the underwriter for a distribution of securitized products.

3. Depositor

A "depositor" is a person or company in a securitized product transaction who receives or purchases pool assets from the sponsor and transfers or sells the pool assets to an issuer of securitized products.

4. Originator

An "originator" is a person or company that originates receivables, loans or other financial assets that are pool assets.

1.6 Issuer

Describe the following:
(a) the permissible activities and restrictions on the activities of the issuer under its governing documents, including any restrictions on the ability to issue or invest in additional securities, to borrow money or to make loans to other persons;

1.7   Servicer

A "servicer" is a person or company responsible for the management or collection of pool assets or making allocations or payments to a holder of a securitized product, but does not include a trustee of an issuer of securitized products or trustee for the securitized product that makes allocations or payments.

POOL OF ASSETS

1. General information regarding pool asset types and selection criteria

Describe the following:

(a) each type of pool asset that will be securitized, including a general description of the material terms of the pool assets;

(b) the method and criteria used by each originator to originate the assets in the pool, or by each sponsor to select the pool assets to be purchased for the pool, and any changes to the method or criteria and whether the method or criteria can be modified or overridden;

(c) any exceptions to the criteria in paragraph (b), including a quantification of such exceptions;

(d) the origination channel and origination process for the pool assets, including:
  (i) information about how the originator acquired the asset;
  (ii) the level of origination documentation that was required;

(e) the cut-off date or similar date for establishing pool compositions;

(f) any specific due diligence performed on the selection of the pool assets, including verification and risk assurance practices that have been performed by the arranger, sponsor or originator;

(g) the jurisdiction whose laws and regulations govern the pool assets and the effects of any relevant legal or regulatory provisions that may materially affect pool performance or payments or expected payments on the securitized products;

(h) whether the pool assets have been reviewed for compliance with selection criteria or are the subject of a report by a third party to verify the accuracy of the loan or other asset information disclosed in the prospectus;

(i) if the pool assets have been reviewed for compliance or are the subject of a report by a third party, the identity of the reviewer or third party, the scope of the review or report, and the results or findings of the review or report.

2. Pool characteristics

(1) Provide an introductory overview of the material pool characteristics that includes:
  (a) the methodology used in determining or calculating the characteristics;
  (b) a description of any terms or abbreviations used.

(2) Describe the material characteristics of the pool assets, including, to the extent applicable:
  (a) the legal nature of each type of pool asset;
  (b) the number of each type of pool asset;
  (c) the original balance and outstanding balance or other reasonable measurement of pool asset size, at date of origination, and as of the designated cut-off date;
  (d) interest rate or rate of return;

(e) any cap or floor on interest rates;

(f) any significant installment at loan maturity;

(g) any increased installment rate;

(h) capitalized or uncapitalized accrued interest;

(i) age, maturity, expiry date, remaining term, average life, current payment or prepayment speed, applicable payment grace periods and pool factors;

(j) service distribution, if different servicers service different pool assets;

(k) amortization period;

(l) loan purpose;

(m) loan status;

(n) average payment rate of receivables;

(o) for revolving financial assets, information about:

    (i) the monthly payment rate;

    (ii) maximum credit lines;

    (iii) average account balance;

    (iv) yield percentage;

    (v) type of assets;

    (vi) finance charges, fees and other income earned;

    (vii) balance reductions granted for refunds, returns, fraudulent charges or other reasons;

    (viii) percentage of full-balance and minimum payments made.

(p) for an asset pool containing one or more commercial mortgages, the following information, to the extent material:

    (i) For each commercial mortgage:

        (A) The location and present use of each mortgaged property.

        (B) Net operating income and net cash flow information, as well as the components of net operating income and net cash flow, for each mortgaged property.

        (C) Current occupancy rates for each mortgaged property.

        (D) The identity, area occupied by and lease expiration dates for the three largest tenants at each mortgaged property.

        (E) The nature, amount and priority of all other material mortgages, liens or encumbrances against each mortgaged property.

    (ii) For each commercial mortgage that represents, by dollar value, 10% or more of the asset pool, measured as of the cut-off date:

        (A) Any proposed program for the renovation, improvement or development of the mortgaged properties, including the estimated cost of the program and the method of financing to be used.

        (B) The general competitive conditions to which the properties are or may be subject.

        (C) The management of the properties.

        (D) The occupancy rate expressed as a percentage for each of the five years before the date of the prospectus.

        (E) The principal business, occupations and professions carried on in, or from the properties.

        (F) The number of tenants occupying 10% or more of the total rentable square footage or meterage of such properties, the principal nature of business of each such tenant, and the principal provisions of the leases with those tenants including, but not limited to: rental per annum, expiration date, and renewal options.

(G) The average effective annual rental per square foot, square meter or unit for each of the three years prior to the date of the prospectus and the year to date for the year in which the prospectus dated.

(H) The lease expirations, in the form of a schedule, for each of the previous ten years starting with the year in which the prospectus dated, stating:

1. The number of tenants whose leases will expire.
2. The total area in square feet or square meters covered by such leases.
3. The annual rental represented by such leases.
4. The percentage of gross annual rental represented by such leases.

(q) whether pool assets are secured or unsecured, and if secured, the type of collateral;

(r) information about the collateral underlying the loans in the pool, including:

   (i) the type or use of the underlying property, product or other collateral;

   (ii) loan-to-value ratio;

   (iii) the existence of insurance for real estate;

   (iv) if a valuation has been performed on the collateral, who performed the valuation, when it was performed or updated, and the standard used in measuring the valuation;

(s) credit score of obligors and other information regarding obligor credit quality;

(t) billing and payment procedures, including frequency of payment, payment options, fees, charges and origination or payment incentives;

(u) geographic distribution of the pool assets, including any economic or other factors specific to any jurisdiction, region or sector where a significant portion of the pool assets are or will be located that may materially impact the pool assets or cash flows from the pool assets;

(v) priority on collateral in event of default.

3. Delinquency and loss information

"Delinquent", for purposes of determining if an asset in a pool that collateralizes one or more series or classes of securitized products is delinquent, means a pool asset that is more than 30 or 31 days or a single payment cycle, as applicable, past due from the contractual due date, as determined in accordance with any of the following:

(a) the transaction agreements for the securitized products;

(b) the delinquency recognition policies of the sponsor, any affiliate of the sponsor that originated the pool asset, or the servicer of the pool asset;

(c) the delinquency recognition policies applicable to that pool asset established by the regulator primarily responsible for supervising the financial condition of the sponsor, any affiliate of the sponsor that originates the pool asset, or the servicer of the pool asset, or established by the program or regulator that oversees the program under which the pool asset was originated "Non-performing", for purposes of determining if a pool asset that backs one or more series or classes of securitized products is non-performing, means a pool asset if any of the following is true:

   (i) the pool asset would be treated as wholly or partially charged-off under the requirements in the transaction agreements for the securitized products;

   (ii) the pool asset would be treated as wholly or partially charged-off under the charge-off policies of the sponsor, an affiliate of the sponsor that originates the pool asset, or a servicer that services the pool asset;

   (iii) the pool asset would be treated as wholly or partially charged-off under the charge-off policies applicable to such pool asset established by the regulator primarily responsible for supervising the financial condition of the sponsor, an affiliate of the sponsor that originates the pool asset, or a servicer that services the pool asset, or established by the program or regulatory entity that oversees the program under which the pool asset was originated;

Provide the following information on delinquencies and losses on the asset pool for each pool asset type as of the cut-off date for the securitized product transaction, or in the case of a master trust, the date specified in the prospectus:

(a) delinquency experience in 30 or 31 day increments, as applicable, beginning at least with assets that are 30 or 31 days delinquent, as applicable, through the point that assets are written off or charged off as uncollectable;
(b) the total amount of delinquent and non-performing assets as a percentage of the aggregate asset pool;
(c) other significant loss and cumulative loss information;
(d) how delinquencies and non-performance are defined or determined, including whether the criteria used for such definition or determination can be modified or overridden, and whether they are consistent with market practice;
(e) other material information regarding delinquencies, losses and non-performance particular to the pool asset type, including to the extent applicable information regarding:
   (i) repossession;
   (ii) foreclosure;
   (iii) renegotiation or modification

4. Sources of pool cash flow

If the cash flows that support the securitized products come from more than one source, such as both lease payments and the sale of the residual asset at the end of a lease, describe:

(a) the specific sources of funds and their uses, including the relative amount and percentage of funds that will be derived from each source;
(b) any assumptions, data, models and methodology used to derive the amounts in paragraph (a).

5. Representations and warranties and repurchase obligations

(1) Summarize any representation and warranty made concerning the pool assets by each sponsor, originator or any other party, including an affiliate of the foregoing, in connection with the securitized product transaction, and briefly describe the remedies available if a representation and warranty is breached. State whether there is any representation and warranty relating to fraud in the origination of the pool assets.
(2) If material, for each originator and affiliate of the originator that is required to repurchase or replace a pool asset for breach of a representation and warranty pursuant to the transaction agreements, provide the following disclosure on a pool-by-pool basis for each of the three years prior the date of the prospectus, but only in respect of pool assets of the same class as those collateralizing the securitized products being distributed, and that were securitized in connection with a distribution of securitized products under a prospectus:
   (a) the amount of pool assets that the originator or an affiliate of the originator originated that were the subject of demands to repurchase or replace for a breach of a representation and warranty pursuant to the transaction agreements;

(b) the amount of pool assets described in paragraph (a) in respect of which the demands were resolved, and the nature of the resolution;

(c) the amount of pool assets described in paragraph (a) in respect of which the demands were not resolved, and the status of the demands as of a date that is not more than 60 days before the date of the prospectus;

(d) where the originator rejected a demand to repurchase or replace pool assets on the basis that the assets did not violate a representation and warranty concerning the pool assets, whether an opinion of a third party not affiliated with the originator had been furnished to the trustee or issuer that confirmed that the assets did not violate the representation and warranty.

(3) If material, for each party that is required to repurchase or replace a pool asset for breach of a representation and warranty pursuant to the transaction agreements, provide the following disclosure on a pool-by-pool basis for each of the three years prior the date of the prospectus, but only in respect of pool assets of the same class as those collateralizing the securitized products being distributed, and that were securitized in connection with a distribution of securitized products under a prospectus:

(a) the amount of pool assets that were the subject of demands to repurchase or replace for a breach of a representation and warranty pursuant to the transaction agreements;

(b) the amount of pool assets described in paragraph (a) in respect of which the demands were resolved, and the nature of the resolution;

(c) the amount of pool assets described in paragraph (a) in respect of which the demands were not resolved, and the status of the demands as of a date that is not more than 60 days before the date of the prospectus;

(d) where the party rejected a demand to repurchase or replace pool assets on the basis that the assets did not violate a representation and warranty concerning the pool assets, whether an opinion of a third party not affiliated with the originator had been furnished to the trustee or issuer that confirmed that the assets did not violate the representation and warranty.

(4) Provide information regarding the financial condition of any party with a repurchase or replacement obligation, to the extent that there is a significant risk that the party's financial condition could have a material impact on its ability to comply with the provisions relating to the repurchase or replacement obligations

6. Claims on pool assets

(1) Disclose if any parties other than the securitized products holders have a material direct or contingent claim on any pool assets.

(2) Describe any material cross-collateralization or cross-default provisions relating to the pool assets.

7. Revolving periods and prefunding accounts

(1) For a securitized product transaction that contemplates a prefunding or revolving period, describe the following:

(a) the term or duration;

(b) the aggregate amounts and percentages of the pool assets involved;

(c) the triggers that would limit or terminate such period;

(d) how pool assets may be added, removed or substituted;

(e) the acquisition or underwriting criteria for additional pool assets;

(f) the identity of any party that makes determinations in respect of changes to the asset pool;

(g) any minimum requirement to add or remove pool assets;

(h) the procedures and standards for temporary investment of funds pending use;

(i) whether and how an investor would be notified of any changes to the asset pool.

8. Modification of terms

Describe any provisions in the transaction agreements governing the modification of the terms of any pool asset, including how modification may affect cash flows from the pool assets or payments on the securitized products being distributed.

STATIC POOL INFORMATION

1. General

(1) Provide static pool information if it would be material.

(2) If static pool information is provided, provide an introductory overview of the information including:

(a) the methodology used in determining or calculating the characteristics of the static pool;

(b) a description of any terms or abbreviations used;

(c) a description of how the assets in the static pool differ from the pool assets underlying the securitized products;

(d) an explanation of material trends.

(3) If no static pool information is provided, explain why no static pool disclosure is included. If alternative disclosure is included, explain why the alternative disclosure provides more useful information to a prospective investor in understanding and analyzing the securitized product.

2. Amortizing asset pools

(1) For amortizing asset pools, if material, provide static pool information regarding delinquencies, cumulative losses and prepayments in respect of the following:

(a) for a sponsor with three or more years experience securitizing assets of the type included in the current securitized product transaction, each prior pool of such assets securitized within the last five years;

(b) for a sponsor with less than three years experience securitizing assets of the type included in the current securitized product transaction, such assets by vintage origination year for the period the sponsor has been originating or purchasing such assets.

(2) Provide delinquency, cumulative loss and prepayment information for each prior pool or vintage origination year disclosed under paragraph (1) over the life of the prior pool or vintage origination year. Present delinquency and loss information in the manner set out in Item 3.3.

(3) Provide the following summary information for the original characteristics of each prior pool or vintage origination year disclosed under paragraph (1) if material and applicable:

(a) debt-to-income ratio;

(b) number of pool assets;

(c) original pool balance;
(d) weighted average original pool balance;
(e) weighted average interest or note rate;
(f) weighted average original term;
(g) weighted average remaining term;
(h) weighted average and minimum and maximum standardized credit score or other applicable measure of obligor credit quality;
(i) product type;
(j) loan purpose;
(k) loan-to-value information;
(l) distribution of assets by loan or note rate;
(m) geographic distribution of assets.

3. Revolving asset master trusts

For revolving asset master trusts, provide the following information in appropriate separate increments based on the date of origination of the pool assets, if material and applicable:

(a) delinquencies;
(b) cumulative losses;
(c) prepayments;
(d) payment rate;
(e) yield;
(f) standardized credit score or other applicable measure of obligor credit quality;
(g) average payment term;
(h) the percentage of assets originated by each obligor.

DESCRIPTION OF THE STRUCTURED PRODUCTS

Describe each securitized product being distributed, including:

(a) its type and category;
(b) how principal and interest on each class of securitized products is calculated and payable;
(c) amortization;
(d) performance or similar triggers or effects, and their effects on the securitized product transaction if triggered;
(e) overcollateralization, cross-default or cross-collateralization provisions;
(f) voting requirements to amend the transaction agreements or other relevant documents;
(g) minimum standards, restrictions or suitability requirements regarding ownership of the securitized product.

RETENTION OF THE SECURITIZED PRODUCTS

Disclose whether any person or company for which disclosure has been provided under Items 1.2 to 1.9, including any affiliate of such person or company, is retaining a portion of a tranche or tranches, and if so, specify the amount retained for each tranche. State whether that person or company has directly or indirectly hedged, or taken any other action, that seeks to transfer in whole or in part the credit risk associated with a retained portion.

1. Structure of the transaction

Describe the material features and assumptions of the flow of funds for the securitized product transaction, including:

(a) payment allocations, rights and distribution priorities among all classes and within each class of securitized products, with respect to:
    (i) cash flows;
    (ii) credit enhancement;
    (iii) any other structural features in the transaction;
(b) any requirements directing cash flows, such as reserve accounts or cash collateral accounts, and the purpose and operation of those requirements.

2. Distribution frequency and cash maintenance

Disclose:

(a) the frequency of the distribution dates for the securitized product;
(b) the collection periods for the pool assets;
(c) any arrangement for cash held pending use, including the length of time that cash will be held pending a distribution to a holder of a securitized product;
(d) the identity of the parties with access to cash balances and the authority to make decisions regarding their investment and use.

3. Fees and expenses

(1) Describe the following:
    (a) all fees and expenses to be paid or payable out of the cash flows from the pool assets;
    (b) each party that is receiving such fees or expenses, and the general reasons for the receipt;
    (c) the source of funds for such fees or expenses, if different from other fees or expenses or if such fees or expenses are to be paid from a specified portion of the cash flows;
    (d) the distribution priority of such fees or expenses;
    (e) if the amount of fees or expenses is not fixed, the formula used to determine the amounts payable.
(2) Provide any additional information necessary to help investors understand the timing and amount of the fees or expenses, including:
    (a) any restrictions or limits;
    (b) whether and how fees or expenses could change in certain circumstances;
    (c) whether and how fees or expenses could be changed without notice to, or approval by, securitized products holders;
    (d) any restrictions on the ability to change a fee or expense amount, such as due to a change in transaction party.

4. Excess cash flow

Describe the following:

(a) the disposition of residual or excess cash flows;

(b) the identity of any person or company who owns any residual or retained interests in the cash flows and who also satisfies either of the following:

 (i) is affiliated with, any person or company for which disclosure has been provided under Items 1.2 to 1.9;

 (ii) has rights that may alter the transaction structure beyond receipt of residual or excess cash flows;

(c) any requirements to maintain a minimum amount of excess cash flow or spread from, or retained interest in, the transaction and the effects on the transaction if the requirements are not met;

(d) if material, any arrangements to facilitate a securitization of the excess cash flow or retained interest from the securitized product transaction, including whether any material changes to the transaction structure may be made without the consent of the holders of the securitized products in connection with such securitization;

(e) any conditions on the payment of excess cash flows, such as priority in payment to certain tranches;

(f) any investment policies and restrictions in respect of residual or excess cash flows.

5. Master trusts

If one or more additional series or classes of securitized products have been or may be issued that are backed by the same asset pool backing the securitized products being distributed, describe the additional securities, providing all material information including the following:

(a) the relative priority of the additional securities to the securities being distributed and their respective rights to the underlying pool assets and their cash flows;

(b) the allocations of cash flow from the asset pool and any expenses or losses among the various series or classes;

(c) the terms under which additional series or classes may be issued and pool assets increased or changed;

(d) the terms of any required security holder approval or notification of such additional securities;

(e) which party has the authority to determine whether such additional securities may be issued;

(f) if there are conditions to an issuance of such additional securities, whether or not there will be an independent verification of the exercise of authority or determinations made by the party in paragraph (e).

6. Optional or mandatory redemption or termination

If any class of the securitized products includes an optional or mandatory redemption or termination feature, describe the following:

(a) the terms for triggering the redemption or termination;

(b) the identity of any person or company who holds the redemption or termination option or obligation, and whether that person or company is affiliated with any person or company for which disclosure has been provided under Items 1.2 to 1.9;

(c) the amount of the redemption or repurchase price;

(d) the redemption or termination procedures, including any notices required to be provided to holders of the securitized products.

7. Prepayment, maturity and yield considerations

Describe the following:

(a) any material models used to identify cash flow characteristics with respect to the pool assets, including a description of material assumptions and limitations;

(b) if material, the degree to which each class of securitized products is sensitive to changes in the rate of payment on the pool assets and the consequences of such changing rate of payment, including provision of statistical information about such consequences such as the effect of prepayments on yield and weighted average life.

(c) any special allocations of prepayment risks among the classes of securities and whether any class protects other classes from the effects of the uncertain timing of cash flow with respect to the pool assets.

CREDIT ENHANCEMENT AND OTHER SUPPORT

(1) Describe any material external credit enhancement or other support intended to ensure that the securitized products or pool assets will pay in accordance with their terms in the normal course, including:
   (a) any bond insurance, letters of credit or guarantees;
   (b) any liquidity facilities, lending facilities, guaranteed investment contracts or minimum principal payment agreements;
   (c) any derivatives that provide insurance against losses on the assets in the pool.

(2) Describe any material internal credit enhancement or other support that is a result of or is part of the structure of the transaction, and that is intended to increase the likelihood that payments will be made on one or more classes of the securitized products in accordance with their terms in the normal course, including:
   (a) subordination provisions;
   (b) overcollateralization;
   (c) reserve accounts;
   (d) cash collateral accounts or spread accounts;
   (e) transactions in which receivables may be purchased at a discount or on a deferred basis.

(3) For each credit enhancement or other support, describe the following:
   (a) any limits on the timing or amount of the enhancement or support;
   (b) any conditions that must be met before the enhancement or support can be used;
   (c) any provisions regarding the substitution of the enhancement or support.

(4) Identify each entity or group of affiliated entities that provides credit enhancement or other support and is liable or contingently liable to provide payments representing 10% or more of the cash flow supporting one or more classes of securitized products being distributed, and describe:
   (a) its form of organization;
   (b) the general character of its business.

(5) If any entity or group of affiliated entities that provides credit enhancement or other support is liable or contingently liable to provide payments representing 10% or more, but less than 20%, of the cash flow supporting one or more classes of securitized products being distributed, provide all of the following:
   (a) the selected annual financial information required by Item 1.3 of Form 51-102F1;

(b) the same selected financial information for any subsequent interim period that ended more than 60 days before the date of the prospectus.

(6) If any entity or group or affiliated entities that provide credit enhancement or other support is liable or contingently liable to provide payments representing 20% or more of the cash flow supporting a class or series of securitized products being distributed, provide the financial statements of the entity or group of affiliated entities that would be prescribed under securities legislation and described in the form of prospectus that the entity or group would be eligible to use at the date of the prospectus, if the entity or group was distributing securities under a prospectus.

CERTAIN DERIVATIVE INSTRUMENTS

(1) For each derivative instrument used to alter the payment characteristics of the payments made on the securitized products, and the primary purpose of which is not to provide credit enhancement or other support as described in Item 8, provide the following information:
   (a) the identity of the derivative counterparty;
   (b) its form of organization;
   (c) the general character of its business;
   (d) the operation and material terms of the derivative instrument, including any limits on the timing or amount of payments or any conditions to payments;
   (e) the minimum requirements regarding the counterparty;
   (f) any material provisions regarding termination or substitution of the derivative instrument;
   (g) the significance percentage.

(2) For purposes of paragraph (1)(g), the "significance percentage" is the percentage referred to in paragraph (b) calculated as follows:
   (a) determine the financial significance of the derivative instrument using a reasonable good faith estimate of the maximum probable exposure of the derivative counterparty that is made in substantially the same manner as that used in the sponsor's internal risk management process in respect of similar instruments;
   (b) determine the percentage that the amount in paragraph (a) represents of the aggregate principal balance of the pool assets, or, if the derivative instrument relates only to certain classes of securitized products, of the aggregate principal of those classes.

(3) If the aggregate significance percentage for one or more derivative instruments for which any entity or group of affiliated entities is acting as a derivative counterparty is 10% or more, but less than 20%, provide all of the following:
   (a) the selected annual financial information specified by Item 1.3 of Form 51-102F1;
   (b) the same selected financial data for any subsequent interim period that ended more than 60 days before the date of the prospectus.

(4) If the aggregate significance percentage for one or more derivative instruments for which any entity or group of affiliated entities is acting as a derivative counterparty is 20% or more, provide the financial statements for that entity or group of affiliated entities that would be prescribed under securities legislation and described in the form of prospectus that the entity or group would be eligible to use at the date of the prospectus, if the entity or group was distributing securities under a prospectus.

CREDIT RATINGS

Disclose the following:

(a) whether the issuance or sale of any securitized products being distributed is conditioned on the assignment of a credit rating by one or more credit rating agencies;

(b) the identity of each credit rating agency that will be used and the minimum rating that must be assigned as a condition of the securitized product transaction;

(c) any arrangements to have the rating assigned be monitored while the securitized products are outstanding;

(d) if a credit rating agency used in connection with the securitized product transaction has undertaken an analysis of market risks that may have an impact on the credit rating, such as changes in interest rates or prepayment risk, the nature of the market risk that the credit rating agency has identified;

(e) the name of each credit rating agency whose rating is disclosed and the definition or description of the category in which the class of securities was rated;

(f) any preliminary credit rating obtained by a sponsor or arranger for any class of the securitized products being distributed;

(g) whether any credit rating agency has refused to assign a credit rating to a class of securitized products being distributed, and the reasons for refusal if it is related to the structure or the financial viability of the securitized product transaction.

REPORTS

Describe the following reports or documents that relate to the securitized products:

(a) each report or other document to be provided to holders of the securitized products being distributed that is required under the transaction agreements, including provision of the following information:
  (i) the information that will be contained in the report or other document;
  (ii) the schedule and manner of distribution or other availability;
  (iii) the entity or entities that will prepare and provide the report or other document;
  (iv) whether the report or other document will be available to the public on a Web site, and if so, how to access the Web site and the report or other document;
  (v) whether one or more parties to the securitized product transaction will provide electronic or paper copies of the reports or documents without charge upon request.

(b) any report or other document to be filed with a securities regulatory authority, including an explanation of how the public can access the report or other document.

LEGAL PROCEEDINGS AND REGULATORY ACTIONS

Provide the disclosure required by Item 23 (Legal Proceedings and Regulatory Actions) of Form 41-101F1 for each party for which disclosure has been provided under Items 1.2 to 1.9.

Appendix 14: Financial Ratios

Short-term Liquidity

Current ratio	Current assets ÷ Current liabilities
Quick ratio (also acid test)	(Cash + Marketable securities + Accounts receivable) ÷ Current liabilities
Operating cash flow to current liability	Cash flow from operations (net of taxes) ÷ Average current liabilities
Days receivable outstanding	365 days × (Average receivables ÷ Net credit sales)
Days inventory outstanding	(365 days × Average inventories) ÷ Cost of goods sold
Accounts receivable turnover	Net sales ÷ Average accounts receivable
Working capital	Current assets – Current liabilities
Working capital turnover	Sales ÷ (Current assets – Current liabilities)
Days' purchases in accounts payable (also Days' payable outstanding)	365 days ÷ Accounts payable turnover, where Accounts payable turnover = Purchases ÷ Average payables or, 365 days of Inventory purchases ÷ Average accounts payable
Average net trade cycle (also Cash conversion cycle)	Number of days' sales in: (Accounts + Inventories) – Days in accounts payables
Inventory turnover	Cost of sales ÷ Average inventory

Capital Structure and Solvency

Total long-term debt to assets	Long-term debt ÷ Total average assets
Total debt ratio	Total liabilities ÷ Total assets
Long-term debt to equity	Long-term debt ÷ Equity capital
Current liabilities to Total liabilities	Current liabilities ÷ Total liabilities
Pretax GAAP earnings to fixed Charges	Pre-tax income + Interest expensed on income statement + $\frac{1}{3}$ operating lease payment (rent expense) – Undistributed equity in earnings of affiliates or, Total interest expense incurred + $\frac{1}{3}$ Operating lease payment

(*continued*)

Continued

Financial Leverage Index (FLI)	ROCE ÷ Total ROA
Cash flow to fixed charges	Cash flow from operations + Current tax expense + Interest expense + $\frac{1}{3}$ Operating lease payment or, Interest expense + $\frac{1}{3}$ Operating lease payment
Times Interest Earned coverage ratio (TIE)	Operating income before taxes and interest expense ÷ Interest expense or (Pre-tax income + Interest expense) ÷ Interest expense
Cash flow to liabilities	Operating cash flow ÷ Average total debt
Financial Leverage Ratio (FLR)	Total average assets ÷ Total average common equity

Return on Invested Capital

Total Return on Assets (ROA)	((Net income + Interest expense) × (1 – Tax rate)) ÷ Average total assets
Return on Common Equity (ROCE)	(Net income – Preferred dividend) ÷ Average common equity
Earnings per share	(Net income – Preferred dividend) ÷ Average number of common shares outstanding
Total asset turnover	Sales ÷ Average total assets
Desegregation of the Return on Common Equity	*The product of the following 3 ratios equals the rate of return on common equity and shows how and why it changed.*
Adjusted net profit margin on each dollar of sales that belongs to common equity	(Net income – Preferred dividends) ÷ Sales
Total Asset Turnover Ratio	Sales ÷ Average total assets
Financial Leverage Ratio (Financial Structure)	Average total assets ÷ Average common shareholders' equity = ROE
Equity growth rate	(Net income – Dividends paid) ÷ Average common equity
Common earnings leverage	(Net income – Preferred dividends) ÷ (Net income + Interest expense (1 – Tax rate))

Operating Performance – Profit Margin Analysis

Gross profit margin (before taxes)	Net sales – Cost of goods sold ÷ Net sales
Operating profit margin (before taxes)	Income before taxes and interest expense ÷ Net sales
Net profit margin	Net income ÷ Sales

Asset Utilization (Turnovers)

Accounts receivable turnover	Sales ÷ Average accounts receivable
Inventory turnover	Sales ÷ Average inventories
Fixed asset turnover	Sales ÷ Average fixed assets
Total asset turnover	Sales ÷ Average total assets

Source: Felix Lessambo.

Appendix 15: Sample Business Plan Outline (Start-Up)

This is a sample outline for a business plan to be used by a start-up operation to request funding. In most cases, it is equally appropriate for existing businesses and those not pursuing funding. There is no single *right* way to lay out a business plan – feel free to add, subtract, and rearrange as is appropriate to your business and writing style. (If you do delete sections, make sure that the information involved either does not apply to your business or is addressed sufficiently in other sections of the plan.)

I. EXECUTIVE SUMMARY

Finish this section after you have finished the others. (You may wish to **begin** this section first, however, to help organize the major issues in your mind.) Use this section to summarize the major points to be addressed in the rest or the plan. You can follow the outline for the rest of the plan for the format of your executive summary. If you do, summarize each subsection with a bullet-point sentence or two.

II. CAPITAL PLAN

A. Sources of Funds

How much money will you need? From what sources? Under what terms?

B. Uses of Funds

How will you use the money? Begin with a table that outlines the major use of funds categories (such as building purchase, build-out, equipment, franchise fees, working capital reserves, etc.) and amounts required, then follow it up with a paragraph or two describing each use of funds category in greater detail. If possible, explain how the expenditure will help you become more profitable. (For example, if you are buying inventory, explain how much revenue that inventory can support. If purchasing real estate, calculate the estimated rent expense saved over the life to the loan.)

C. Repayment of Funds

Illustrate your ability to repay the loan from operating cash flow by presenting a chart that compares projected annual cash flow with projected annual loan payments.

Briefly describe the total values of personal and business assets available for use as collateral in securing the loan.

If you or your spouse will continue to receive a paycheck from an employer after the establishment of your business, discuss it here.

III. BACKGROUND INFORMATION

A. Ownership & Corporate Format

What kind of business (such as sole proprietor, LLC, S-Corporation) is it/will it be? When was it/will it be established? In what state is it/will it be chartered? Who are the owners and what percentage do/will they own?

B. History of the Business

For existing businesses: talk about the major milestones of development including opening, break-even, major changes to products/services, important personnel additions, and relocations. For new businesses: talk about the preparations and planning you've done so far in anticipation of opening the company.

C. Industry Overview

What is the size, growth, and overall trends of the industry?

D. Objectives

Explain your quantitative (such as profit and sales targets) as well as qualitative (such as market position) goals for your company. If possible, briefly explain your overall strategies for reaching those goals.

E. Implementation Timeline

What are the major tasks and milestones to be reached as you move forward. For each, provide an estimate of how long it will take to accomplish.

F. Future Opportunities

Use this section to describe future opportunities you hope to pursue, but don't yet know enough about the hows, whens, and ifs to include them in your financial projections.

IV. PRODUCTS AND SERVICES

A. Overview

Briefly provide a basic overview of the products and services your company will provide.

B. Description of Products/Services by Category

For each major product/service category, describe: the nature of the products/services in the category, pricing and pricing policies, direct costs involved.

   DO THE MATH: If you will provide a limited number of standard products/services, provide a chart projecting annual totals for projected unit sales within each category, average prices for each category, and projected sales based on projected units and pricing.

V. MANAGEMENT, STAFFING, STRATEGIC PARTNERS, AND PROFESSIONAL SUPPORT

If feasible, provide a table that summarizes your projected staff and payroll for each of the first three years of operations.

A. Management Team

Provide a profile for each owner who will participate in operations as well as each major manager. Discuss major job responsibilities as well as specific skills and experiences of each manager that qualify them to handle the job at hand. Touch on career highlights here and include complete résumés in the attachments. Discuss compensation.

B. Staffing

If your staff numbers will be modest, provide descriptions of each job title here. If you have particular people already selected for these positions, discuss their qualifications. If not, discuss the qualifications required for successful candidates. Discuss how staffing needs will change as the company grows. Discuss compensation.

C. Strategic Partners

Strategic partners are others who have a major effect on the way you do business, but are not part of your organization. These can include vendors, general contractors (if you are a subcontractor), subcontractors, landlords, collaborative marketing partners, and others.

D. Professional Support

Briefly list professionals you will use and describe how you will use them. These can include attorneys, accountants, bookkeepers, payroll services, consultants, insurance brokers, graphic designers, and others. A sentence or two for each is sufficient.

VI. OPERATIONS

A. Hours and Days of Operation

How will your hours and days of operation be configured to meet the needs of your customers?

B. Location and Facilities

Location – where will the business be located? Is location important to the success of your operation? How will this location contribute to that success? What businesses and potential customers are nearby? For retail businesses, provide traffic counts if you can.

Facilities – describe the actual location, including total square footage, allocation of space, parking (if appropriate). Discuss office and computer equipment, as well as other equipment and vehicles required. If renting, describe the lease. Describe how your facilities needs will change as the business grows.

C. Licensing, Permitting and Other Regulatory Issues

Describe the regulatory requirements for doing business, including any certifications, licenses, permits, registrations. Also discuss any zoning or building regulations. For home-based businesses, discuss any homeowners' association restrictions. Discuss your current status in regard to those requirements.

D. Other Operational Issues

Address any other operational issues that have not been covered in other sections. Retitle this section and add others as appropriate.

VII. MARKETING

A. Marketing Targets

Provide as much detail as possible about your most likely customers. Who are they? What is important to them? Where are they? Do they have things in common that make it possible to efficiently reach them with marketing messages?

   Also, don't forget about past and current customers as a productive source of business. Referral sources should also be a marketing target.

B. Distribution

Discuss how your products and services will get into the hands of their users. Will you sell direct? With you sell through retailers? Wholesalers? Many companies use a combination of these approaches. Talk about the relative merits and challenges of each distribution model you will use. If you will use wholesalers and/or retailers and have identified specific candidates, discuss them and your expected relationship with them.

C. Competitive Environment and Positioning

Discuss your major direct competitors and your comparative strengths and weaknesses. Remember, very few businesses truly have "no competition" – even if no one in the marketplace provides exactly what you do, customers often have the option of simply not buying from anyone, buying alternative types of product or service, or buying over the Internet. How will you position yourself against these options as well as your direct competitors?

D. Marketing Tactics

What tools will you use to promote your products and services? Create a section for each major marketing tactic (such as advertising, internet promotions, direct mail, trade shows, etc.) as well as subsections (such as print advertising, TV advertising, radio advertising, etc.), as applicable. Describe how and when you will use these tools and how your tactics will interact for cohesive, organized marketing campaigns.

VIII. FINANCIAL SUMMARY

A. Sales

Present a chart summarizing your annual projections for total sales in each of the next three years. If appropriate, make it a "stacked" chart providing a visual presentation of each sales category's contribution to total annual sales.

B. Profits

Present a chart summarizing your annual projections for total sales, gross profits, and net profits in each of the next three years.

C. Expenses

Based on three-year projected totals and the equation [income = expenses + profits], provide a pie chart that presents the percentage of total income equalled by each major expense category (such as costs of sales, rent, payroll, minor expenses combined into a single "all other expenses" category), and profits.

D. Break-Even

Based on three-year projected annual averages and the equation [profits = variable cost % x sales – fixed costs], provide a chart illustrating projected profit at various potential sales levels. If your cost structure will change dramatically from year to year, you may need to provide a separate break-even analysis for each year.

ATTACHMENTS

A. Projected Income Statement (Cash Basis) – 3 years, monthly
   Minimum requirements: 1 year monthly, plus 2 years quarterly. It's easier just to do all three years on a monthly basis. Include a cash flow calculation section after profit calculations.
B. Projected balance sheet, 3 years
C. Résumés
D. Others, could include: product information, Letters of Interest/sales contracts, reprints, marketing materials, etc.

Appendix 16: Selected IRC Sections (M&A)

Section 332. Complete liquidations of subsidiaries

(a) General rule
No gain or loss shall be recognized on the receipt by a corporation of property distributed in complete liquidation of another corporation.
(b) Liquidations to which section applies
For purposes of this section, a distribution shall be considered to be in complete liquidation only if –
  (1) the corporation receiving such property was, on the date of the adoption of the plan of liquidation, and has continued to be at all times until the receipt of the property, the owner of stock (in such other corporation) meeting the requirements of section 1504(a)(2); and either
  (2) the distribution is by such other corporation in complete cancellation or redemption of all its stock, and the transfer of all the property occurs within the taxable year; in such case the adoption by the shareholders of the resolution under which is authorized the distribution of all the assets of such corporation in complete cancellation or redemption of all its stock shall be considered an adoption of a plan of liquidation, even though no time for the completion of the transfer of the property is specified in such resolution; or
  (3) such distribution is one of a series of distributions by such other corporation in complete cancellation or redemption of all its stock in accordance with a plan of liquidation under which the transfer of all the property under the liquidation is to be completed within 3 years from the close of the taxable year during which is made the first of the series of distributions under the plan, except that if such transfer is not completed within such period, or if the taxpayer does not continue qualified under paragraph (1) until the completion of such transfer, no distribution under the plan shall be considered a distribution in complete liquidation.

   If such transfer of all the property does not occur within the taxable year, the Secretary may require of the taxpayer such bond, or waiver of the statute of limitations on assessment and collection, or both, as he may deem necessary to insure, if the transfer of the property is not completed within such 3-year period, or if the taxpayer does not continue qualified under paragraph (1) until the completion of such transfer, the assessment and collection of all income taxes then imposed by law for such taxable year or subsequent taxable years, to the extent attributable to property so received. A distribution otherwise constituting a distribution in complete liquidation within the meaning of this subsection shall not be considered as not constituting such a distribution merely because it does not constitute a distribution or liquidation within the meaning of the corporate law under which the distribution is made; and for purposes of this subsection a transfer of property of such other corporation to the taxpayer shall not be considered as not constituting a distribution (or one of a series of distributions) in complete cancellation or redemption of all the stock of such other corporation, merely because the carrying out of the plan involves (A) the transfer under the plan to the taxpayer by such other corporation of property, not attributable to shares owned by the taxpayer, on an exchange described in section 361, and (B) the complete cancellation or redemption under the plan, as a result of exchanges described in section 354, of the shares not owned by the taxpayer.

(c) <u>Deductible liquidating distributions of regulated investment companies and real estate investment trusts</u>

If a corporation receives a distribution from a regulated investment company or a real estate investment trust which is considered under subsection (b) as being in complete liquidation of such company or trust, then, notwithstanding any other provision of this chapter, such corporation shall recognize and treat as a dividend from such company or trust an amount equal to the deduction for dividends paid allowable to such company or trust by reason of such distribution.

Internal Revenue Code Section 351

Transfer to corporation controlled by transferor.

(a) <u>General rule</u>. No gain or loss shall be recognized if property is transferred to a corporation by one or more persons solely in exchange for stock in such corporation and immediately after the exchange such person or persons are in control (as defined in section 368(c)) of the corporation.

(b) <u>Receipt of property</u>. If subsection (a) would apply to an exchange but for the fact that there is received, in addition to the stock permitted to be received under subsection (a), other property or money, then –

    (1) gain (if any) to such recipient shall be recognized, but not in excess of –

        (A) the amount of money received, plus

        (B) the fair market value of such other property received; and

    (2) no loss to such recipient shall be recognized.

(c) <u>Special rules where distribution to shareholders.</u>

    (1) In general. In determining control for purposes of this section, the fact that any corporate transferor distributes part or all of the stock in the corporation which it receives in the exchange to its shareholders shall not be taken into account.

    (2) Special rule for section 355. If the requirements of section 355 (or so much of section 356 as relates to section 355) are met with respect to a distribution described in paragraph (1), then, solely for purposes of determining the tax treatment of the transfers of property to the controlled corporation by the distributing corporation, the fact that the shareholders of the distributing corporation dispose of part or all of the distributed stock, or the fact that the corporation whose stock was distributed issues additional stock, shall not be taken into account in determining control for purposes of this section.

(d) <u>Services, certain indebtedness, and accrued interest not treated as property</u>. For purposes of this section, stock issued for –

    (1) services,

    (2) indebtedness of the transferee corporation which is not evidenced by a security, or

    (3) interest on indebtedness of the transferee corporation which accrued on or after the beginning of the transferor's holding period for the debt, shall not be considered as issued in return for property.

(e) <u>Exceptions</u>. This section shall not apply to –

    (1) Transfer of property to an investment company. A transfer of property to an investment company. For purposes of the preceding sentence, the determination of whether a company is an investment company shall be made –

        (A) by taking into account all stock and securities held by the company, and

        (B) by treating as stock and securities –

           (i) money,

          (ii) stocks and other equity interests in a corporation, evidences of indebtedness, options, forward or futures contracts, notional principal contracts and derivatives,

         (iii) any foreign currency,

         (iv) any interest in a real estate investment trust, a common trust fund, a regulated investment company, a publicly-traded partnership (as defined in section 7704(b)) or any other equity interest (other than in a corporation) which pursuant to its terms or any other arrangement is readily convertible into, or exchangeable for, any asset described in any preceding clause, this clause or clause (v) or (viii),

          (v) except to the extent provided in regulations prescribed by the Secretary, any interest in a precious metal, unless such metal is used or held in the active conduct of a trade or business after the contribution,

         (vi) except as otherwise provided in regulations prescribed by the Secretary, interests in any entity if substantially all of the assets of such entity consist (directly or indirectly) of any assets described in any preceding clause or clause (viii),

         (vii) to the extent provided in regulations prescribed by the Secretary, any interest in any entity not described in clause (vi), but only to the extent of the value of such interest that is attributable to assets listed in clauses (i) through (v) or clause (viii), or

        (viii) any other asset specified in regulations prescribed by the Secretary.

The Secretary may prescribe regulations that, under appropriate circumstances, treat any asset described in clauses (i) through (v) as not so listed.

    (2) Title 11 or similar case. A transfer of property of a debtor pursuant to a plan while the debtor is under the jurisdiction of a court in a title 11 or similar case (within the meaning of section 368(a)(3)(A)), to the extent that the stock received in the exchange is used to satisfy the indebtedness of such debtor.

(f) <u>Treatment of controlled corporation</u>. If –

    (1) property is transferred to a corporation (hereinafter in this subsection referred to as the "controlled corporation") in an exchange with respect to which gain or loss is not recognized (in whole or in part) to the transferor under this section, and

    (2) such exchange is not in pursuance of a plan of reorganization, section 311 shall apply to any transfer in such exchange by the controlled corporation in the same manner as if such transfer were a distribution to which subpart A of part I applies.

(g) <u>Nonqualified preferred stock not treated as stock.</u>

    (1) In general. In the case of a person who transfers property to a corporation and receives nonqualified preferred stock –

        (A) subsection (a) shall not apply to such transferor, and

        (B) if (and only if) the transferor receives stock other than nonqualified preferred stock –

          (i) subsection (b) shall apply to such transferor; and

         (ii) such nonqualified preferred stock shall be treated as other property for purposes of applying subsection (b).

(2) Nonqualified preferred stock. For purposes of paragraph (1) –

    (A) <u>In general.</u> The term "nonqualified preferred stock" means preferred stock if –

        (i) the holder of such stock has the right to require the issuer or a related person to redeem or purchase the stock,

        (ii) the issuer or a related person is required to redeem or purchase such stock,

        (iii) the issuer or a related person has the right to redeem or purchase the stock and, as of the issue date, it is more likely than not that such right will be exercised, or

        (iv) the dividend rate on such stock varies in whole or in part (directly or indirectly) with reference to interest rates, commodity prices, or other similar indices.

    (B) <u>Limitations.</u> Clauses (i), (ii), and (iii) of subparagraph (A) shall apply only if the right or obligation referred to therein may be exercised within the 20-year period beginning on the issue date of such stock and such right or obligation is not subject to a contingency which, as of the issue date, makes remote the likelihood of the redemption or purchase.

    (C) <u>Exceptions for certain rights or obligations.</u>

        (i) In general. A right or obligation shall not be treated as described in clause (i), (ii), or (iii) of subparagraph (A) if –

           (I) it may be exercised only upon the death, disability, or mental incompetency of the holder, or (II) in the case of a right or obligation to redeem or purchase stock transferred in connection with the performance of services for the issuer or a related person (and which represents reasonable compensation), it may be exercised only upon the holder's separation from service from the issuer or a related person.

        (ii) Exception. Clause (i)(I) shall not apply if the stock relinquished in the exchange, or the stock acquired in the exchange is in –

           (I) a corporation if any class of stock in such corporation or a related party is readily tradable on an established securities market or otherwise, or

           (II) any other corporation if such exchange is part of a transaction or series of transactions in which such corporation is to become a corporation described in subclause (I).

(3) Definitions. For purposes of this subsection –

    (A) <u>Preferred stock</u>: The term "preferred stock" means stock which is limited and preferred as to dividends and does not participate in corporate growth to any significant extent. Stock shall not be treated as participating in corporate growth to any significant extent unless there is a real and meaningful likelihood of the shareholder actually participating in the earnings and growth of the corporation. If there is not a real and meaningful likelihood that dividends beyond any limitation or preference will actually be paid, the possibility of such payments will be disregarded in determining whether stock is limited and preferred as to dividends.

    (B) <u>Related person</u>: A person shall be treated as related to another person if they bear a relationship to such other person described in section 267(b) or 707(b).

(4) Regulations. The Secretary may prescribe such regulations as may be necessary or appropriate to carry out the purposes of this subsection and sections 354(a)(2)(C), 355(a)(3)(D), and 356(e). The Secretary may also prescribe regulations, consistent with the treatment under this subsection and such sections, for the treatment of nonqualified preferred stock under other provisions of this title.

(h) Cross references.
   (1) For special rule where another party to the exchange assumes a liability, see section 357.
   (2) For the basis of stock or property received in an exchange to which this section applies, see sections 358 and 362.
   (3) For special rule in the case of an exchange described in this section but which results in a gift, see section 2501 and following.
   (4) For special rule in the case of an exchange described in this section but which has the effect of the payment of compensation by the corporation or by a transferor, see section 61(a)(1).
   (5) For coordination of this section with section 304, see section 304(b)(3).

Sec. 1.354-1: Exchanges of stock and securities in certain reorganizations.

(a) Section 354 provides that under certain circumstances no gain or loss is recognized to a shareholder who surrenders his stock in exchange for other stock or to a security holder who surrenders his securities in exchange for stock. Section 354 also provides that under certain circumstances a security holder may surrender securities and receive securities in the same principal amount or in a lesser principal amount without the recognition of gain or loss to him. The exchanges to which section 354 applies must be pursuant to a plan of reorganization as provided in section 368(a) and the stock and securities surrendered as well as the stock and securities received must be those of a corporation which is a party to the reorganization. Section 354 does not apply to exchanges pursuant to a reorganization described in section 368(a)(1)(D) unless the transferor corporation –
   (1) Transfers all or substantially all of its assets to a single corporation, and
   (2) Distributes all of its remaining properties (if any) and the stock, securities and other properties received in the exchange to its shareholders or security holders in pursuance of the plan of reorganization. The fact that properties retained by the transferor corporation, or received in exchange for the properties transferred in the reorganization, are used to satisfy existing liabilities not represented by securities and which were incurred in the ordinary course of business before the reorganization does not prevent the application of section 354 to an exchange pursuant to a plan of reorganization defined in section 368(a)(1)(D).
(b) Except as provided in section 354 (c) and (d), section 354 is not applicable to an exchange of stock or securities if a greater principal amount of securities is received than the principal amount of securities the recipient surrenders, or if securities are received and the recipient surrenders no securities. See, however, section 356 and regulations pertaining to such section. See also section 306 with respect to the receipt of preferred stock in a transaction to which section 354 is applicable.
(c) An exchange of stock or securities shall be subject to section 354(a)(1) even though –
   (1) Such exchange is not pursuant to a plan of reorganization described in section 368(a), and
   (2) The principal amount of the securities received exceeds the Principal amount of the securities surrendered or if securities are received and no securities are surrendered--

Sec.356. Receipt of additional consideration

(a) <u>Gain on exchanges</u>
 (1) Recognition of gain
  If –
   (A) section 354 or 355 would apply to an exchange but for the fact that
   (B) the property received in the exchange consists not only of property permit-
    ted by section 354 or 355 to be received without the recognition of gain but
    also of other property or money then the gain, if any, to the recipient shall
    be recognized, but in an amount not in excess of the sum of such money and
    the fair market value of such other property.
 (2) Treatment as dividend
  If an exchange is described in paragraph (1) but has the effect of the distribution
  of a dividend (determined with the application of section 318(a)), then there
  shall be treated as a dividend to each distributee such an amount of the gain
  recognized under paragraph (1) as is not in excess of his ratable share of the
  undistributed earnings and profits of the corporation accumulated after February
  28, 1913. The remainder, if any, of the gain recognized under paragraph (1) shall
  be treated as gain from the exchange of property.
(b) <u>Additional consideration received in certain distributions:</u> If –
 (1) section 355 would apply to a distribution but for the fact that
 (2) the property received in the distribution consists not only of property permitted
  by section 355 to be received without the recognition of gain, but also of other
  property or money, then an amount equal to the sum of such money and the fair
  market value of such other property shall be treated as a distribution of property
  to which section 301 applies.
(c) <u>Loss</u>
 If –
 (1) section 354 would apply to an exchange or section 355 would apply to an
  exchange or distribution, but for the fact that (2) the property received in the
  exchange or distribution consists not only of property permitted by section 354
  or 355 to be received without the recognition of gain or loss, but also of other
  property or money, then no loss from the exchange or distribution shall be
  recognized.
(d) <u>Securities as other property</u>
 For purposes of this section –
 (1) In general
  Except as provided in paragraph (2), the term "other property" includes securities.
 (2) Exceptions
  (A) Securities with respect to which non-recognition of gain would be permitted. The term "other property" does not include securities to the extent that,
   under section 354 or 355, such securities would be permitted to be received
   without the recognition of gain.
  (B) Greater principal amount in section 354 exchange If –
   (i) in an exchange described in section 354 (other than subsection (c)
    thereof), securities of a corporation a party to the reorganization are sur-
    rendered and securities of any corporation a party to the reorganization
    are received, and
   (ii) the principal amount of such securities received exceeds the princi-
    pal amount of such securities surrendered, then, with respect to such

securities received, the term "other property" means only the fair market value of such excess. For purposes of this subparagraph and subparagraph (C) if no securities are surrendered, the excess shall be the entire principal amount of the securities received.

(C) Greater principal amount in section 355 transaction If, in an exchange or distribution described in section 355, the principal amount of the securities in the controlled corporation which are received exceeds the principal amount of the securities in the distributing corporation which are surrendered, then, with respect to such securities received, the term "other property" means only the fair market value of such excess.

(e) Nonqualified preferred stock treated as other property

For purposes of this section –

(1) In general

Except as provided in paragraph (2), the term "other property" includes nonqualified preferred stock (as defined in section 351(g)(2)).

(2) Exception

The term "other property" does not include nonqualified preferred stock (as so defined) to the extent that, under section 354 or 355, such preferred stock would be permitted to be received without the recognition of gain.

(f) Exchanges for section 306 stock

Notwithstanding any other provision of this section, to the extent that any of the other property (or money) is received in exchange for section 306 stock, an amount equal to the fair market value of such other property (or the amount of such money) shall be treated as a distribution of property to which section 301 applies.

(g) Transactions involving gift or compensation

For special rules for a transaction described in section 354, 355, or this section, but which –

(1) results in a gift, see section 2501 and following, or

(2) has the effect of the payment of compensation, see section 61(a)(1).

Section 361: Non-recognition of gain or loss to corporations; treatment of distributions

(a) General rule

No gain or loss shall be recognized to a corporation if such corporation is a party to a reorganization and exchanges property, in pursuance of the plan of reorganization, solely for stock or securities in another corporation a party to the reorganization.

(b) Exchanges not solely in kind

(1) Gain

(2) If subsection (a) would apply to an exchange but for the fact that the property received in exchange consists not only of stock or securities permitted by subsection (a) to be received without the recognition of gain, but also of other property or money, then –

(A) Property distributed

If the corporation receiving such other property or money distributes it in pursuance of the plan of reorganization, no gain to the corporation shall be recognized from the exchange, but

(B) Property not distributed

If the corporation receiving such other property or money does not distribute it in pursuance of the plan of reorganization, the gain, if any, to the corporation shall be recognized.

The amount of gain recognized under subparagraph (B) shall not exceed the sum of the money and the fair market value of the other property so received which is not so distributed.

(3) Loss

If subsection (a) would apply to an exchange but for the fact that the property received in exchange consists not only of property permitted by subsection (a) to be received without the recognition of gain or loss, but also of other property or money, then no loss from the exchange shall be recognized.

(4) Treatment of transfers to creditors

For purposes of paragraph (1), any transfer of the other property or money received in the exchange by the corporation to its creditors in connection with the reorganization shall be treated as a distribution in pursuance of the plan of reorganization. The Secretary may prescribe such regulations as may be necessary to prevent avoidance of tax through abuse of the preceding sentence or subsection (c)(3). In the case of a reorganization described in section 368(a)(1)(D) with respect to which stock or securities of the corporation to which the assets are transferred are distributed in a transaction which qualifies under section 355, this paragraph shall apply only to the extent that the sum of the money and the fair market value of other property transferred to such creditors does not exceed the adjusted bases of such assets transferred.

(c) Treatment of distributions

(1) In general

Except as provided in paragraph (2), no gain or loss shall be recognized to a corporation a party to a reorganization on the distribution to its shareholders of property in pursuance of the plan of reorganization.

(2) Distributions of appreciated property

(A) In general

If –

(i) in a distribution referred to in paragraph (1), the corporation distributes property other than qualified property, and

(ii) the fair market value of such property exceeds its adjusted basis (in the hands of the distributing corporation), then gain shall be recognized to the distributing corporation as if such property were sold to the distributee at its fair market value.

(B) Qualified property

For purposes of this subsection, the term "qualified property" means -

(i) any stock in (or right to acquire stock in) the distributing corporation or obligation of the distributing corporation, or

(ii) any stock in (or right to acquire stock in) another corporation which is a party to the reorganization or obligation of another corporation which is such a party if such stock (or right) or obligation is received by the distributing corporation in the exchange.

(C) Treatment of liabilities

If any property distributed in the distribution referred to in paragraph (1) is subject to a liability or the shareholder assumes a liability of the distributing corporation in connection with the distribution, then, for purposes of subparagraph (A), the fair market value of such property shall be treated as not less than the amount of such liability.

(3) Treatment of certain transfers to creditors

For purposes of this subsection, any transfer of qualified property by the corporation to its creditors in connection with the reorganization shall be treated as a distribution to its shareholders pursuant to the plan of reorganization.

(4) Coordination with other provisions

Section 311 and subpart B of part II of this subchapter shall not apply to any distribution referred to in paragraph (1).

(5) Cross reference

For provision providing for recognition of gain in certain distributions, see section 355(d).

Appendix 17: Report of the New York Stock Exchange Commission on Corporate Governance, September 23, 2010

Ultimately, and notwithstanding the broad diversity of views among the various Commission members, the Commission was able to achieve a consensus on a number of principles, which are summarized below and detailed in Section IV below:

Principle 1 *The board's fundamental objective should be to build long-term Sustainable growth in shareholder value for the corporation, and the board is accountable to shareholders for its performance in achieving this objective.*

This is an important first principle to guide corporate boards at this time because boards have come under increased pressure in recent years as shareholders with competing interests and investment time horizons have sought to influence corporate behavior. The Commission believes that a board has the responsibility, subject to its fiduciary duties, to steer the corporation towards policies supporting long-term sustainable growth in shareholder value. It follows that corporate polices which encourage excessive risk-taking for the sake of short-term increases in stock price performance are inconsistent with sound corporate governance. Additionally, the board and management should establish compensation plans that incorporate goals aligned to various degrees based upon long-term value creation. Consistent with this principle, it is also important for the corporation to establish relationships with a core base of long-term oriented investors who understand the corporation's long-term strategy and recognize that long-term decisions by their very nature will take time to produce results. While many factors other than board performance may affect long-term shareholder value, the Commission believes that shareholders have the right and responsibility to hold a board accountable for its performance in achieving long-term sustainable growth in shareholder value.

Principle 2 *While the board's responsibility for corporate governance has long been established, the critical role of management in establishing proper corporate governance has not been sufficiently recognized. The Commission believes that a key aspect of successful governance depends upon successful management of the company, as management has primary responsibility for creating an environment in which a culture of performance with integrity can flourish.*

In recent years the debate over what constitutes "good" corporate governance has focused upon the board's scope of authority and the proper relationship between the board and shareholders. This discussion may improperly ignore the critical role of management in corporate governance. The Commission believes that successful governance depends heavily upon honest, competent and industrious managers. Management's role in corporate governance includes, among other things, establishing and monitoring processes and procedures for risk management and proper internal controls, as well as evaluating executive talent according to high ethical standards, having systems for open

321

internal communication about problems without the fear of retaliation, and promoting accountability through tailored incentive compensation that encourages, among other things, disciplined and transparent risk taking. Management's role also includes providing accurate information to the board and developing and communicating the corporation's strategic plan to shareholders and the market. Consistent with this principle, management should understand that directors may need access to various sources of information in order to fully understand the viewpoints of all major constituencies, and may also disagree with management over strategy or decisions, and that this "constructive tension" between the board and management is a characteristic of good corporate governance so long as debate is conducted within the context of a collegial and productive discussion.

Principle 3   *Shareholders have the right, a responsibility and a long-term Economic interest to vote their shares in a thoughtful manner, in recognition of the fact that voting decisions influence director behavior, corporate governance and conduct, and that voting decisions are one of the primary means of communicating with companies on issues of concern.*

The Commission believes that the right to vote the shares of a company is a basic right and duty of share ownership, and that shareholders should vote their shares in a reasoned and responsible manner. This is even more important now because of the significantly increased ability of shareholders to influence corporate conduct, including through the election of directors. Consistent with this principle, institutional investors should establish and disclose their corporate governance guidelines and general voting policies. These investors should also engage in dialogue with companies on their corporate governance and voting policies, processes and philosophy. The Commission also recognizes the need that some institutional investors have to use third party proxy advisory services, and while this decision should generally be left to the discretion of the institution, the Commission believes that such a decision does not relieve institutions from discharging their responsibility to vote constructively, thoughtfully and in alignment with the interests of their clients.

Principle 4   *Good corporate governance should be integrated with the company's business strategy and objectives and should not be viewed simply as a compliance obligation separate from the company's longterm business prospects.*

The Commission believes that sound corporate governance should be a core element of a company's business strategy, as it includes independent and objective oversight of strategy and management by boards; alignment of interests among shareholders, management and the board; accountability of the board to shareholders and accountability of management to the board; compensation programs that incentivize long-term growth; establishment of criteria that are aligned with the company's business goals; prudent risk management; a culture of integrity; and consideration of the impact of the corporation's activities on society overall. Corporate governance thus must be seen as an integral part of the basic operation of the corporation, and not just a compliance obligation. Yet there is a risk that the number of new governance mandates and "best practice" recommendations over the last decade can lead even the best boards to adopt a "check the box" mentality when trying to adopt and comply with certain corporate governance requirements. This risk is increased by the reality that being a director is still generally not considered a full-time job, and that directors must also have the time to address issues in addition to monitoring and oversight.

Principle 5 *Legislation and agency rulemaking are important to establish the basic tenets of corporate governance and ensure the efficiency of our markets. Beyond these fundamental principles, however, the Commission has a preference for market based governance solutions whenever possible.*

The Commission recognizes that legislation and appropriate rulemaking are critical to ensuring that fundamental principles of corporate governance are established and maintained. However, the Commission believes over-reliance on legislation and agency rulemaking may not be in the best interests of shareholders, companies or society. The Commission believes that corporate governance problems can and should be constructively solved through collaboration and dialogue resulting in market-based reforms. This approach results in practices that are customized to individual companies, providing more flexibility, as well as more practical and sustainable solutions. As set forth in Principle 3, shareholders should not be regarded as adversaries of a company; rather, all corporate constituencies should be encouraged toward a common goal of building companies that generate value over an extended period of time. The Commission believes that ideally legislation and rulemaking should operate to set broad principles that encourage such collaboration and dialogue among the corporate constituencies.

Principle 6 *Good corporate governance includes transparency for corporations and investors, sound disclosure policies and communication beyond disclosure through dialogue and engagement as necessary and appropriate.*

The Commission recognizes that transparency is a critical element of good corporate governance, and that companies should make regular efforts to ensure that they have sound disclosure policies and practices. While disclosure is the primary method of communication with shareholders, the Commission understands that, where appropriate, management or directors should engage in direct dialogue with investors on governance, performance or strategy concerns. Companies and shareholders should develop best practices to ensure that such conversations are meaningful to the participants, result in increased understanding and trust among boards, shareholders and management, and are conducted in compliance with applicable rules and regulations. Investors should also be held to appropriate levels of transparency and be required to disclose holdings, including derivative or other security ownership, on a timely and equal basis, subject to the recognition that certain information relating to trading and investment strategies may be proprietary.

Principle 7 *While independence and objectivity are necessary attributes of board members, companies must also strike the right balance between the appointment of independent and non-independent directors to ensure that there is an appropriate range and mix of expertise, diversity and knowledge on the board.*

The Commission fully supports the NYSE's listing requirements on the importance and role of independent directors. At the same time, the Commission notes that in recent years it has become common to have the company's CEO as the only non-independent director on the board. The Commission recognizes that the NYSE's listing requirements do not limit a board to only one non-independent director, and believes that the appointment of a minority of directors who possess in-depth knowledge of the company and its industry could be helpful for the board as it assesses the company's strategy, risk profile, competition and alternative courses of action. The Commission does not wish to imply that an independent director cannot have equally deep knowledge of the company as a non-independent director. Rather, the Commission believes that, as provided for under the NYSE's listing standards, a properly functioning board can include more than one non-independent director.

Principle 8   *The Commission recognizes the influence that proxy advisory firms have on the market, and believes that such firms should be held to appropriate standards of transparency and accountability. The Commission commends the SEC for its issuance of the Concept Release on the U.S. Proxy System, which includes inviting comments on how such firms should be regulated.*

Although many large investors use proxy advisory services primarily as a source of information and research, that is not necessarily the practice of all institutional investors, and there is an increased level of concern regarding the impact of advisory firms. As a result, the Commission believes that the SEC should engage in a study of the role of proxy advisory firms to determine their potential impact on, among other things, corporate governance and behavior and consider whether or not further regulation of these firms is appropriate. At a minimum, such firms should be required to disclose the policies and methodologies that the firms use to formulate specific voting recommendations, as well as all material conflicts of interest, and to hold themselves to a high degree of care, accuracy and fairness in dealing with both shareholders and companies by adhering to strict codes of conduct. The advisory services should also be required to disclose the company's response to its analysis and conclusions.

Principle 9   *The SEC should work with the NYSE and other exchanges to ease the burden of proxy voting and communication while encouraging greater participation by individual investors in the proxy voting process.*

The SEC should work with all parties to the proxy system to ensure that companies and investors are able to communicate about proxy voting issues on a timely basis without undue costs or burdens, recognizing that there are privacy and other concerns from investors regarding the proprietary nature of their investment strategies. As a part of this process, the Commission believes that the SEC should establish a committee of market participants and outside experts, including representatives of the various constituencies, to consider its recent concept release on improving the proxy process. In addition, in light of the declining participation of individual investors in recent years, the SEC should consider whether there are more effective and efficient ways for individual investors to participate in the system, as well as providing such investors with pertinent information to help ensure they make informed decisions.

Principle 10   *The SEC and/or the NYSE should consider a wide range of views to determine the impact of major corporate governance reforms on corporate performance over the last decade. The SEC and/or the NYSE should also periodically assess the impact of major corporate governance reforms on the promotion of sustainable, long-term corporate growth and sustained profitability.*

As summarized in Section III of this Report, the past decade has seen a significant amount of regulatory and other initiatives designed to improve corporate governance with the goal of improving performance. The Commission recognizes that it is difficult to measure the impact of corporate governance regulations given that performance is impacted by many factors. Nevertheless, the Commission believes that because of the significance of these reforms, and because of the numerous entities involved in regulating corporate governance in the United States, the SEC and other regulators should consider a wide range of views and perspectives before adopting new regulations, including the practical implications of new regulations on directors' ability to perform their existing duties, the potential costs and benefits to the company and its shareholders and the efficacy of existing regulations. The Commission notes that being a director is not a full-time job, and that creating new mandates risks limiting the time directors can spend on other tasks. Accordingly, the Commission believes the SEC should also consider the expanded use of "pilot" programs, including the use of "sunset provisions," and phased-in implementation dates to identify any implementation problems before a program is fully rolled out. The next section of this Report describes our charter, the membership of the Commission and a brief review of the process leading to our detailed principles. Section III reviews some of the most significant developments in corporate governance and the broader market in the last decade that have put significant strains on traditional concepts of corporate governance. Section IV contains our specific principles, including detailing the separate principles applicable to the board, management and shareholders.

Bibliography

Apostolik, Richard (2009) *Foundations of Banking Risk*, Wiley Finance.

Baker, James (2002) *The Bank for International Settlements*, Quorum Books.

Baladi, André (2009) *Globalization and the Reform of the International Banking and Monetary System*, Palgrave Macmillan.

Banks, Eric (2005) *Liquidity Risk, Management Asset and Funding Risk*, Palgrave-Macmillan.

Crouhy Michel (2006) *The Essentials of Risk Management*, McGraw-Hill.

Doenberg, Richard (2007) *International Taxation*, Thompson West.

de Haan, Jacob (2011) *The European Central Bank at Ten*, Springer.

Graetz, Michael (2003) *Foundations of International Income Taxation*, Foundation Press.

Guiliano, Iannota (2009) *A Guide to Underwriting and Advisory Services*, Springer.

Lessambo, Felix (2010) *Fundamentals of Hedge Funds*, Dorrance Publishing.

Maude, David (2006) *Global Private Banking and Wealth Management*, Wiley Finance.

Okina, Kunio (2004) *Functions and Operations of the Bank of Japan*, IMES.

Robinson, Roland (1962) *The Management of Bank Funds*, 2nd edition, McGraw-Hill.

Rothbard, Murray (2005) *A History of Money and Banking in the United States: The Colonial Era to World War II*, Ludwig Von Mises Institute.

Saunders, Antony (2009) *Financial Markets & Institutions*, McGraw-Hill.

Sheller, Hanspeter (2006) *The European Central Bank: History, Role and Functions*.

Steger, Ulrich (2004) *Mastering Global Corporate Governance*, John Wiley & Sons Ltd.

Stiglitz, Joseph (2010) *Free Fall, America Free Markets, and the Sinking of the World Economy*, W. W. Norton & Company.

Taleb, Nassim (2007) *The Black Swan*, Random House.

Uyemura, Dennis (1993) *Financial Risk Management in Banking*, Irwin.

Glossary of Terms

Adjustable-rate mortgage (ARM) A mortgage rate which ties the borrower's interest rate to some market interest rate or interest rate index.

Alpha Risk management tool that a fund manager uses to measure its performance against that of a risk-free investment, such as a Treasury bill. Alpha is also the difference between the predicted return on an investment and the actual return.

American Deposit Receipt (ADR) A negotiable certificate or receipt issued in the US, representing ownership of securities of a non-US-based company, issued in a foreign market.

Appreciation (or strengthening) of a currency The increase in value of a currency spot rate relative to other currencies.

Ask price The offer or sale price of an asset such as a share or bond.

Asset transformation The process of creating a new asset (loan) from liabilities (deposits) with different characteristics by converting small denomination, immediately available, and relatively risk-free bank deposits into loans – a new, relatively risky, large denomination asset – that are repaid based on a set schedule.

Asset-backed security Is a financial security backed by a loan, lease, or receivables against assets other than real estate and mortgage-based securities.

Balloon payment Large final payment paid in an installment loan.

Basel Accord An agreement that requires the imposition of risk-based capital ratios on banks in major industrialized countries.

Beta Risk management tool that gauges the risk of a portfolio by measuring the volatility of its past returns in relation to the returns of a benchmark, such as the S&P 500.

Bid-ask spread The standard measure of transactions costs in many financial markets.

Broker An intermediary person or firm, function of which consists of arranging purchases and sales of securities, commodities or derivatives, for a commission.

Call option An option that gives a purchaser the right, but not the obligation, to buy an underlying asset from the writer, at a fixed strike price, on a pre-specified date.

Capital adequacy Refers to the amount of equity capital and other securities a bank holds as reserves against risky assets to reduce the probability of a bank failure.

Capital-to-assets ratio The relationship between risk-weighted assets and the regulatory capital.

Cash sweep An automated process whereby all or a portion of the available cash is moved from a non-interest bearing account into an interest bearing account or an interest bearing instrument.

Central bank Is the principal monetary authority of a country, or a group of countries, which exercises regulatory and/or supervisory authority over banks within its jurisdiction.

Clearinghouse An independent entity that stands between the counterparties to secure all the trades processed in an organized market.

Collateral A lien against property placed by the lender until the loan is fully paid off.

Commercial banks Banks where the core activities consist of taking deposits and extending loans.

Commercial paper A type of fixed-maturity unsecured short-term negotiable debt issued generally in bearer form and primarily by non-banks, with a maturity between 1 day to 270 days.

Core banking services Refers to the main activities of a commercial or investment bank, such as deposit collection, underwriting, and payment services.

Correspondent banks Banks with reciprocal accounts and agreements.

Counterparty credit risk The risk that a bank's trading or business partner might fail to fulfill its contractual obligations.

Country risk Refers to the probability that unexpected events occur in a specific country that will affect the ability to repay loans or to repatriate dividends.

Credit approval Refers to the loan approval procedure within a lending institution.

Credit enhancement Refers to internal and external facilities designed to reduce the credit risk to the investor with the goals of achieving higher ratings on and improving the marketability of investor certificates.

Credit rating An opinion about the likelihood of default of either an issuer or an issue made by that issuer.

Credit risk The potential for financial loss if a borrower or counterparty in a transaction fails to meet its obligations.

Crime risk Refers to risks due to embezzlement, robbery, fraud, and identity theft.

Cross-default An event default which leads to the loan becoming immediately repayable.

Cross trade A transaction executed on the floor of an exchange by just one Member who is both buyer and seller. Cross trades must be executed at market price.

Daily position The maximum open position a dealer is authorized to assume during the trading day.

Derivative security: A financial security or commodity whose payoff is linked to another previously-issued asset.

Default risk The potential loss due to default by the borrower.

Delta Market measure in options to buy or sell stocks. It is the measure of how the value of the derivatives would change compared with the underlying stock or other assets. The term has evolved to refer to how banks customize a security for a client, such as ETFs, and closely replicate it on the bank's books.

Deposit Money entrusted in a bank for safekeeping in a bank account that allows the depositor to withdraw the funds and interest thereon at any time.

Deposit rates The rates at which commercial banks pay the public in return for deposits.

Depreciation (or weakening) of a currency The decrease in value of a currency spot rate relative to another currency.

Discount window The facility through which Federal Reserve banks issue loans to depository institutions.

EBIT Earnings before interest and taxes.

Economic exposure The extent to which the value of a firm would be affected by unanticipated changes in exchange rates.

Edge Act Bank (Corporation) Federally chartered subsidiaries of US banks that are physically located in the US and are allowed to engage in a full range of international banking activities.

Eurocurrency A time deposit of money in an international bank located in a country other than that which issues the currency.

Exchange risk Refers to the probability of loss due to fluctuation in currency prices.

Exchanged traded funds (ETF) Securities that resemble mutual funds but trade like stocks, and are commonly designed to replicate the movement of an index.

Externalities Situations where a market exchange imposes costs or benefits on others who are not party to the exchange.

Fed funds rate The interest rate on short-term funds transferred between financial institutions, usually one day.

Financial asset Consists primarily of obligations to make cash payments.

Foreign exchange risk The risk of losses resulting from changes in foreign exchange rates.

FOREX Foreign exchange market from spot or forward exchange dealings.

Forward contract An agreement between counterparties to buy or sell an asset, at an agreed price, on a future date.

Functional currency The currency of the primary economic environment in which the entity operates. It is often the local currency of the country in which the entity conducts most of its business.

Go Shop provision A provision that grants the target board the right to negotiate a sale of the company with one buyer, while meeting the Revlon duties, subject to receiving a better offer during that period.

Gross Domestic Product (GDP) The standard measure of the sum of all the goods and services produced in the economy.

Haircut A value discount of a portfolio based upon the value and nature of an asset. Haircuts are mostly based on the quality and type of assets and tend to provide the degree to which an asset can be sold or pledged in a relatively short time period to raise liquidity.

Hedging Risk management technique consisting of protecting against potential or perceived losses.

Hedging instrument A contract that reduces an institution's exposure to a change in risk or interest rate.

Hurdle return The minimum amount of return an investor requires prior to making an investment decision.

Impaired loan A loan that the management believes can no longer be reasonably assured.

Initial Public Offer (IPO) The first public issue of financial instruments by a firm.

Insolvency risk Risk that liabilities would exceed assets or threaten to bring the bank under.

Institutional investor A financially sophisticated organization such as a publicly traded company, a bank, an insurer company, a hedge fund, or private equity firm.

Interest rate margin The difference between the interest income the bank earns on its assets and the interest expense it pays on its liabilities.

Interest rate risk The impact changes in interest rates could have on margins, earnings, and economic value. Put differently, it refers to the probability that changes in interest rates will adversely affect the value of the net worth.

International bank A large commercial investment or merchant bank with operations in different countries.

International banking facility A separate banking center in a US domestic bank or office, authorized by the Federal Reserve Board in 1981 to participate in Eurocurrency lending through a separate set of accounts.

Investment bank A bank which deals predominantly with corporate and institutional customers, issues financial securities in the financial and capital markets, provides advice on transactions such as mergers and acquisitions, manages investments, and trades on its own account.

Issuance The process of creating and distributing securities.

Junk bond A bond rated as speculative or less than the investment grade by bond-rating agencies.

Lead/lag strategy Currency management strategy which consists of reducing transaction exposure by paying or collecting foreign financial obligations early (lead) or late (lag) depending on whether the currency is hard or soft.

Lending rates The rates at which commercial banks charge the public when lending.

Leverage Consists of increasing an investment's value or return without increasing the amount invested.

Letter of credit A guarantee from the importer's bank that it will act on behalf of the importer and pay the exporter for the merchandise if all relevant documents specified in the L/C are presented according to the terms of the L/C.

Liabilities A bank's deposits and its borrowings.

LIBOR The London Interbank Offered Rate is used to set interest rates on items such as corporation debt, car loans, etc. It is supposed to reflect the rates that banks charge one another for loans.

Liquidity risk The risk that a counterparty to a transaction will not settle an obligation for full value when due, but will do so on some unspecified day afterwards.

Marked-to-market An accounting method consisting of valuing assets on an entity's books, in part by requiring holders of financial instruments to assign a value to the instruments based on their current market price.

Market risk The potential for loss from changes in the value of financial instruments. The value of a financial instrument can be affected by changes in interest rates, foreign exchange rates, equity and commodity prices, and credit spreads.

Master netting agreement An agreement between two counterparties with multiple and reciprocal derivative contracts that provides for a single payment, in a single currency, in the event of default on or termination of any one contract.

Mezzanine A second level of debt, below the senior debt, which ranks behind the senior debt, generally secured by second ranking charges and governed by a priority deed.

Monetary policy Refers to the actions undertaken by a central bank to influence the availability, cost, and release of reserves at depositary institutions, which in turn loosens or tightens the money supply.

Monetary policy transmission mechanism The process through which monetary policy decisions affect the economy in general, and the price level in particular.

Money markets Markets that trade debt securities or instruments with maturities of less than one year.

Money supply Refers to the sum of all money in a particular country. Every state has its own means of measuring money supply, but in general money supply is an aggregate figure that includes M1 (physical currency and demand deposits), M2 (M1 plus time deposits, saving deposits, non-institutional money-market funds and small CODs), and M3 (M2 plus large savings and time deposits over $100K, and institutional money-market funds).

Moral hazard Occurs when insurance, in the form of deposit insurance or lender-of-last resort action, encourages a financial institution to take risks rather than discourages it from so doing.

NASDAQ National Association of Securities Dealers Automatic Quotation System.

Notional principal A reference amount of principal used for determining payments under various derivative contracts.

Off-balance-sheet asset An asset kept outside the balance sheet until a specified event occurs. When the contingent event occurs, the asset – item or activity – moves onto the asset side of the balance sheet, or income is realized on the income statement.

Off-balance-sheet activity Activities not recorded on the bank balance sheet, that include asset, debt, or financing-related activities such as derivatives or loan commitments and other contingent exposures that could pose a risk to the bank.

Off-balance-sheet liability A liability kept outside the balance sheet until a specified event occurs. When the specified event occurs, the liability moves onto the liability side of the balance sheet, or an expense is realized on the income statement.

Open market operations Purchases or sales of securities in the nation's money and bond markets that affect the level of reserves held by financial institutions.

Operational risk The risk of loss resulting from inadequate or failed internal processes, people, and systems, or from external events.

Outright open market transactions Operations where the Euro system buys and sells eligible assets outright on the market. They imply a full transfer of ownership from the seller to the buyer with no connected reverse transfer of ownership.

Over-the-counter markets Transactions executed directly between private parties, without an organized existing market.

Personal banker Retail branch office personnel who acquire, retain, and expand relationships with new and existing customers rby assessing their needs and recommending and selling appropriate banking products and/or services.

Price stability A year-on-year increase in the Harmonized Index of Consumer Prices (HICP).

Primary market Markets in which corporations raise funds through new issues of securities.

Prime mortgage Mortgage loans that have low default risk, made to borrowers with good credit records.

Private equity An asset class consisting of equity securities in operating companies that are not publicly traded on a stock exchange.

Private placement Issue placed with one or a few large institutional investors.

Prompt corrective action The action the supervisory authority should take when a bank's capital ratio falls below the thresholds.

Put option A derivative contract that grants the holder of the option the right, but not the obligation, to sell an underlying asset at a fixed strike price.

Qualified institutional buyer A sophisticated investor who owns and invests at least $100 million in securities.

Qualified special purpose vehicle (QSPV) The entity that issues the certificates in a two-step securitization structure.

Quantitative easing Refers to a monetary policy that consists of boosting the money supply through large-scale asset purchases in order to meet the inflation target in the medium term.

Rediscount rate The rate at which the central bank charges commercial banks with discount notes.

Repurchase agreements (REPOs) A secured financing effected through a short-term sale of securities to a cash provider with the commitment to repurchase the same or similar securities at an agreed-upon price in the future.

Reserve requirement The proportion of deposits commercial banks put aside as reserves in their central bank accounts.

Retail bank A bank that primarily services individuals or consumers, and small and medium sized enterprises.

Return on Assets (RoA) A measure of the bank's profitability linked to the size of its assets.

Return on Equity (RoE) A measure of the amount of net income after taxes earned for each dollar of equity capital contributed by the bank's shareholders. A large drop in equity capital could result in a violation of minimum regulatory capital standards and an increased risk of insolvency.

Reverse termination fee A fee paid in the event a buyer walks away from the signed merger agreement.

Revolving pool securitization The reinvestment of receivables and interest in new receivables to continue the financing.

Rho The change in value of an option for a given change in interest rate.

Risk The possibility that an uncertain outcome or event might have an undesirable consequence.

Risk management Monitoring the portfolio risks to make sure that the portfolio or position would not be evaporated by various risks.

Roadshow A marketing event that precedes a public listing. It is seen as a trial of public opinion for the issuer's business plan.

Secondary market A market in which investors buy or sell securities to other investors; the original issuer is not involved in these trades. A secondary market provides marketability and valuation.

Securitization The process by which a set of cash flows from a retail portfolio is transformed into the payouts of securities through various legal and financial engineering procedures.

Settlement price The average price at which a contract trades, calculated at both the open and the close of each trading day.

Sharpe ratio A ratio that measures the amount of return on an investment (less the return of a risk-free asset) per unit of risk, which is proxied by its standard deviation.

Shelf registration Process whereby a firm can offer multiple issues of securities over a two-year period to submit one registration statement summarizing the firm's financing plans for the period.

Short selling The selling of a security that the seller does not own, or any sale that is completed by the delivery of a security borrowed by the seller.

Sovereign risk The risk of lending to the government or government-controlled agency of a sovereign nation.

Special Purpose Vehicle (SPV) A bankruptcy-remote entity whose operations are limited to the acquisition and financing of specific assets. It is usually a subsidiary company with an asset and liability structure and legal status that makes its obligations secure even if the parent company goes bankrupt.

Speculative risk Refers to risk from which either a profit or a loss can occur.

Spot Price for immediate delivery (in foreign exchange two days from date of trade).

Spot foreign exchange rate The rate for exchanging two currencies (usually two business days).

Spread The difference between the yields on two financial assets.

Statement of cash flow A statement which reconciles movements in cash between two accounting periods.

Straddle Refers to put and call options with the same strikes and maturities.

Stress test A scenario that measures market risk under unlikely but plausible events in abnormal markets.

Sub-prime mortgage Refers to mortgage loans which have one or more high risks, usually extended to customers with poor credit histories.

Supervisory review A process used by national bank regulatory or supervisory authorities to evaluate a bank's capital adequacy in relation to the risks and capital of the bank.

Swap An agreement between the counterparties to exchange assets or a series of cash flows for a specific period of time, at specified intervals.

Syndicate A group of banks participating in a single credit facility.

Synthetic CDO Securitization whereby the investors do not have direct exposure to a portfolio of customary cash producing financial assets, but rather to a credit default swap that references financial assets.

Term loan A loan with a fixed drawdown period and a repayment schedule, where the principal is normally repaid in equal installments.

Theta The change in value of an option as time elapses, all else factors remaining the same.

Tombstone An advertisement which lists the managers and underwriters and sometimes the providers to a recently-completed facility or issue.

Treasury bills Short-term obligations of the US government, issued to cover government budget deficits and to refinance maturing government debt.

Underwriter The investment bank assisting in the issuance of new securities.

Underwriting Consists of assessing the borrower's eligibility to receive a credit, a loan or a bond by analyzing financial and other information furnished by the potential borrower, or obtained from third parties.

Underwriting spread The difference between the price to the public printed on the prospectus and the price the corporate issuer receives.

Universal bank International bank which provides a large range of services including foreign exchange, swap financing, and cash management. Universal banks complement their offering of core banking services with a wide range of other financial services, including insurance.

Value-at-Risk (VaR) A risk management model that is supposed to protect the expected extreme loss in an institution's portfolio that can occur over a specific time frame at a specified level of confidence.

Vega The change in the value of an option for a given change in volatility.

Venture capital Money given to corporate and other new high-risk enterprises by investors who seek above-average returns and are willing to take illiquid positions.

Warrants Securities that entitle the holder to exercise the right, on predetermined conditions, to buy mainstream securities, usually equity.

Wholesale bank A bank that serves as an investment bank, or merchant bank, and advisory services.

Withholding tax A tax levied on the gross amount of a passive or investment income. Withholding tax is mainly a mechanism through which tax is levied.

Working capital The difference between current assets and current liabilities.

Yankee bond (stock) Bond (stock) directly sold to US investors by foreign companies.

Yield The return on an investment, taking into account the amount invested and the expected future cash flows.

Zero-coupon bond A bond that pays no-coupon interest and simply returns the face value at maturity.

Notes

1. Representative Carter Glass (1858–1946) of Virginia, and Senator Robert Owen of Oklahoma played significant roles in the debate surrounding the institution of the Federal Reserve System in the US Congress.
2. James C. Baker (2002) *The Bank for International Settlements*, p. 149.
3. http://www.federalreserve.gov/pf/pdf/pf_complete.pdf
4. http://www.federalreserve.gov/pf/pdf/pf_complete.pdf
5. http://www.federalreserve.gov/pf/pdf/pf_complete.pdf
6. http://www.answers.com/topic/fed-federal-reserve-system#cite_note-mpb-85
7. http://www.answers.com/topic/fed-federal-reserve-system#cite_note-mpb-85
8. http://www.answers.com/topic/fed-federal-reserve-system#cite_note-mpb-85
9. Murray N. Rothbard (2005) *A History of Money and Banking in the United States: The Colonial Era to World War II*, Ludwig Von Mises Institute, p. 264.
10. Murray N. Rothbard (2005) *A History of Money and Banking in the United States: The Colonial Era to World War II*, Ludwig Von Mises Institute, p. 336.
11. Federal Reserve Act, section 10.
12. Patricia S. Pollard (2003) *A Look Inside Two Central Banks: The ECB and the Federal Reserve*, The Fed of St. Louis, p. 15.
13. http://www.answers.com/topic/fed-federal-reserve-system#cite_note-mpb-85
14. The Federal Reserve Act of 1913. O. M. W. Sprague, *The Quarterly Journal of Economics*, Vol. 28, No. 2 (Feb., 1914), pp. 213–254 Published by The MIT Press Stable. URL: http://www.jstor.org/stable/1883621
15. The Federal Reserve Act of 1913. O. M. W. Sprague, *The Quarterly Journal of Economics*, Vol. 28, No. 2 (Feb., 1914), pp. 213–254 Published by The MIT Press Stable. URL: http://www.jstor.org/stable/1883621
16. http://www.answers.com/topic/fed-federal-reserve-system#cite_note-mpb-85
17. http://www.federalreserve.gov/pf/pdf/pf_complete.pdf
18. http://www.house.gov/jec/fed/fed/fed-impt.htm#endnotes
19. http://www.house.gov/jec/fed/fed/fed-impt.htm#endnotes
20. http://www.house.gov/jec/fed/fed/fed-impt.htm#endnotes
21. http://www.house.gov/jec/fed/fed/fed-impt.htm#endnotes
22. http://www.answers.com/topic/fed-federal-reserve-system#cite_note-mpb-85
23. http://www.answers.com/topic/fed-federal-reserve-system#cite_note-mpb-85
24. http://www.answers.com/topic/fed-federal-reserve-system#cite_note-mpb-85
25. http://www.answers.com/topic/fed-federal-reserve-system#cite_note-mpb-85
26. The Federal Reserve Act of 1913, O. M. W. Sprague, *The Quarterly Journal of Economics*, Vol. 28, No. 2 (Feb., 1914), pp. 213–254 Published by The MIT Press Stable. URL: http://www.jstor.org/stable/1883621
27. The Federal Reserve Act of 1913, O. M. W. Sprague, *The Quarterly Journal of Economics*, Vol. 28, No. 2 (Feb., 1914), pp. 213–254 Published by The MIT Press Stable. URL: http://www.jstor.org/stable/1883621
28. http://www.house.gov/jec/fed/fed/fed-impt.htm#endnotes
29. http://www.answers.com/topic/fed-federal-reserve-system#cite_note-mpb-85
30. http://www.answers.com/topic/fed-federal-reserve-system#cite_note-mpb-85

31. http://www.answers.com/topic/fed-federal-reserve-system#cite_note-mpb-85
32. http://www.answers.com/topic/fed-federal-reserve-system#cite_note-mpb-85
33. http://chir.ag/papers/ind-fed-final.shtml
34. http://chir.ag/papers/ind-fed-final.shtml
35. http://www.frbsf.org/publications/federalreserve/monetary/structure.html
36. Joseph Stiglitz (2010) *Free Fall: America Free Markets, and the Sinking of the World Economy*, p. 142.
37. http://mpra.ub.uni-muenchen.de/18977/1/MPRA_paper_18977.pdf
38. Joseph Stiglitz (2010) *Free Fall: America Free Markets, and the Sinking of the World Economy*, p. 52.
39. http://mpra.ub.uni-muenchen.de/18977/1/MPRA_paper_18977.pdf
40. Marc Sumerlin, The Fed's dual mandate is not the problem, in *WSJ*, Dec. 28, 2010.
41. Marc Sumerlin, Opcit.
42. Otto Hieronymi (2009) *Gobalization and the Reform of the International Banking and Monetary System*, Palgrave Macmillan, p. 26.
43. Mario Draghi is the third president of the ECB, but the most qualified for the job.
44. Hanspeter K. Sheller (2006) *The European Central Bank: History, Role and Functions*, p. 42
45. Jacob de Haan (2011) *The European Central Bank at Ten*, Springer, p. 145.
46. Jacob de Haan (2011) *The European Central Bank at Ten*, Springer, p. 33.
47. Jacob de Haan (2011) *The European Central Bank at Ten*, Springer, p. 89.
48. Expansionary monetary policy is used when the economy is slow and the ECB wants to boost activity. It does so by raising money supply and lowering the interest rates with the expectation of encouraging investment and/or boosting employment.
49. Contractionary monetary policy aims to reduce a heating economy by reducing the money supply and/or raising the interest rates.
50. Non-marketable assets are not used by the Euro system for outright transactions.
51. Reverse transactions refer to operations where the Euro system buys and sells eligible assets under repurchase agreements or conducts credit operations against eligible assets as collateral.
52. The acronym PIIGS stand for: Portugal, Ireland, Italy, Greece, and Spain.
53. Hanspeter K. Sheller (2006) *The European Central Bank: History, Role and Functions*, pp. 85–86.
54. ECB: Monetary Policy before, during and after the financial crisis available at: http://www.ecb.int/press/key/date/2009/html/sp091109.en.html
55. Thomas F. Cargill, (2005) Is the Bank of Japan's financial structure an obstacle to policy?, *IMF Staff Papers*, Vol. 52, p. 320.
56. Dieter Gerdesmeier, Franesco P. Mongelli, and Barbara Roffia (2009) The Fed, the Eurosystem, and the Bank of Japan, *VoxEU*, p. 3.
57. Only three or less are members of the BoJ Officers.
58. A few Counsellors.
59. Kunio Okina (2004) Functions and Operations of the Bank of Japan, *IMES*, p. 108.
60. Kunio Okina (2004) Functions and Operations of the Bank of Japan, *IMES*, p. 111.
61. Alvaro Angeriz and Philip Arestis, *Monetary Policy in the UK*, Cambridge Centre for Economic and Public Policy, p. 26.
62. Alvaro Angeriz and Philip Arestis, *Monetary Policy in the UK*, Cambridge Centre for Economic and Public Policy, p. 16.
63. Kalin Nikolov (2002) *Monetary Policy Rules at the Bank of England*, p. 5.
64. The Sterling Monetary Framework refers to the Bank of England's operations to support both monetary and financial stability objectives as the two are intimately linked.

65. Bank of England (2011) The Framework for the Bank of England's Operations in the Sterling Money Market, p. 11.
66. Bank of England (2011) The Framework for the Bank of England's Operations in the Sterling Money Market, p. 13.
67. Bank of England (2011) The Framework for the Bank of England's Operations in the Sterling Money Market, p. 14.
68. These banks (big four) account for over 80% of the total banking system assets and more than one third of the financial system's assets.
69. Paul Conway (2010): Reforming China's Monetary Policy Framework to Meet Domestic Objectives, OECD Economics Department Working paper No. 822, p. 4.
70. On December 23, 2008, the PBoC cut the lending and deposit rates by 27 basis points, and on November 27, 2008, it cut the same rates by 108 basis point.
71. That is because China's financial calendar is made of 360 days (not 365 as in the U.S.), and also because the Chinese cherish the number "9" which, according to their tradition, bears longevity.
72. In a documentary referred to as "Inside Jobs", the author establishes the fact that most of the academic or think-tank circles are producing opinion to promote a specific viewpoint despite the reality of the situation.
73. Reserve Bank of India at www.rbi.org.in., p. 5
74. Reserve Bank of India at www. rbi.org. in., p. 21.
75. Direct instruments include: cash reserve ratio (CRR); statutory liquidity ratio (SLR); and refinance facilities. Indirect instruments include: liquidity adjustment facility (LAF); open market operations (OMO); market stabilization scheme (MSS); Repo/reverse Repo rate; bank rate.
76. Ila Patnaik (2001) *The Indian Foreign Exchange Market and the Equilibrium Real Exchange Rate of the Rupee*, NCAER, Delhi.
77. Reserve Bank of India at: www.rbi.org.in. p. 60.
78. Central Bank of Russia Guidelines, 2009, 2008, p. 4.
79. IMF (2010) *Russian Federation: Financial Sector Stability Assessment Update*, Country Report, N0. 10/96.
80. Seija Lainela and Alexey Ponomarenko (2012) Russian financial markets and money policy instruments, *BOFIT*, pp. 14–16.
81. Seija Lainela and Alexey Ponomarenko (2012) Russian financial markets and money policy instruments, *BOFIT*, p. 20.
82. Inna Vysman (1993) New banking legislation in Russia: Theoretical adequacy, practical difficulties, and potential solutions, *Fordham Law Review*, Volume 63, Issue 1, p. 274.
83. Law N0. 4.595 of December 31, 1964.
84. Source: http:www.bcb.gov.br.
85. Royal Decree N0. 30/4/1/1046 of April 20, 1952.
86. Muhammad Al-Jasser (2011) Global imbalances: The perspective of the Saudi Arabian Monetary Agency, *Banque de France- Financial Stability Review* N0. 15, p. 9.
87. Muhammad Al-Jasser and Ahmed Banafe, Monetary policy instruments and procedures in Saudi Arabia, p. 212.
88. IMF Country Report N0. 06/199: Saudi Arabia: Financial System Stability Assessment, p. 21.
89. The 10 founders included: the central banks of Belgium, France, Germany, Italy, Japan, and the United Kingdom along with three leading commercial banks from the United States (J.P. Morgan Chase & Co., First National Bank of New York, and First National Bank of Chicago).
90. Bank for International Settlements, Archive guide, 2007, p. 2.

91. Murray N. Rothbard, *A History of Money and Banking in the United States: The Colonial Era to World War II*, Ludwig Von Mises Institute, 2005, p. 276.
92. James C. Baker (2002) *The Bank for International Settlements*, Quorum Books, p. 141.
93. James C. Baker (2002) *The Bank for International Settlements*, Quorum Books, p. 143.
94. James C. Baker (2002) *The Bank for International Settlements*, Quorum Books, p. 167.
95. James C. Baker (2002) *The Bank for International Settlements*, Quorum Books, p. 5.
96. The Guardian BEIJING, May 19, 2010.
97. James C. Baker (2002) *The Bank for International Settlements*, Quorum Books, pp. 51–52.
98. Michael Graetz (2003) *Foundations of International Income Taxation*, Foundation Press, p. 335.
99. George H. Bossy (1964) Edge Act and Agreement Corporations in International Banking and Finance, Bank & Law.
100. The International Banking Act of 1978.
101. Neil Pinsky, Edge Act and Agreement Corporations, Federal Reserve Bank of Chicago, p. 26.
102. Joseph Stiglitz (2010) Free Fall, America Free Markets, and the Sinking of the World Economy, p. 217.
103. Famous dictators, such as Mobutu from the former Zaire, Omar Bongo Odimba from Gabon, and Ben Ali from Tunisia looted their countries with the expertise of unscrupulous financiers. Calls from the West to freeze dictators' accounts are a joke as their own legislators created, covered, and lobbied for the system. Those lobbyists openly finance our political parties.
104. Joseph Stiglitz (2010) Free Fall, America Free Markets, and the Sinking of the World Economy, p. 160.
105. EU Saving Tax Directive of 2005 entered into effect on July 1, 2005 and applies to natural persons only, resident in an EU country, on interest received on saving instruments, deposit accounts, etc.
106. The IBF concept originated in July 1978, with the New York Clearing House Association.
107. Tier 2 is also known as supplemental capital.
108. James C. Baker (2002) *The Bank for International Settlements*, Quorum Books, pp. 75–76.
109. The probability of default (PD) is the likelihood that a borrower will default.
110. The loss given default (LGD) is the actual loss a lender suffers in the wake of a default. LGD is function of the borrower recovery rate (RR) and its exposure at default (EAD).
111. The exposure at default (EAD) is the total exposure a lender (bank) could have at the time of default.
112. The expected loss (EL) is the LGD times the PD.
113. Bank for International Settlements (2009) Revisions to the Basel II market risk framework, p. 1.
114. Bank for International Settlements (2009) Revisions to the Basel II market risk framework, p. 2.
115. Bank for International Settlements (2009) Revisions to the Basel II market risk framework, p. 11.
116. www.reuters.com, November 4, 2010.
117. BIS, Triennial Central Bank Survey, December 2010, p. 6.
118. BIS, Triennial Central Bank Survey, December 2010, p. 6.
119. BIS, Triennial Central Bank Survey, December 2010, p. 8.
120. Foreign Exchange is double counted as transactions involve two currencies.
121. For further developments on swap as derivative, see Chapter 10: Hedge Funds Investing in Derivatives.

122. The first ISO currency is called the base currency, and the second ISO currency quoted is called the quote currency.
123. There are various ways to measure the momentum, such as the relative strength index (RSI), the commodity channel index (CCI), and the scholastic oscillator.
124. Dennis G. Uyemura (1993) *Financial Risk Management in Banking*, Irwin, p. 219.
125. For further details over these instruments, see Chapter 9: Banks' Transactions in Derivatives.
126. Dennis G. Uyemura (1993) *Financial Risk Management in Banking*, Irwin, p. 224.
127. Fundamental analysis takes into account all the aspects of a given country (e.g., interest rates, unemployment rate, inflation rate).
128. The Deficit Reduction Act of 1984 (DEFRA), Pub.L. 98-369.
129. Mark D. and Jennifer L. Summuit v. CIR, 134 T.C. N0. 12, May 20, 2010.
130. The Bank for International Settlements (2009–2010) Annual Report.
131. Seung Jung Lee, and Jonathan D. Rose (2010) Federal Reserve Bulletin, p. A25.
132. James C. Baker (2002) *The Bank for International Settlements*, Quorum books, p. 112.
133. Joseph Stiglitz (2010) *Free Fall: America Free Markets, and the Sinking of the World Economy*, p. 169.
134. The four main types of barrier options are:

    1. Up-and-out: the price of the instrument starts below the barrier level and has to move up for the option to be knocked out.
    2. Down-and-out: the price starts above the barrier level and has to move down for the option to become invalid.
    3. Up-and-in: the price starts below the barrier level and has to move up for the option to be activated.
    4. Down-and-in: the price starts above the barrier level and has to move down for the option to become activated.

135. Guiliano Iannota (2009) *A Guide to Underwriting and Advisory Services*, Springer, p. 69.
136. Mary L. Schapiro (2011) Remarks Before the American Securitization Forum, June 22, 2011.
137. Securities Industry and Financial Markets Association Research and Statistics, 2009, at: http: www.sifma.org/uploadedFiles/Research/Statistics/SIFMA_USKeyStats.xls
138. Over-collateralization consists of issuing securities with a par value that is lesser than the par value of the underlying assets in the pool. The excess resulting from the par value of the underlying assets over the par value of ABS constitutes a credit enhancing technique. It can be used to absorb losses.
139. Reserve funds are whether the cash reserve funds or the excess spread funds. Cash reserve funds are a portion of the issuance proceed set aside and invested in money market instruments.
140. The Act also requires the SEC and federal banking agencies to allow exceptions and exemptions pursuant to hedging prohibition.
141. Al Yoon, *The Wall Street Journal*, July 29, 2011, C-6.
142. As of January 2008, 64,000 asset-backed-securities were rated Triple A. However, over 90% of these Triple A ratings given to sub-prime RMBS originating between 2006 and 2007 were later downgraded by the same rating agencies to junk status.
143. Dwight M. Jaffee (2011) Reforming the U.S. Mortgage Market Though Private Market Incentives.
144. Equity is the difference between the appraised value of the home and the outstanding mortgage balance.

145. Anthony Saunders (2009) *Financial Markets & Institutions*, McGraw-Hill, p. 202.
146. National Housing Act of 1934, 12 U.S.C., section 1716 et seq.
147. For further details concerning theses hedging instruments, see: Chapter 9: Banks' Transactions in Derivatives.
148. Smith v. Van Gorkhom, 448 A.2d 858 (Del. Supr. 1985).
149. Revlon, Inc v. MacAndrews & Forbes Holding, Inc. 506 A.2d. 173 (Del. 1985).
150. Unocal Corp. v. Mesa Petroleum Co. 493 A.2d 946 (Del. 1985).
151. Paramount Communications, Inc. v. QVC Network, Inc. 637 A.2d 34 (Del. 1994).
152. To satisfy this standard, the directors must prove that they were informed and acting in good faith.
153. The second condition requires the board to prove two things: (1) That the response was not "coercive" or "preclusive", and (2) the response was within a range of reasonableness.
154. Phelps Dodge v. Cyprus Amax Minerals Co., CA N0. 17398 (Del. Ch. Ct. 27 September, 1999)
155. Mills Acquisition Co. v. Macmillan, Inc., 559 A 2d. 1261 (Del. 1989).
156. Omnicare v. NCS Healthcare Inc., 818 A.2d 914 (Del. 2003).
157. The term "poison pill" comes from the domain of espionage and refers to the cyanide pill spies were instructed to swallow rather than face capture. In the field of corporate takeover, the poison pill is a device used to by a corporate board to resist inadequate hostile takeover.
158. Moran v. Household International, Inc., 500 A.2d 1346 (De. 1985).
159. Air Products and Chemicals, Inc. v. Airgas, Inc. (Del. Ch., C.A. N0. 5249-CC, 2/15/2011).
160. Often the discount is within the range of 50% to 60%.
161. In Rev. Rul. 2001-25, 2001-22 I.R.B. 1291, the Service has ruled that the "substantially" all test was satisfied even when the target company has sold half of its assets prior to the merger, since the proceed of those assets were retained by the target company.
162. Helvering v. Minnesota Tea Co., U.S. 378 (1935).
163. Rev. Proc. 77-37, 1977-2 C.B 568 § 3.02.
164. Treas. Regs., § 368-1(e)(2)(v), Example 1.
165. Treas. Regs., § 368-1(e)(2)(v), Example 6.
166. Treas. Regs., § 368-1(e)(7).
167. Treas. Regs., § 368-1(d)(2).
168. Treas. Regs., § 368-2(g).
169. Felix I. Lessambo (2003) BNA, *Tax Planning International – Mergers & Acquisitions*, November, p. 13.
170. The mere existence of a cash option disqualifies the transaction, even when at least 80% of voting stock is actually used.
171. Roosvelt Hotel Co. v. Commissioner, T.C 399 (1949).
172. Felix I. Lessambo, BNA,*Tax Planning International – Mergers & Acquisitions*, November, p. 14.
173. Rev. Rul. 66-365, 1966-2 C.B. 116.
174. Rev. Rul. 55-440, 1955-2 C.B. 226, and Rev. Rul. 68-285, 1968-1 C.B. 147.
175. Felix I. Lessambo (2003) BNA, *Tax Planning International – Mergers & Acquisitions*, November, p. 15.
176. Spin-off is a transfer of the assets of the parent corporation (typically the assets of a division or line of business) to a newly-formed corporation and dividend of the stock of the newly-created corporation to the parent corporation's shareholders.

177. Split-up is a transfer of the assets of the parent corporation to two or more newly-formed corporations and dividend of the stock of the newly-created corporations to the parent corporation's shareholders. The parent corporation liquidates and the stockholders hold shares in the two or more newly-formed companies.

178. Split-off is an exchange offer in which the stockholders of the parent corporation exchange their stock in the parent for stock in a new entity.

179. Felix I. Lessambo (2004) BNA, Tax Planning International – Mergers & Acquisitions: Tax-free Spin-off and the Active Conduct of Business, May, p. 8.

180. Rev. Ruling 98-27, 1998-1 C.B. 1159; Rev. Ruling 2003-18, 2003-7 IRB. 467; and Rev. Ruling 2003-38, 2003-17 IRB 811.

181. Felix I. Lessambo, BNA, *Tax Planning International – Mergers & Acquisitions*, November, p. 15.

182. Felix I. Lessambo (2004) BNA, Tax Planning International – Mergers & Acquisitions: Tax-Free Spin-Off Within a Pre-arranged Series of Transactions, April, p. 12.

183. Rev. Rul. 90-95, 1990-2 C.B. 67.

184. Senate Report N0.1622, Eighty-third Congress, p. 52.

185. Felix I. Lessambo (2004) BNA, *Tax Planning International – Mergers & Acquisitions*, January, p. 11.

186. Illinois Tool Works & Subs. v. Commissioner, 117 T.C., N0 4, July 31, 2001.

187. Hort v. Commissioner of internal Revenue, US. S.Ct.. 313 US 28 (1941).

188. Felix I. Lessambo (2004) BNA, *Tax Planning International – Mergers & Acquisitions*, January, p. 12.

189. New Colonial Ice Co. v. Helvering, S.Ct. 292 US 435 (1934).

190. Libson Shops, Inc. v. Koehler, S.Ct. 353 US. 382 (1957).

191. Felix I. Lessambo (2004) BNA, *Tax Planning International – Mergers & Acquisitions*, January, p. 13.

192. Richard L. Doenberg (2007) *International Taxation*, Thompson West, pp. 435–440.

193. IRC section 6038B provides a penalty for failure to file information with respect to certain transfers of property by a U.S. person to certain foreign persons. Form 8865, Schedule O, Transfer of Property to a Foreign Partnership, and Form 926, Return by a U.S. Transferor of Property to a Foreign Corporation, are used for reporting purposes.

194. Richard L. Doenberg (2007) *International Taxation*, Thompson West, pp. 435–440.

195. Thomas Liaw (2006) *The Business of Investment Banking*, John Wiley & Sons, p. 65.

196. *Private Equity Analyst Newsletter*, 2011.

197. IRC section 7704(c).

198. Felix Lessambo (2011) *Fundamentals of Hedge Funds*, RoseDog Books, Chapter 3.

199. Felix Lessambo (2011) Fundamentals of Hedge Funds: Alternative Investment Vehicles, Rosedog Books.

200. David Maude (2006) *Global Private Banking and Wealth Management*, John Wiley & Sons, p. 27.

201. David Maude (2006) *Global Private Banking and Wealth Management*, John Wiley & Sons, p. 236.

202. Sara Schaeffer Munoz, *The Wall Street Journal*, July 28, 2011, C-3.

203. FDIC Quarterly Banking Profile, 2007.

204. CAMELS is an acronym, which encompasses C = Capital adequacy; A = Asset quality; M = Management; E = Earnings; L = Liquidity; and S = Sensitivity to market risk. The rating scales are from 1 to 5. 1 = sound in every respect; 2 = fundamentally sound, but with modest weaknesses that can be corrected; 3 = moderately severe to unsatisfactory weaknesses that make the business vulnerable if there is a downturn; 4 = many serious

weaknesses that have not been addressed – failure is possible but not imminent; 5 = high probability of failure in the short term. CAMELS ratings are disclosed to bank management, but not to the public. Therefore, readers of bank financial statements can be sure that they do not have inside information from the management, and would need to demonstrate specific skills in assessing these financial statements.

205. For information on US banks, please visit: http://www2.fdic.gov/idasp/index.asp
206. Seung Jung Lee and Jonathan D. Rose (2009) Profits and Balance Sheet Developments at U.S. Commercial Banks in 2009, *Federal Reserve Bulletin*, January 2010.
207. Seung Jung Lee and Jonathan D. Rose (2009) Profits and Balance Sheet Developments at U.S. Commercial Banks in 2009, *Federal Reserve Bulletin*, January 2010, p. A17.
208. Seung Jung Lee and Jonathan D. Rose (2009) Profits and Balance Sheet Developments at U.S. Commercial Banks in 2009, *Federal Reserve Bulletin*, January 2010, p. A19.
209. Commercial banking stands as the less profitable activity of JP Morgan Chase, contributing only 5% of the firm's overall income in 2009. Treasury and securities services, which contributed 10% of the overall income generated in 2009, are discussed in Chapter 10.
210. Felix Lessambo (2011) *Hedge Funds: Alternative Investment Vehicles*, Dorrance Publishing.
211. The three levels are defined as follows. Level 1: inputs to the valuation methodology are quoted prices (unadjusted) for identical assets or liabilities in active markets. Level 2: inputs to the valuation methodology include quoted prices for similar assets and liabilities in active markets, and inputs that are observable for the asset or liability, either directly or indirectly, for substantially the full term of the financial instrument. Level 3: one or more inputs to the valuation methodology are unobservable and significant to the fair value measurement.
212. Akinari Horii (2010) *The Financial Crisis and the Ensuing Reform: Neglected Wisdom*, Harvard University Asia Center, p. 5.
213. Erik Banks (2005) *Liquidity Risk*, Palgrave, p. 12.
214. Andre Baladi (2009) *Globalization and the Reform of the international Banking and Monetary System*, Palgrave Macmillan, p. 176.
215. Richard Apostolik (2009) *Foundations of Banking Risk*, Wiley Finance, p. 231.
216. Ulrich Steger (2004), *Mastering Global Corporate Governance*, John Wiley & Sons Ltd, p. 13.
217. S. Johnson, P. Boone, A. Breach, E. Friedman (2000) Corporate governance in the Asian financial crisis, 2000, *Journal of Financial Economics*, 58, pp. 141–186.
218. Bank for International Settlements (2006) *Enhancing Corporate Governance for Banking Organizations*, BIS, February, p. 4.
219. Francis v. New Jersey Bank, 432 A.2d 814 (N.J. 1981).
220. In Re Walt Disney Co. Derivative Litigation, Del. Ch. 2003.
221. Grant Kirkpatrick (2009) *The Corporate Governance Lessons from the Financial Crisis*, OECD, p. 19.
222. Francesco Guerra and Peter Thal-Larsen (2008) Gone by the Board? Why Bank Directors Did Not Spot Credit Risks, *Financial Times*.
223. Grant Kirkpatrick (2009) *The Corporate Governance Lessons from the Financial Crisis*, OECD, p. 22.
224. Best Practice for the Hedge Fund Industry (2009) Report of the Asset Manager's Committee to the President of the Working Group on Financial Markets, p. 22.
225. SEC (2003) Implications of the Growth of Hedge Funds, SEC, September, p. 67.
226. McKinsey & Company (2008) Turning risk management into a true competitive advantage, Number 5. p. 2.

227. Michel Crouhy (2006) *The Essentials of Risk Management*, McGraw-Hill, p. 29.
228. Lars Jaeger (2003) *The New Generation of Risk Management for Hedge Funds and Private Equity*, Institutional investor Books, p. 112.
229. Deng Xiaoping:(1904–1997) Chinese prominent political leader from the 1970s until his death in 1997. He reformed the Chinese Communist Party by abandoning many orthodox communist doctrines and introduced a significant dose of Western liberal (free-market) concepts in China's economic reforms.
230. Michel Crouhy (2006) *The Essentials of Risk Management*, McGraw-Hill, p. 154.
231. Michel Crouhy (2006) *The Essentials of Risk Management*, McGraw-Hill, p. 156.
232. Bank for International Settlements (2011) Interpretive Issues with Respect to the Revisions to the Market Risk Framework.
233. The IMF has been using stress tests in the last decade to assess the ability of banking systems to withstand major adverse developments. Indeed, virtually all of the Fund's Financial System Stability Assessment reports include stress tests of banking systems.
234. Basel Committee on Bank Supervision (2000) *Sound Practices for Managing Liquidity in Banking Organizations*, p. 1.
235. Bank for International Settlements (2008) *Principles for Sound Liquidity Risk and Supervision*, BIS.
236. McGladrey (2009) Liquidity Risk Management, McGladrey, pp. 1–11.
237. Roland I. Robinson (1962) The Management of Bank Funds, 2nd edition, McGraw-Hill.
238. Yasuyuki Fuchita (2010) *Prudent Lending Restored – Securitization After the Mortgage Meltdown*, Brooking Institution Press, p. 191.
239. Nassim Taleb (2007) *The Black Swan*, Random House, pp. 132 et seq.
240. Erik Banks (2005) *Liquidity Risk, Management Asset and Funding Risk*, Palgrave Macmillan, p. 145.
241. Erik Banks (2005) *Liquidity Risk, Management Asset and Funding Risk*, Palgrave Macmillan, p. 146.
242. Erik Banks (2005) *Liquidity Risk, Management Asset and Funding Risk*, Palgrave Macmillan, pp. 124 et seq. Despite the development already mentioned, credit risk is the core of any business, and particularly the banking industry.
243. The working capital ratio, the quick ratio, the liquidity ratio are among the most used.
244. Dennis G. Uyemura (1993) *Financial Risk Management in Banking*, Irwin, p. 214.
245. Dennis G. Uyemura (1993) *Financial Risk Management in Banking*, Irwin, p. 214.

Reader's Notes

Index